THE READING-WRITING
CONNECTION

THE READING-WRITING CONNECTION

Ninety-seventh Yearbook of the National Society for the Study of Education

PART II

Edited by

NANCY NELSON and ROBERT C. CALFEE

Editor for the Society

KENNETH J. REHAGE

19 **NSSE** 98

Distributed by THE UNIVERSITY OF CHICAGO PRESS • CHICAGO, ILLINOIS

The National Society for the Study of Education

Founded in 1901 as successor to the National Herbart Society, the National Society for the Study of Education has provided a means by which the results of serious study of educational issues could become a basis for informed discussion of those issues. The Society's two-volume Yearbooks, now in their ninety-seventh year of publication, reflect the thoughtful attention given to a wide range of educational problems during those years. Each year the Society's publications contain contributions to the literature of education from scholars and practitioners who are doing significant work in their respective fields.

An elected Board of Directors reviews proposals for Yearbooks, selects the proposals that seem suitable for a Yearbook, and appoints an editor, or editors, to oversee the preparation of manuscripts for the projected volume.

The Society's publications are distributed each year without charge to members in the United States, Canada, and elsewhere throughout the world. The Society welcomes as members all individuals who desire to receive its publications. Information about current dues and a listing of its publications that are still in print may be found in the back pages of this volume.

This volume, *The Reading-Writing Connection*, is Part II of the Ninety-seventh Yearbook of the Society. Part I, published at the same time, is entitled *The Adolescent Years: Social Influences and Educational Challenges*.

ISSN: 0077-5762

Published 1998 by
THE NATIONAL SOCIETY FOR THE STUDY OF EDUCATION

5835 Kimbark Avenue, Chicago, Illinois 60637
© 1998 by the National Society for the Study of Education

First Printing

Printed in the United States of America

Acknowledgments

The National Society for the Study of Education is greatly indebted to Professors Nancy Nelson and Robert C. Calfee, editors of this volume, to each of the authors who have contributed chapters, and to all who provided external reviews of the chapters. We realize that their work on the book was done on top of already busy schedules.

Professors Nelson and Calfee planned the volume, requested highly competent authorities to prepare chapters, and are themselves the authors of chapters. Striving for a book of high quality, they arranged for review of all manuscripts by still other authorities. As editors, they have given thoughtful and diligent attention to the tasks that must be performed to bring a book to completion.

Professor Margaret Early read each chapter with great care and offered valuable comments and suggestions as the manuscripts were undergoing final editing.

Jenny Volpe, assistant in the NSSE office, prepared the name index with her usual attention to detail.

To all who have had a part in enabling us to add this volume to the NSSE series of Yearbooks, we express our deepest appreciation.

KENNETH J. REHAGE
Editor for the Society

Editors' Preface

The National Society for the Study of Education has devoted a number of its yearbooks—about twenty—to literacy education. Early NSSE books, such as G. P. Brown and Emerson Davis's *On the Teaching of English in Elementary and High Schools*, published in 1903, Earl Hudelson's *English Composition: Its Aims, Methods, and Measurements*, published in 1923, and the reports on reading instruction from national committees chaired by William S. Gray, published in 1925 and 1937, were influential publications in their day and are rich historical sources for educators today. Since those early years, the Society has published at least one major yearbook each decade on some aspect of literacy education. Recent volumes, published in the 1980s, include *The Teaching of Writing*, edited by Anthony Petrosky and David Bartholomae, and *Becoming Readers in a Complex Society*, edited by Alan Purves and Olive Niles. We are honored to edit in 1998 a NSSE yearbook that has this kind of lineage.

Our volume focuses on a longstanding and pedagogically significant issue in literacy education: the reading-writing connection. The organization of instruction in literacy was an important concern in the early decades of this century, when the various school subjects were being established and those "classic" yearbooks were published, and it continues to be a major issue today. What sorts of knowledge used in reading are also used in writing? How does the reading process relate to the writing process? Should the two processes be taught separately, or should they be integrated in instruction?

Despite many obvious connections between the two, reading and writing have tended to be taught as separate, and even unrelated, subjects in United States schools. This instructional separation has often been the case for students throughout the educational spectrum: from the elementary years, when there are separate periods for reading and writing, through the college years, when there are separate composition courses and literature courses. In the field of literacy education, specializations in reading and writing have developed with different theories and different terminologies, and scholars and educators are known as "reading people" or "writing people." Although these separations have been—and still are—quite pervasive, literacy education has experienced, and is now experiencing, movements toward integration.

We begin our book with a history of literacy instruction that traces trends of connection and disconnection across the various levels of education and across the various school subjects and disciplines devoted to written language. As our readers will note, the forces toward integration tend to pull together more than reading and writing; they also interrelate written with oral uses of language.

After our historical introduction, authors of the other eleven chapters deal with three kinds of contexts in which the connections between reading and writing can be easily seen and fostered. First is the author-audience context, which has been a major focus of rhetorical study. Writers "read" their audiences, anticipating how their texts will be received, and readers "read" authors as well as texts, construing those authors' intentions and motives for various choices they made in writing. Second is the classroom context in which reading and writing are used together for communicative purposes. When attention is on what is being communicated, instead of on reading and writing as subjects of study, students (and teacher) move readily from the role of writer to that of reader, and vice versa, making use of what they have read in their own writing. And third is the context of an academic discipline. When engaging in the practices of a particular disciplinary community, students read and transform texts written by others as they produce their own texts, and the boundaries between reading and writing are blurred.

A major goal, as we conceived the book, was to provide readers with a broad perspective on the topic. We wanted our treatment to cut across the various subject areas and disciplines that focus on literacy education, and thus invited authors from various specializations, which include reading education, language arts/English education, English, rhetoric, and communications, to contribute chapters. We also wanted to portray a broad developmental spectrum in education, from the early years of schooling through graduate education, since the disconnections and connections between reading and writing can be seen at all levels of education. Although individual chapters tend to emphasize particular levels of education (elementary, secondary, or college), our authors have considered the development that comes before—and, in many cases, after—the years of schooling that receive their major attention.

A number of people have contributed to this volume, and we want to acknowledge those contributions. We are grateful to Courtney Cazden, Margaret Early, and P. David Pearson, each of whom read and responded to a number of chapters. Our appreciation also goes to the following individuals who reviewed single chapters: Russel Durst, Richard Enos, Linda Flower, Sarah Warshauer Freedman, Angela Lunsford, Christine Oravec, David R. Russell, and Mark Sadoski. The thoughtful comments and suggestions of all these people were quite helpful to us and the other authors as we prepared final versions of the chapters. Most of all, we want to thank Kenneth Rehage, secretary/treasurer and editor for NSSE, for his guidance, patience, and wisdom throughout the project.

NANCY NELSON
ROBERT C. CALFEE

Table of Contents

Section One
The Historical Context

CHAPTER

Section Two
The Author-Audience Context

Section Three
The Classroom Context

Section Four
The Disciplinary Context

Section One
THE HISTORICAL CONTEXT

CHAPTER I

The Reading-Writing Connection Viewed Historically

NANCY NELSON AND ROBERT C. CALFEE

Why a volume on the connection between reading and writing? Why is this topic significant? These are reasonable questions to be asked by readers of this NSSE yearbook, who already know that literacy includes both reading and writing, that a measure of one is often used as an index of proficiency in the other, that writing is produced to be read, that both are included in English and language arts. Why, then, the significance of this topic, the reading-writing connection? It is significant because historically the two components of literacy have been largely *dis*connected in education in the United States. Despite numerous points of contact through the years and various efforts to connect the two, a schism has often existed between reading and writing in theory and research, and reading and writing have often been taught as unrelated subjects. If it were not for this long-standing separation, so much importance would not be given to possible connections. This chapter on historical context is intended to demonstrate the significance of the topic as well as to highlight points of convergence and divergence between reading and writing in American education.

We begin with a synoptic history of literacy education from colonial to more recent times. Our broad sweep includes trends at the college level as well as elementary and secondary, since curricular changes at the lower levels are influenced by developments at upper levels, and vice versa. Also included are trends in rhetoric and literary studies, since these subjects overlap with subjects known as reading

Nancy Nelson is Professor in the College of Education at Louisiana State University, where she is also Director of the LSU Writing Project. Robert C. Calfee is Professor of Education in the School of Education, Stanford University.

and composition. For readers, who, like the two of us, claim literacy studies as a disciplinary specialization, this is a look at our shared intellectual history—our roots, our ancestors, our culture. For readers with other specializations, here is an opportunity to understand such puzzling features of literacy education as: Why the different terminology for reading and writing education? Why such different approaches to instruction? Why the wars between literature (reading) people and composition (writing) people in English departments?

As we will show, some historical developments draw reading and writing (and often oral uses of language as well) together, toward some common "center," and other developments push them apart and away from the common center. In describing these patterns, we speak of those developments that consolidate reading and writing as *centripetal* and those that maintain or further the separation as *centrifugal*. The center metaphor works well, we think, for visualizing these patterns. It is a familiar way of "seeing" curriculum (e.g., subject-*centered* curriculum, child-*centered* approaches) that runs through many discussions, and it has also been used in accounts of the quest of English studies to find a unifying theme—a *center*.[1]

After this initial review, which takes us to the 1970s, we slow the pace to concentrate on centripetal and centrifugal developments during the last three decades. We focus first on five integrative movements: the comprehension-as-construction movement, which, in dramatic fashion, transformed reading education; three other movements—reader response, "process" writing, and whole language—so interrelated they might even be viewed as a single movement; and, finally, a discourse community movement, which is becoming increasingly influential. These five movements entail ways of thinking and talking about reading and writing as well as ways of teaching them. After discussing these integrative developments, we consider the centrifugal forces—political, historical, and theoretical—that are operating concurrently with the centripetal forces. In conclusion, we summarize overall patterns in the relation between reading and writing and introduce the chapters that follow.

The Colonial Curriculum

READING AND WRITING INSTRUCTION FOR AMERICAN CHILDREN

The curricular separation of reading and writing in American schools is not a recent development. Actually, the separation goes back to colonial times, when the first two Rs were taught as separate subjects to children, whether in common primary schools, private schools, or private tutoring.² Even then, the separation was characterized by two features that have persisted through the years: (a) the emphasis of reading over writing in schooling and (b) the delay of writing instruction until the rudiments of reading have been acquired.

Reading instruction, which focused on identification of letters, syllables, and words, as well as oral reading of brief texts, came first and might last only a few weeks but could continue for two or three years. Some children who had been taught to read would then receive instruction in writing, focused on transcription and penmanship, often from a different teacher. Seventeenth-century New England sometimes offered separate schools for reading and writing, in accordance with European custom. The writing schools, which were considered more advanced, included some practice—but typically no instruction—in the rudiments of reading.

The Protestant settlers of colonial America valued the ability to read, particularly for reading the Bible and other religious selections and the common law. In the early colonial years instructional materials consisted mainly of hornbooks, wooden boards displaying the alphabet, some words, and some religious excerpts; but by the end of the seventeenth century the hornbooks were replaced by primers, most notably *The New England Primer*, first printed in the 1680s for the Puritans. Primers—and reading instruction—moved from smaller to larger units: letters to syllables to words (one-syllable, two-syllable, three-, four-, and five-syllable words) and on to brief passages and prayers, all accompanied by much drill and repetition. In colonial times and for decades after the Revolution, spelling was a major component of reading. After memorizing the alphabet, children learned to read by saying the letters that comprise syllables and words. This alphabetic-spelling method led children to infer the pronunciation of a syllable or word by saying its component letters.

Writing instruction followed reading because writing was thought to depend on the ability to read and to be more difficult than reading. The ability to write was considered less important for most people, particularly girls. Writing would be needed for certain kinds of employment and for college studies, and, since girls were not typically employed outside the home and would not receive a college education, they were not as likely to be taught to write. Writing instruction focused on techniques and tools and involved copying and dictation, again with much drill and repetition. A major link between reading and writing was spelling, as students would often say letters aloud as they wrote them.

There were pragmatic, utilitarian reasons for acquiring literacy in the vernacular language, which for most colonists was English. However, the vernacular was not considered the basis for a *real* education—which at that time meant a *classical* education. What a person needed in order to pursue an education in college and become an "educated" person was a knowledge of the classical languages, particularly Latin but also Greek, which together constituted the foundation for learning and literature needed by anyone preparing for a profession. For learning these languages, the colonists had the Latin grammar schools, which were modeled after similar European schools. At these schools, college-bound males studied the structure of the classical languages.[3] Within a focus on features of the language itself, grammar instruction provided some instructional linkage between reading and writing. This came through the models approach that was often employed: students read and analyzed written sentences and then imitated them through writing the patterns they saw. In addition to grammar, some schools included classwork in oral reading and elocution.

During the eighteenth century, with the establishment of English as the shared language in America, English grammar schools were also developed. The language studied there was English, but the approach was much the same as in the Latin schools. In addition to English grammar, the English schools typically offered a more expansive curriculum including such subjects as science, mathematics, and geography as well as commercial subjects. By the middle of the eighteenth century, a third type of school emerged: the academy, which combined the curriculum of both types of schools and became a prototypical secondary school until the public high school appeared a century and a half later. Secondary education for women would begin after the Revolution, when some coeducational academies and some seminaries for girls were established.[4]

RHETORIC IN COLONIAL COLLEGES

At the college level, language education was more integrated than at lower levels. Rhetoric filled a centripetal function in the curriculum of the colonial colleges, whose major mission was preparing men for the clergy and other "learned" professions. Here in this college subject was a center—the focus on social aspects of communication—that tied together the productive and receptive aspects of language. The classical rhetoric of Aristotle, Cicero, and Quintilian was then, and still is today, concerned with author and audience: an author producing a text intended to have particular effects on an audience.[5] The classical conception, discussed in more detail by James Murphy later in this volume, divides rhetorical production into five parts, each with its own principles: invention (*inventio*), arrangement (*dispositio*), style (*elocutio*), memory (*memoria*), and delivery (*pronuntiatio*). Of these parts, the first three concern the creation of a text and the latter two its presentation. Rhetoric deals with the relation between producing and understanding texts, which may be a listening-speaking, reading-writing, listening-writing, or reading-speaking connection, since texts can be either oral or written. With respect to text production, the major attention during colonial times was on texts to be presented orally; nevertheless, the principles applied also to written texts.

One connection was the relation between author and audience. In Aristotle's conception audience was important to authors even in the invention, the generation, of content. A speaker or writer would attempt to discover material that would affect a particular audience in particular ways. These might be appeals to knowledge of the subject matter (*logos*), to emotions of the audience (*pathos*), or to one's own character (*ethos*). A second connection was the generality of the principles, which could be applied to the understanding and analysis of others' texts as well as the production of one's own. To learn the principles, students often read and analyzed texts produced by others and sometimes (as in studying grammar) they would imitate those examples. This imitation of models in rhetoric is often associated with Quintilian, who argued that an orator can learn much from studying and imitating the style of others, building through such study a *copia*, a bank of expressions and words. The use of models, which continues to be a major means of relating writing and reading, has gone through periods of disfavor, particularly in the 1970s when the "old" product-oriented instruction was set in opposition to a "new" process-oriented instruction. At that time, process advocates considered the imitation of models to be a product-oriented method that ignored the strategic nature of composing.[6]

Today, several concepts from classical rhetoric run through the talk about reading-writing connections. Reference may be made, for instance, to the relation between author and audience, to the discourse knowledge that is applied in both composing and comprehending, and to the role of reading in writing development.[7]

The classical conception dominated rhetoric in colonial times, although for a while a truncated version, known as Ramist rhetoric, was influential in some American colleges. Invention, the generation of content, was not included in this treatment of rhetoric, which emphasized style and delivery.[8] As with other subjects, the teaching of rhetoric, whether the full classical version or Ramist, involved substantial memorization and recitation. These practices were in accordance with the notion of mental discipline—that the mind develops through exercise, much as muscles develop—which undergirded instruction in the colleges as it did instruction at lower levels of education. The classical version remained the major focus of rhetorical study until after the Revolution, when it was reconceived, mainly through the theories of two Scottish scholars.

Formation of English as a Single Discipline and Subject, 1776-1900

The subject of English, conceived as the study of literature and writing of essays, is now so entrenched in the American curriculum that it is difficult to conceive of secondary or college education without it. However, English conceived thusly was not always included in the curriculum, and it took some effort on the part of early educators to get it there. From the colonial years through the nineteenth century, English underwent several transformations before it eventually became a discipline (and department) dealing with written language in universities and colleges and became a school subject at secondary and elementary levels. Here we review those transformations, and we also point out that, despite its status in the curriculum, English did not become an integrative center for reading and writing, since, from its beginnings as a discipline and subject, it was a curricular collection.

In discussing these changes, we begin with the college level and then move to secondary and elementary. This is to highlight how developments at college level influenced lower grades. Some might call this influence "trickle down," but the term suggests too passive a process. The influence was more "push down," as college personnel actively pressured the lower levels of education to make certain changes.

FROM RHETORIC TO COMPOSITION AND LITERARY CRITICISM

After the Revolution, rhetoric continued to be integrative—centripetal—with respect to the composition and understanding of texts, but the rhetoric of Aristotle, Cicero, and Quintilian was being modified, as mentioned above, by the new rhetoric developed by two Scottish scholars. These eighteenth-century rhetoricians, George Campbell and Hugh Blair, retained most of the components of the classical version of rhetoric but made them more consistent with the psychologies of their day. For Campbell, a major psychological theory was associationism, as he considered the various kinds of links (e.g., cause-effect, resemblance) between ideas and their function in communication; but for Blair it was aesthetics, as he considered factors affecting taste (e.g., color, shape, novelty).[9] Of those five parts of classical rhetoric (invention, arrangement, style, memory, and delivery), these rhetoricians focused mainly on arrangement and style, giving much attention to an author's presentation of material for an audience but little to the invention of material for an audience.

These Scottish rhetoricians and other rhetoricians of their day continued the two kinds of reading-writing connections that we pointed out earlier for classical rhetoric: the relation between author and audience and the use of rhetorical principles in understanding as well as producing texts. Campbell focused mainly on the former, giving much attention to the psychological effects that particular organizational or stylistic features would have on readers. Blair focused mainly on the latter, formulating rhetoric as a critical theory. With his attention on literary texts, he attempted to show how rhetorical principles are used in analyzing, interpreting, and appreciating the texts of others. He put it this way: "The same instructions which assist others in composing, will assist them in judging and relishing the beauties of composition."[10] For teaching the principles, both rhetoricians employed models. Students were taught rhetorical principles by seeing them demonstrated by well-respected writers, whose works were often included in the text.

For much of the nineteenth century, rhetoric continued to provide an integrative theory—a center holding together the understanding of texts and the composing of texts. Other rhetoricians followed Campbell and Blair in presenting rhetorical principles for analyzing and critiquing others' texts and also producing one's own texts.[11]

However, the center that rhetoric had provided began to break apart toward the end of the century. This happened as rhetoric courses were becoming composition courses. Colleges and universities, dissatisfied with the job the academies were doing with respect to students' writing, instituted more instruction in composition.[12] At first, the "rhetoric" label was combined with "composition" to create "rhetoric-composition" courses and then it was often eliminated as the courses became simply "composition." College-level composition courses, often viewed as remedial work, emphasized rules for mechanical correctness and began to include grammar too. Although some rhetorical principles for arrangement and style were typically included, little attention was given to strategies authors use in analyzing audiences and adapting to them.

What about the reading, or interpretive, component of rhetoric? As scholarship became more specialized, criticism was being attached to literature, and literary criticism was being established as a separate component of English. Even though some critical study was still included in the composition courses, textual criticism was developing apart from any connection to students' own writing. Literature scholars were becoming responsible for the reading of texts, and those in composition were becoming responsible for the writing of texts. The literature component combined rhetorical principles with the aesthetic of belles lettres, whereas the composition component combined rhetorical principles with rules for correct writing and elimination of errors.

ESTABLISHMENT OF "ENGLISH" IN COLLEGES AND UNIVERSITIES

When universities were created in the expansion of higher education that followed the Civil War, a strong scientific influence was felt in all areas, including those concerned with uses of language. At that time of specialization, it was important for disciplines to have a scientific approach and a scientifically developed body of knowledge. If it were to become a university discipline, English needed to be scientific too.

By the 1890s, English did achieve disciplinary and departmental status. This status was not accomplished through literary criticism or through composition, although these two familiar components were included, but through English philology, which had developed rapidly after 1875. Philology, the historical study of a culture and its products, including language, involved meticulous analyses of linguistic artifacts, which sometimes were literary works, and it was this kind of detailed historical investigation that provided the major scientific underpinnings.[13]

At its inception, English was a rather loose collection of separate subjects with different lineages and emphases: philology, literary criticism, rhetoric, and composition. In some universities the collection included oratory too—the oral use of language that eventually went to communications departments as English became a subject focused almost exclusively on written language. Philology appeared in two kinds of courses: the scientific study of the history of the English language and the scientific study of literature (tracking down dates, references, sources, and allusions). However, with respect to the teaching of literature, a more dominant approach than philology was aesthetic criticism, in which literature was studied as art. Students were taught to understand the English "masterworks" through detailed analysis of the authors' workmanship (e.g., plot, characterization, figurative language). Literature was growing in importance, as literature courses became popular in the newly instituted elective system and as a body of scholarship was produced by literature specialists. The integrative subject, rhetoric, which had provided a functional, conceptual link between composing and comprehending, was split, with part going to literary criticism and part to composition. The teaching of composition, directed toward improving student writing, was considered a remedial function of the English department, and faculty in composition had low-status positions, although composition courses had a certain importance to an English department in terms of numbers of students to be taught.

English did not provide an intellectual center for these various branches, which had developed their own traditions and their own turf. In his well-known article "Where Do English Departments Come From?" William Riley Parker argued that, from its beginnings, English was not really a discipline because, out of acquisitiveness, it became a "catchall" for various kinds of studies taught by faculty with different interests and backgrounds.[14]

ENGLISH IN THE SECONDARY SCHOOL CURRICULUM

Now we move to the development of English as a subject in the secondary schools. As our sweep through the colonial period showed, the facet of English established first in the secondary curriculum was grammar, not literature and not composition. After the Revolution the curriculum, including the language curriculum, expanded until by the early decades of the nineteenth century the academies offered various assortments of courses in "English," which in addition to grammar included composition and elocution and eventually, by mid-century, English literature too. Some assortment of courses in the vernacular was also offered in the public high schools, which developed rapidly in the last decade of the century. At that time the curriculum varied widely across schools. The classical subjects persisted, but new subjects, including those focused on English, were established.

"Push down" was the major pattern for curricular development, as the colleges and the new universities exerted influence on the curriculum in secondary schools. Colleges complained about the inadequate preparation of entering students and spelled out requirements for what students should know. Along with complaints about student writing, there was pressure to place more emphasis on literature and on particular literary selections, the beginnings of a canon. Students were to read specific selections, "great works," almost exclusively by British authors—to "know" certain books before entering college and to be able to demonstrate that knowledge by writing analytic essays. These requirements presented a problem for the school curriculum, as the colleges varied somewhat in the particular titles they required.[15]

Eighteen ninety-four was an important year for English. It was then that the Committee of Ten, appointed by the National Education Association (NEA), identified English as a school subject—a *major* school subject. The committee, composed of college as well as school faculty and administrators, had been charged with defining and prioritizing the school subjects and specifying the content of each. The committee's report, so influential it was called a "gospel for the curriculum writers of the burgeoning high schools,"[16] made English a priority in the curriculum by recommending that the subject be studied all four years of high school. It is important to note that English was defined as a single subject with two major facets, both emphasizing written uses of language: the "study of literature and training in the expression of thought." However, despite this dual definition, the curricular emphasis, as reflected in time devoted to the component, was weighted toward literature, the study of works of "good" authors.[17]

By the end of the nineteenth century, the colleges seemed to be getting what they wanted with respect to literature instruction: the study of literature for secondary students in many schools emulated the analytic approach of literary criticism in colleges and universities, and secondary students were reading recommended works. Schools had extensively annotated texts and reading guides for students to use in their analyses of works of "great" authors, and a uniform list of titles had been established.[18]

Many high school faculty were not happy with the situation. They opposed a literature curriculum based on preselected works and a writing curriculum based on composing essays about that literature. Tensions between school and college faculty over college entrance requirements increased after the Committee of Ten made its recommendations and after the uniform requirements were passed. Numbers of high school teachers, particularly in the East, opposed the set curriculum imposed upon them, and created organizations to voice objections. In fact, the National Council of Teachers of English (NCTE) was formed later (in 1911) largely as a means of concerted action on the part of high school English teachers to resist this kind of curriculum and to give more attention to students' interests and experiences in their reading and writing.

READING, WRITING, AND ENGLISH IN THE ELEMENTARY CURRICULUM

For young children, major curricular changes affecting reading and writing would not come until the second half of the nineteenth century. The alphabetic-spelling approach to reading instruction continued after the Revolution, with emphasis still on oral reading and mechanics. As one historian put it, stories "were all read and re-read a hundred times by the millions of boys and girls who toed the mark and spelled in a row."[19] Webster's blue-backed speller had eventually replaced the New England Primer as the major text for beginning reading instruction. Its version of instruction was little different from that of the primer except for one major—and significant—addition: some attention to phonics, the sounds associated with letters. The practice of teaching the rudiments of reading before writing was well established, and writing instruction for elementary students continued to deal almost exclusively with mechanical matters. Any teaching of creative aspects of composition was generally delayed till the secondary years.

After mid-century there were three major developments in reading instruction. One was creation of series of graded readers for children (most notably the hugely successful McGuffey's readers) as they moved through grades in school. A second was more attention to the meaning of reading passages in addition to the focus on word identification. This was reflected in questions on content included in the series. The third change—and the one of most historical interest to many reading educators—was the introduction of other approaches to beginning reading in addition to the alphabetic-spelling method, which was still employed.[20]

There were debates, even then, about the best approach to beginning reading, which foreshadowed the great debates that rage on even today. Among the approaches debated then were two phonic approaches: a synthetic approach, moving from part to whole (symbol/sound to word) and an analytic approach, moving from whole to part (word to sound/symbol). The latter holistic approach was developed by a Frenchman, Jacotot, who argued "*tous est dan tous*" ("all is in all"). In addition to this method, there was an approach that began with larger wholes known as the sentence method. There was also a "write-read method" to beginning instruction that was introduced but received little attention.

In this approach, children wrote and read words that they heard and said. Proponents argued that learning was much easier this way, but opponents argued that it made both reading and writing more difficult by having to learn both at once.[21]

As in higher education and the secondary schools, English was being established in the elementary curriculum as a single but aggregate subject. There was some push-down pressure to make elementary English similar to the college practice by emphasizing literature, in particular, the analytic reading of literature. Some came from the Committee of Ten, which went beyond its original charge to make recommendations for elementary as well as secondary levels. Consider the following recommendation of the committee for *elementary* students' reading:

Due attention should be paid to what are sometimes thoughtlessly regarded as points of pedantic detail, such as the elucidation of involved sentences, the expansion of metaphors into similes and the compression of similes into metaphors, the tracing of historical and other references, and a study of the denotation and connotation of single words. Such details are necessary if the pupil is to be brought to anything but the vaguest understanding of what he reads.[22]

The pushing down of college practices for the reading of literature was not as successful at the elementary level as it was at secondary level. Children's reading instruction was shaped by other influences, which we will discuss shortly.

However, the Committee of Ten did make a very important recommendation for children's writing: that the teaching of composition should begin in the third grade. From our perspective today, third grade may seem late in a child's schooling, but from the perspective of that time it was early. As mentioned earlier, not much was being done throughout the nineteenth century in writing instruction for elementary students, particularly with respect to creative aspects, and instruction in composing was generally delayed till the secondary years. Today we would assume that a book titled *Elementary Composition* would be intended for elementary students, but this title was used at the turn of the century for a text intended for secondary students.[23]

Then along came the Committee of Ten's recommendation to push down the teaching of composition—a recommendation that had more shock value, and a more lasting effect, than the committee's recommendation for children's reading. This authoritative committee established the importance of composition in children's education and moved the onset of such instruction earlier than was customary, even as it observed the long tradition of delaying writing after reading was well underway (which was customary as far back as colonial times). According to the committee's guidelines, composition, when it began in the third grade, should include the writing of narratives and descriptions as well as copying and writing from dictation and memory.

Our review thus far has shown how English was established in colleges and universities as a collection of subjects with different underpinnings, histories, and functions. It has also shown how English was established in secondary schools as a subject composed of two major branches (one of them more major than the other). What about elementary English? In 1895, one year after the report of the Committee of Ten, another NEA committee issued a report on elementary education. This was the Committee of Fifteen, whose charge had been to make recommendations regarding the sequencing of study in school subjects and possible unification of some subjects. Their conception of English, which was called "the center of instruction in the elementary school," preserved the conventional categories for learning English: reading, writing, spelling, and grammar. "Writing" referred to penmanship, but "composition writing" was included in the report as a component of grammar.[24] Even though English was seen as the center of instruction, it was portrayed as a collection of branches or sub-subjects.

Status of Reading and Writing at the End of the Nineteenth Century

By the end of the nineteenth century, English had become a discipline in the colleges and universities. It also became a subject in the subject-centered curriculum of the schools. It was, however, a discipline and a subject without any center holding together its various parts (including reading and writing) other than that its various components dealt in some way with the English language—unless, of course, one sees literature as the center, which the literary scholars often did.

From the colleges and universities to the secondary and elementary school, the major pattern throughout the nineteenth century was separation of reading and writing, even though one might have expected the single label "English" to signal some unity. At the end of the century, the major connection between reading and writing in English came through students writing essays on literature. Rhetoric still provided a theoretical link, particularly at the college level, but it had a diminished role as literature gained in importance. There was, however, another link between reading and writing that was almost invisible, partly because it was so universal: professors in the colleges and universities, who emphasized the "scientific" nature of their disciplines, expected students to produce "research" papers, which involved reading disciplinary texts and using these to write their own texts.[25]

Changes—some of them quite dramatic—were on the horizon. Even though the subject curriculum was becoming more entrenched, there were some evidences near the end of the century that a new philosophy of education was developing, particularly among educators of young people: one that was student-centered rather than subject-centered, that broke boundaries of various types, and that connected reading and writing and oral uses of language. New ideas about pedagogy were coming from Europe and being applied in some American schools. Some ideas advocating student-centered education were associated with Johann Pestalozzi, who emphasized the natural development of the child, and Friedrich Froebel, who brought attention to children's individuality and the benefit of activity. Other ideas about breaking boundaries in the subject-centered curriculum were associated with Johann Friedrich Herbart, who argued the importance of interrelating subjects through correlation.[26] A National Herbart Society was established in 1895, and it was this organization that became the National Society for the Study of Education just after the turn of the century.

During this time several experimental schools were instituting innovative child-centered approaches, based on ideas of Pestalozzi, Froebel, and Herbart. Among them was Francis W. Parker's school in Quincy, Massachusetts, which offered a curriculum integrating the language arts and other subjects as well.[27] A new view of literacy learning was making its way into the literature for teachers. The English subject curriculum would become more fully articulated and more decisively challenged during the first two-thirds of the twentieth century.

Twentieth-Century Challenges to Tradition, 1900-1970

In the early decades of this century, a time of enormous industrial, social, and economic change, the scientific model continued to influence higher education, as newly formed academic disciplines emulated the disciplines of science. The components of various knowledge domains were being identified, defined, and taxonomized, and scientific studies were being conducted to make those domains more complete. Various "isms"—associationism, connectionism,[28] and eventually behaviorism—replaced the old notions of mental discipline. With the influence of Darwinism, growth models were applied to students' learning, and attention was given to individual differences in development.

At that time, two concurrent movements impacted education, both influenced by psychology. One of them, the scientific measurement movement, associated with E. L. Thorndike, had centrifugal effects on reading and writing. The other, the progressive education movement, associated with John Dewey, had centripetal effects on reading and writing.[29] In this section, we review these movements, looking particularly at the impact on reading-writing connections and disconnections, and then we consider the aftermath during the 1950s and 1960s as the public reacted to educational innovations and the federal government became more involved in education.

SCIENTIFIC MEASUREMENT

A couple of decades into the twentieth century, the scientific model, which had been so influential as the university disciplines were created, was also applied to the education of young people. Education was seen as a scientific discipline that could have its parts specified and its knowledge quantified through counts and statistics. E. L. Thorndike, who provided much of the intellectual leadership of the scientific movement, argued the importance of quantification in the 21st NSSE Yearbook, *Intelligence Tests and Their Use*:

> The task of education is to make changes in human beings. We teachers and learners will spend our time this year to make ourselves and others different, thinking and feeling, and acting in new and better ways. These classrooms, laboratories, and libraries are tools to help us change human nature for the better in respect to knowledge and taste and power.
>
> For mastery in this task, we need definite and precise knowledge of what changes are made and what ought to be made. In proportion as it becomes definite and exact, this knowledge of educational products and educational purposes must become quantitative, taking the form of measurements. Education is one form of human engineering and will profit by measurements of human nature and achievement as mechanical and electrical engineering have profited by using the foot-pound, calorie, volt, and ampere.[30]

In concluding the essay, he countered the anticipated criticisms: that only trivial aspects of education could be measured quantitatively, that educational institutions would become "scholarship factories," and that science and measurement would "deface the beauty of life."

Whatever exists, exists in some amount. To measure it, is simply to know its varying amounts. Man sees no less beauty in flowers now than before the day of quantitative botany. It does not reduce courage or endurance to measure them and trace their relations to the autonomic system, the flow of adrenal glands, and the production of sugar in the blood. If any virtue is worth seeking, we shall seek it more eagerly the more we know and measure it.[31]

"Standard deviations and coefficients of correlations were in the air," as Harold Rugg would later describe the circumstances.[32]

As they conducted their studies, educational researchers tended to accept the traditional boundaries between and within the school subjects, and gave their attention to the content of those subjects.[33] They applied quantitative analysis to the various branches of English. Much of the work was descriptive (e.g., what materials were used, how much time was devoted to particular kinds of instruction), but some was transformative. For instance, by calculating high frequency words, researchers could recommend changes in spelling instruction and, by tabulating students' interests, they could advocate changes in reading material. However, a major agenda of the scientific movement was to develop reliable, valid, and specific measures of ability and achievement.

Reading education became a specialized subfield within education, distinctive from the rest of English education, as researchers gave much attention to reading. The work on reading was so vast, even then, that it commanded separate research volumes and review articles. The scientific approach was applied to reading research, most notably by psychologists, including William S. Gray and Arthur Gates, who devoted their research careers almost totally to reading, and Thorndike himself, who studied reading and a number of other subjects.[34] Attention was on measurement—of materials, of aspects of the reading process, of reading abilities, and of curriculum—and great emphasis was put on efficiency, the economical use of time. Research conducted from the 1920s through the 1950s yielded large bodies of knowledge on several components of reading education with which reading educators are so familiar today: reading rate, sight words, content area reading, reading readiness, and so on.

Scientific measurement was integral to development of the new specialization in reading, and, for those of us in reading education, this is an important part of the intellectual history of our field, even though today we might want to undo some of its excesses. Numerous formal and informal measures were developed, and reading instruction became individualized and differentiated for particular students and for groups of students. Instruction was designed to accommodate their assessed abilities, aptitudes, and needs. The medical model was applied, and *diagnosis* (with its underlying "deficit" model, which is now subject to criticism) became an important practice in the field. For reading education, as for much of education, the scientific measurement view was dominant during most of the century. Reading, which had received so much scholarly attention, was considered such an important component of literacy that it required its own instructional period in the elementary curriculum in addition to the time included in English. Reading received more attention, and reading education more authority through this scientific approach.

Writing instruction, whether at the elementary, secondary, or college and university level, did not receive the same attention that reading had and was not taxonomized to the same extent. The scientific measurement approach seemed a better fit with reading, which lent itself more easily to quantification. For reading, the text that was read could be analyzed and quantified in various ways, and responses from reading could also be analyzed, quantified, and judged against the text. For writing, the features that could be counted easily were not necessarily associated with the quality of the piece. Despite numerous attempts to measure the quality of writing, particularly with scales, quantification of quality proved difficult.[35] Nevertheless, in a general way all education, including writing instruction, was transformed, and it continues to be affected profoundly by the concept of scientific measurement through the widescale use of standardized tests and the emphasis on quantification. Educational reforms, even today, often focus on this conception, as they are designed either to diminish it or reify it.

When applied to education, scientific measurement perpetuated the curricular structure of established school subjects and had a centrifugal effect on reading and writing. The divisions among the established components of English were retained as research was conducted, and bodies of specialized knowledge were also created within these categories. Researchers specializing in one particular category, for instance, reading, did not necessarily make connections with a related category, for instance, writing. The major change was a greater division between reading and other aspects of English education; through research accumulated through the scientific measurement approach, reading became a distinct, specialized subfield in education.

PROGRESSIVE EDUCATION

Instead of working within the subject-oriented curriculum as scientific measurement did, progressive education, the other major movement of the same time period, challenged it. Whereas scientific measurement had centrifugal effects on reading and writing, the effects of progressivism were largely centripetal. The progressive education movement, which had begun in the latter decades of the nineteenth century with the experimental programs of such educators as Francis Parker, received its major philosophical foundation early in the twentieth century from the theories of John Dewey and his contemporaries. The movement began to attract much attention in the 1920s, and its influence grew during the 1930s as the country went through the Great Depression. It remained important in the early 1940s, when its focus became life adjustment, but encountered much criticism after World War II. As we will discuss, progressivism did not die at mid-century but has seen a resurgence with other labels during the last three decades.

Dewey had much to say about what should be the center in education. In *School and Society*, published in 1899, he argued for a "Copernican revolution" in thinking about that center. The center should become the child instead of the subject matter, and the role of the school should be to foster the child's growth and to give direction to his or her activities of learning. He continued this argument three years later in *The Child and the Curriculum*, where he argued that the relation between the two elements, child and curriculum, should not be viewed as separate and oppositional: "Subject matter never can be got into the child from without. Learning is active. It involves reaching out of the mind."[36] In his view, subject matter was a part of a student's experience, and teachers should develop appropriate learning experiences, based on their knowledge of the subject matter and the child. He criticized the dominant approaches to beginning reading and writing instruction for being unnatural and mechanical and isolated from other learning. Dewey saw unity where others saw parts. In his organic psychology, mental activity was a continuous whole. In his social theories, development of individuals was also development of society.[37]

Progressive educators promoted instructional approaches that broke conventional boundaries between school subjects and that integrated the components of English. One was William Kilpatrick's project method, which involved students in purposeful activity in a social environment. In performing their projects, students used various language modalities—reading, writing, listening, speaking—as they conducted their work and shared their knowledge with others. Another was the language experience method, in which students used all modalities as they orally recounted an experience, made a written record of their account (often done by the teacher), and read the written accounts.[38] These approaches made students' projects or experiences central in the curriculum. Themes associated with the romanticism of Rousseau and Froebel ran through much of the progressive pedagogy: the emphasis on individuals' self-expression, the value of the unique, and the belief in the child's essential goodness. During the 1930s and 1940s, social processes, such as peer response and conferences, were incorporated into the writing activities of some classrooms. This meant a reading-writing connection was made as students became readers of other students' texts and writers of their own.[39]

Anyone wanting to know more about the origins of the writing workshop approach, which seems so new today, can gain historical perspective by reading *They All Want to Write*, first published in 1939. This book, written by a group of teachers, reports a classroom inquiry these teachers conducted to study their own implementation of a workshop approach.[40]

At the secondary level, the progressives challenged the domination of the established curriculum, advocating such innovations as a correlated curriculum (the combining of subjects, such as English and history) and a curriculum based on students' experiences. They offered other ways of focusing education—other centers—besides the traditional subjects. Pedagogies based on self-expression, holistic experience, and activity were applied to reading and writing processes. Some changes along the progressive lines were effected at the secondary level, but general and long-lasting changes in classroom practice were probably fewer there than they were at elementary level.[41]

NEA, which had done much through the Committee of Ten to establish particular subjects in secondary curriculum according to the college model and to differentiate the various parts of English, now through other committees recommended changes in that curriculum. In 1917 the Committee of Thirty issued a report on Reorganization of English in Secondary Schools, which asserted the independence of the high school curriculum and offered a plan to organize the curriculum around experiences and to develop differentiated programs. The next year the NEA Commission on Reorganization of Secondary Education issued a more general report, *Cardinal Principles of Secondary Education*, which preserved the school subjects but encouraged some integration of learning across subjects and specialized curricula for different groups of students.[42]

NCTE was a major player in the progressive movement. Through various reports it advocated the importance of experiences, the need for correlating subjects, and the value of self expression. This organization, which had been formed in large part to counter the college domination of the high school English curriculum, played a major role in opposing the reading of a particular literature canon and the production of a single kind of writing, an essay based on such reading. One early step was collaboration with NEA on the reorganization report, but other reports would follow.

In 1935, at the height of progressivism, NCTE published *An Experience Curriculum in English*, a committee report undergirded with numerous progressive concepts: experience, correlation and integration, and units as organic wholes.[43] This document is interesting to study because of a contradiction in the committee's position: the committee offered lots of suggestions for integrating English with other subjects but did little to integrate the various parts of English (literature, reading, creative writing, and so on). The next year a related report, *A Correlated Curriculum*, from yet another NCTE committee continued the effort to relate and even fuse English with other subjects. This document, also interesting for study, reflects a tension that English teachers must have felt—a fear that the correlation they advocated could diminish English teaching. Along with the talk about correlation came much affirmation of the specialized disciplinary knowledge associated with the subject known as English. English was seen as the center of any curricular experience, and English teachers were told: "Preserve, at all cost, . . . your specialized knowledge of literature and your special teaching skills" and "Remember the values of English."[44] The document, like *An Experience Curriculum*, shows how difficult it can be to break down the categories belonging to one's own tradition and to risk losing one's turf.

Progressive English teachers, seeking to empower the individual reader and allow self-expression, also challenged the authority of the predominant approaches to literature instruction. In 1939, *Conducting Experiences in English*, yet another NCTE committee report, portrayed reading as an emotional and imaginary experience in which a reader "rewrites" a book through his or her own experience, and, because of "emotional intensity," would want to express himself or herself through extemporaneous writing.[45] A more scholarly book emphasizing literary experiences had been published in the preceding year for the Progressive Education Association: Louise Rosenblatt's *Literature as Exploration*, which has become an important book today.[46] Rosenblatt also centered on the individual as she described literary reading as a reader's aesthetic experience with an artistic work. For her, creativity provided the link between reading and writing: she argued that both processes are creative and advised that students can come to appreciate the artistry of a literary work by engaging in their own creative writing.

CHANGES IN COLLEGE ENGLISH

During the first half of this century, progressivism challenged tradition in the precollegiate curriculum and made connections between reading and writing. At the college level, there was some evidence of push-up influences from progressivism, which had begun at lower levels of education. Progressive notions resulted in some innovative curricula at a few colleges, like Bennington and Sarah Lawrence, as well as correlated courses for freshmen at many colleges and universities that are now known as core courses. However, progressivism—with its integrative impetus—had no major influence on college English at that time.

As the high schools exerted their independence from college requirements, the gap grew larger between university and high school in the teaching of English. Oscar Campbell, chair of Committee on Undergraduate Training for NCTE's Curriculum Commission, contrasted what was done at the college level to what was done in the schools. We quote him at length here because his description shows so clearly two divisions—the division between high school and college and the division between college composition and literature—as well as one link—the student-centered link between written composition and literature reading at high school level:

In composition, college courses for freshmen generally emphasize correctness and exactness in usage and structure. In other words, they stress the disciplinary aspect of the subject. Most [secondary] schools, particularly the so-called "progressive" ones, emphasize the creative aspect of composition. They regard it as an instrument for self-expression. Mastery of the conventions and accuracy of form are expected to attract the student's interest as essential instruments to the desired expression.

In the matter of literature, also, there is frequently complete divergence of aims. Schools are prone to emphasize the cultivation of a taste for reading. Therefore, the high-school student's present likings and immediate interests serve as a basis for the choice of books he is to read. Colleges, on the other hand, devise their first courses in literature either on the theory that literature forms a body of scholarly knowledge in the reading of which the student must learn to apply critical standards hallowed by tradition, or the theory that learning to read implies scholarly and intensive study of a few classics.[47]

During that period, college English experienced increased separation of reading and writing, as programs in literature and composition grew even farther apart. The literature faculty taught interpretation and criticism, and composition instructors focused on organizational and mechanical matters in writing. For a few years after World War II, composition instructors at some universities joined forces with communications instructors to teach courses in oral and written communication, but that collaboration was short-lived. It did, however, result in a professional organization for college writing instructors within NCTE, the Conference on College Composition and Communication. Composition faculty were building a community and a collective identity.

Literary criticism, an eclectic mix of philological, rhetorical, and impressionist approaches, became more unified when the theory known as New Criticism spread in the 1940s and took over the field by the 1950s. In this objectivist approach, attention was on the text itself as critics performed their close readings to see how form and content united into a coherent whole. New Critics avoided what they called the *intentional fallacy*, trying to ascertain authors' intent, and the *affective fallacy*, speculating about how texts affect readers.[48] (The latter crime would have been committed by those secondary teachers who followed Rosenblatt's approach or that advocated in *Conducting Experiences*.) New Criticism was a theoretical orientation toward reading practiced by specialists in literature. This approach, like other types of criticism, entailed some writing: literary scholars wrote critical essays about literary works, and students were evaluated on the bases of their written analyses.

PUBLIC ATTENTION TO LITERACY—READING AND WRITING AT MID-CENTURY

After World War II and with the onset of the Cold War, public attention was directed toward elementary and secondary education through such critiques as *Quackery in the Public Schools* (which declared that "some of the real 'enemies' of the public school are in its ranks") and *Educational Wastelands* (which claimed that "professional educationists have all but forgotten the high aims and ideals of American public education").[49] Many Americans had concerns about nontraditional educational practices in the schools, particularly those associated with progressivism, and had fears about the declining quality of American education. Little attention went to the report of the large-scale Eight Year Study, which showed the value of a progressivist course of study.[50] Centrifugal developments, in particular a movement to identify and foster "the basics" in the 1950s and 1960s, broke some connections that progressivism had made between reading and writing and put them back as separate components of a subject-centered curriculum. A progressive curriculum focused on holistic language experiences, student-centered projects, and correlation of subjects did not fit the public's conception of a traditional and rigorous course of study. What did fit were an elementary curriculum focused on reading and writing as separate subjects and a secondary curriculum focused on literature as the masterworks of American culture and on composition as mechanical correctness.

Much of the attention went to reading education. This was the time of the infamous mid-century "great debate" about the best approach to reading instruction. Debates had occurred before, as we noted earlier, but this time the American public participated along with educators. Rudolf Flesch aroused much public attention in 1955 with his *Why Johnny Can't Read*, in which he argued that students' difficulties in learning to read would be eliminated if teachers were to teach phonics explicitly and synthetically.[51] He saw synthetic phonics as the traditional approach and the analytic "word method" as an innovation. This was a criticism not only of the word approach but also of basals—and of the reading education profession. A year or two before, reading educators began forming a new professional organization, the International Reading Association (IRA), with the merger of two smaller organizations, and the union was effected in 1956. This organization, composed mainly of teachers working at the elementary level, included university researchers and reading educators, most notably William S. Gray, the first president.

After Sputnik challenged America's technological superiority, the federal government put more money into education. Eventually some of it went to English. In 1961 the Cooperative Research Act was expanded to include a program called Project English, which included curriculum development projects and other research relevant to the teaching of English. Some Project English studies, such as Kellogg Hunt's *Differences in Grammatical Structures Written at Three Grade Levels* and Richard Braddock, Richard Lloyd-Jones, and Lowell Schoer's synthesis, *Research in Written Composition*,[52] provided some research tools and a much-needed research base for composition. Hunt's study, based on Noam Chomsky's transformational grammar, generated the T-unit (minimal terminal unit), a construct used in numerous studies in the 1970s and 1980s. This foundation of research was important to the growing field of composition studies.

Federal funds also went specifically to reading education. The First Grade Studies—27 individual studies comparing various approaches to beginning reading—were funded by the Cooperative Research Program from 1964 to 1967. The studies did not identify a single best approach but pointed instead to the importance of teacher and school effects on reading achievement. Title I, initiated in 1965, put money into programs for children considered disadvantaged and employed a large number of teachers whose specialty was reading. The controversy over beginning reading continued, even after Jeanne Chall's notable attempt to sort out research in *Learning to Read: The Great Debate*.[53]

In the late 1960s, as upheavals were occurring in various social spheres, literacy education was looking fragmented. Reading education, which had become a specialized field apart from elementary English, had little theoretical coherence holding together its various parts: reading readiness, content area reading, and so on. What was needed, most of all, was a theory of comprehension that went beyond listing skills in some taxonomy. Elementary English itself was undergoing a name change to "language arts," but this too was often a collection, which included writing, speaking, listening, and a special kind of reading (literary) with little theoretical integration.

English as a discipline was experiencing an identity crisis. What made it a discipline? What held it together? At that time, when there was much interest in structure, including the structure of the disciplines, English did not seem to have a structure in the sense that some other disciplines did. The best anyone could come up with was a tripod model with literature, composition, and language as the three legs.[54] This metaphor provided no center for English as it simply affirmed the parts, the separate components. John Mayher has recently commented on the implications of the tripod, which is still influential:

Teachers could go on . . . teaching literature, grammar, and writing in separate compartments, usually on different days of the week, and letting whatever integration is required happen in the minds of the student rather than in the practices of the classroom.[55]

The quest to find a center for English resulted in the Dartmouth Conference, held in 1966 and attended by English and language arts educators from the United States and the United Kingdom. At that event—about which there is such nostalgia today—progressive notions met with the greatest approval for unifying English and creating a "new" English. In particular, personal growth—a theme from the work of James Britton, one of the participants—was favored by many members of the group, who also looked favorably at such practices as organizing courses around themes from human experience and creating a "language community" in which students' writings become the "literature."[56]

READING AND WRITING AT THE END OF THE 1960S

At this point, to set up the next section focusing on recent developments, we summarize the status of reading and writing at the end of the 1960s. During the first five decades of the twentieth century, reading and writing had been connected in some visions and practices of education and disconnected in others. Centripetal developments associated with progressivism brought together reading and writing (and oral uses of language) through some common central theme, such as experience, self-expression, and performance of projects. These developments were challenges to the subject-centered curriculum. Centrifugal developments, associated with the scientific measurement movement and disciplinary specializations, maintained or furthered the separation of reading and writing into distinct subjects—a separation that sharpened with the back-to-the-basics movement of the 1950s. The 1960s closed with much unrest within education and much public attention on education. Some favored the "traditional" curriculum, which meant the curriculum of the turn of the century, while others critiqued that vision and sought alternatives, often in some of the themes associated with progressivism.[57]

Recent Developments, 1970-1998

In this section, we discuss five influential movements that have fostered connections between reading and writing during the last three decades and that continue today: the comprehension-as-construction movement, the reader response movement, the process writing movement, the whole language movement, and the discourse community movement. For each, we consider the theoretical orientation as well as the pedagogical practices—all of which are important for understanding history and provide a foundation for this volume. We follow that discussion by mentioning some other evidences of the current trend toward integration. After that initial emphasis on connections, we conclude this section with a description of counter-trends toward separation of reading and writing, which have been, and continue to be, important too.

FIVE CENTRIPETAL MOVEMENTS

Comprehension and composition as construction. When the cognitive revolution impacted on education in the 1970s, reading education was transformed dramatically as people from various disciplines and fields—psychology, artificial intelligence, linguistics, and literacy—converged on reading as the focus of their studies of cognitive processes and as educators looked outward at these other disciplines. The study of reading was still "scientific," but the scientific emphasis was now on larger concerns: the nature of knowledge and understanding. John Bransford's pioneering work showed that, to understand a text, a reader has to bring meaning to it rather than simply take meaning from it. His early studies showed that comprehension was much more than simply decoding words. It involved much adding, much filling in. To understand a text, a reader had to make inferences on the basis of relevant prior knowledge. Many others began contributing to a unifying and overarching theory describing reading as a process of building—building mental meanings from textual cues.[58]

Reading, viewed thusly, had connections with writing, which was—more obviously than reading—a constructive process. Attention was going again, as it had in rhetoric, to the functional aspects of language, to the guidance writers provide their readers for organizing, selecting, and connecting content. Attention was also given to readers' knowledge—world knowledge, topic knowledge, discourse knowledge—as the material from which meaning is built. During the 1970s, cognitive models of reading were introduced, such as David Rumelhart's interactive model, which illustrated various kinds of knowledge operating in concert during interpretation.[59]

Since the mid-1970s considerable research has been guided by this shared constructivist conception. Much of it has focused on the effectiveness of various strategies in meaning making—strategies for comprehension monitoring, for identifying organizational patterns, and for locating particular information in a text. A major role in this work has been played by the Center for the Study of Reading at the University of Illinois, which was funded as a national center by the federal government from 1976 to 1991. The center, established with comprehension as its research agenda, presented some of its work for the public and policymakers in *Becoming a Nation of Readers*, written by Richard Anderson, Elfrieda Hiebert, Judith Scott, and Ian Wilkinson. The major claim was that "reading is a constructive act" and should be taught accordingly.[60]

Several reading-writing connections have been made within this broad constructivist orientation. In particular, an important conceptual link has been made between reading and writing. These processes have some similarities—both involve the active construction of meaning— rather than being the inverse of each other. For instance, P. David Pearson and Robert Tierney have noted parallels between the reading process and the writing process, as it was described by John R. Hayes and Linda Flower in their cognitive process model of writing.[61] Corre- lations between reading and writing abilities have been studied, some showing, for instance, that reading and writing abilities tend to develop concurrently, rather than sequentially.[62] Knowledge has been gained about writers' cues and readers' processes, as researchers pursue the same issue that interested the Scottish rhetoricians in the eighteenth century: how particular choices made by a writer influence readers' understanding. For instance, some studies have shown that particular organizational configurations work better for readers who know much about a topic and others work better for readers who know less, and other studies suggest that it is more important for authors to specify some kinds of connections (*however, but*) for their readers than other kinds of connections (*because*), which can be more easily inferred.[63]

Attention has also gone to acts of literacy that include both reading and writing, such as summarization, in which writers reduce and re- present other writers' texts; critiquing, in which writers comment upon other writers' texts; and discourse synthesis, in which writers use multiple texts written by others to produce their own. Some of the studies in critiquing and discourse synthesis, discussed in chapters in this volume by Maureen Mathison and by Nancy Nelson, were con- ducted by researchers at the Center for the Study of Writing, which was established at the University of California, Berkeley, and Carnegie Mellon University from 1986 to 1996.[64] (It is worth noting that a national center for writing research was established a decade after the center for reading research.)

Social factors have been a major focus of this work dealing with cognitive processes. One factor of interest is the socially acquired knowledge that people use in reading and writing, including their knowledge of discourse conventions and forms associated with mem- bership in various social groups. Another is the rhetorical relationship between writer and reader. This includes both (a) how a writer's perception of audience influences the writing and (b) how a reader's perception of author influences the reading. The research on writers' awareness of audience is discussed further in Donald Rubin's chapter in this volume, and the work focused on readers' awareness of author is discussed further in two other chapters—one by Timothy Shanahan and the other by Margaret McKeown and Isabel Beck. The term "rhetorical reading" was coined by Christina Haas and Linda Flower for reading that involves much attention to the author and to the context in which the author worked.[65]

Reader response. Reader response is one of three interrelated movements—which also include process writing and whole language—that have collectively pulled reading and writing together toward common centers. As our review will show, these three share themes characteristic of the progressive era in education: growth, experience, and self-expression.

The label *reader response* is given to an interrelated set of theories offered in the 1970s that collectively impacted literary studies at the college level. Particularly important were the theories of three Americans—David Bleich, Stanley Fish, and Norman Holland—and the theory of Wolfgang Iser in Europe. Louise Rosenblatt built upon her earlier theoretical position in *Literature as Exploration* with another book, *The Reader, the Text, the Poem*—a book that, as it turned out, became more influential in secondary and elementary schools than in higher education.[66] This book too repeated the themes of the progressive educators: experience, expression, and organic growth. Reader-response theory countered the objectivist position of the New Criticism, which was so powerful in college literature classes. It privileged individual readers' unique responses, in contrast to the New Criticism, which downplayed readers' individual and subjective responses to texts.

The most visible reading-writing connection came in practice that followed from this theoretical orientation. In classrooms incorporating reader response theory, students were likely to produce expressive writing through composing response papers or keeping journals. Expressive writing was different from the analytic essays associated with literature courses based on literary criticism (New Critical or otherwise). Actually what was being done in the classrooms had some similarities to the procedure used by researchers in the 1960s before these theorists produced their influential works. During that decade there had been a number of response studies, usually conducted by soliciting and analyzing written pieces after people had read a work.[67]

This movement is not so important today in college literature classes, now that poststructuralists have critiqued subjectivity and literary scholars have moved to other models, such as feminism and cultural studies. However, reader response, particularly Rosenblatt's version, is quite influential in elementary and secondary settings. It has more of a social slant today as teachers have students share their responses and develop responses with others. Here Bleich has been helpful, as he gave emphasis to the negotiation among members of a classroom community. A social emphasis can also be seen in Rosenblatt's earlier work. In his chapter in this volume, Richard Beach uses reader response as a point of departure for a different conception of literary response based on a conversational metaphor.

A social orientation to responsive reading has guided the work of the National Research Center on Literature Teaching and Learning located at the State University of New York at Albany from 1991 to 1997. Of particular importance is the work of Judith Langer, who has discussed the various stances that readers take in response to literature and encouraged the use of writing (e.g., logs and letters) as well as oral conversations to foster response.[68]

The writing process and process writing. In 1971 Janet Emig drew attention to the writing process with publication of *The Composing Processes of Twelfth Graders*, which was followed by several other studies of the composing processes of students at various levels of education, including Donald Graves's study of *The Composing Processes of First Graders*.[69] Using composing-aloud procedures, Emig studied the behaviors (prewriting and planning, starting, composing aloud, stopping, contemplating the product, reformulating) of a small number of students as they moved recursively, backward as well as forward, through the process of writing. She built on prior work from *Project English*: Braddock et al.'s synthesis and also a study by Gordon Rohman and Albert Wlecke, who had reinstated the organic plant metaphor from the Romantic poets and used it to describe the writing process. She made connections not only with the theory of John Dewey but also with the work of James Britton, whose growth model, so important at the Dartmouth Conference, was a model of composing as well.[70]

Other important studies of the writing process were conducted by Flower and Hayes, whose work was mentioned above. Their studies, like Emig's and the studies that followed hers, showed the recursive, rather than linear, nature of writing, with writers moving back and forth from one subprocess to another. There were other studies as well, including some that focused on a single aspect of composing, such as revision strategies or computer-assisted invention.[71]

At the same time, a new pedagogy was developing across all levels of schooling that fostered the writing process and was loosely related to the ongoing research in the composing process. Major influences during the 1970s were books about empowerment of students as writers, such as Peter Elbow's *Writing without Teachers* and Ken Macrorie's *Telling Writing* and books providing guidance for teachers, such as James Moffett and Betty Jane Wagner's *Student-Centered Curriculum*. Later, in the 1980s, Graves's *Writing: Teachers and Students at Work* would become sort of a bible for many elementary teachers, and Nancie Atwell's *In the Middle* would be read by high school teachers and elementary teachers as well as its intended audience of middle school teachers.[72] As in the progressive pedagogies of earlier decades, students were encouraged to develop their own voices, express their own thoughts, and choose their own topics, and were given social support through such means as peer response groups and teacher conferences. Through this workshop approach reading and writing were connected, as students moved back and forth between roles as reader and writer.

A new model for faculty development of writing teachers appeared when the Bay Area Writing Project held its first summer institute for teachers in 1974, evolving into the National Writing Project (NWP) in 1977. NWP projects continue to operate under the same set of assumptions, of which one figures prominently: teachers become better teachers of writing by becoming writers themselves. Social processes have always been important, as teachers participating in institutes respond to one another's writing and publish anthologies of writing for others to read.[73]

In the 1970s some of the attention that had gone to reading was now directed to writing. Among educators there was much enthusiasm and confidence that the new attention to writing would solve the problems in students' writing that were noted by authors of such pieces as "Why Johnny Can't Write" and *The Great American Writing Block*.[74]

Associated with the writing process movement are programs in *writing across the curriculum* (WAC), which began in the United States in the 1970s with ties to language-across-the-curriculum programs in England. The latter were described in the Bullock report, for which James Britton was one of the authors.[75] As George Newell mentions in his chapter in this volume, features of the process-oriented pedagogy have been incorporated into content fields in schools and disciplines in colleges and universities. An empirical base, including studies by Arthur Applebee, Judith Langer, George Newell, Russel Durst, and their colleagues, has provided some justification for using analytic writing assignments to promote learning. These studies, discussed by Newell, have demonstrated advantages for extended writing (i.e., essays) over restricted writing (i.e., summaries, notes).[76] WAC now faces a number of challenges which, according to Barbara Walvoord, include not only providing evidence of effectiveness but also establishing a more secure place in the structure of schooling, where interdisciplinary programs tend to come and go but compartmentalization remains.[77]

The writing process movement has become somewhat amalgamated with reader response, with which it has some philosophical affinities, particularly through the progressive influence of Rosenblatt. In fact, Emig, when addressing writing researchers, called Rosenblatt "our closest intellectual ally in literature research" because of Dewey's influence and other theoretical similarities.[78] This movement has also become somewhat amalgamated with whole language, which we discuss next.

Whole language. "Whole language" refers to a conception of language learning that emphasizes holistic aspects of language and learning, including the following: (a) the modalities of language (listening, speaking, reading, writing) develop in concert with one another; (b) they develop in holistic, naturalistic situations, as children perform communicative acts; and (c) learning often moves from whole to part. The whole language movement, which began in the 1970s, is associated with particular individuals, such as Kenneth and Yetta Goodman, but it has, as Patrick Shannon has noted, some similarities to the progressive literacy education of earlier decades, which was also holistic.[79] The great reading debates of the 1950s and 1960s are being reenacted today with instruction in phonics (which many consider the "traditional" approach) opposing a larger opponent, whole language, instead of whole word.

The knowledge base supporting whole language includes studies of emergent literacy, which show that literacy starts developing when children are quite young, as they are read story books and encounter print in their environment and attempt to produce texts of their own. Through such experiences, children begin learning literate forms of language that they will use in reading and writing.[80] Other research in emergent literacy shows that children seem to go through "pretend" forms of literacy, scribbling and pretending to read, before the more conventional forms. This body of work also includes some studies of children who learn to read without formal instruction.[81] The emergent literacy notion, which presents literacy learning as a gradual process without a clear beginning point, contrasts with the earlier notion of reading readiness, which assumed that there was a kind of dividing line between the time a child was not ready and the time he or she was ready to learn to read.

Whole language, as its advocates explain, is a set of beliefs, not a particular approach or approaches to education. Nevertheless, adherents are likely to adopt certain practices in their classrooms and avoid others. Whole-language teachers working with young children are likely to provide students with shared-book experiences through which they emulate the kind of storybook reading that occurs in home settings. "Natural" is a hallmark of whole language: the materials of instruction are almost certain to be natural—children's literature as well as other authentic forms of communication. These materials serve as models—"natural" models, not the prescriptive models of past times— connecting reading and writing, as children learn, through their own reading, the conventions and styles of writing that writers use. Whole-language teachers would avoid practices and materials that fragment language processes, such as synthetic phonics lessons.

The whole-language orientation is compatible with reader response and process writing approaches. Thus, some people, such as John Willinsky, consider them a single movement, "the new literacy," even though their recent origins seem to differ and different people have been instrumental in their development.[82] Reader response and process writing have obvious links to progressivism of earlier times with their emphasis on experience, activity, and expression, and theorists associated with both pedagogies credit Dewey for some of their ideas. The progressive link is not so explicit to whole language, since whole language advocates do not typically cite Dewey and other progressives. However, as noted earlier, other scholars have linked whole language positions and progressivism.

Discourse communities. The final integrative development we include here is the discourse community movement. The concept of community is not novel in education, but what is new is the centrality of the community notion in the thought and practice of many literacy educators. Here, as in the cognitive construction movement, the focus is also on constructive processes and constructed products, but, instead of being tied to individuals, these processes and products of meaning making are tied to groups. Emphasis is on the social construction of meanings for texts as well as the social construction of genres, conventions, and even knowledge.[83]

A discourse community is a group of people held together by a common interest who make contributions to communal discourse through the group's forums and who follow the group's own particular discourse conventions.[84] A community can be as large as the number of people in a particular discipline, such as psychology, or subfield within it, such as ecological psychology, or it can be as small as a discussion group that communicates regularly by e-mail. Becoming a member of a discourse community involves taking on what James Gee has called an identity kit, a "saying (writing)-doing-being-valuing-believing" combination.[85] Over time, an individual adopts the ways of "speaking" (which often includes writing) and the ways of knowing used by that community and begins to participate in its practices. Such participation can be likened to joining a conversation—a conversation that can extend, chainlike, across long distances of space and time—in which texts are responses to other texts. This is the sort of conversation implicit in Mikhail Bakhtin's dialogic conception of communication.[86]

This community conception has done much to unify reading, writing, and the oral uses of language, particularly with respect to disciplinary discourse. A community is seen as constructing a body of knowledge as its members read one another's texts and build upon one another's work in producing one's own—thus blending roles of author and audience. It is an authoring community, but is also, to use Stanley Fish's term, an interpretive community.[87] The discourse community notion provides a rationale for the WAC movement in higher education that differs from that associated with process writing. Actually it is more a justification of writing *within* the disciplines than of writing *across* the disciplines. Instead of personal involvement, its focus is on the kind of enculturation that is involved in learning a discipline, as noted in Mathison's chapter in this volume. To learn a discipline, a student needs to learn how people in that discipline support their arguments, present their research, and so on. Learning can result from working on research papers in a discipline, which, if guidance is provided, afford opportunities for students to acquire discourse conventions and to find how various community members align themselves on particular issues.

To people interested in elementary education, all this talk about disciplinary discourse may seem far removed from the elementary

classroom, but the community conception has been important in discussions of children's literacy learning too. Frank Smith has popularized the notion in his discussion of children's joining the "literacy
club."[88]

A number of researchers, informed by Dell Hymes's discussion in
the 1970s of language communities and communicative competence,
have studied conventional practices in children's schooling.[89] The idea
here is that a particular class, composed of students and a teacher, is a
community embedded within the larger community of American
schooling and, as such, follows its conventions in producing oral and
written discourse. This includes such matters as who fills what role
and who has speaking rights. However, as a community unto itself as
well, a class also constructs its own more idiosyncratic conventions for
its discourse, such as rules for the kinds of comments that can be made
after a class member reads his or her writing to the group. Two chapters in this volume, one by Melanie Sperling and one by Paul Prior,
discuss social patterns associated with teachers' responses to student
writing, a pedagogical practice associated with process writing.

Some ethnographic studies have shown that the discourse patterns
that children learn before starting school can match fairly well or can
contrast sharply with the discourse patterns of American schooling.
For instance, in her well-known study conducted in the Piedmont Car-
olinas, Shirley Brice Heath found that mainstream, middle-class children learn a kind of recitation discourse during storybook reading time
with their parents—a pattern quite similar to that used in oral and
written discourse practices in American schooling—and have a kind of
head start when they begin schooling.[90] Studies by Heath and others
have found that children whose home cultures do not match so well
often experience difficulties that can be attributed, not to the vocabulary or syntax, but to the pragmatics of language, to their not knowing
who is supposed to speak and what kind of contribution is expected.

The discourse community conception has integrated reading and
writing in two ways: first, by including reading and writing as well as
oral uses of language in a larger endeavor, the social construction of
knowledge, and, second, by describing larger patterns that subsume
both production and reception of discourse.

Additional evidence of centripetal trends. Besides these linkages in
thought and practice, there are other evidences of centripetal trends, as
a broader conception—literacy education—sometimes replaces reading
education and English/language arts education. NCTE and IRA, with

overlapping memberships and with some of the same people in leadership roles in both organizations, have recently collaborated on recommendations for National Standards for English/Language Arts. Three of the standards they proposed are particularly integrative: two that deal with research and inquiry ("gather, evaluate, and synthesize data from a variety of sources," and "use a variety of technical and informational resources . . . to gather and synthesize information and to create and communicate knowledge") and one that deals with the collaborative nature of learning ("participate as knowledgeable, reflective, creative, and critical members of a variety of literacy communities").[91]

Several name changes reflect a broader conception: the National Conference on Research in English is now the National Conference on Research in Language and Literacy, and the National Reading Conference (NRC) now calls its publication *Journal of Literacy Research* instead of *Journal of Reading Behavior*. Also one of the first titles in a new monograph series, *Literacy Studies*, to be produced by two "reading" organizations, NRC and IRA, deals with writing instruction. Many universities, which had separate programs titled Reading Education and English Education/Language Arts, now offer programs with such titles as Literacy Education or Language and Literacy Education.

CURRENT CENTRIFUGAL INFLUENCES

Concurrent with these centripetal trends, literacy education is also experiencing centrifugal influences. The traditional subject-centered curriculum, with its historical divisions, is still quite powerful in elementary, secondary, and higher education, defining academic specialities for faculty as well as curriculum for students.

Today, teacher educators in literacy education are often still identified as either reading people or writing people. Despite the overlapping memberships in large professional organizations, the divisions are still quite apparent in individuals' scholarly endeavors. For instance, the American Educational Research Association has a Special Interest Group (SIG) on Basic Research in Reading and Literacy and a SIG on Writing and Literacies, both of which sponsor paper sessions at the annual conference. The groups have different participants and different types of papers, despite the inclusion of *literacy* in both names to reflect broader interests.

College English, a discipline that still lacks a center, is populated by literature (reading) people and composition (writing) people who have experienced different kinds of graduate education, who cite different authors, who use different terminology, and who publish in different journals; and turf wars still rage. Attempts to create a more integrated discipline are often resisted out of fear that a group other than one's own might gain more power than it already has. For example, at the English Coalition Conference, held in 1987, two decades after the Dartmouth Conference, members of the college contingent came up with the idea of recommending a two-semester course for college freshmen that dealt with both reading and writing. However, composition people feared that literature folks would see that kind of course as an opportunity to return to the domination of literature in the discipline.[92] Parity has come about, in large part, because composition now has an impressive body of scholarship, sometimes called the "new rhetoric," which started accumulating in the 1970s and which includes studies of the composing process, research in the discourse community, and also work in rhetorical theory. Within composition today, there is attention to reading, but this composition version of reading differs from the literary reading that belongs to the other part of the English department.

In the precollegiate curriculum of elementary and secondary schools, the course called language arts/reading or English is often still a collection of separate components, each with its own traditions, theoretical underpinnings, and terminology. It is not unusual for elementary and secondary teachers, who have themselves been schooled without linkages, to shift traditions and theories when moving instruction from one component to another and to mark the shift with different terminology. For instance, an elementary teacher might teach students about "main idea" when teaching reading and about "topic sentence" when teaching writing—without pointing out any overlap. The very fact that "integrated language arts" is still considered novel is evidence that the arts are not yet integrated.[93]

"Back to the basics," a recurring theme in the public discourse about education, continues to be a centrifugal influence on reading and writing. Grounded in a subject-centered conception of curriculum, the agenda of basics advocates is a return to—and intensification of—past educational practices. The calls for returning to the basics are calls for familiar categories and practices—a "traditional" curriculum with the long-established subject divisions. For elementary students, in addition to arithmetic, this would be reading (approached through phonics) and writing (emphasizing grammar, mechanical correctness, and conventional spelling), with the two taught separately. For secondary students, this would be English with its two major components—literature (limited to the literary "canon") and composition (emphasizing correctly written sentences, paragraphs, and "themes")—

as well as science, history, and mathematics. Basics advocates want learning to be monitored closely through testing, grades, and report cards, and they favor such methods as drill and recitation in the classroom and homework outside of it.[94] Integrative practices (e.g., reading-writing workshops) associated with the five integrative movements just discussed do not fit in this conception, and some integrative notions, such as whole language and portfolios, are perceived as threats.

Like back-to-the-basics movements, with which they are sometimes associated, accountability movements on the part of policymakers tend to have centrifugal influences on reading and writing. These influences are largely due to the measurement tools that are used: tests in which reading and writing are typically tested as totally separate kinds of knowledge. Achievement is measured for reading and writing as well as mathematics and other subject contents, and comparisons are made across students, across teachers, across schools, across communities, and even across states in local report cards, state report cards, and a national report card. The current accountability wave, which began in the 1970s and escalated in the 1980s, when *A Nation at Risk* appeared, brought a dramatic increase in statewide testing. States began setting standards and developing means of assessing progress toward them, and national goals were established for America 2000. The movement continues in the 1990s with implementation of the Goals 2000: Educate America Act.[95]

What sorts of tests are employed? For reading, the typical standardized test provides relatively brief passages, each followed by multiple-choice questions. The questions are often classified according to particular comprehension "skills" (e.g., inference questions, sequencing questions) so that a student can be given a profile of scores according to the various skills as well as an overall score. This approach, which has been around for decades, predated the constructivist conception of comprehension that developed since the 1970s. Although this type of test dominates, there have been some attempts, most notably in Illinois and Michigan, to develop reading tests that are more consistent with the comprehension research and with a conception of reading as meaning making.[96] These newer process-oriented tests assess such aspects of reading as the strategies students use at particular points in the process and the approaches they take to arrive at particular interpretations. As for composition, a writing test in the fairly recent past would not have even required students to write, but instead would have had them identify errors or select the "correct" way of saying something from a set of options. Increasingly, though, testmakers have moved beyond this sort of indirect measure to direct measures of writing, in which each student produces a piece of writing in response to a prompt and the writing is judged for quality by raters.

In many cases, different theoretical frameworks undergird the tests of reading and writing used in large-scale assessments. For example, when the state writing assessment was developed in Texas, James Kinneavy's neoclassical theory of discourse was used for designating the types of writing to be measured.[97] Writing to be produced by students was distinguished according to mode (narration, description, and classification) and purpose (expressive, informative, and persuasive). However, that mode-purpose framework was not used at all in the reading portion, even though the writing framework was derived from a theory of *discourse*, not simply a theory of writing, and was thus applicable also to reading. The reading test was based on a skills conception.

We should, at this point, acknowledge recent attempts to develop more integrative measures, particularly through what is called "performance assessment." Maryland, which has taken the performance approach in its School Performance Assessment Program, provides students with "authentic," consequential literacy tasks, which require integration of reading and writing.[98] For instance, students might be asked to generate some new text (e.g., a written version of a talk to be given to a club meeting) from a set of materials, which might include a full-length informative text, a story, and some graphic materials. The emphasis is on how well students solve problems and how well they can apply what they learn, but there are also scores for reading and writing. Performance is judged by raters using rubrics.

High-stakes tests, such as the state assessments, can have a profound impact on curriculum, as administrators and teachers align curricula to the conception of literacy implicit in the test, even when it contrasts sharply with the stated instructional framework of the school district or with individual teachers' preferences.[99] Teachers do often teach to the test when the stakes are high. Materials similar to those on the test are selected or are developed if they are not available commercially, and conditions of testing are sometimes replicated in the classroom so that students have practice in the procedures. The major pattern of influence from accountability movements has been centripetal, not because a demand for accountability *has* to lead to a division between reading and writing, but because most measurement tools now available reflect that longstanding division in American schooling and because assessment guides instruction.

Summary and Conclusion

The history of literacy instruction can be viewed, as we have viewed it here, as an interplay of centripetal and centrifugal developments. Reading and writing tend to become more unified when the center becomes something other than one of the major school subjects (English, reading, language arts) that are so familiar to Americans today. However, the subject called rhetoric, which emphasizes social aspects of communication, has been and can be integrative, as it deals with the relationship between author and audience and with rhetorical principles to be used in understanding as well as producing texts. The various foci of the progressive educators of the 1920s, 1930s, and 1940s, such as growth, self-expression, and experience, were integrative, as they encompassed various language modalities. In progressive classrooms students assumed roles as writers and readers of their own work and as readers of other students' work as they expressed themselves and shared experiences. The neoprogressive movements of more recent times—reader response, process writing, and whole language—have brought back a focus on personal growth, self-expression, and experience, and the new attention to emergent literacy has pointed out additional relations in development. Reading educators' conception of comprehension as cognitive construction of meaning has highlighted parallels between reading and composition, and the current focus on social construction of knowledge has blurred some boundaries between the modalities, since writers build their own contributions on the work of others. This writing from reading occurs with electronic texts as well as paper texts.

Concurrently with these centripetal developments that pull reading and writing together, centrifugal trends have pushed reading and writing apart. Earlier in this century, the scientific measurement movement, with its acceptance of subject boundaries, including those between reading and writing, coincided with the progressive movement; and today a back-to-the-basics movement and an accountability movement co-occur with the five integrative movements we discussed. Conflicting theories, different traditions, and turf issues persist. They characterize our complex field and motivate many of our discussions.

This history has shown, first, that connections between reading and writing are not all new and, second, that disconnections are not all old. Despite our emphasis on integrative developments for this volume on connections, we have tried to guard against any inclination to present this history as an evolutionary process in which reading and writing, which were separated in past times, have now finally, and happily, come together. We have also avoided presenting literacy instruction in terms of a simple cyclical pattern in which an integrative conception of literacy is developed, only to be replaced by a divergent conception, and so on. Rather, we have tried to show how both connections and separations are manifested, often at the same time, as some people see and treat reading and writing as connected and others see and treat them as separate. At some points the convergence has seemed most prominent, and at other points it is the divergence that is most noticeable.

If we are to understand current movements, such as reading-writing connections, it is important to know the historical context in which relevant theories and practices have emerged. When discussing the "essential tension" between innovation and tradition, Thomas Kuhn pointed out that "new theories are not born *de novo*. On the contrary, they emerge from old theories and within a matrix of old beliefs."[100]

Overview of the Volume

The eleven chapters that follow this introductory chapter treat, in more depth, some of the developments and issues we have introduced. The chapters are grouped according to three kinds of connections between reading and writing (author-audience connections, classroom connections, and connections within a discipline or domain), although any one of the chapters could probably fit in either of the other categories. We have arranged them where they have the most obvious fit.

A major strength of this collection, we think, is the broad developmental perspective that is taken. In this chapter we set the stage by reviewing historical patterns of education in literacy from the early years through college. In the chapters that follow, authors deal with specific topics or issues that are central to considerations of reading-writing connections today, but, as they do so, they discuss relevant work conducted with students of various ages as well as implications for instruction at various levels. That is true even for those whose chapters are primarily reports of studies conducted at a particular level of schooling.

The next four chapters, written by Donald Rubin, James Murphy, Timothy Shanahan, and Margaret McKeown and Isabel Beck, all deal in some way with the relationship between writer and reader. Collectively, they show the importance of emphasizing those intersubjective elements of communication that, during much of this century, have received little attention in American education, particularly when the study of rhetoric decreased in importance in the colleges and universities. As these authors all emphasize, texts are social products: the products of human authors, who draw on prior social experiences in their writing and who write purposely to accomplish goals with their readers, who have their own purposes and goals and bring their own social experiences to their reading. For the chapters comprising this section we have used the label "The Author-Audience Context."

In "Writing for Readers: The Primacy of Audience in Composing," Rubin presents support for his argument that audience is the central element in composing. He gives particular attention to the role of audience in the composing process and to developmental aspects of writers' awareness of, and adaptation for, audience. That fairly recent work relates to many of the concerns of classical rhetoric, which Murphy discusses in the following chapter, "What Is Rhetoric and What Can It Do for Writers and Readers?" In classical times, rhetoric emphasized the pragmatic aspects of communication: the use of language in particular situations with particular audiences for particular reasons. This pragmatic emphasis can also be seen in literacy studies today. After an overview of major rhetorical principles, Murphy describes the Roman educational system, particularly its integrated approach to the teaching of rhetoric, in which speaking and writing were taught in concert with listening and reading.

In contrast to Rubin and Murphy, who focus mainly on the author's relationship with audience, Shanahan looks the other direction, from audience to author, to consider "Readers' Awareness of Author." He points to the recent attention to author in two bodies of work: one dealing with the reading of literary texts and the other with the reading of informational, disciplinary texts. Studies of both kinds of reading suggest a linkage between heightened awareness of author and expertise in reading. Shanahan concludes with a discussion of development factors in author awareness, and provides illustrations from interviews he conducted with school children. That chapter is followed by a related piece, "Talking to an Author: Readers Taking Charge of the Reading Process," by McKeown and Beck, who present an instructional approach designed to increase students' awareness of author as they read textbooks and stories. That approach, which McKeown and Beck have used with elementary students, was motivated by their own prior research into children's difficulties in understanding their textbooks, which tend to be authoritative as sources of knowledge but almost "authorless" in terms of writing style.

The next four chapters by Melanie Sperling, Paul Prior, George Newell, and Robert Calfee are grouped together in a section called "The Classroom Context." This kind of social context is currently receiving a great deal of attention in research and pedagogy, as we noted earlier, and is often discussed in terms of classroom communities and the cultural patterns tied to them. These authors consider what happens when particular instructional practices (e.g., providing assignments for writing and learning, responding as readers to students' writing) are implemented in classroom settings. All four chapters deal with the interrelations of reading and writing (and often listening and speaking too) as language is used in the practices associated with schooling.

Both Sperling and Prior consider teachers' responses to students' writing—a topic of much interest to teachers in most areas of the curriculum and all levels of education. In her discussion of "Teachers as Readers of Student Writing," Sperling examines the classroom practices and shifting roles in a classroom community as teachers respond to students' writing. She shows how teachers assume different roles, read for various purposes, and respond in multiple voices. Her chapter considers both written comments and oral response, and it includes research conducted with students of various levels of schooling, although her extended examples come from secondary classrooms. Prior continues the discussion in "Contextualizing Teachers' Responses to Writing in the College Classroom" as he also argues for a more expansive perspective on response. In contrast to Sperling's emphasis on multiplicity of responses in classroom contexts, Prior's emphasis is on the temporal dimension, the history of a classroom. He shows how, over time, various kinds of classroom interactions, most of which involve reading, shape students' interpretations of their writing tasks and also influence teachers' responses to students' performances. Although his insights come from research in graduate seminars, Prior sketches general implications for teachers at all levels of instruction who give writing assignments to their students.

Newell's chapter, " 'How Much Are We the Wiser?' Continuity and Change in Writing and Learning in the Content Areas," responds to a question raised by James Britton, a major figure in the writing process movement. After discussing the theory on which writing-to-learn is based, Newell assesses how much is now known about writing as a means of learning, and he sketches new directions that research should take. He gives much attention to specific tasks of writing and learning, including those in which students read informational texts and use them as sources when they compose their own. In the following chapter, "Leading Middle-Grade Students from Reading to Writing," Calfee examines a number of common classroom practices that lead either to integration or to separation of reading and writing. His major attention, however, is on the integrative potential of two particular tasks requiring students to produce compositions based on their reading. These tasks are known as the *book report*, and the *research paper*. Calfee considers their current status in the education of middle-grade students and suggests ways for teachers to present them to their students.

The final three chapters by Richard Beach, Maureen Mathison, and Nancy Nelson, which are grouped together in a section entitled "The Disciplinary Context," all consider connections between reading and writing as they are performed in contexts that are larger and more abstract than the rhetorical context of author and audience and the social context of the classroom. These authors show how students' reading and writing fit into ongoing traditions, including those of the academic disciplines.

Beach and Mathison both consider forms of writing that are associated with the practices of particular academic communities. For Beach, the context is that of the discipline of English, in which students are often expected to respond in writing to the literature they read. His piece, "Writing about Literature: A Dialogic Approach," is a contribution to a long-running conversation among English and language arts educators about the kind of writing students should do when responding to literature. Beach suggests that, instead of writing essays that constrain interpretation, students should be encouraged to explore the multiple, competing meanings of a text. His Bakhtinian approach to reading and writing involves writers' reflecting on conflicts and tensions that are raised by a text. In the following chapter, "Students as Critics of Disciplinary Texts," Mathison also considers a form of writing that is based on reading. This form is the critique. After reviewing the history of critique in the scientific and social-scientific tradition, Mathison focuses on the place of critique in the current discourse practices of sociology and in the education of students learning sociology. Using illustrations from a recent study, she shows how sociologists' expectations for critique can differ from students' realizations, and she draws some implications for schooling.

In the concluding chapter, "Reading and Writing Contextualized," Nelson calls into question three conceptual boundaries in literacy education: the boundary between reading and writing, the boundary between writer and reader, and the boundary between texts. Examples of various types—from classroom discourse to disciplinary discourse to electronic discourse—show that in many acts of literacy people are both readers and writers, constructing meanings for the texts they write while they construct meanings for the texts they read. In this larger context, one's identity as a reader and writer is constructed through social relationships with other readers and writers.

NOTES

1. The center metaphor has been employed in other histories of academic disciplines, for example, Irwin Altman, "Centripetal and Centrifugal Trends in Psychology," *American Psychologist* 42 (1987): 1058-1069, and Gerard Radnitzky, ed., *Centripetal Forces in the Sciences* (New York: Paragon House, 1987).

2. For general treatments of this period, see R. Freeman Butts and Lawrence A. Cremin, *A History of Education in American Culture* (New York: Holt, Rinehart and Winston, 1953); Joel Spring, *The American School, 1642-1985* (New York: Longman, 1986); and Colyer Meriwether, *Our Colonial Curriculum, 1607-1770* (Washington, D.C.: Capital Publishing, 1907). For articles and books that deal specifically with the history of literacy instruction, see Jennifer Monaghan, "Readers Writing: The Curriculum of the Writing Schools of Eighteenth Century Boston," *Visible Language* 21 (1987): 167-213; Jennifer Monaghan and E. Wendy Saul, "The Reader, the Scribe, the Thinker: A Critical Look at the History of American Reading and Writing Instruction," in *The Formation of School Subjects: The Struggle for Creating an American Institution*, ed. Thomas S. Popkewitz (New York: Falmer, 1987); H. Alan Robinson, ed., *Reading and Writing Instruction in the United States: Historical Trends* (Newark, Del.: International Reading Association, 1977); Nila Banton Smith, *American Reading Instruction* (New York: Silver, Burdett and Co., 1934); and Geraldine Jonçich Clifford, "A Sisyphean Task: Historical Perspectives on Writing and Reading Instruction," in *Collaboration through Writing and Reading*, ed. Anne Haas Dyson (Urbana, Ill.: National Council of Teachers of English, 1989), pp. 25-83.

3. See Susan Hunter and Ray Wallace, eds., *The Place of Grammar in Writing Instruction: Past, Present, Future* (Portsmouth, N.H.: Boynton/Cook, 1995) for discussions of the role of grammar in American schooling.

4. Harriet Webster Marr, *The Old New England Academies* (New York: Comet, 1959).

5. Major works in classical rhetoric include Aristotle's *Rhetoric*, Cicero's *On Invention and On Oratory and Orators*, and Quintilian's *Institutes of Oratory* (or *Education of the Orator*); also important is the *Rhetorica ad Herennium*, which incorporates many of Cicero's concepts but was not written by him. All are available in various translations and editions. Historical treatments of classical rhetoric include George A. Kennedy, *Classical Rhetoric and Its Christian and Secular Tradition from Ancient to Modern Times* (Chapel Hill: University of North Carolina Press, 1980) and Edward P. J. Corbett, *Classical Rhetoric for the Modern Student*, 2nd ed. (New York: Oxford University Press, 1971).

Rhetoric in colonial colleges is discussed in James J. Murphy, ed., *A Short History of Writing Instruction from Ancient Greece to Twentieth-Century America* (Davis, Cal.: Hermagoras Press, 1990) and Frederick Rudolph, *Curriculum: A History of the American Undergraduate Course of Study since 1636* (San Francisco: Jossey-Bass, 1981).

6. See discussion in Erika Lindemann, *A Rhetoric for Writing Teachers* (New York: Oxford University Press, 1982), pp. 242-245. Donald Murray argued the process position in "Teach Writing as Process not Product," *The Leaflet of the New England Association of Teachers of English* (November, 1972): 11-14.

7. See review by Robert J. Tierney and Timothy Shanahan: "Research on the Reading-Writing Relationship: Interactions, Transactions, and Outcomes," in *Handbook of Reading Research*, vol. 2, ed. Rebecca Barr, Michael L. Kamil, Peter Mosenthal, and P. David Pearson (New York: Longman, 1991), pp. 246-280.

8. Ramus assigned invention to the province of logic rather than rhetoric. The work of Ramus includes *Institutiones Dialecticae* and also the *Rhetorica* (which is sometimes attributed to him and sometimes to his colleague, Omer Talon).

For a discussion of Ramist rhetoric and its influence, see Walter J. Ong, S. J., *Ramus: Method and the Decay of Dialogue* (New York: Octogon Books, 1979). The importance of Ramism in New England and in the Harvard curriculum was documented in Samuel Eliot Morrison's histories, *The Founding of Harvard College* (Cambridge, Mass.: Harvard University Press, 1935) and *Harvard College in the Seventeenth Century* (Cambridge, Mass.: Harvard University Press, 1936) and Perry Miller's history, *The New England Mind: The Seventeenth Century* (New York: Macmillan, 1939).

9. George Campbell, *The Philosophy of Rhetoric* (New York: Harper and Brothers, 1846; first edition, 1776); Hugh Blair, *Lectures on Rhetoric and Belles Lettres* (Philadelphia: T. Ellwood Zell, 1867; first edition, 1783).

10. Blair, *Lectures*, p. 13.

11. Compare Richard Whately's *Elements of Rhetoric* (New York: Sheldon, 1867; first edition, 1828), which continued the rhetorical tradition of Campbell and Blair, with John Franklin Genung's *The Practical Elements of Rhetoric* (Boston: Ginn, 1892), which accompanied the movement to composition.

The transformation of rhetoric during the nineteenth century has been the subject of three histories: James A. Berlin, *Writing Instruction in Nineteenth-Century American Colleges* (Carbondale: Southern Illinois University Press, 1984); Nan Johnson, *Nineteenth-Century Rhetoric in North America* (Carbondale: Southern Illinois University Press, 1991); and Albert R. Kitzhaber, *Rhetoric in American Colleges, 850-1900* (Dallas, Tex.: Southern Methodist University Press, 1990).

12. For instance, there were the "Harvard Reports" in the 1890s about the poor quality of students' writing. These reports are now collectively bound in *Reports of the Visiting Committees of the Board of Overseers of Harvard College* (Cambridge, Mass.: Harvard College, 1902). Paul Prior's chapter in this volume begins with an excerpt from one of them.

13. Kitzhaber, *Rhetoric in American Colleges*, pp. 36-37.

14. William Riley Parker, "Where Do English Departments Come From?" *College English* 28 (1967): 339-351. For detailed descriptions of departmental structures at the end of the nineteenth century, see William Morton Payne, ed., *English in American Universities by Professors in the English Departments of Twenty Representative Institutions* (Boston: D. C. Heath, 1895).

15. See Edna Hayes, *College Entrance Requirements in English: Their Effects on the High Schools* (New York: Teachers College, Columbia University, 1936). Arthur N. Applebee discusses these and other developments in secondary English in *Tradition and Reform in the Teaching of English: A History* (Urbana, Ill.: National Council of Teachers of English, 1974) and in *Curriculum as Conversation: Transforming Traditions of Teaching and Learning* (Chicago: University of Chicago Press, 1996).

16. *Report of the Committee of Ten on Secondary School Studies* (New York: American Book Company for the National Education Association, 1894); Theodore R. Sizer, *Secondary Schools at the Turn of the Century* (New Haven, Conn.: Yale University Press, 1964), p. xi.

17. *Report of the Committee of Ten*, p. 86. The recommendations were for three hours of literature a week for all four years and two hours of composition a week for two years and one hour a week for one year. Included also were recommendations for an hour of grammar each week for one year and an hour of rhetoric each week during another year.

18. See Francis H. Stoddard, "Conference on Uniform Entrance Requirement in English," *Educational Review* (1905): 375-383.

19. Rudolph R. Reeder, "Historical Development of School Readers and of Method in Teaching Reading," *Columbia University Contributions to Philosophy, Psychology, and Education*, vol. 8, no. 2 (New York: Macmillan, 1900).

20. Edmond Burke Huey, *The Psychology and Pedagogy of Reading* (New York: Macmillan, 1908); G. Stanley Hall, *Educational Problems*, vol. 2 (New York: D. Appleton, 1911), pp. 397-492.

21. Hall, *Educational Problems*, vol. 2.

22. *Report of the Committee of Ten*, p. 89.

23. *Report of the Committee of Ten*; Fred Newton Scott and Joseph Villiers Denney, *Elementary English Composition* (Boston: Allyn and Bacon, 1900).

24. *Report of the Committee of Fifteen on Elementary Education* (New York: American Book Company for National Education Association, 1895).

25. David R. Russell, *Writing in the Academic Disciplines, 1870-1990: A Curricular History* (Carbondale: Southern Illinois University Press, 1991).

26. Johann Heinrich Pestalozzi, *Letters on Early Education*, trans. R. Sherwood (London: Sherwood, Gilbert and Piper, 1827); idem, *How Gertrude Teaches Her Children*, trans. Lucy E. Holland and Francis C. Turner and ed. Ebenezer Cook (Syracuse, N.Y.: C. W. Bardeen, 1898); Friedrich W. Froebel, *The Education of Man*, trans. W. N. Hailmann (New York: Appleton, 1903); Johann Friedrich Herbart, *Outlines of Educational Doctrine* (New York: Macmillan, 1913).

27. Francis W. Parker, *Talks on Teaching* (New York: E. L. Kellogg, 1883); idem, *Talks on Pedagogics* (New York: E. L. Kellogg, 1884).

28. See Edward L. Thorndike, *Educational Psychology*, 3 vols. (New York: Teachers College Press, Columbia University, 1913 and 1914) for this early form of connectionism, which focused on connections between individuals' responses and the situations that influence them.

29. The two traditions are discussed in Applebee, *Tradition and Reform*; Patrick Shannon, *Broken Promises: Reading Instruction in Twentieth-Century America* (Granby, Mass.: Bergin & Garvey, 1989); and Harold Rugg, "Curriculum-Making and the Scientific Study of Education since 1910," in *The Foundations and Technique of Curriculum Construction*, ed. Harold Rugg, Twenty-sixth Yearbook of the National Society for the Study of Education, Part I (Bloomington, Ill.: Public School Publishing Company, 1926), pp. 67-82. For a discussion of the theories that undergird various curricula, see William F. Pinar, William M. Reynolds, Patrick Slattery, and Peter M. Taubman, *Understanding Curriculum: An Introduction to the Study of Historical and Contemporary Curriculum Discourses* (New York: Peter Lang, 1995).

Actually the term "progressive" was also used for the scientific measurement movement, since it too broke with tradition. However, we decided to follow current conventions and limit the term to the work of Dewey and like-minded educators.

30. Edward L. Thorndike, "Measurement in Education," in *Intelligence Tests and Their Use: The Nature, History, and General Principles of Intelligence Testing*: Twenty-first Yearbook of the National Society for the Study of Education, Part I (Bloomington, Ill.: Public School Publishing Company, 1922), p. 1.

31. Ibid, p. 99.

32. Rugg, "Curriculum-Making," p. 67.

33. This point was also made by Geraldine Jonçich Clifford in *The Sane Positivist: Edward L. Thorndike* (Middleton, Conn.: Wesleyan University Press, 1968), 392-393: "Like the curriculum scientists—to whom he is an inspiration—Thorndike accepts the traditional school subjects as givens, without accepting their contents." This acceptance of school subjects can also be seen in the reviews included in early volumes of the *Review of Educational Research*. See, for instance, volume 4 (1934).

34. William S. Gray, *Summary of Investigations Relating to Reading* (Chicago: University of Chicago Press, 1925); Gray, chair, *Report of the National Committee on Reading*, Twenty-fourth Yearbook of the National Society for the Study of Education, Part I (Bloomington, Ill.: Public School Publishing Company, 1925); Gray, chair, *Second Report on Reading: Report of the National Committee on Reading*, Thirty-sixth Yearbook of the National Society for the Study of Education, Part I (Bloomington, Ill.: Public School Publishing Company, 1937); Arthur I. Gates, *The Improvement of Reading: A Program of Diagnostic and Remedial Methods* (New York: Macmillan, 1927); Edward L. Thorndike, "Reading as Reasoning: A Study of Mistakes in Paragraph Reading," *Journal of Educational Psychology* 8 (1917): 323-332.

35. Milo B. Hillegas, "A Scale for the Measurement of Quality in English Composition by Young People," *Teachers College Record* 13 (4) (1912): 29; James Fleming Hosic, "Composition Standards in the Elementary School, Arranged to Show the Minimal Performance Essential in Grades Two to Eight," in *Third Report of the Committee on the Economy of Time in the Schools*, Seventeenth Yearbook of the National Society for the Study of Education, Part I (Bloomington, Ill.: Public School Publishing Company, 1918), pp. 46-59; Earl Hudelson, *English Composition: Its Aims, Methods, and Measurement*, Twenty-second Yearbook of the National Society for the Study of Education, Part I (Bloomington, Ill.: Public School Publishing Company, 1923).

36. John Dewey, *School and Society* (Chicago: University of Chicago Press, 1899); idem, *The Child and the Curriculum* (Chicago: University of Chicago Press, 1902), p. 14.

37. John Dewey, "The Reflex Arc Concept in Psychology," *Psychological Review* 3 (1891): 357-370; idem, *Democracy and Education: An Introduction to the Philosophy of Education* (New York: Macmillan, 1916).

38. William Kilpatrick, "The Project Method," *Teachers College Record* 19 (1918): 319-325; Lillian A. Lamoreaux and Dorris May Lee, *Learning to Read through Experience* (New York: D. Appleton-Century, 1943).

39. For descriptions of the social processes in writing instruction, see Barbara von Bracht Donsky, "Trends in Elementary Writing Instruction, 1900-1959," *Language Arts* 61 (1984): 795-803; idem, "Writing as Praxis: 1900-1959," *Visible Language* 21 (1987): 237-251.

40. Alvina Treut, Doris C. Jackson, June D. Ferebee, and Dorothy Olton Saunders, *They All Want to Write* (Indianapolis, Ind.: Bobbs-Merrill, 1939).

41. Larry Cuban, *How Teachers Taught, 1890-1980*, 2d ed. (New York: Teachers College Press, 1993).

42. *Reorganization of English in Secondary Schools*, Report of the Hosic Committee of Thirty, U.S. Bureau of Education, Bulletin No. 2, 1917; National Education Association, *Cardinal Principles of Secondary Education*, A Report of the Commission on the Reorganization of Secondary Education (Washington, D.C.: Government Printing Office, 1918).

43. *An Experience Curriculum in English*, Report of the Curriculum Commission of the National Council of Teachers of English (New York: D. Appleton-Century, 1935).

44. *A Correlated Curriculum*, Report of the Committee on Correlation of the National Council of Teachers of English (New York: D. Appleton-Century, 1936), pp. 283-284.

45. *Conducting Experiences in English*, Report of the Committee of the National Council of Teachers of English (New York: D. Appleton-Century, 1939), p. 6.

46. Louise M. Rosenblatt, *Literature as Exploration* (New York: D. Appleton-Century, 1938).

47. Oscar James Campbell, *The Teaching of College English* (New York: D. Appleton-Century, 1934), pp. 18-19.

48. Cleanth Brooks and Robert Penn Warren, *Understanding Poetry*, rev. ed. (New York: Holt, Rinehart and Winston, 1950); William K. Wimsatt, Jr., and Monroe C. Beardsley, "The Intentional Fallacy," *Sewanee Review* 54 (1946): 468-488; Monroe C. Beardsley and William K. Wimsatt, Jr., "The Affective Fallacy," *Sewanee Review* 57 (1949), 31-55.

49. Albert Lynd, *Quackery in the Public Schools* (Boston: Little, Brown, 1953), p. 9; Arthur Bestor, *Educational Wastelands: The Retreat from Learning in Our Public Schools* (Urbana: University of Illinois Press, 1953), p. 5.

50. Wilford M. Aiken, *The Story of the Eight-Year Study* (New York: Harper & Brothers, 1942).

51. Rudolf Flesch, *Why Johnny Can't Read—and What You Can Do about It* (New York: Harper & Brothers, 1955).

52. Kellogg W. Hunt, *Differences in Grammatical Structures Written at Three Grade Levels* (Tallahassee: Florida State University, Office of Education Cooperative Research Project No. 1998, 1964); Richard Braddock, Richard Lloyd-Jones, and Lowell Schoer, *Research in Written Composition* (Champaign, Ill.: National Council of Teachers of English, 1963). For an account of the Project English curriculum development projects, see Erwin R. Steinberg, "Research on the Teaching of English," *Publication of the Modern Language Association* 79 (1964): 50-76.

53. U.S. Office of Education, "First Grade Reading Studies," *Reading Teacher* 19 (1966): 463-675; *Reading Teacher* 20 (1967): 6-42, 341-545; Jeanne S. Chall, *Learning to Read: The Great Debate* (New York: McGraw-Hill Book Company, 1967).

54. The Commission on English, appointed by the College Entrance Examination Board, offered the tripod model in its report, *Freedom and Discipline in English* (New York: College Entrance Examination Board, 1965). The three-part conception had been used earlier in a series of conferences at Yale University, which are discussed in Edward J. Gordon and Edward S. Noyes, *Essays on the Teaching of English: Reports of the Yale Conferences on the Teaching of English* (New York: Appleton-Century-Crofts, 1960) and at the Conference on Basic Issues in the Teaching of English, whose documents are published in *Issues, Problems, and Approaches in the Teaching of English*, ed. George Winchester Stone, Jr. (New York: Holt, Rinehart and Winston, 1961), pp. 2-22, 234-246.

55. John S. Mayher, *Uncommon Sense: Theoretical Practice in Language Education* (Portsmouth, N.H.: Heinemann, 1990), p. 27.

56. John Dixon, *Growth through English* (London: Cox & Wyman Ltd., 1967). For a critique of personal growth as a center for English, see Frances Christie, "The 'Received Tradition' of English Teaching: The Decline of Rhetoric and the Corruption of Grammar," in *The Insistence of the Letter: Literacy Studies and Curriculum Theorizing*, ed. Bill Green (Pittsburgh: University of Pittsburgh Press, 1993), pp. 75-106.

57. The latter included the critiques by John Holt, *How Children Fail* (New York: Dell, 1964); Jonathan Kozol, *Death at an Early Age* (Boston: Houghton Mifflin, 1967); Neil Postman and Charles Weingartner, *Teaching as a Subversive Activity* (New York: Delacorte, 1969).

58. John D. Bransford, "Contextual Prerequisites for Understanding," *Journal of Verbal Learning and Verbal Behavior* 11 (1972): 717-726. Particularly important collections of articles based on constructivist research are Richard C. Anderson, Rand J. Spiro, and William E. Montague, eds., *Schooling and the Acquisition of Knowledge* (Hillsdale, N.J.: Lawrence Erlbaum, 1977), and Rand J. Spiro, Bertram C. Bruce, and William F. Brewer, eds., *Theoretical Issues in Reading Comprehension* (Hillsdale, N.J.: Lawrence Erlbaum, 1980). For a review of the body of work, see Nancy Nelson Spivey, *The Constructivist Metaphor: Reading, Writing, and the Making of Meaning* (San Diego, Cal.: Academic Press, 1997), pp. 57-95.

59. David E. Rumelhart, "Toward an Interactive Model of Reading," in *Attention and Performance VI*, ed. Stanislav Dornic (Hillsdale, N.J.: Lawrence Erlbaum, 1977), pp. 573-603.

60. Richard C. Anderson, Elfrieda H. Hiebert, Judith A. Scott, and Ian A. G. Wilkinson, *Becoming a Nation of Readers* (Washington, D.C.: National Institute of Education, 1985), p. 9.

61. P. David Pearson and Robert J. Tierney, "On Becoming a Thoughtful Reader: Learning to Read Like a Writer," in *Becoming Readers in a Complex Society*, Eighty-third Yearbook of the National Society for the Study of Education, Part I, ed. Alan Purves and Olive S. Niles (Chicago: University of Chicago Press, 1984), pp. 144-173; John R. Hayes and Linda Flower, "Identifying the Organization of Writing Processes," in *Cognitive Processes in Writing*, ed. Lee W. Gregg and Erwin R. Steinberg (Hillsdale, N.J.: Lawrence Erlbaum, 1980), pp. 3-28; Linda Flower and John R. Hayes, "A Cognitive Process Theory of Writing," *College Composition and Communication* 32 (1981): 365-387.

62. See Timothy Shanahan and Richard G. Lomax, "An Analysis and Comparison of Theoretical Models of the Reading-Writing Relationship," *Journal of Educational Psychology* 78 (1986): 116-123; and the review in Tierney and Shanahan: "Research on the Reading-Writing Relationship."

63. Wolfgang Schnotz, "Comparative Instructional Text Organization," in *Learning and Comprehension of Text*, ed. Heinz Mandl, Nancy L. Stein, and Tom Trabasso (Hillsdale, N.J.: Lawrence Erlbaum, 1984): pp. 53-74; John D. Murray, "Logical Connectives and Local Coherence," in *Sources of Coherence in Reading*, eds. Robert F. Lorch, Jr., and Edward J. O'Brien (Hillsdale, N.J.: Lawrence Erlbaum, 1995), pp. 107-125.

64. Nancy Nelson Spivey and James R. King, "Readers as Writers Composing from Sources," *Reading Research Quarterly* 24 (1989): 7-26; Spivey, "The Shaping of Meaning: Options in Writing the Comparison," *Research in the Teaching of English* 25 (1991): 390-418; John Ackerman, "Reading, Writing, and Knowing: The Role of Disciplinary Knowledge in Comprehension and Composing," *Research in the Teaching of English* 25 (1991): 133-178; Linda Flower et al., *Reading to Write: Exploring a Cognitive and Social Process* (New York: Oxford University Press, 1990); Stuart Greene, "The Role of Task in the Development of Academic Thinking through Reading and Writing in a College History Course," *Research in the Teaching of English* 27 (1993): 46-75.

65. Christina Haas and Linda Flower, "Rhetorical Reading Strategies and the Construction of Meaning," *College Composition and Communication* 39 (1988): 167-183; Linda Flower, "The Construction of Purpose in Writing and Reading," *College English* 50 (1988): 528-550.

66. David Bleich, *Readings and Feelings: An Introduction to Subjective Criticism* (Urbana, Ill.: National Council of Teachers of English, 1972); Stanley Fish, "Literature in the Reader: Affective Stylistics," *New Literary History* 2 (1970): 123-162; Norman Holland, *Five Readers Reading* (New Haven, Conn.: Yale University Press, 1975; Wolfgang Iser, *The Act of Reading: A Theory of Aesthetic Response* (Baltimore, Md.: John Hopkins University Press, 1978): Louise M. Rosenblatt, *The Reader, the Text, the Poem: The Transactional Theory of the Literary Work* (Carbondale: Southern Illinois University Press, 1978).

67. For example, see James R. Squire, *The Responses of Adolescents While Reading Four Short Stories*, Research Report No. 2 (Champaign, Ill.: National Council of Teachers of English, 1964).

68. Judith A. Langer, "Rethinking Literature Instruction," in *Literature Instruction: A Focus on Student Responses*, ed. Judith A. Langer (Urbana, Ill.: National Council of Teachers of English, 1992), pp. 35-53.

69. Janet Emig, *The Composing Processes of Twelfth Graders*, Research Report No. 13 (Urbana, Ill.: National Council of Teachers of English, 1971); Donald Graves, "An Examination of the Writing Process of Seven Year Old Children," *Research in the Teaching*

of English 9 (1975): 227-241; Sharon Pianko, "A Description of the Composing Processes of College Freshmen Writers," *Research in the Teaching of English* 13 (1979): 5-22; Sondra Perl, "The Composing Processes of Unskilled College Writers," *Research in the Teaching of English* 13 (1979): 317-336.

70. D. Gordon Rohman and Albert O. Wlecke, *Pre-writing: The Construction and Application of Models for Concept Formation in Writing* (East Lansing: Michigan State University, U.S. Office of Education Cooperative Research Project No. 2174, 1964; ERIC Document ED 001 273); James Britton, Tony Burgess, Alexander McLeod, and Harold Rosen, *The Development of Writing Abilities, 11-18* (London: Macmillan Education, 1975).

71. For example, Nancy I. Sommers, "Revision Strategies of Student Writers and Experienced Writers," *College Composition and Communication* 31 (1980): 378-388; Hugh Burns, "Stimulating Invention in English Composition through Computer-Assisted Instruction" (Ph.D. diss., University of Texas, 1979).

72. Peter Elbow, *Writing without Teachers* (Oxford: Oxford University Press, 1973); Ken Macrorie, *Telling Writing*, 2nd ed. (Rochelle Park, N.J.: Hayden, 1976); James Moffett and Betty Jane Wagner, *Student-Centered Language Arts and Reading, K-13: A Handbook for Teachers* (Boston: Houghton-Mifflin, 1968); Donald Graves, *Writing: Teachers and Students at Work* (Portsmouth, N.H.: Heinemann, 1983); Nancie Atwell, *In the Middle: Writing, Reading, and Learning with Adolescents* (Montclair, N.J.: Boynton/Cook, 1987).

73. Mary Ann Smith, "The National Writing Project after 22 Years," *Phi Delta Kappan* 78 (1996): 688-692.

74. Merrill Shiels, "Why Johnny Can't Write," *Newsweek 86*, no. 23 (December, 1975): 58-65; Thomas C. Wheeler, *The Great American Writing Block* (New York: Penguin, 1979).

75. *A Language for Life*, Report of the Committee of Inquiry Appointed by the Secretary of State for Education and Science under the Chairmanship of Sir Alan Bullock (The Bullock Report) (London: Her Majesty's Stationery Office, 1977).

76. Arthur N. Applebee, *Contexts for Learning to Write: Studies of Secondary School Instruction* (Norwood, N.J.: Ablex, 1984); Judith A. Langer and Arthur N. Applebee, *How Writing Shapes Thinking: A Study of Teaching and Learning*, Research Report No. 22 (Urbana, Ill.: National Council of Teachers of English, 1987); George E. Newell, "Learning from Writing in Two Content Areas: A Case Study/Protocol Analysis," *Research in the Teaching of English* 18 (1984): 265-287; Russel K. Durst, "Cognitive and Linguistic Demands of Analytic Writing," *Research in the Teaching of English* 21 (1987), pp. 347-376.

77. Barbara Walvoord, "The Future of WAC," *College English* 58 (1996), pp.58-79.

78. Janet Emig, "The Tacit Tradition: The Inevitability of a Multi-Disciplinary Approach to Writing Research," in *Reinventing the Rhetorical Tradition*, ed. Aviva Freedman and Ian Pringle (Conway, Ark.: L&S Brooks, 1980), p. 13.

79. Kenneth Goodman, *What's Whole in Whole Language* (Portsmouth, N.H.: Heinemann, 1986); Yetta M. Goodman, "Roots of the Whole Language Movement," *Elementary School Journal* 90, no. 2 (1989): 113-127; David B. Doake, *Literacy Learning: A Revolution in Progress* (Bothell, Wash.: Wright Group, 1995); Shannon, *Broken Promises*; Shannon, *The Struggle to Continue: Progressive Reading Instruction in the United States* (Portsmouth, N.H.: Heinemann, 1990).

80. Marie Clay, "Emergent Reading Behavior" (Ph.D. diss., University of Auckland, New Zealand, 1966); William Teale and Elizabeth Sulzby, eds., *Emergent Literacy: Reading and Writing* (Norwood, N.J.: Ablex, 1986).

81. Elizabeth Sulzby, "Children's Emergent Reading of Favorite Storybooks: A Developmental Study," *Reading Research Quarterly* 20 (1985): 458-481; Dolores Durkin,

Children Who Read Early: Two Longitudinal Studies (New York: Teachers College Press, 1966).

82. John Willinsky, *The New Literacy* (New York: Routledge, 1990).

83. Peter L. Berger and Thomas Luckmann, *The Social Construction of Reality* (New York: Doubleday, 1966); John Seely Brown, Allan Collins, and Paul Duguid, "Situated Cognition and the Culture of Learning," *Educational Researcher* 18, no. 1 (1989): 32-42. For historical roots of social constructivism, see Spivey, *The Constructivist Metaphor*, pp. 5-26.

84. James E. Porter, "Intertextuality and the Discourse Community," *Rhetoric Review* 5 (1986): 34-47.

85. James Gee, *Social Linguistics and Literacies: Ideology in Discourses* (London: Falmer Press, 1990), p. 142.

86. Mikhail Bakhtin, *The Dialogic Imagination*, ed. Michael Holquist and trans. Caryl Emerson and Michael Holquist (Austin: University of Texas Press, 1981). See also V. N. Voloshinov, *Marxism and the Philosophy of Language*, trans. Ladislav Matejka and I. R. Titunik (Cambridge, Mass.: Harvard University Press, 1986).

87. Stanley Fish, *Is There a Text in This Class? The Authority of Interpretive Communities* (Cambridge, Mass.: Harvard University Press, 1980).

88. Frank Smith, *Joining the Literacy Club: Further Essays into Education* (Portsmouth, N.H.: Heinemann, 1988).

89. Dell Hymes, "Ways of Speaking," in *Explorations in the Ethnography of Speaking*, ed. Richard Bauman and Joel Sherzer (London: Cambridge University Press, 1974), pp. 433-451; Courtney B. Cazden, Vera P. John, and Dell Hymes, eds., *Functions of Language in the Classroom* (New York: Teachers College Press, 1972).

90. Shirley Brice Heath, *Ways with Words: Language, Life, and Work in Communities and Classrooms* (New York: Cambridge University Press, 1982).

91. *IRA/NCTE Standards for the English Language Arts* (Newark, Del.: International Reading Association and Urbana, Ill.: National Council of Teachers of English, 1996), p. 25.

92. See Peter Elbow, *What Is English?* (New York: Modern Language Association, 1990).

93. For example, Leslie Mandel Morrow, Jeffrey K. Smith, and Lousie Cherry Wilkinson, eds., *Integrated Language Arts: Controversy to Consensus* (Boston: Allyn and Bacon, 1994). Integrated instruction was a major focus of the National Reading Research Center at the University of Georgia and the University of Maryland from 1991 to 1996. See, for instance, John T. Guthrie and Allan Wigfield, eds., *Reading Engagement: Motivating Readers through Integrated Instruction* (Newark, Del.: International Reading Association, 1996).

94. Ben Brodinsky, "Back to the Basics: The Movement and Its Meaning," *Phi Delta Kappan* 58 (1977): 522-527.

95. National Commission on Excellence in Education, *A Nation at Risk: The Imperative for Educational Reform* (Washington, D.C.: The Commission, 1983); *Goals 2000: A World-Class Education for Every Child* (Washington, D.C.: U.S. Department of Education, Office of Educational Research and Improvement, 1994); *National Education Summit* (1996, March). Policy statement available at http://www.summit96.ibm.com.

96. Charles W. Peters, Karen K. Wixson, Sheila W. Valencia, and P. David Pearson, "Changing Statewide Reading Assessment: A Case Study of Michigan and Illinois," in *Policy Perspectives on Educational Testing*, ed. Bernard R. Clifford (Norwell, Mass.: Kluwer, 1992), 295-385. See also Robert C. Calfee and Elfrieda H. Hiebert, "Classroom Assessment of Reading," in *Handbook of Reading Research*, vol. 2, ed. Rebecca Barr, Michael L. Kamil, Peter B. Mosenthal, and P. David Pearson (New York: Longman, 1991), pp. 281-309.

97. James L. Kinneavy, *A Theory of Discourse* (Englewood Cliffs, N.J.: Prentice-Hall, 1971).

98. Barbara A. Kapinus, Gertrude V. Collier, and Hanna Kruglanski, "The Maryland School Performance Assessment Program: A New View of Assessment," in *Authentic Reading Assessment: Practices and Possibilities*, ed. Sheila W. Valencia, Elfrieda H. Hiebert, and Peter Afflerbach (Newark, Del.: International Reading Association, 1994), pp. 255-276. See also the attempts at integrative assessment in New Standards, *Performance Standards* (Rochester, N.Y.: National Center on Education and the Economy, 1997).

99. Peter Afflerbach, ed., *Issues in Statewide Reading Assessment* (Washington, D.C.: ERIC Clearinghouse on Tests, Measurement, and Evaluation, 1990).

100. Thomas S. Kuhn, *The Essential Tension: Selected Studies in Scientific Tradition and Change* (Chicago: University of Chicago Press, 1977), p. 234.

Section Two
THE AUTHOR-AUDIENCE CONTEXT

CHAPTER II

Writing for Readers: The Primacy of Audience in Composing

DONALD L. RUBIN

Welcome to our chapter.

I use "our" because in some very important ways you and I will be co-constructing this text. In fact, we're already underway. You have already started, no doubt, thinking about me, your author. And I have been thinking long and hard (too long, my editors would probably say) about you, my audience. As I compose, read, and recompose the words I have set out for you to read, I am ever trying to anticipate how you will react. I am trying to write and read through your eyes as well as through my own. I am trying to assay whether your responses will match my intentions.

If some of my assumptions miss the mark about you as a reader, I hope you will nonetheless find a way to temporarily inhabit the roles and attitudes I am inviting you to try on, and in that way become the audience for this chapter.

What is odd about the preceding rumination is that I chose to exteriorize it. While writers usually keep thoughts like the above to themselves, they are nonetheless driven by audience considerations. I want to make a very strong claim about the preeminence of audience in composing: writing is at its essence a social act, a rhetorical act, an act of communication,[1] and thus affecting an audience in one way or another is the very point of writing. Audience considerations can affect those other aspects of writing typically included in models of composing, such as retrieving prior knowledge about subject matter, inventing or discovering new content, and applying knowledge of discourse patterns and conventions.[2]

Donald L. Rubin is Professor in the Department of Speech Communication and the Department of Language Education at the University of Georgia.

Perhaps this grand thesis about audience and writing appears obvious. Even so, it is on no account trivial. For if you agree that audience considerations are central to writing, certain instructional corollaries follow. Of particular relevance to a book about reading-writing connections, for example, the principle of audience primacy dictates that we elevate the role of revision when we teach writing. We would teach students to write like readers,[3] re-visioning even their emerging meanings through the eyes of their audience. Developing skill at reading one's own text should be as important to writing instruction as is skill in generating text.

The Status of Audience-based Composition in the Schools

To be sure, progressive teachers of writing are more concerned with issues of audience and revision than was the case a generation ago, before the composing process "revolution" found its way into commonly adopted language arts textbooks and curricula. Still, there is little reason to believe that prevailing practice in public schools and colleges in the United States is geared toward teaching students to work in any profound way with the concept of audience. For example, the majority of eighth grade English teachers surveyed in 1992 (the most recent national sample available) reported spending fewer than one hour per week on writing instruction. About 30 percent of eighth grade students indicated that their teachers never asked them to think about audience and purpose in performing writing assignments. Over 40 percent of these students said that they never or hardly ever write essays or letters to persuade others. The majority of their teachers admitted that they never or hardly ever use group work or peer review as part of writing instruction.[4] Under these circumstances, it is not likely that students are receiving instruction in writing as a rhetorical act.

In their 1975 treatise, which remains a major influence on how we conceive the role of audience awareness in writing, James Britton and his associates examined over two thousand British classroom essays and writing assignments.[5] On the basis of that corpus, they induced a taxonomy of audience which students address in school writing. The five superordinate audience categories are (1) self, (2) teacher, (3) wider audience—known, (4) unknown audience, and (5) miscellaneous categories. Within the category of teacher audience, they further distinguished four subcategories: (2.1) child to trusted adult, (2.2) pupil to teacher in the sense of teacher-learner dialogue, (2.3) pupil to teacher who shares a specific interest, and (2.4) pupil to teacher as examiner. According to their tabulations, 95 percent of all the writings they collected were addressed to teacher audiences. Of these, half were addressed to teachers as examiners. To the degree that these findings can be extrapolated, it appears that students are often exposed to notions of audience that are impoverished indeed.[6]

One impediment to audience-centered writing instruction is a rather rigid notion about scope and sequence in teaching writing that is implicit in some teachers' curricula: the idea that students must master sentence structure before they are permitted to try their hands at paragraphs, and master paragraphs before attempting longer, more natural discourse. Even educators who subscribe to a view of writing as communication may not relate audience considerations to their teaching of sentence-level and paragraph-level writing.[6]

I would argue that even the most prosaic of sentence-level skills—punctuation—can be usefully analyzed from a rhetorical perspective that gives attention to audience.[7] Consider, for example, the issue of restrictive and nonrestrictive relative clauses. This is a distinction that has convinced masses of students (and their teachers) that they are ignorant about their own language. But the point about restrictiveness is easily presented with minimal reference to grammatical jargon simply by asking writers to think about what their audiences can be expected to know. In the sentence, *Jeff chose to read the novel which had pictures*, the need for any internal punctuation depends on what the audience knows prior to encountering this news about Jeff. If the audience can be presupposed to know,[8] by reading the text up to that point or by prior knowledge, that Jeff was choosing between two novels and only one was illustrated, then the sentence is fine as it stands. It will be properly read by that audience as a single unit of essential information. On the other hand, if the audience can be presupposed to know that Jeff was choosing between a particular novel and, say, a particular book of essays, then the sentence will need a comma. It needs a comma to signal a break between what will be two distinct units of information for the audience, the first of which is essential to the audience (Jeff chose the novel) and the second of which will constitute an interesting extra detail to that audience (the novel happens to have pictures). There are no absolute "rules" for punctuation in this case. There is only the need to read the sentence from the perspective of the audience.

But other than being enjoined to "make sure your writing is grammatically correct so people will not think you are ignorant," students are rarely trained to think in any serious way about rhetorical or reader-based foundations for writing conventions like punctuation.

What Is an Audience?

WRITERS' CONSTRUCTIONS OF AUDIENCE

We live and write in the midst of social contexts populated by individuals, some of whom may read the texts we have written while others will not. The social context is also a function of broader social and political vectors—differing access to economic well-being, to literacy skills, to power, to information, to our texts—which exert pervasive effects on our writing (and reading). But the social context of a particular writing episode establishes no action potential except as it is represented in the mind of the writer.[9] Writers do not adapt to social contexts directly, but rather to their *understandings* of social context. More particularly, writers do not adapt to their readers directly, but to their cognitive representations of their intended readers.

I use the term "reader" in this chapter to denote an individual who in some real-time episode actually accesses and processes a writer's text. I use the term "readership" to denote the population of potential readers who are likely (by virtue of opportunity and interest) to access and process a writer's text. But the identity of particular individuals who happen to become readers of any given text is historically contingent. (For example, your letter is properly addressed, the mail room clerk routes it to a particular office, the secretary decides to place it in his boss's in-box, the boss happens to have a free moment because of a canceled video conference, she recently had a conversation with her friend about the same topic, she skims the first paragraph and becomes intrigued . . . she becomes your reader.) I reserve the term "audience," in contrast, to denote a writer's cognitive representation of intended readers or readerships. Audiences do not come prepackaged; writers must mentally construct them, engage in social inferencing, "read" their intended readers.[10]

To represent their audiences, writers engage in social cognitive processes.[11] For example, in coming to a sense of audience, writers must draw upon their repertoire of role constructs, their internal catalogue of person attributes which are available for categorizing and characterizing specific audiences. A considerable body of research now documents that strong writers are those who can mobilize abstract role constructs ("intelligent" rather than "eats a chocolate bar for lunch each day"), more differentiated constructs across individuals ("Sally is wise and Betty is quick-witted"), and constructs that acknowledge variability in targets' dispositions ("When Sally makes a bad decision, it is usually because she is distracted by chocolate").[12] The process of constructing a coherent—and perhaps accurate—representation of an audience involves selecting relevant cues about the audience (e.g., level of education), and then inferring the associated role constructs (e.g., has or has not read Proust) from one's repertoire.

The great difficulty in adapting to an audience occurs when one has limited experience with an intended audience and therefore lacks adequately differentiated audience constructs, lacks inference rules for selecting constructs, and lacks a rich body of cues (information) from which to draw social inferences. This is precisely the plight of many novice college students who are asked to write with the authority of a scholar to an audience of scholars about whom they can have but a vague representation.[13] Because it helps overcome the problem of the hard-to-represent audience, writing to peers—and especially peers who can give immediate and concrete response—is fundamental to learning audience adaptation skills.

While some audiences may be more difficult to represent than others, after writing the first sentence or two, the writer need never be at a total loss about audience characteristics. That is because the writer has at least begun to create a shared text-world with the audience. The writer can predict at least something about the audience's knowledge state at any given point by virtue of the information presented in the preceding text. This essential activity between writer and audience,[14] however, sometimes fails to contribute to the novice writer's representation of the audience. The novice writer may be unskilled at taking the role of a reader processing the ongoing text. Thus the novice (and all writers are novices to one degree or another) neglects to define an idiosyncratic term here or repeats an item of information there, just because of some slippage in taking the reader's role.

INVENTED AUDIENCES

In *The Rhetoric*, Aristotle presents detailed psychological profiles of various audiences (rich, poor, young, old) and prescribes persuasive strategies correlated to each type. For Aristotle, the audience is composed of flesh-and-blood individuals. The beliefs and emotions of each individual may be swayed toward the speaker's purpose, but only if the speaker is mindful of the listeners' more-or-less immutable traits. Current instruction in audience analysis (that is, when students *are* taught about audience at all) tends to equate audiences with incarnate individuals (or congregations of such individuals) imbued with stable interests or demographic identities.

In our efforts to teach writing as rhetoric we may give assignments like, "Explain why you oppose Atlanta's 11ᵖ o'clock curfew on people under the age of sixteen. Assume that you are writing to the local chapter of Mothers Against Drunk Driving." Critics of this type of assignment claim that it encourages students to develop caricatured audience specifications based on shallow stereotypes, with resulting prose that is stilted and enervated.[15] And indeed, studies of writing prompts in large-scale assessments have consistently failed to find any advantage for instructions which elaborate for students a rich rhetorical context, including detailed audience specifications.[16]

In "The Writer's Audience Is Always a Fiction," Walter Ong stakes out the alternative stance to the classic Aristotelian approach to audience analysis.[17] Ong notes that works of fiction make use of stylistic devices to invite their readers to adopt particular audience roles, particular relationships with the narrator and the events narrated (e.g., the use of pronouns with no textual antecedents—as when some writer of Spillanesque detective stories begins a story with "It was just his dumb luck, to get stuck in that dive, with those palookas, and with HER, of all dames. . . ."). No less so, according to Ong, authors of the perennial grammar school essay on "What I Did During My Summer Vacation" need to envision an interested audience who can be enticed to become involved in their compositions. Faced by the dreary institutional reality of a teacher who will read the essays only to assign grades, the effective student writer will *invent* a more convivial audience. All writers create fictional audiences, and it is to these idealized readers that they bend their styles.

The notion of writers fictionalizing their audiences has important implications for competent reading behavior. If authors invent the audiences to whom their writing is addressed and adjust their writing for those intended audiences, then the competent reader is one who recognizes the author's textual cues and at least tentatively adopts the implied reader stance. If I pick up a detective novel by Elmore Leonard, the choppy syntax and the references to "joints" and "guys" signal to me that this author is asking me to suspend any belletristic norms I may hold, and to adopt the sort of slack-jawed, gum-popping, "what-me-worry" stance of a comic book reader. If I can adopt that audience stance, the book may be an enjoyable read. Nor need I read exclusively from the fictionalized audience stance which Leonard has presupposed. I can simultaneously adopt other audience roles which run in the background: the analyst of style who appreciates a certain linguistic craft, or the sneering intellectual snob who is only temporarily slumming.

The distinction between Aristotle's incarnate audience (which the writer must analyze) and Ong's fictional audience (which the writer must presuppose) is captured by the paired terms "audience addressed" and "audience invoked."[18] I have already stated that assignments which ask students to contort their intentions in order to address specified audiences can result in stilted writing. By the same token, writing curricula which give students practice only in invoking "constructed" audiences—to the neglect of addressing living, breathing audiences—likewise shortchange students, who after all do need to learn to write love letters, sales reports, policy proposals, and PTA announcements in ways which will affect their intended readers. No doubt, optimal writing curricula would provide students opportunities to address both incarnate audiences and invoked or fictionalized ones, as well as to switch midstream when one type of audience proves inhibiting and to cast about for a more inviting one.

DETERMINATE AND INDETERMINATE AUDIENCES

It is easy to conceptualize addressed or invoked audiences that have nameable characteristics: your Aunt Beatrice who hoards the family keepsakes, the two or three hundred people who will attend your high school reunion, people who think Proust was the greatest of stylists. It is likewise easy to appreciate the role of audience awareness in writing when you are directly and deliberately trying to affect those readers in some way: to convince them to hand over a family heirloom, to honor a beloved teacher, or to admire an exquisite syntactic construction. The relationship between author and audience is more opaque, however, for many other types of writing—especially types that predominate in schools. If I am assigned to write a biographical sketch of Edgar Allan Poe, what plausible audience can I invoke and how shall I conceive my rhetorical purpose vis à vis that audience? Isn't writing a competent biographical sketch in grade school simply a matter of conforming to some set of rules or expectations for that discourse type? (e.g., tell where born, childhood influences, two greatest accomplishments, date of death, then sit down.)

To state that writers must simply conform to rules and expectations for particular discourse types is to elevate the import of genre knowledge over sense of audience, at least in the case of some types of writing.[19] The instructional corollary is that students are well served simply by learning forms and conventions for those genres: The Five Paragraph Theme, The Term Paper, The Book Report. It is helpful for students to appreciate that many genre conventions are not merely arbitrary rules. Rather, these "rules" encapsulate generalizations about audience adaptation. Genre conventions like "State your thesis in your first paragraph" are typically shorthand prescriptions for meeting audience needs. It is considerate to readers, for example, when writers provide them with organizing frames early in the discourse. The "rule" is not "law," though unfortunately it is often presented that way in textbooks as well as in a teacher's response to writing ("No thesis statement" instead of "I would have been less confused about the purpose of the first half of the paper if you had told me your topic right off the bat.").

In such cases, the audience to which we adapt by conforming to genre conventions is an indeterminate audience, a generalized other, sometimes called "the universal audience."[20] It is an audience which is not compelled to read since it shares no prior interpersonal bonds with the author. The "universal audience" is an audience about which the author can make few presuppositions about prior knowledge. It is therefore an audience for which the text-world created by the author must carry an especially great burden. Though the notion of a truly "autonomous text" has been debunked (all text requires some degree of context for making meaning; no text can be context-free),[21] writing for indeterminate audiences is often presented to students as the ideal for academic discourse. Developmentally, it does appear that students are first able to conceptualize and adapt to determinate audiences who are well known to them (e.g., peers and other intimates). Only later can they extend themselves to write effectively for remote, indeterminate audiences.[22]

"Discourse community," discussed briefly in the preceding chapter, is a concept of considerable currency which is related in some ways to the notion of the indeterminate audience.[23] Through the warp and woof of intertextual "conversations" in which discourse community members participate in one way or another, sociolinguistic norms are negotiated, propagated, and continually renegotiated. These norms might include what is to count as a legitimate topic, or which literary allusions are canonical, or what acronyms can we assume everybody recognizes. A discourse community might be relatively closed and specialized (e.g., breeders of Manx cats, or owners of asphalt-laying companies, or researchers in plasma physics), or it might be quite broad (e.g., citizens concerned about school reform or scholars in the humanities).

When you are an authentic member of a discourse community, you do not need to puzzle about discourse norms; they are *your* norms. Thus, it would seem that audience adaptation is not much of an issue when writing within one's own community; all you have to do is act naturally. Writing across discourse communities is another matter, of course. Some would claim that to do so, authors must be socialized into the norms of those new communities, primarily by immersion in their disciplinary conversations. One problem with the notion of discourse community is that it seems to rob the author of personal agency. The motivations, the ideas, the language strategies for writing all seem extrinsic to, and controlling of, individual writers. In the most radical of social constructionist positions, the line between writer and social context is erased; a piece of writing can never be attributed to a single individual. But even if one holds to the view that individual writers are indeed authors of their own texts,[24] it is still necessary to understand how those authors represent their communities to themselves. The discourse community is, after all, one more type of audience.

THE SELF AS AN AUDIENCE

One reason I feel comfortable asserting the primacy of audience in writing is that I accept a very broad notion of what constitutes an audience. As in the audience taxonomy developed by Britton and colleagues, for example, I contend that *the self* constitutes a plausible audience for writing. Indeed, the self is a particularly important audience. How is it possible that writers can be their own audiences? Reflect on how one goes about composing even the simplest of texts, a shopping list for one's own use. Presumably you know what you need to purchase at the supermarket; perhaps the weather is turning brisk, and you'd like to have oatmeal on hand for an occasional bracing breakfast this season. Since memory capacity is limited, you prudently write the word "oatmeal" on your shopping list. But in the act of writing "o-a-t-m-e-a-l" you recall a particular kind of oatmeal—the steel-cut Irish variety—that you had decided you'd like to use for breakfast cereal. Any garden variety of oatmeal might do for baking oatmeal cookies, but not for the hearty breakfast you are envisioning. To be sure you don't slip at the store and purchase the wrong type of oatmeal, you revise your shopping list/text; you elaborate the entry "oatmeal" by inserting some specific modifier like "the good stuff."

Why is it necessary to revise such a simple text when it is for your own consumption? Because the reader "you" is not quite the same entity as the writer "you." The two "yous" exist in different contexts, different knowledge states, and different motivational states. In a manner similar in kind (if not in degree) to addressing a wholly different reader, you-as-author need to make some guesses about you-as-audience, and adapt your text accordingly. Writing in one's diary presents a more complex illustration of casting a self-as-audience. Whom does one address with the salutation "Dear Diary" if not the self cast as "the other"—the self-as-audience?

The view that writing for oneself is really just a special case of writing for an audience is crucial to promoting the primacy of audience in composing. This is because much writing that we value in schools is not ostensibly directed toward communicating ideas to some other reader. We value so-called "personal" writing for the purposes of helping the writer make sense of the world, to discover one's own point of view, to express or vent one's feelings. Even in these inner-directed kinds of writing, however, writers establish a distance between self in the here-and-now (that is, author) and self in the potentially-distinct-context (that is, audience). Else why bother encoding one's sense making, discovery, or venting in the time-binding medium of writing? Why not just think the thought?

The opposing point of view is expressed by Peter Elbow's compelling essay, "Closing My Eyes as I Speak: An Argument for Ignoring Audience."[25] As the title of the article signifies, Elbow contends that too much consideration for audience—or thinking about audience at the wrong stage of composing—often undermines writing, that writing sometimes attains strength when writers are oblivious to audience. After considering arguments similar to those I have been making about the primacy of audience, Elbow "tentatively . . . resist[s]" the theory that all discourse is social as well as the view that "all private writing is really communication with the '*audience of self*.'" Though I take issue with Elbow's overall thesis, I want to draw attention to valuable points he makes about the richness of the audience construct and about the author's choice in selecting a sense of audience. Elbow writes, "First, even if there is no getting away from *some* audience, we can get relief from an inhibiting audience by writing to a more inviting one. Second, audience problems don't come only from *actual* audiences, but also from phantom 'audiences in the head'."[26] To assert, as does Elbow, that audiences may be inviting or inhibiting, actual or phantom, and in some way at the discretion of the author is to imply that an audience is something considerably more complex than the physical reality of a reader or readers.

MULTIPLE AUDIENCES

It is easy to lapse into referring to "*the* audience" for a particular text; and, when we do teach students about audience, we most often ask them to think about their audience as if that were some singular entity. But quite often authors write with several audiences in mind. This has become most apparent as researchers on writing have begun to examine composing outside the academy such as in the worlds of commerce and government. Thus, for example, a researcher at a pharmaceutical company might write a memo to a laboratory supervisor requesting new equipment to pursue some promising breakthrough in acne medication. At the same time, the researcher knows that the memo will likely be used to bolster the lab's standing with the manager of new over-the-counter product development. It might even find its way into the hands of someone in the marketing department. And surely the memo will reside in the company's files, where in the worst-case scenario of litigation over product liability the legal department will have recourse to it at some future time. The competent memo writer (trained primarily as a pharmacologist though she may be) might formally address the memo to a single individual—her direct supervisor—but will adapt to each of the other audiences as well. Indeed, one interesting analysis attributes the Three Mile Island nuclear power plant disaster to a series of engineering memoranda that were not equally well adapted to each of their various audiences (i.e., engineers at the plant's construction company vs. the technicians who actually operated the plant).[27]

In a similar fashion, most school writing asks students to write for at least a double audience. The teacher audience lurks in the background even when the ostensible assignment targets a celebrity or a community leader or an audience of the student's own choice. The multiple-audience feature in these writing assignments may not be an altogether negative factor, for it can introduce students to one realistic demand of writing outside the academy. But in discussing these more rhetorically rich writing assignments, we must help students understand the nature of multiple audiences, and not to pretend that secondary and perhaps tertiary (parents) audiences do not exist. Indeed, perhaps the cure for deadly saccharin or stereotyped student writing is to encourage students to write for multiple audiences that include themselves as well as other named and unnamed audiences. Inclusion of the self-as-audience conveys to students that they must write in a way that interests themselves as well as other projected audiences.

How Does Awareness of Audience Figure in Composing Processes?

WRITING AS A RECURSIVE PROCESS

Writing is a process. It occurs in real time. A writing episode does have a starting point and an end point (though both points can sometimes be difficult to specify). The process is irreversible in the sense that you cannot unwrite a text; you can only rewrite it. Therefore, it is tempting to portray composing processes as linear—beginning with something like "prewriting discovery" and ending with "publication," with "drafting" and "revision" plunked down in the middle. But common experience belies a linear model, or even any neat spiral or helix. We may still be trying to discover the basic structure of our essay even as we begin drafting. At some point we may take a break from the hard work of drafting and switch to the relatively mindless job of copy-editing, and simultaneously at some other level of consciousness we may be inventing new subject matter. We may show our work to several people in several formats at different points in its progress, and thus "publish" it repeatedly.

Revision cannot be tied to a particular "phase" of composing, since it can occur at any point in the process. Most effort-full writing tasks (as opposed to, say, formulaic memoranda or spontaneous diary entries) require us to revise in an ongoing fashion. Moreover, not all revision is as tangible as the scratching out of a word or the dragging-and-pasting of a computer cursor. Much revision is pretextual, that is, accomplished mentally by operating on plans rather than on realized text.[28] The competent writer has already begun revising before ever setting down a first word. Students may continue revising right on through emendations in reading their "final" drafts aloud to the class.

Given the highly recursive and even simultaneous nature of composing processes, it is quite natural that audience considerations pervade every phase and aspect of writing. Certainly publication is audience-directed. Indeed, for many writing teachers, publication of student work—whether by distributing class magazines or by posting class work on bulletin boards or by mailing out letters to public figures or just by reading it aloud—takes on great importance as a means for encouraging students to take care with their writing. Assignments to produce writing which is never read, or which is scanned only in a cursory hunt for errors, do not engage most students. Applying editorial conventions, I have argued earlier in this chapter, can also be taught as an audience-directed process. Drafting becomes audience-centered when teachers transform their assignments from "a five-page paper that describes . . ." or "500 words on . . ." to "Tell me what you think I need to know in order to . . ." or "What would interest a fourth grade student in Ukraine?"

AUDIENCE AWARENESS AND INVENTION

One view of the invention or discovery (sometimes called "prewriting") processes of composing is that they are private, interiorized, and conducted as solo missions. If my assignment is to write about the contribution of Michael Faraday to the study of chemistry, I closet myself with my reference works and immerse myself in phlogiston theory. I emerge, ready perhaps to share with an audience, once I have committed my thoughts to prose.

This sort of Platonic account of generating subject matter, according to Karen LeFevre,[29] misses the essentially social nature of invention. LeFevre notes that invention is social in at least three ways. When we engage in an *internal dialogue* with another "self," that inner conversation is constituted by views and voices we have internalized from social influences and other individuals. When we *collaborate* with others, we depend upon direct interaction with others in creating content about which to write. Very often our collaborators are our first other readers; reading to collaborate is a particular function of reading that differs in important ways from reading for information or reading for pleasure. Oftentimes—especially in the world of work outside the academy—the production of a single text is from the very onset a corporate effort, and not in the least attributable to a single mind working in isolation. Collaborative writing activities in the classroom can therefore be seen as very realistic preparation for real-world demands on students. However, schools in the United States generally place a premium on "original" work and assessment of individual abilities, and these values militate against the kinds of group work that are typical in government and industry. Finally, when writing is seen as a broadly *collective* act that is enabled only by participation in a discourse community, invention is regarded as a process of an author tapping into and drawing upon currents that course through that community.

The notion that audience considerations help shape invention processes is confirmed by studies of writers who are asked to think aloud as they compose. Strong writers are extensive planners; they often work to construct a rhetorical "problem space" for their compositions before setting the first word on paper. And their plans, in contrast with those of novice writers, generally manifest a rich sense of audience.[30] For example, an English teacher asked to compose a presentation about his career for high school students reflects,

[H]ow am I supposed to tell these people who are in the midst of a technological revolution, dioxiden poisoning, gas shortages, energy blackouts that my career as an English teacher is rewarding, which I think it is. O.K. What I think I'll emphasize is that my career allows flexibility and change.[31]

Audience awareness, then, can be a heuristic and constructive force in helping writers generate subject matter. Experienced writers learn that the question, "What shall I write?" is almost always intertwined with the question, "To whom shall I write?"

Revision is bleak territory for many writers.[32] The research indicates that many student writers do not revise; they only copy over or engage in only the most cosmetic correction of errors. Paradoxically, several studies found that students might be better off *not* revising; first drafts are many times superior to revised drafts. Strong writers revise no more extensively than do poor writers (at least this holds true for manifest revisions to the text). To revise effectively, writers must read and represent their texts to themselves. They must also represent to themselves their intentions for writing. When there is a mismatch between the two, the dissonance should cause the writer to detect a problem. After detecting a problem, the writer must be able to diagnose it at some level of metacognitive awareness. Finally, after diagnosis, the writer must have available the knowledge for remediating it. Revision can fail at any one or more of these subprocesses.

For example, revision can fail when writers fail to accurately or adequately represent their texts to themselves. The text that must be represented, if effective revision is to take place, is the one which the reader will encounter, not necessarily the one which the writer intended to write. For all writers—mature as well as novice—the inevitable press of egocentrism tends to conflate those two representations. Thus, we read a sentence over and over again and fail to notice the repeated word. Or we reread our turgid paragraph and deem it brilliantly illuminating, oblivious that any other audience would demand a concrete illustration to lower the level of abstraction a notch or two.

One old saw for overcoming the force of egocentrism, for reading our own texts more objectively, is to set our work aside for some period of time before revising. With the passage of time, we hope we can reread our writing with fresh eyes, those of the naive reader. Unfortunately, there is no empirical evidence that this sequestering strategy makes any difference whatsoever.[33] On the other hand, a procedure which asks students to evaluate each sentence of their composition, one at a time, from the perspective of their audience (e.g., "Mr. Lewis will think this gets away from the main point. Mr. Lewis will find this interesting.") does appear to encourage close reading, which, in turn, leads to more revision.[34]

Indeed, between-draft revision seems to be a particularly apt point at which to feed writers additional information about their audiences.[35]

That is, it can be particularly helpful for teachers to provide students with rich audience information just at the point when students are about to begin a second draft. The additional audience specification can facilitate revision in several other ways. Making audience more salient at that point may help reinforce the writer's rhetorical intentions, against which the text is judged. Thus, the student writer becomes a better critic of his or her own writing. Additional audience information could also suggest some strategies for remedying diagnosed deficiencies. For example, if a writer who was having a hard time adequately depicting the character of a storm at sea discovered that her intended audience worked as a soda jerk, she might decide that the malted milk machine would provide a metaphor with which to augment the description.

How Do Audience Awareness and Adaptation Develop?

SOCIAL COGNITION AND DEVELOPMENT OF ORAL COMMUNICATION

Children's oral communication develops from largely spontaneous to more strategic, from mainly egocentric to mainly sociocentric, from privately meaningful to publicly accessible. To communicate in a listener-adapted fashion, children must become proficient in assuming the perspectives of those listeners, to decenter from their own idiosyncratic perspectives on a situation.[36] A young child speaking on the telephone must learn that pointing to an object does a listener in another location no good. In a game which requires an encoder to describe abstract shapes to a decoder, the child must learn that idiosyncratic descriptions like "Mommy's hat last Sunday" may be accurate but carry no information of value to the listener.

To achieve the breakthrough to listener-adapted communication, children must first be able to differentiate their own perspectives from those of others. They must learn to infer the perspective of another who does not share the child's own point of view, learn to put themselves in someone else's shoes. Then they must struggle to maintain their perspectivism (the ability shift and change perspectives) against the ever-threatening intrusion of their own immediate perceptual field. At advanced levels of social cognitive development, children learn to take the role of a generalized other: "People would probably say . . .," "Society would consider this. . . ."

Growth in social cognition is fostered by experiencing different perspectives. The experience of interpersonal conflict, in which others' opposing points of view are forcefully argued, is especially helpful in this respect. Cognitive maturation also plays a role. A child must attain a degree of general cognitive development to be able to simultaneously entertain multiple perspectives on a single event. Early theories of ego-centrism proposed stage models; children were first egocentric and then decentered. A more defensible view is that egocentrism is a response set rather than an irreversible stage. We all behave with greater or lesser degrees of egocentrism, depending on such contextual factors as difficulty of task. If I am trying to explain a very complicated situation to you, I may very well lose my perspectivism and lapse into egocentric speech.

Social cognition is a necessary, but not sufficient, condition for listener-adapted communication. When a young child is directly told that a listener does not understand a description of a picture, say, the child may nevertheless repeat the identical description. At first, children insist that listeners bear all the responsibility for successfully decoding a message; so for them it is perfectly natural to repeat a message until it penetrates. But even older children, who do understand the speaker's onus for listener-adapted speech, sometimes do nothing to remedy patent communication failure. Sometimes, when playing a communication game, children may predict messages will fail, and nevertheless repeat the same inadequate message. What is happening is that they simply lack the communication tools to adapt their discourse. Their repertoire of discourse strategies lags behind their social awareness.

SOCIAL COGNITION AND WRITING DEVELOPMENT

If social cognition is important for oral communication develop-ment, it is that much more important for development in written communication. In writing, after all, the audience rarely shares the same physical and temporal context as the author. Exchanges of ongo-ing and immediate feedback are rarely possible. Audiences can be quite indeterminate. Therefore, the writer may be even more depen-dent on social perspective-taking than the speaker. Several studies confirm that the same kinds of ill-adapted messages one sees in speech are also evident in early writing, that social cognitive development and writing ability progress hand-in-hand, and that better writers are usu-ally more advanced in social cognitive ability than are "basic" or devel-opmental writers of the same age.[37]

Early research on social cognition and writing tended to depict young writers and basic writers as trapped in egocentric expression. However, when task constraints of writing assignments ease, students even in early elementary grades do seem able to write in audience-cen-tered ways. Marion Crowhurst concludes, in particular, that audience adaptation is facilitated when children write for audiences younger than themselves, when they write in modes that promote the salience of audience (e.g., persuasion), and when audiences are real rather than imagined.[38]

Just as social cognition is necessary but not sufficient for listener-adapted speech, so is sense of audience only in part responsible for audience-adapted writing. Sometimes students are capable of saying a great deal about their audiences, but do not tailor their writing accordingly. This failure of audience adaptation could be due to students' lack of rhetorical strategies for translating their audience knowledge into discourse. Alternatively, young writers may not know—perhaps because they are not taught—that writing can function as a medium of communication with audiences.[39]

CULTIVATING AUDIENCE AWARENESS THROUGH READING AND RESPONSE

Children can be trained in social perspective taking. Often this training takes the form of asking them to create skits in which they serially enact each of the varying roles. After each role enactment, the students are asked to describe their responses.[40] This role-taking training procedure does not vary in principle from what happens in peer-response circles in the language arts classroom. Students serially enact the roles of writer and reader. Writers get to hear serially from several readers, each of whom may have a somewhat different perspective on the text. In this way students learn to decenter from their own representations of their texts and to assimilate varying social perspectives on the very same text. Peer response, then, is perhaps the major classroom tool available for cultivating a sense of audience and imparting tools for audience adaptation. It is most effective when it is structured in a manner that demands *descriptive* responses rather than *evaluative*. That is, it can improve audience awareness when a writer hears a peer respond, "When I read line 14, I finally figured out which brother you thought was the hero." A response like, "I really liked the older brother, I thought he was cool," is less useful in that respect.

A relevant instructional experiment is reported by Karen Schriver, who gave college students problematic texts, and then asked them to predict the difficulties readers would have with these texts.[41] Next, students had a chance to peruse think-aloud transcripts of people actually reading the problem texts. After a diet of such tasks, predicting reading difficulties and then seeing actual reading protocols, students became better able to predict difficulties readers would have with texts.

Educators have proposed a wide variety of direct instruction and indirect exercises for cultivating audience awareness and adaptation.[42] These include audience checklists, strategies for questioning peers, role-switching improvisations, and mock debates. Each of these can be a valuable element for nurturing audience-centered writing. Ultimately, however, encouraging students to read closely and sensitively may be the best of all instructional approaches for fostering audience awareness in writing. Donald Murray writes of revising for audience, "I believe that if I attend to the draft, read it carefully, and listen to what it says, the draft will tell me what a reader needs."[43] Reading and writing merge in this way when we regard audience as the primary component of composing.

NOTES

1. In this chapter I deal with one aspect—the audience-centered aspect—of the premise that writing is at its essence a social act. For a more broad-ranging survey of that premise, see Donald L. Rubin, "Introduction: Four Dimensions of Social Construction in Written Communication," in *The Social Construction of Written Communication*, eds. Bennett A. Rafoth and Donald L. Rubin (Norwood, N.J.: Ablex, 1988), pp. 1-33.

2. See, for example, Judith A. Langer, *Children Reading and Writing: Structures and Strategies* (Norwood, N.J.: Ablex, 1986).

3. P. David Pearson and Robert J. Tierney, "On Becoming a Thoughtful Reader: Learning to Read Like a Writer," in *Becoming Readers in a Complex Society*, Eighty-Third Yearbook of the National Society for the Study of Education, Part 1, eds. Alan Purves and Olive S. Niles (Chicago: University of Chicago Press, 1984), pp. 144-175.

4. Arthur N. Applebee, Judith A. Langer, Ina V. S. Mullis, Andrew Latham, and Claudia Gentile, *NAEP 1992 Writing Report Card* (Princeton, N.J.: National Assessment of Educational Progress, 1990), pp. 139, 144, 177.

5. James Britton, Tony Burgess, Nancy Martin, Alex McLeod, and Harold Rosen, *The Development of Writing Abilities (11-18)* (London: Macmillan Education, 1975).

6. See, for example, Erika Lindemann, *A Rhetoric for Writing Teachers*, 3rd edition (New York: Oxford University Press, 1995), p. 142.

7. John Dawkins, "Teaching Punctuation as a Rhetorical Tool," *College Composition and Communication* 46 (1995): 533-548.

8. I use the term "presuppose" to denote a language user's making a working assumption about another's knowledge or beliefs. The reader/writer acts *as if* that assumption were true, but he or she does not really *know* if the assumption is true. Sometimes it doesn't even matter. For example, if I say, "My cat thinks he deserves an apology when you shove him off the kitchen table," you understand me by acting as if cats possessed some sense of social etiquette, conscious cognition, and so on. You may disagree with those presuppositions, or you may think I am joking (i.e., I don't seriously believe cats care about manners), but you understand what presuppositions must be apprehended if my utterance is to be taken as sensible. For a fuller discussion, see George Lakoff, "Presupposition and Relative Well Formedness," in *Semantics*, eds. Dan Steinberg and L. Jacobovitz (London: Cambridge University Press, 1971), pp. 329-340.

9. This is essentially a social constructivist position, and is more adequately explicated in Linda Flower, *The Construction of Negotiated Meaning: A Social-Cognitive Theory of Writing* (Carbondale: Southern Illinois University Press, 1994); in Nancy Nelson

Spivey, *The Constructivist Metaphor: Reading, Writing, and the Making of Meaning* (San Diego, Cal.: Academic Press, 1997), pp. 313-330; and in Rubin, "Four Dimensions of Social Construction."

10. For similar reasons I distinguish between the terms "writer" and "author." I used the former to denote the historically contingent person or persons who actually produced the text in real-time composing processes. The latter refers to the persona or role implied by the text and likely to be inferred by the audience. Wayne Booth makes a similar distinction between the historical and implied author in The Rhetoric of Fiction (Chicago: University of Chicago Press, 1961).

11. Donald L. Rubin, "Social Cognition and Written Communication," *Written Communication* 1 (1984): 211-245.

12. See a review in Curtis J. Bonk, "A Synthesis of Social Cognition and Writing Research," *Written Communication* 7 (1990): 136-163. See also, Kathryn Heltne Swanson, "Ultimatum and Negotiation: Gender Differences in Student Writing," in *Composing Social Identity in Written Communication*, ed. Donald L. Rubin (Hillsdale, N.J.: Lawrence Erlbaum, 1995), pp. 203-220.

13. David Bartholomae, "Inventing the University," in *When a Writer Can't Write*, ed. Mike Rose (New York: Guilford, 1985), pp. 134-165; Patricia Bizzell, "What Happens When Basic Writers Come to College?" *College Composition and Communication* 13 (1986): 294-301.

14. Martin Nystrand, *The Structure of Written Communication: Studies in Reciprocity between Writers and Readers* (Orlando, Fl.: Academic Press, 1986).

15. For example, Russell C. Long, "The Writer's Audience: Fact or Fiction?" in *A Sense of Audience in Written Communication*, eds. Gesa Kirsch and Duane Roen (Newbury Park, Cal.: Sage Publications, 1990), pp. 73-84; Barry M. Kroll, "Writing for Readers: Three Perspectives on Audience," *College Composition and Communication* 35 (1984): 172-185.

16. Gordon Brossell, "Rhetorical Specification in Essay Examination Topics," *College English* 45, no. 2 (1983): 165-173.

17. Walter Ong, "The Writer's Audience Is Always a Fiction," *Publication of the Modern Language Association* 90 (1975): 9-21. For a related concept, see Edward Black, "The Second Persona," *Quarterly Journal of Speech* 56 (1970): 109-119.

18. Lisa Ede and Andrea Lunsford, "Audience Addressed/Audience Invoked: The Role of Audience in Composition Theory and Pedagogy," *College Composition and Communication* 35 (1984): 140-154. For a critique of their own earlier conceptualization, see Andrea Lunsford and Lisa Ede, "Representing Audience: 'Successful' Discourse and Disciplinary Critique," *College Composition and Communication* 47 (1996): 167-179.

19. See, for example, Brent Burleson and Katherine E. Rowan, "Are Social Cognitive Ability and Narrative Writing Skill Related? A Response to Rubin et al.," *Written Communication* 2 (1985): 25-43.

20. Chaim Perelman and L. Olbrechts-Tyteca, *The New Rhetoric: A Treatise on Argumentation*, trans. John Wilkinson and Purcell Weaver (South Bend, Ind.: Notre Dame University Press, 1969).

21. Martin Nystrand, Anne Doyle, and Margaret Himley, "A Critical Examination of the Doctrine of Autonomous Texts," in Nystrand, *The Structure of Written Communication*, pp. 81-108.

22. Rubin, "Social Cognition and Written Communication."

23. James E. Porter, "Intertextuality and the Discourse Community," *Rhetoric Review* 5 (1986): 34-47; Bennett A. Rafoth, "Discourse Community: Where Writers, Readers, and Texts Come Together," in *The Social Construction of Written Communication*, eds. Rafoth and Rubin, pp. 131-146.

24. For a view that effaces the distinctions between author, audience, and discourse community, see Louise Wetherbee Phelps, "Audience and Authorship: The Disappearing Boundary," in *A Sense of Audience in Written Communication*, eds. Kirsch and Roen, pp. 153-174.

25. Peter Elbow, "Closing My Eyes as I Speak: An Argument for Ignoring Audience," *College English* 49 (1987): 50-69.

26. Ibid., 62-63.

27. Carl G. Herndyl, Barbara A. Fennell, and Carolyn R. Miller, "Understanding Failures in Organizational Discourse: The Accident at Three Mile Island and the Shuttle Challenger Disaster," in *Textual Dynamics of the Professions: Historical and Contemporary Studies of Writing in Professional Communities*, ed. Charles Bazerman and James Paradis (Madison: University of Wisconsin Press, 1991), 279-305.

28. Jill Fitzgerald, "Research on Revision in Writing," *Review of Educational Research* 57 (1987): 481-506; Stephen Witte, "Revising, Composing Theory, and Research Design," in *The Acquisition of Written Communication: Response and Revision*, ed. Sarah W. Freedman (Norwood, N.J.: Ablex, 1985), pp. 250-284.

29. Karen LeFevre, *Invention as a Social Act* (Carbondale: Southern Illinois University Press, 1987).

30. Linda Flower and John R. Hayes, "Plans That Guide the Composing Process," in *Writing: Process, Development, and Communication*, eds. Carl Frederiksen and Joseph Dominic (Hillsdale, N.J.: Lawrence Erlbaum, 1981), pp. 39-58; Sondra Perl, "Understanding Composing," *College Composition and Communication* 31 (1980): 363-369.

31. These data are quoted in Carol Berkenkotter, "Understanding a Writer's Sense of Audience," *College Composition and Communication* 32 (1981): 391.

32. See reviews of research in Fitzgerald, "Research on Revision in Writing" and Witte, "Revising, Composing Theory, and Research Design." A model of revision appears in Linda Flower, John R. Hayes, Linda Carey, Karen Schriver, and James Stratman, "Detection, Diagnosis, and the Strategies of Revision," *College Composition and Communication* 37 (1986): 16-55.

33. Randall W. Stowe, "Effects of Delay of Final Revision on Writing Quality" (Ph.D. diss., University of Georgia, 1988).

34. Donald L. Rubin and John O'Looney, "Facilitation of Audience Awareness: Revision Processes of Basic Writers," in *A Sense of Audience in Written Communication*, eds. Kirsch and Roen, pp. 280-292.

35. Bennett A. Rafoth, "Audience and Information," *Research in the Teaching of English* 23 (1989): 273-190; Duane H. Roen and R. J. Willey, "The Effects of Audience Awareness on Drafting and Revising," *Research in the Teaching of English* 22 (1988): 75-88.

36. See an authoritative discussion of perspective taking in John Flavell, *Cognitive Development* (Englewood Cliffs, N.J.: Prentice Hall, 1977).

37. Bonk, "A Synthesis of Social Cognition and Writing Research." See also, Noel Gregg and Patricia McAlexander, "The Relations between Sense of Audience and Specific Learning Disabilities: An Exploration," *Annals of Dyslexia* 39 (1989): 206-226.

38. Marion Crowhurst, "The Developmental Stylistics of Young Writers' Communicative Intentions," in *Composing Social Identity in Written Language*, ed. Donald L. Rubin (Hillsdale, N.J.: Lawrence Erlbaum, 1995), 189-240.

39. Sheryl I. Fontaine, "Using What They Know: 9-, 13-, and 18-Year-Olds Writing for Different Audiences," in *The Social Construction of Written Communication*, cds. Rafoth and Rubin, pp. 99-116.

40. See, for example, R. J. Iannotti, "Effect of Role-Taking Experiences on Role Taking, Empathy, Altruism, and Aggression," *Developmental Psychology* 15 (1978): 119-124.

41. Karen Schriver, "Teaching Writers to Anticipate Readers' Needs," *Written Communication* 9 (1992): 179-208.

42. For example, Donald L. Rubin and William Dodd, *Talking into Writing: Exercises for Basic Writers* (Urbana, Ill.: National Council of Teachers of English, 1987); Jan Youga, *The Elements of Audience Analysis* (New York: Macmillan, 1989).

43. Donald M. Murray, *The Craft of Revision* (Fort Worth, Tex.: Holt, Rinehart, and Winston, 1991), p. 85.

CHAPTER III

What Is Rhetoric and What Can It Do for Writers and Readers?

JAMES J. MURPHY

The term "rhetoric" is easily misunderstood today because it has, unfortunately, so many negative connotations based on past misunderstandings and modern biases. Dictionary definitions reflect such usage. For example, *The American College Dictionary* includes this phrase in its definition: "the use of exaggeration and display, in an unfavorable sense." The same dictionary defines the adjectival form, "rhetorical," as "belonging to or concerned with mere style." And it is common to hear someone describe an opponent's language as "mere rhetoric"—that is, language not worth listening to. Such pejorative and narrow uses of the term "rhetoric" and "rhetorical" miss the very essence of rhetoric: its breadth and its integrativeness. Rhetoric offers a broad, integrative conception of language use that includes what writers and speakers do to create texts and what listeners and readers do in understanding them. It includes attention to style, but it is much more than simply style.

Rhetoric has been a major subject of study in Western culture since the earliest days of Greek civilization. It dominated language study for more than two thousand years, right into this century. Every important philosopher from Plato and Aristotle to Friedrich Neitzche and Jurgen Habermas has found it necessary to account for the role of rhetoric in language and human affairs. Moreover, since the end of World War II there has been an explosive increase in the interest accorded the matters which rhetoric treats. In other words, rhetoric has been much reviled and much studied, much deplored and much used. Clearly, it is a subject worth considering, even if only to understand it.

In this chapter I will first discuss the nature of rhetoric and its traditional use in teaching, before turning to the implications for the writing-reading relationship.

James J. Murphy is Professor Emeritus of English and of Rhetoric and Communication at the University of California, Davis.

What Is Rhetoric?

The most important place to start is to offer a definition of rhetoric which will adequately describe its essence, while at the same time accounting for the historical variations which have appeared over the centuries. Rhetoric can be defined as "the study of the means for producing future discourse." Writers/speakers use rhetoric in preparing to create future language.[1] Rhetoricians typically explain how ideas can be found, how they can be organized, and how they can be put into words for presentation to an audience. For example, an instructor might discuss how writers of research papers can use certain kinds of documents as proofs and can organize papers in, say, a five-part plan. Sometimes rhetoricians delineate existing texts as examples, showing how previous writers and speakers have accomplished these tasks; this analytic reading of examples is then used to illustrate possible strategies for future use of language. Lincoln's *Gettysburg Address* or William Faulkner's *The Bear*, for instance, can be used to demonstrate to a student certain language strategies useful in his or her own language planning.

The history of rhetoric shows that, while rhetoric developed originally in ancient Greece for the use of orators, the Romans came to base their whole educational system on an interrelated program of reading, listening, and writing as well as speaking. The Roman process continued through the Middle Ages and was developed even further in the Renaissance in Europe, from whence it was exported to America and dominated language education for three centuries. Thus, very early there was concern for readers of the written word as well as listeners to the spoken word. The shaper of future language needed to keep all four of these elements in mind.

This *future* direction is what distinguishes rhetoric from other language arts. Grammar and linguistics describe language as it is, while logic formalizes the rule for making language match mental expression. Both grammar/linguistics and logic exist for present analysis. Rhetoric, on the other hand, looks to *future* language. The future is, of course, imponderable and unpredictable. Its variables are potentially infinite. The question becomes: how does one prepare, now, in the present, for a future with infinite possibilities?

As a consequence, rhetoric has traditionally sought to identify the basic principles of oral and written composition that will apply to a wide range of future uses of language. Rather than try to predict the unpredictable, though, the rhetorician prepares the writer/speaker to have a keen sense of adaptability coupled with a broad spectrum of knowledges and skills, as preparation for meeting the unpredictable. It is not the rhetoric that writes or speaks, but the user of rhetoric who does. It is the writer/speaker, now, in the present, who learns from the study of rhetoric how to act well in the future. To put it another way, rhetoric analyzes every element in what might be called "situational linguistics"—that is, the use of language employed for some particular reason in some particular situation. It is important to note that this study of language, instead of focusing on language as it is, focuses on language as it might be used in the future.

Table 1 displays the four elements in such instances of purposeful use of language. "Literacy" in rhetoric requires personal command by the agent of all the elements involved—not mere competence in one or more—to enable production of the appropriate language in a given situation. Every communicative event involves all four of these elements. In the speaking situation, these elements tend to occur simultaneously; in the writing situation they may be separated by time and space, since the reader may meet the text in some other place or some time later.

TABLE 1

ELEMENTS OF SITUATIONAL LINGUISTICS INVOLVED IN
FUTURE PURPOSEFUL USE OF LANGUAGE

Language user/Agent (e.g., writer, speaker)
    Motive for language use
    Choice of speaking or writing
    Perception by audience

Language receiver (audience)
    General nature of audiences
    Particular audiences

Language (verbal or nonverbal)
    Nature of language (linguistic)
    Types of language ("styles")
    Effects of language

Situations (response to "exigencies")
    Characterizable (legal, political, occasional)
    Noncharacterizable

These might seem like very abstract terms; so rather than continue with abstract discussion, it might be useful to examine in more detail the ways that these elements have been handled throughout the history of rhetoric.

The Rhetorical Tradition

The foundations of Western rhetorical theory were laid in ancient Greece.[2] Although some contributions were made by the so-called "sophists" (teachers like Gorgias, Protagoras, and Isocrates) and although the philosopher Plato discussed rhetoric in several of his dialogues, the first systematic treatment of the subject was that of Aristotle, who died in 322 B.C.E.

Aristotle's *Rhetoric*,[3] which focuses on oral production, defines rhetoric as "the faculty of discovering the available means of persuasion in a given case." The key term here is "faculty," or the human ability to act regularly in a certain way—a meaning close to the modern term "habit." (The Roman educator Quintilian later was to identify this concept as the basic principle of Roman schools.) For Aristotle, the good rhetorician is one who is able to analyze all the elements in a situation and then choose from mental and linguistic resources the right thing to say, and the right way to say it ("right" with respect to having the desired effect on the audience).

For Aristotle, the purpose of knowing how to devise future language is to know how to "prove" what one says, to make an audience accept what you say as true. Aristotle says, "There are only two parts to a speech: you make a statement and you prove it" (III.13). He lays out three kinds of proof: *ethos*, derived from the person of the speaker as the audience perceives it (today we might say "credibility"); *pathos*, derived from the nature of the audience (e.g., age, status, emotional state); and *logos*, derived from the speech itself (logical and paralogical argument).

Under logical proof, Aristotle discusses "topics" (*topoi*) and "enthymemes"—two of the most influential concepts in the long history of rhetoric. Topics are avenues of mental self-examination which provide a speaker with a means to recall to a conscious level knowledge that is already possessed; each topic is also a "line of argument" to construct enthymemes. In his *Rhetoric* Aristotle gives twenty-eight examples of topics; some of his examples are Definition, Motives of Actions, Consequences of Action, Parts of a Subject, Cause and Effect, and Meanings of Words. Modern textbooks for written composition often promote the use of certain of these topics for "paragraph development" without noting their ancient origins.

Aristotle states that an enthymeme is a type of syllogism, or logical construct which compares two propositions to produce a third proposition (a "conclusion"). He says that, since all people wish to regard themselves as logical, and also take pleasure in reaching conclusions for themselves even if they are not literally presented to them by a speaker, then a speaker can achieve proof by leading the hearers into a "line of argument" which the hearers finish for themselves in their own minds. The enthymeme, then, is a sort of cooperative syllogism in which audience and speaker interact to reach the conclusion desired by the speaker.

Aristotle also describes three types of speaking situations: the deliberative (political), where some action is chosen; the forensic (legal), where accusation and defense are the modes; and epideictic (occasional), where praise or blame is assigned. Each of these has its own specific challenges to the orator; for example, the forensic speaker needs to know about wrongdoing and the law, while the deliberative speaker needs to know what an audience perceives as "the good" and conducive to its happiness, and an epideictic speaker needs to know about virtue (for praise) and vice (for blame). These are examples of the situational concerns of rhetoric.

No brief summary of Aristotle's *Rhetoric* can possibly do justice to this remarkably sophisticated book. By drawing on many of his other works on ethics, logic, political science, and psychology, Aristotle demonstrates the wide range of knowledge and skills one needs to prepare for future discourse. Above all, it presents for the first time a manageable way for speakers to cope with the four fundamental elements of purposeful language use.

The next major development was the Roman rhetorical system, which approached the problem in a different way. A little more than two centuries after the death of Aristotle, two books appeared in Rome almost simultaneously. They laid out a new set of rhetorical precepts. One, titled *On Invention* (*De inventione*), was by the young Marcus Tullius Cicero; the other, titled *A Book of Rhetoric Addressed to Herennius* (*Rhetorica ad Herennium*), was by an unknown author.[4] Both set out virtually identical doctrines, indicating that a uniform "Roman" approach to rhetoric was already established by about 100 B.C.E.

The Roman system is based on two premises: first, that the production of discourse proceeds through five progressive steps or "parts"; and, second, that these parts can be studied either separately or as a whole.

The first four parts are internal, and the last is external. The *Rhetorica ad Herennium* (I.ii.3) defines the five parts as follows:

Invention is the devising of matter, true or plausible, that would make the case convincing.
Arrangement is the ordering and distribution of the matter, making clear the place to which each thing is to be assigned.
Style is the adaptation of suitable words to the matter devised.
Memory is the firm retention in the mind of the matter, words, and arrangement.
Delivery is the graceful regulation of voice, countenance, and gesture.

All of these, the author adds, can be acquired through Theory, Imitation, and Practice.

Both this unknown author and Cicero accept Aristotle's division of speaking situations into Deliberative, Forensic, and Epideictic. Cicero's *De inventione* treats only Invention, though he outlines the rest of the theory, saying he will treat each of the other parts in other books (which, in fact, he never composed). Both authors also urge the study of "issues" (stock questions) pertaining to each type of speaking, and they follow Aristotle's concept of invention through topics. (Cicero produced a book, *Topica*, which deals specifically with the latter aspect of rhetoric.) The idea is that the speaker can look to a "topic" as means of dredging the memory for knowledge related to the topic; some frequently cited topics are Definition, Comparison, Names, Cause and Effect, Relation, Motive, Opposites, and Correlation.

This Roman system dominated Western rhetoric for two millennia, and still appears in fragmented form in many textbooks on written composition and in others on public speaking. The Roman educational system helped to spread the Roman rhetorical system throughout Europe in ancient times; then it was revived during the Renaissance and transmitted to America with the earliest colonists in the seventeenth century. Given its long influence, it is important to understand the nature of that educational system.

The Roman Educational System as Described by Quintilian

The Romans inherited from the Greeks the idea of "school," that is, a designated place for learning from an expert adult. But the Romans went far beyond the Greeks by supporting institutional learning centers, with a replicable curriculum, that could be spread geographically to extend Latin influence. Roman emperors beginning with Vespasian in 88 C.E. gave public financial support to schools; provinces and cities followed suit, so that for almost four centuries the schools were a common feature of every Roman settlement. So pervasive was the system that it survived the Empire itself, lasted through the Middle Ages, had an even greater revival in the Renaissance, and came to America in modified form with the earliest English colonists.

The best description of the Roman school system is the *Institutes of Oratory (Institutio oratoria)*[5] published in 95 C.E. by Marcus Fabius Quintilianus, a lawyer turned teacher. Table 2 provides a summary. The system Quintilian describes was already known to Cicero nearly two centuries earlier, and it reappears in other ancient accounts (e.g., Saint Augustine in 426 C.E.), in the Middle Ages and Renaissance, and in descriptions of rhetorical education in America from the colonial period on. In other words, he describes an educational system of major importance in the history of Western civilization.

TABLE 2

OVERVIEW OF ROMAN TEACHING METHODS AS DESCRIBED
IN *INSTITUTIO ORATORIA* OF QUINTILIAN

1. Precept: a method and system of speaking, focusing on five components:
   a. Invention
   b. Arrangement
   c. Style
   d. Memory
   e. Delivery

2. Imitation: the use of models to learn how others have used language. Specific exercises include:
   a. Reading aloud (*lectio*)
   b. Master's detailed analysis of a text (*praelectio*)
   c. Memorization of models
   d. Paraphrase of models
   e. Transliteration (prose/verse or Latin/Greek)
   f. Recitation of paraphrase or transliteration
   g. Correction of paraphrase or transliteration

3. Composition exercises (*progymnasmata* or *praeexercitamenta*): a graded series of exercises in writing and speaking themes. Each succeeding exercise is more difficult and incorporates what has been learned in preceding ones. The following twelve were common by Cicero's time:
   a. Retelling a fable
   b. Retelling an episode from a poet or a historian
   c. *Chreia*, or amplification of a moral theme
   d. Amplification of an aphorism (*sententia*) or proverb
   e. Refutation or confirmation of an allegation
   f. Commonplace, or confirmation of a thing admitted
   g. Encomium, or eulogy (or dispraise) of a person or thing
   h. Comparison of things or persons
   i. Impersonation (*prosopopeia*), or speaking or writing in the character of a given person
   j. Description (*ecphrasis*), or vivid presentation of details
   k. Thesis, or argument for/against an answer to a general question (*quaestio infinita*) not involving individuals
   l. Laws, or arguments for or against law

4. Declamation (*declamatio*), or fictitious speeches in two types:
   a. *Sausoria*, or deliberative (political) speech arguing that an action be taken or not taken
   b. *Controversia*, or forensic (legal) speech prosecuting or defending a fictitious or historical personal in a law case

5. Sequencing, or the systematic ordering of classroom activities to accomplish two goals:
   a. Movement from the simple to the more complex
   b. Reinforcement, by reiterating each element of preceding exercises as each new one appears

Source: Adapted from James J. Murphy, ed., *Quintilian: On the Teaching of Speaking and Writing, Translations from Books One, Two, and Ten of the "Institutio oratoria"* (Carbondale, Ill.: Southern Illinois University Press, 1987). Copyright © 1987 by the Board of Trustees, Southern Illinois University. Reprinted with permission of the Southern Illinois University Press.

The Roman educational system started a boy at about age six, and for a dozen years prepared him for "facility" in language use, both spoken and written. The primary objective was to enable the student to develop a "habit" of language use—to become so familiar with his own mental and linguistic resources that he could react almost instinctively to speak or write well in any situation. Quintilian calls this faculty "a wise adaptability" (II.xiii.2).

Rhetoric was at the core of the "curriculum"—and, indeed, the very concept of a standardized teaching methodology was basically a Roman invention—but the program included as well the formal process of Imitation and a variety of composition exercises like Progymnasmata and Declamation.[6] The system was built around the integrated use of reading, writing, speaking, and listening. Quintilian points out that the "public" school—i.e., one with many students rather than a single student taught by a single tutor—enables the students to hear each other's speaking and read each other's writing and, in turn, to have their own compositions heard and read. All the imitations and exercises aim at multiple uses of language. The *Institutio oratoria* is studded with admonitions about the relations between the language modes, for instance, "By writing we speak with greater accuracy and by speaking we write with greater ease" (X.7.29). And he says of writing, reading, listening, and speaking that all are so important that no one can be called more important than the others (X.1.1).

The same care for relations among the modes appears in the process known as Imitation. This is a process much misunderstood today, but was for the Roman classroom a specific set of activities designed to have students acquire a wide range of linguistic skills by imitating the methods used by others; the models could be speeches, histories, epics, biographies, or any number of other types. There were typically seven steps: reading the text aloud; the teacher's detailed analysis of the text; student paraphrases of the text; transliteration of the text (i.e., prose into verse, Latin into Greek); public recitation of paraphrases or transliterations; and, finally, correction of the student compositions by the teacher. Students used both writing and speaking in their assignments, with reading and listening an integral part of the exercises.

The same can be said about the Progymnasmata, a set of twelve graded (i.e., progressively more difficult) composition exercises which ranged from the simple retelling of a fable to analyzing the complex structures of laws. Every day the student had to engage in writing, speaking, reading, and listening in what we might today call an "interactive" classroom. It was preparation for the day when he had to use these skills as an adult.

The most advanced exercise was the Declamation, which called for the student to make an actual speech in response to an assigned question. Here again, reading of assigned texts and critical listening played an important part; the most complicated declamations involved interpretive readings of laws to choose an appropriate response.

For the many thousands of Roman students and those who followed them in this system over the centuries, rhetoric provided an integral connection not only between speaking and writing but between reading and listening as well. This rhetorical tradition continued for students in American colleges beginning with the colonial period, and it was only toward the end of the nineteenth century that these four elements began to be separated in higher education in the United States. The separation between reading and writing occurred at Harvard and other liberal arts colleges, and it became entrenched as English departments were established in the universities. (Prior to the 1880s hardly anyone would have questioned the relation between writing and reading, since it was universally accepted—based both on tradition and experience—that rhetoric prepared for writing and reading as well as speaking and listening.[7])

Implications for Speaking, Writing, Listening, and Reading

In various ways over the centuries rhetoric has tried to provide ways to cope with the four elements involved in language use: the language user, the language receiver, the language itself, and the situation which calls for writing or speaking. To a great extent, traditional rhetorical theory has followed basic Greek and Roman tenets. There have, of course, been variations, for example, the application of Ciceronian rhetoric to the writing of poetry during the Middle Ages, and the numerous versions of rhetorical theory today. But it is fair, I think, to point to a rhetorical tradition with some consistency of approach in analyzing the problems involved in language use.

It is extremely important, though, to understand that rhetoric does not provide "rules" for linguistic behavior. All rhetorical precepts or principles are in the nature of contingent advice—contingent, that is, on the agent, the audience, the occasion, the purpose. The would-be writer or speaker thus has an arsenal of advices, coupled with whatever practical skills he or she has amassed through constant practice in trying out such advice.

Nevertheless, the search for rules of language goes on. Note the approach of the linguist Noam Chomsky and then that of the sociologist

Jurgen Habermas. Chomsky defines "competence" as knowledge of universal rules by which we construct sentences; Habermas goes beyond "competence" to a second level of knowledge of rules by which we use "speech acts" to accomplish our purposes.[8] In both cases, the operative term is "rules." This is a kind of geometry of language; rhetoric is instead a calculus. Just as geometry proceeds deductively from axioms and postulates, so grammar strives to identify fixed principles governing language use. On the other hand, rhetoric provides for language use in varied and changing circumstances, just as differential calculus deals with the rate of change of a variable function.

From a rhetorician's viewpoint, it is tempting to conclude that the first four "parts" of the Roman theory, the internal parts (Invention, Arrangement, Memory, Style), must be common to both speaking and writing, and that only Delivery by voice, facial expression, and gesture separates speaking from writing. We could say that "orthography," or the physical act of writing, is equivalent to spoken "delivery," all else being the same.

Yet there are questions about differences between oral and written discourse. From the point of view of rhetoric, writing is a minimalist medium, since it offers only the visible language itself; this, in turn, places a burden on the reader to extract intention and meaning from the text without recourse to sound of a voice or sight of a speaker. Given the modern habit of teaching related subjects separately from each other—in this case, reading, speaking, and writing (listening is rarely taught)—perhaps it is not surprising that the role of rhetoric as unifier is seldom recognized. In the absence of rhetorical consciousness, we are left to individual questions about fragmentary issues.

Does a writer devise ("invent") ideas in the same way a speaker does? If so, we can with confidence use topical invention to explore our knowledge base, or pursue an issues approach. Does the speaking situation with its audience-centered, immediate presentation place different mental demands on the language user than that same person would face in a leisurely writing situation with only an imagined audience in mind? (Is "stage fright" the same as "writer's block"?) Is the ability to redraft a written text before publication an advantage over the speaker whose words once uttered cannot be recalled? Many written forms have prescribed formats (i.e., patterns of "arrangement") that relieve the writer of worrying about this aspect of language use; some examples are business letters, sonnets, haiku, and contracts. Is this an advantage or a restriction?

I was once shown an interesting experiment with some implications for the question at hand.[9] The tester asks a writer to use an inkless stylus on a sheet of paper which has a carbon sheet under it. When writers try to write a full page without being able to see what they have written, virtually no one is able to complete the page coherently. The page under the carbon sheet, of course, shows what was actually traced by the stylus. Yet the same person could speak coherently for a much longer period of time than was spent on the writing. (This is similar to the problem often encountered in writing by computer, when previously written sections shown on the monitor scroll out of sight.) One possible answer may be that the writer's expectation is different from the speaker's, in that a lifetime of dependence on seeing the previously written text leads to paralysis in its absence. No such expectation is present when relying on memory while speaking.

Another type of question is whether writing and speaking aid each other. Writing is more deliberate, speaking is more immediate. Is Quintilian correct when he says that speaking makes writing easy and writing makes speaking more accurate? From experience, I would tend to agree with him. A parallel question is whether listening is easier or more efficient than reading. Even more important, does listening skill improve with use just as reading skills seems to do? Studies consistently show that children who are read to at home (i.e., who listen to the written text) tend to become better readers, though it is not clear why. Perhaps it is their knowledge of language patterns of written texts, their awareness of written orthography, and their familiarity with the practices associated with literacy. Perhaps it is their increased motivation.

How does the mode of reception influence the approach to production? A great deal of historical research has been done on the changing nature of reading over the centuries.[10] In the Middle Ages, before the advent of printing, readers equipped with expensive, and therefore rare, texts tended to read them slowly and aloud; correspondingly, medieval writers often tended to use oratorical cadences that fit an oral language. Punctuation was sparse, since the oral style supplied the equivalent of pauses and other directives for the reader. With the explosive growth of printed texts, however, faster reading was necessary to keep up with the quantities of text available, and oral reading faded out fairly quickly in the fifteenth and sixteenth centuries. Silent reading required expanded punctuation, including paragraphing, to replace oral marks like pauses and vocal emphasis. The reader of a text to be read silently was provided more guidance by the writer. Modern writing now differs from speaking in that its audience's reception mode has changed: the writer can usually count on the reading of his or her product to be done silently.[11]

Plato worried that writing would destroy memory and, moreover, would prevent the acquisition of knowledge because the reader would be unable to question the writer.[12] A speaker in the presence of an audience can adjust to that audience, change oral tones, add emphasis, even change arrangement plans in mid-speech, if necessary to make a point; the audience, on the other hand, sees and hears a human being whose motives and intelligence can be assessed during the speech. The reader of a written text, on the other hand, has much less information about the author, and can only deduce motive indirectly. The success of a piece depends, to a large extent, on the linguistic choices a writer makes in order to lead a reader to "meaning"; that is, it depends on the writer's being "clear" enough to avoid potential ambiguities in the perception the reader gains. Rhetoric, in assessing all the factors involved in preparing future discourse, has to acknowledge all these considerations.

A Conclusion

From my perspective, the question educators should be asking is not "How can reading and writing be connected?" Instead, their question should be "Where do reading and writing fit into learning about language and its uses?"

We have seen that rhetoric was defined above as the study of the means for producing future discourse. Rhetoric began in ancient Greece with a concern for spoken discourse, but over the centuries has produced principles which seem to be applicable to every kind of discourse including the written. Until a little more than a century ago, American education, particularly at the college level, recognized the unifying force of a rhetoric which correlated reading, writing, speaking, and listening. There was common agreement with the Roman view that no one of the four was more important than the others.

Then came the literature movement in college and university English departments, when the critical evaluation of literature became the major focus of college English courses, and separate (often remedial) composition courses were created to deal with the production of written language. At the secondary level, both literature and composition were to be emphasized, but they were becoming separate components of the subject English. Although listening faded out of the secondary curriculum, speaking was included in English until it became a separate subject of study in the early decades of this century. That division followed a climactic scene at the 1917 meeting of the National Council of Teachers of English when speech teachers walked out to form their own association. In these circumstances rhetoric was no longer a unifying force.

One is reminded of an early statement about rhetoric, an inscription on a wall in Greece four centuries before Christ: "He who does not study rhetoric will be a victim of it." The same has been said many times about another subject, history. Ignorance of the history of American education makes it impossible today to grapple with the parts, as if there never were, or ever could be, a whole. The ever-increasing specialization of curricula has students dealing with fragmentary questions about increasingly smaller facets of life.

Some modern forces, like television and the computer, are impossible to comprehend unless seen in the larger context of human communication. Both strike to human impulses of stimulation and control. For example, the remote control and the keyboard open up avenues of pleasure that Aristotle would have recognized as being based on every person's desire to think of himself or herself as intelligent—the root principle of the rhetorical "enthymeme." The effects of mass media cannot be studied in isolation, and can be grasped only when the observer knows about audiences in general and audiences in particular, about needs, about situations, about intention—in short, about rhetoric as a whole.

Clearly, many more examples could be adduced. The point, however, is that it would be useful for American educators to step back, take a look at their own history, and then gauge whether there might be some values overlooked in a curriculum characterized by specialization and fragmentation. In particular, they might well reexamine the role of rhetoric. No one would suggest that we return to the ancient terminology of Cicero or Quintilian or their successors or try to reinstate all the practices associated with the classical program, but it does seem fair to try to identify the educational *principles* which made rhetoric a unifying force for so many centuries.

Above all, rhetoric can provide its users with a sensitivity not only to language but to the circumstances in which language is used. The writer who knows the complexities of composition and its reception will surely be in a better position to make the right linguistic choices than someone who simply writes as if in a vacuum. By the same token, the reader familiar with the rhetorical exigencies faced by writers will be in a better position to understand and evaluate any text. The same can be said of speakers and listeners. There are, of course, some interesting questions about the exact relation of the four modes—speaking, reading, writing, and listening—but, in the last analysis, the rhetorician would say that his or her task is to help people prepare for future language use—whatever the mode.

Notes

1. There is no single definitive history of rhetoric. However, three recent surveys may be of interest: Thomas M. Conley, *Rhetoric in the European Tradition* (New York: Longman, 1990); George A. Kennedy, *Classical Rhetoric and Its Christian and Secular Tradition from Ancient to Modern Times* (Chapel Hill, N.C.: University of North Carolina Press, 1980); and Brian Vickers, *In Defense of Rhetoric* (New York: Oxford University Press, 1988). See also, Winifred Bryan Horner, ed., *The Present State of Scholarship in Historical and Contemporary Rhetoric*, rev. ed. (Columbia, Mo.: University of Missouri Press, 1990), and Theresa Enos, ed., *Encyclopedia of Rhetoric and Communication* (New York: Garland, 1996).

2. See James J. Murphy and Richard A. Katula, eds., *A Synoptic History of Classical Rhetoric*, 2d ed. (Davis, Cal.: Hermagoras Press, 1995), and George A. Kennedy, *A New History of Classical Rhetoric* (Princeton, N.J.: Princeton University Press, 1994).

3. Aristotle, *Rhetoric*, trans. W. Rhys Roberts (New York: Modern Library, 1954); idem, *Poetics*, trans. Friedrich Solmsen (New York: Modern Library, 1954).

4. Cicero, *De inventione, De optimo genere oratorum, Topica*, trans. H. M. Hubbell (Cambridge, Mass.: Loeb Classical Library, Harvard University Press, 1949); *Ad C. Herennium de ratione dicendi*, trans. Harry Caplan (Cambridge, Mass.: Loeb Classical Library, Harvard University Press, 1954).

5. *The Institutio oratoria of Quintilian*, 4 vols., trans. H. E. Butler (Cambridge, Mass.: Loeb Classical Library, Harvard University Press, 1954).

6. For a detailed description of the Roman curriculum, see James J. Murphy, ed., *A Short History of Writing Instruction* (Davis, Cal.: Hermagoras Press, 1990), pp. 19-76.

7. See William Riley Parker, "Where Do English Departments Come From?" *College English* 18 (1967): 339-351, and Donald C. Stewart, "Two Model Teachers and the Harvardization of English Departments," in James J. Murphy, ed., *The Rhetorical Tradition and Modern Writing* (New York: Modern Language Association, 1982).

8. See Noam Chomsky, *Syntactic Structures* (Hawthorne, N.Y.: Mouton de Gruyter, 1978). For Habermas, see Sonja K. Foss, Karen A. Foss, and Robert Trapp, *Contemporary Perspectives on Rhetoric*, 2d ed. (Prospect Heights, Ill.: Waveland Press, 1991), pp. 241-272. The latter is a valuable study of contemporary rhetorical theories, discussing also I. A. Richards, Richard M. Weaver, Stephen Toulmin, Chaim Perelman, Ernesto Grassi, Kenneth Burke, and Michel Foucault.

9. I am indebted to Nancy Nelson for the information that this exercise is described in James Britton, "The Composing Processes and the Functions of Writing," in Charles R. Cooper and Lee Odell, eds., *Research on Composing: Points of Departure* (Urbana, Ill.: National Council of Teachers of English, 1978), pp. 13-28.

10. See, for example, Elizabeth L. Eisenstein, *The Printing Press as an Agent of Change: Communications and Cultural Transformations in Early-Modern Europe* (New York: Cambridge University Press, 1980).

11. It is interesting, and somewhat ironic, that the American Educational Research Association feels obliged to furnish conference speakers with a sheet urging them not to read their papers aloud in a monotone as if there were no audience.

12. Plato, *Phaedrus*, trans. W. D. Hembold and W. G. Rabinowitz (Indianapolis, Ind.: Library of Liberal Arts, Bobbs-Merrill, 1954), sections 274-275.

CHAPTER IV

Readers' Awareness of Author

TIMOTHY SHANAHAN

In 1895, the first edition of *Leaves of Grass* was published. Its author, Walt Whitman—then an unknown poet—was not cited on the title page. His photograph appeared in place of his name. Whitman believed that this device would allow him to have a closer and more direct encounter with his readers.[1] The idea that authors think deeply about how to reach out to their reading audiences is well accepted by rhetoricians, and has been explored both theoretically and empirically. But how do readers reach out to authors and from where do they learn to form such relationships?

Composition researchers have devoted great attention to the social aspects of communication in reading and writing, and much of their work deals with writers' relationships with their audiences.[2] Such work has demonstrated that audience considerations can play a major role in the writing process, leading to modifications in text, including changes in author's syntax and quality of writing. Issues such as the status, distance, and authenticity of the audience influence writers' conceptions of their messages as well as particular language choices. Although audience awareness seems to increase with age and experience, some studies have shown that young writers in the elementary grades have some sensitivity to the needs of different readers and can revise texts accordingly. However, these young writers and even mature, fairly experienced writers can be taught to give more attention to the specific needs of their readers. As Melanie Sperling has noted, "Learning to write means . . . learning to anticipate that (and how) one's words will be read—that (and how) one's assumptions about language and meaning relate the understandings of those reading one's work."[3] Composition researchers have developed a rich and informative body of work on how authors think about readers. Reading research has not developed an equivalent collection of investigations concerning how readers think about authors, but such work is now beginning.

Timothy Shanahan is Professor of Education in the College of Education, University of Illinois at Chicago, where he is also Director of the Center for Literacy.

Rhetorical issues will be the focus of this chapter. Instead of the more typical focus—how writers think about readers—I will consider how readers come to think of authors and what difference such thinking makes in their understandings of the texts they read. I will examine (1) the place of the author in literary theory, (2) the role of the author in disciplinary discourse, (3) features of text that make the author more visible, and (4) the concept of author in children's literacy development. These growing bodies of scholarship are evidence that our field is developing an expansive view of social factors in written communication.

The Place of the Author in Literary Theory

During the last half of the twentieth century, literary theorists have hotly contested the relevance and value of the author construct in reading.[4] They have at various times embraced, sometimes warily, or they have vociferously rejected the value of author and, consequently, authorial intentions as worthwhile interpretive constructs. Although the debates in literary theory conducted at the college level have had little direct influence over reading education, especially at the elementary levels, these controversies provide both a theoretical backdrop and a hint at the complexity and subtlety of the author concept that children must acquire in order to become powerful readers.[5]

Historical-biographical approaches to literature were prominent in the early part of the century as literary criticism became a major branch of study in departments of English in colleges and universities. In these approaches, which situated text meaning in the author's historical context, far beyond the boundaries of the text, the ultimate meaning of a text was thought to reside in the biographical details of the author's life that gave rise to it. As a result, meaning was likely to be accessible only to the literary scholar who could spend a career investigating the ontogenesis of the text.

The historical-biographical approach was stultifying and eventually gave way to the (somewhat) more democratic New Criticism in literary theory.[6] New Critics placed the text at the center of their interpretive universe, and relegated the author's life history to the dustbin. For the New Critics, meaning was embedded in the text and accessible to anyone who knew the correct rules or methods of reading. New Criticism marked a kind of reformation both in its belief that meaning was to be found within the text and in its rejection of the need for an interpretive priesthood. Attention to author was not within the purview of the reading methods proposed. In fact, anyone daring enough to consider author's purpose ran the risk of being accused of committing the "intentional fallacy,"[7] since New Critics considered the author's intent to be unknowable and also irrelevant to the interpretive process.

The New Critics in their turn were displaced by the reader-response theorists and poststructuralists. Reader-response theorists, such as David Bleich, Norman Holland, Stanley Fish, Wolfgang Iser, and Louise Rosenblatt, do not exhibit so much an aversion to author awareness as an inattentiveness to the construct.[8] These theorists have usually been so intent on foregrounding the reader's actions, personal associations, felt experiences, and subjectivity in reading that the author as interpretive construct has usually been ignored. Reader-response theorists, unlike the New Critics, have been willing to concede authors some importance, however. For instance, Bleich wrote that "even the greatest works of literature are most comprehensively understood as expressions of the personalities of the authors."[9] Rosenblatt conceded that the reader is always aware "that the words of the author are guiding him; he will have a sense of achieved communication, sometimes, indeed, of communion with the author."[10] But author awareness and inferences of the author's intentions are not important components of reader-response theory. Reader-response theorists have championed reader-constructed meaning, and their attentions are devoted to the interpretive activities of readers rather than to specific text or author factors, although they concede that readers may reach out to authors.

Poststructuralism in literary theory, which began in France in the late 1960s and became influential in the United States concurrently with reader response in the 1970s, critiques notions of subjectivity, including the concept of a subjective author. Poststructuralists have argued the role of author in reading, mainly to reject the notion of a subjective author as a source of meaning and to reconceptualize author as an abstract multivocal construct. For instance, Roland Barthes in his provocatively titled essay, "The Death of the Author," declared an end to the traditional concept of the author behind the text:

We know now that a text is not a line of words releasing a single "theological" meaning (the "message" of the Author-God) but a multi-dimensional space in which a variety of writings, none of them original, blend and clash. The text is a tissue of quotations drawn from innumerable centers of culture.[11]

Barthes dismissed the long-standing idea of a human author who is tied in any ongoing and discernible way to a text. Instead he postulated a multivocal space or source, the author as abstract ventriloquist rather than as creative god.

Michael Foucault also contributed to the demise of the traditional conception of author when he argued for a different conception: author as a function.[12] His idea was that the notion of author serves a kind of organizing function, giving readers a means of tying together a particular body of work. The traditional author concept—the author as a "who"—might be dead, but attention to the interconnections within an author's *oeuvre*—the author as a "what"—was still a part of how we read.

Despite all their claims about an end to the author, the poststructuralists have given much attention to author—so much that the concept has remained very much alive. In fact, Barthes discussed awareness of author when considering the pleasures of reading. For instance, after claiming that reading is pleasurable primarily because it is a solitary, asocial event, he made the point that

lost in the midst of text . . . there is always the other, the author. As institution, the author is dead: his civil status, his biographical person have disappeared; dispossessed, they no longer exercise over his work the formidable paternity whose account, literary history, teaching, and public opinion had the responsibility of establishing and renewing; but in the text, in a way, I desire the author: I need his figure (which is neither his representation nor his projection), as he needs mine.[13]

Barthes echoed here the aversion to author-centered reading that has reverberated throughout literary studies for more than fifty years, but then surrendered to the concept of author as an abstract force. He conceded the value of seeking a kind of human or social "otherness" in reading—through the author's words rather than through his or her biography—because of his belief that it is this, ultimately, that makes reading joyful.

In recent years, the author has made a strong return to literary theory through a revival of such rhetorical concepts as voice, invention, purpose, and through a new interest in discourse communities. Voice and social intercourse play major roles in the theoretical contributions of Mikhail Bakhtin, a Russian scholar whose work preceded and influenced the poststructuralists.[14] When discussing the works of particular authors, such as Rabelais and Dostoevsky, Bakhtin noted multiple voices for each text, instead of a single authorial voice. He went on to argue that an author speaks with the voices of other people whose texts the author has read or heard, and even maintained that the reader's voice can be discerned within an author's utterance. "The term 'voice' serves as a constant reminder that mental functioning in the individual

originates in social, communicative process. . . . When a speaker produces an utterance, at least two voices can be heard simultaneously."[15]
Bakhtin's work is particularly attractive because it emphasizes author
awareness without deprecating the importance of the reader. This
Bakhtinian conception puts the author-audience relationship at the
central point in literary interpretation, as Richard Beach demonstrates
in a later chapter in this volume.

The rhetorical notion of invention is now being applied to reading
processes. Just as a writer is thought to "invent" readers, by making
various inferences about them, a reader is said to "invent" the author.
For instance, Robert Scholes has argued for an approach to interpretation in which the reader's quest for author becomes a major creative
aspect of reading. "I must invent the author, invent his or her intentions, using the evidence I can find to stimulate my creative process."[16]
Scholes does not hark back to either the biographical-historical
approach, in which readers try to find the one true meaning of text
through learning about an author's life, or the New Criticism, in
which they try to remove a text from the context in which it was written. Instead, he calls for readers to use various kinds of evidence as
they surmise an author's purpose for writing. Harold Bloom echoes
this idea: "As we read any literary work, we necessarily create a fiction
or metaphor of its author. The author is perhaps our myth, but the
experience of literature partly depends upon that myth."[17] In his commentary on *The Book of J*, thought to be a source for the Hebrew Bible,
he discussed why he inferred that J was a woman (i.e., various differences between J and other biblical authors) and why he attributed various personality traits to her (e.g., wittiness from her wordplay).

An emphasis on author's rhetorical purpose can be seen in the
"point-driven reading," discussed by Douglas Vipond and Russell
Hunt.[18] They argue that, just as tellers of oral stories have "points" to
make through their stories, authors of written stories, including those
considered "literature," also have points to make. Authors are telling
the story for some purpose; they are "getting at" something. And, just
as listeners sometimes try to discern speakers' motives as they listen,
readers sometimes try to discern those of authors as they read. Vipond
and Hunt's classification scheme for types of literature reading
includes, along with point-driven reading, two other types: informa-
tion-driven (i.e., to remember material) and story-driven (i.e., to have
a "good read"). In a study of 150 undergraduate students reading a
short story, about 5 percent of the students imputed motives to the
author. Vipond and Hunt's claim is not that point-driven reading is the

"best" or most "advanced" kind of reading but that it is a "useful addition" to a reader's repertoire.

However, there is some evidence from a study by Barbara Graves and Carl Frederiksen suggesting that heightened awareness of author and attention to author's purpose are a facet of the "expert" reading of literary scholars.[19] These researchers compared the reading of college English faculty members with that of sophomore students. Experts made frequent references to the author as well as to the reader and to the author-audience relationship, and they tended to see particular language choices, even those that led to ambiguity, as purposeful behavior. When unusual language was used or puzzling situations were presented, they assumed that the uncertainties were temporary and would be cleared up eventually. Students, on the other hand, who did not do the same thinking about rhetorical factors, assumed that lack of clarity was due to their own inadequacy.

There is also some evidence that this sort of literary reading is associated with extensive reading of literature. David Miall and Don Kuiken included items relevant to author in their new measure of literary response. The author factor, replicable across subsamples, included "reflects interest in the author's distinctive perspective, themes, and style"; it also included recognition of the author's place in a literary or intellectual tradition."[20] Students who scored high on this factor frequently read novels and poetry and showed an interest in fine arts beyond literature.

The discourse community notion so important in rhetoric today is yet another way in which social concerns are being applied to literary theory. An important contribution has been made here by Stanley Fish, who moved from the reader-response perspective to a social orientation with his notion of "interpretive community."[21] Constructing meaning for a particular text is said to be a community endeavor in which consensus is reached through collaboration. Into Fish's social constructivist conception, Peter Rabinowitz has incorporated notions of author: that reading with a sense of author is not only a way to read but also a way to talk about reading that is used by members of a literary discourse community. He suggests that readers who successfully join this social arrangement do so by trying to suppose the author's perspective, which includes determining the kind of audience that the author wrote for, and sorting out who is speaking (author, narrator, character) at any point in time.[22]

We see from this brief review of literary theory that author awareness is indeed making a comeback in current conceptions of reading. A number of scholars consider sophisticated reading of literature to involve thinking about the author, hearing an authorial voice, inferring an author's purposes, and even, in a sense, inventing the author. Some are even claiming that this kind of reading is the sort of reading that literary scholars themselves do and serves as a kind of marker between those who belong and those who do not belong to a literary discourse community.

The Role of the Author in Disciplinary Discourse

In addition to the work with literary texts, attention to author has also come from researchers studying disciplinary discourse. Numerous scholars have begun examining the specialized genres and conventions produced in the discourse communities associated with the academic disciplines.[23] Since authorship plays a major role in the activities of disciplines, much attention is on such matters as the social dynamics of getting published, getting grants, and getting one's work recognized and cited. Also of interest to some scholars is the role that author plays in readers' understanding and evaluation of disciplinary texts.

The latter body of work shows how important author can be in representations that specialists in a particular discipline make of texts written by others in their discipline. For instance, Charles Bazerman's study of physicists reading disciplinary journals to keep up with their specialized topics showed that those individuals made decisions about what to read on the basis of author.[24] They knew other authors' work so well that they could briefly skim articles or simply look at the title and perhaps the references to know what would be said. In work focused on another discipline, philosophy, Cheryl Geisler studied two philosophers reading a number of texts on the same topic that were written by different authors.[25] She used a think-aloud procedure in which the participants verbalized their thoughts as they read; later she analyzed the protocols they produced. These protocols included frequent mentions of author and remarks about the authorship of particular claims. Geisler likened their reading to participation in a conversation, in which people take different positions. From her sociocognitive perspective, philosophers keeping up with a particular topic enter into a conversation, and, by writing their own pieces, they make their own contributions.

The conversation analogy was also used by Samuel Wineburg, a researcher who has conducted a number of studies in the discipline of history.[26] His work has shown that, when reading a historical text, the historians participating in a long-distance "conversation" not only read the literal text but also "read" a subtext. The latter involves making inferences about why the author has chosen particular words or phrasings, has positioned certain material in particular ways, and has used particular punctuation marks. Historians, as readers, put themselves in the place of an author making such choices, and they also consider how such choices would affect the intended audience. Thus, a historical text is a *rhetorical artifact*, Wineburg claims, because it is the product of an author who wrote with purposes, intentions, and goals, and made authorial choices in order to have particular effects on an audience. It is also a *human artifact*, according to Wineburg, because it can also reveal much about the author's own biases, assumptions, convictions, attitudes, values, and ways of seeing the world.

Wineburg's data came from eight historians who verbalized their thoughts as they read eight historical texts, all dealing with the Battle of Lexington, which ranged from firsthand accounts to historical fiction to a textbook version. As they read, they made inferences about why authors handled language in particular ways, such as putting quotation marks around "rebels" (to indicate that the colonists mentioned should not be considered rebels in the usual sense), and they made assumptions about the character of the author himself or herself, such as concluding one author was a "classist" because of a haughty tone. Historians viewed people, not textual objects, as the sources of the material, and they demonstrated a "sourcing heuristic" which involved looking first at the source before reading the text.

Both Geisler and Wineburg examined differences between experts (the philosophers in Geisler's study and the historians in Wineburg's study) and novices (undergraduates for Geisler and high-achieving high school students for Wineburg). Geisler found that, in comparison to the philosophers, the college students made fewer references to author as they read and verbalized their thoughts, and they made less use of authors as they distinguished among the various claims. In Wineburg's study, the high school students gave almost no attention to author as they focused on learning and remembering the facts, unlike the historians who were "reading" the texts as rhetorical and human artifacts. Wineburg pointed out that the difference could not be attributed to differences in factual knowledge about the battle, as one might think, since he had tested for such knowledge before the participants read. The students had a great deal of factual information about the battle, and the historians were not specialists in that facet of American history.

An interesting sidelight to Wineburg's study came from a ranking task he gave the students and the historians: they ordered the various texts according to trustworthiness. The students rated the textbook version, with its invisible author, as most trustworthy, because to them it straightforwardly reported the facts. In contrast, the historians rated it least trustworthy. Despite its factual tone, they thought its subtext reflected a strong authorial bias (making Americans heroes).

These two studies show some differences in author awareness that are related to different levels of expertise in an academic discipline. In contrast to these expert-novice comparisons, a different approach has been taken by Christina Haas in her longitudinal exploration of developmental differences.[27] For her case study, situated in the discipline of biology, Haas followed a female student majoring in biology throughout her undergraduate career. The study began during the student's freshman year, when she rarely referred to author and, if she referred to what she read, she made such comments as "the book says." From the first year her studies required her to read research articles, but it was not until her junior year that she began to see authors of research articles as scientists and began to attribute motives to them. By her senior year she was much more attentive to author in her reading and also to the dates of publication; in addition, she showed that she had created different representations of different kinds of authors, such as the active scientists who authored journal articles and the senior scholars who authored textbooks.

The literature reviewed here shows that the author is very much alive in current conceptions of disciplinary discourse as in literary theory. Awareness of author seems to play a major role in specialists' reading of the texts in their discipline, and heightened awareness of author has been associated with growing expertise in a discipline.

Text Features That Make the Author More Visible

Thus far, we have considered the role of author in disciplinary and literary discourse. In disciplinary discourse, specialists in the discipline might know something about and, in some cases, be personally acquainted with some authors they read. Nevertheless, they get to know those people better and get to know others through their reading. In literary reading, readers may know authors by reputation or even personally but often do not know them at all before reading. Readers come to know authors and to make assumptions about them through their texts. How do authors project their personality through their texts, and how do readers discern a human author from linguistic material?

Today there is interest in such questions from the point of view of readers: Which features of texts make authors more "visible" (i.e., make readers think about authors and think about them in particular ways—as having particular traits, as projecting a particular kind of persona)? David Olson suggests that the cognitive history of literacy has been a story of the development of devices that compensate for the loss of the speaker's presence.[28] He reasons that anything—eye contact, hand movement, stance—that cannot be represented directly on the page must be reconstructed by the reader. He attempts to prove that various intellectual inventions such as the separation of literal and interpretive readings have arisen from the physical absence of the author and the reader's need to reconstruct this author. Olson analyzes various devices, such as figures of speech, sarcasm, irony, understatement, and hyperbole, showing that each depends on our ability to go beyond the text to consider authorial intentions, stance, voice, and tone.

It makes sense, for example, that authors would be more apparent to a reader when they make such moves as referring to themselves as "I" or to themselves and the reader as "we," when they express their attitudes about the ideas they present, when they speak directly to the reader or engage in a dialogue with the reader. In contrast, authors would seem to be less apparent when they use the third person pronoun, avoid expressing their attitudes, and do not address the reader.[29] As a number of researchers have noted, textbooks, particularly those for elementary and secondary students, tend to be written as if they are authorless; there is little sense of a human hand in their writing. Comparisons indicate textbooks provide little authorial evaluation of the material presented (e.g., "*Unfortunately*, most Americans do not vote as often as they could") or statements of its saliency (e.g., "*Still more important* as a call to reform were . . .") and few hedges (e.g., *Perhaps*, worst of all was the corruption in the cities") or emphatics (e.g., "This, *of course*, is an oversimplification of the slavery problem").[30]

In a recent study, Susan Nolen compared the reading of passages from two books dealing with statistics, one with a visible, personal author and the other with a more invisible author. The former was Stephen Jay Gould's *The Mismeasure of Man*, and the latter was Gene Glass and Kenneth Hopkins's *Statistical Methods in Education and Psychology* (2nd edition).[31] Nolen reasoned that, since the study of statistics makes many students anxious, a text-visible author could provide them with a "comforting presence."

Gould was visible in various ways: expressing attitudes about ideas (i.e., how he felt about a particular idea and how certain he was about it), putting himself as major agent in clauses with specified actions, disclosing information about himself (e.g., "I was a bratty little kid like

that"; "I know something of the biology of the situation," and addressing readers directly (e.g., "Consider the relationship between my age
and the price of gas."[32] His writing contrasted sharply with that of
Glass and Hopkins, who kept themselves out of the picture by using
third person exclusively, providing many agentless clauses, and by not
discussing views.

Nolen found that, indeed, the female students participating in her
study noticed Gould more often. Readers of the *Mismeasure* passage
mentioned the presence of author six times more frequently during
and after their reading than did students reading the passage from the
work by Glass and Hopkins. She also found that the visible author was
well received by some students but not by others. Responses to him
ranged from "caring" (e.g., "The author seemed to do a lot. . . . A lot
of examples and a lot of real life experiences and trying to implement
them in there") to "paternalistic" (e.g., "I don't think he'd care to
make anybody understand").[33] The kind of reception he received
seemed to be related to students' sense of self-efficacy: those readers
who were more confident in their ability to understand statistics saw
him positively; those with less confidence did not. Authors who
emerge from the text may be welcomed, if students believe them to be
generally helpful and supportive. But because human relationships are
inherently unpredictable, we cannot assume that this will be the case.
Students may perceive a visible author to be obstructive, inept, or
manipulative—in short, the author (that "I person") may be seen as
the reason the reader doesn't understand.[34] This study suggests that
the author can become a useful excuse, a figure who can be blamed for
a reader's failures. The visible author gave confidence and enjoyment
to those who understood the chapter, but frustration and disappointment to those who did not.

Some educators who are concerned about the quality of school children's textbooks have been examining factors associated with author,
such as voice. Can textbooks be improved by making them more
"voiced"? Would students learn and remember more from a voiced
text than from a more typical textbook account? This comparison was
made by Isabel Beck, Margaret McKeown, and Jo Worthy,[35] who
defined voice as a property of text based on three components: activity
(active verbs), orality (conversational tone, dialogue, colloquialisms),
and connectivity (addressing the reader directly)—all features pur-
ported to reveal the author behind the text. Before modifying textbook passages, they studied various versions of historical events. For
instance, they contrasted a trade book account of British taxation on

American colonists with a textbook account of the same topic. The former, considered to be voiced, is from Jean Fritz's *Can't You Make Them Behave, King George?*:

> England had been fighting a long and expensive war, and when it was over, the question was how to pay the bills. Finally a government official suggested that one way to raise money was to tax Americans.
> "What a good idea!" King George said. After all, the French and Indian part of the war had been fought on the American soil for the benefit of Americans, so why shouldn't they help pay for it?

The latter, considered lacking in voice, is from a fifth grade textbook published by Silver Burdett:

> The British lawmaking body was and still is called Parliament. The colonists were not members. The British started passing laws to tax the colonies. Britain thought the colonies should pay their share of the cost of the French and Indian War.[36]

Beck and her colleagues wanted to see if textual changes, including voicing, would help students learn more and remember better what they had read. Passages from fourth grade social studies books were revised to add to a greater sense of voice as well as coherence, and comparisons were made between the effectiveness of the revised versions and the originals. The modified versions resulted in higher comprehension and learning, but we do not know if the students became more aware of author.

In a related study conducted with sixth graders, Avon Crismore failed to find much effect by manipulating text variables that would help establish a relationship between readers and author. In social studies texts, she varied a feature she called voice and another she referred to as "attitudinal metadiscourse."[37] The voicing variable was defined in a more limited way in this study than it had been defined in the study by Beck et al.; here it was defined only in terms of the person (first, second, third) used in the writing. An interpersonal voice was manifest through the use of first and second person pronouns (e.g., "My thesis here is that . . ."; "You will see that . . ."), in contrast with impersonal voice, which used the third person rather than first or second (e.g., "It is the case that . . ."). The attitudinal variable included hedges, emphatics, and evaluatives. The results suggested that interpersonal voice had different effects on different groups of students and also interacted with other text variables. For instance, students who were least comfortable with learning in social studies remembered more when interpersonal voice was used in telling the reader about the structure of the text (e.g., "In Part One I review for you the early Middle Ages. The way I do this is by describing what life was like during that time. The main idea I am trying to get across to you here is that the early Middle Ages was a time without learning and freedom for most people"),[38] whereas those who were comfortable about the course did less well when the interpersonal voice was used. There was also some evidence that such features can be overdone, as students responded negatively to texts with the most visible author.

Crismore suggested that the crucial factor may not be the extensiveness of such features but instead what specific features are added, where they are located, and also how they are used. She added that much would depend on readers' familiarity with the topic and their prior knowledge. In other words, for a text to work for an audience, the author needs to do much thinking about his or her readers and adapt the text accordingly—what they know, where they will have difficulties, how they will respond.

Does changing various text features change readers' impressions of the author? That question was addressed in a study conducted by Jill Hatch, Charles Hill, and John R. Hayes.[39] These researchers took a set of personal essays students produced as part of the application procedure to a university—to be sure, a highly specialized type of reading where constructing an author's persona would be especially valuable. Two preliminary studies reported in the same article had shown that readers, reading independently, formed similar notions of the writers' personalities from the essays and that the personality characteristics thus inferred were associated with different admissions outcomes. Positive traits included such things as maturity, sensitivity to people, likeability, and being down to earth, whereas negative traits included such things as dullness, narrowness, and naivete. For the experiment, the researchers created a second set of essays by changing some text features (e.g., pretentious language, creative moves) that seemed linked to negative and positive traits. The study, comparing readers' impressions of original and revised versions, showed that readers' positive and negative impressions were associated with the identified text features and that a different persona would be suggested by a different version of the text.

The studies focused on linguistic features show (1) that there are particular features that make readers more aware of author, (2) that a highly visible author can be received in contrasting ways, welcomed by some readers and not by others, (3) that textbook materials, which

seem authorless, can be changed to have more voice, and (4) that texts
that project a certain kind of author persona can be changed to project
another by transforming some features of texts.

Children's Awareness of Author

Increasingly, teachers and curriculum designers have been recommending instructional activities that could help students develop more
awareness of author. One approach has students learn about authorship by becoming "authors" themselves. Don Graves and Jane Hansen
have, for instance, popularized the idea of "author's chair"—a feature
of classrooms set up as writing workshops in which students have their
work published as books, become "author of the week," and respond
to each others' writing.[40] Students and their teacher sit in the chair to
share their own compositions or to stand in for the author of published works in student discussions. In a year-long investigation with
first graders in a classroom emphasizing these practices, Graves and
Hansen noted three phases through which children seem to move in
developing a concept of author: (1) knowing that authors write books,
(2) seeing themselves as authors because they too write books, and (3)
becoming aware that authors have choices. This is how Graves and
Hansen summarized their conclusion: "Children's concept of author
changes from a vague notion about some other person who writes
books to the additional perception of themselves as authors to the
realization that they have choices and decisions to make as authors."[41]

There seems to be some connection between author-oriented
activities in writing workshops and the development of reading ability.
For instance, Robert Tierney and his colleagues found higher reading
achievement for children who were placed in the role of author (i.e.,
engaging in extensive writing and participating in workshop activities,
such as revision conferences) than for children not placed in that
role.[42] It is possible, though, that student writers do better with reading because of the development of other more text-related skills than
through any deeper insights about authorship.

Recommendations have been made for various ways of knowing
authors—author-student phone conversations, visiting-author programs, dialogue journals, and methods that direct students to consider
an author's assumptions—but there has not been much empirical evaluation of the effectiveness of such activities.[43] There has also been a
recent attempt to provide students with some explicit instruction in
how to use the author concept in their reading. Beck, McKeown, and

Worthy, who conducted the "voicing" study discussed earlier, created a reading strategy, "Questioning the Author," and found that it enhanced reading comprehension. The procedure is based on the idea that meaning must be negotiated with an author and such negotiation cannot proceed effectively if the author is hidden and seemingly above criticism. Students are taught to actively interrogate the text by asking questions such as "What is the author trying to tell you? Why is the author telling you that? Is that said clearly? How could the authors have said the ideas in clearer ways?"[44] This approach is discussed in the following chapter in this volume.

These approaches emphasizing author are relatively recent ideas and most have not been widely used, so it is doubtful that such techniques have, as yet, exercised a significant impact on the learning of many children. It is also doubtful that much learning about author has been derived from working with traditional basal readers either, given their (until recently) authorless stories, the infrequent opportunities they offer students for reading more than a single selection by an author, and their dearth of instructional activities focused on author. Authors are much more in evidence in the newer basals but still they provide little interpretive direction in this regard, and many schools have not as yet updated their materials. This suggests that most elementary readers have not been taught much about the idea of author— or its connection to theme, voice, persona, tone, style, irony, sarcasm, and so on—in any formal way until recently.

At this time, we actually know very little about children's concepts of author. How do children construe author, if they do such construing? How does it develop? The developmental work, cited earlier, has . given little attention to young children. Instead, thus far it has focused mainly on college students, particularly by comparing their lack of awareness of author with the greater awareness of experts in a discipline. In an earlier paper, I reported on an interview with a young child that revealed an almost total lack of awareness of author or of any nonegocentric reasons for why text is written.[45] Since then, I have been conducting more interviews with children at various grade levels and I believe these investigations are providing a clearer understanding of children's awareness of author and a description of how their conceptions of author are used to make sense of the text.[46]

Recently I interviewed a diverse group of children at two grade levels (twelve third and thirteen seventh graders) from an inner city magnet school. These interviews focused on children's ability to construct authors of stories that they had listened to in their classrooms.

Although I collected interesting responses that provide some insights, I cannot make strong claims about grade level differences from this informal study. One reason is that, even though I selected these children randomly, I later found out that the third grade students were higher achievers in reading relative to grade level norms than the seventh graders were relative to their grade level norms. The groups might have been quite different in ways other than age. Another reason is that I used different stories with the two groups to ensure that all of the students would be working with age-level appropriate text. Although there were important similarities between these stories (i.e., both were written in first person, both were modern, realistic fiction, neither had any obvious authorial commentary or asides), it is always possible that subtle differences exist in the texts with regard to any feature. Thus, it is possible that one of the stories might have been more conducive to fostering a particular conception of author. Nevertheless, despite already noted differences between the two groups and the fact that different stories were used, the study does provide some insights into patterns that might be associated with age.

Meeting individually with the students, I read *Miss Rumphius* by Barbara Cooney to the younger students and Walter Dean Meyer's "Trombones" (from *Fast Sam, Cool Clyde, and Stuff*) to the older ones.[47] The authors of the stories were neither named nor mentioned. After my reading, we talked about the stories. I asked whether the students had enjoyed them, and they described the parts they had liked best. Students were then asked to write about the author; they were encouraged to describe the author, tell whether it was a man or a woman, and indicate if they would like to spend time with the author. When they finished, I asked each student several specific questions about the author.

It should be noted that none of these students questioned the validity of my questions. No child seemed to find the task to be unreasonable or even especially difficult, though they sometimes had difficulty providing clear rationales for particular answers. For these students, discussing the author of a work without biographical information seemed to be neither problematic nor confusing. Of course, this does not prove that these students constructed the author while listening to my reading, though some students claimed to have done so. These students said that certain aspects of authorship, such as gender, had been created at the time of the reading, while other aspects were constructed only as a result of my questioning.

All the students, no matter what their age or reading level, appeared to recognize the existence of author, unlike the younger child in my previously reported interview. When students were asked where stories come from, they sometimes gave answers like "far-off places," "England," or "part of the United States." But more frequently they provided explanations like the following: "People write them, they illustrate them, and they write them and do a lot of nice things with them," or "From the mind of the author—that he's trying to show what he thinks life should be or it happened to him." Even those who responded with a location to this question could demonstrate their awareness of authors in their other answers. One third grader had to go through a whole series of questions before I could be certain of her awareness. Her first response was that stories come from the library. I asked her where the library gets them, and she told me, "Gets them from a company." "Where does the company get them?" I asked. "Company gets them from the author and the author gets them from his mind." A long process, but one that eventually showed that she knew books are written by authors.

My questions included "Why would someone write stories like that?" and "Why did the author write that story?" In response to them, almost all the seventh graders and more than half of the third graders stated author purposes that were communicative in nature. However, an interesting difference seemed to lie in their ideas about what the author was trying to communicate—a difference that seems relevant to Vipond and Hunt's notion of "points" in reading.[48] In talking about "Trombones," the seventh graders said things like "He wrote it to tell people that you should never give up and to try to do things." Almost all of the seventh grade students conveyed a sense of the author's thematic message, whereas such responses were less likely for third graders. Third graders were more likely to suggest that the author of *Miss Rumphius* might write this kind of story "because they think kids will like it" or "for children to read 'cause they wanted adventure . . . for kids to see adventure." These statements indicate a nascent understanding that authors write with an eye toward reader responses, but they do not refer to thematic intentions.

These third graders were talking about a person who often writes just for himself or herself and who has only general purposes for what is written (such as making a living or making readers happy). Most of the seventh graders, despite their relatively low academic standing, showed some awareness that the author was trying to communicate with readers and that the theme or main idea of a text is the chief means of conveying this purpose. Although their individual comprehension might vary in quality or insight, these seventh graders appeared to be approaching author from an advantageous perspective that might be as much due to their social development as to the reading instruction that they received at school. It is possible, though, that the "Trombones" story had a theme that was more apparent or one that resonated more with the children.

The third graders' comments included more reference to authors' writing for themselves. For example, one student said, "Maybe they are talking about someone they know or they always wanted to write a story about that. They always wanted to be imaginative. I always wanted to write about my sister. . . . [The story] would be called 'The Weird Sister.' You just like to." Or another, after listening to *Miss Rumphius*, said: "Because they like flowers." And still another, "To become famous. For everybody to like her." These purposes are directed toward the author's self, and the readers' part of the transaction seemed to be incidental at best. Almost half of the third graders said that authors write for self-directed purposes, while only a tenth of the seventh graders offered this sort of answer.

The responses also suggested something about the kind of voice students believed they could sense. I asked them about the author's gender to try to get at the extent to which they construct authors as the "people behind the text." All students, without hesitation, named a gender for the author, and they could usually explain their answers. Most students from both grades indicated that they used the gender of the character or narrator to infer an author's gender; however, the responses suggest that one's own gender could be a key element in making such determinations as well—at least when the messages are positive and the stories are appealing. Most third graders said that *Miss Rumphius* had been written by a woman, which it was. For example, a child who thought *Miss Rumphius* was written by a woman attributed this judgment to the female main character: "Mostly guys write about men instead of about women." Only a few of the third-grade boys thought that that story was written by a man. Most of the seventh graders indicated that "Trombones" was written by a man, again correct, and only some of the seventh grade girls thought it to be written by a woman. It was interesting to see how confident the children seemed to be about the gender of the author. Other studies suggest that many adults think they can accurately attribute author gender on the basis of text alone but are unable to do so reliably when put to the test.[49]

Students invented gendered authors, and they were able to provide textually and socially based explanations for their inventions. The major kind of explanation was the gender of the main character or narrator, but there were other explanations too. One third grader, believing Rumphius to be an accurate characterization of a woman, was certain that the author had been female: "Men don't really know about women that well." However, another girl figured that it must be a man because of men's interest in women. One seventh grader concluded that the "Trombones" story was written by a man because the main character gets an F on his report card and the student thought women are smarter than men.

In addition, sometimes the gendered attributions were tied to the content or theme of the stories relative to their beliefs about the real social roles of men and women. Some children were sure that *Miss Rumphius* was written by a woman because "usually women think of mellow stuff like flowers and how to make the world beautiful and stuff like that." A boy thought it was authored by a woman because he thought the travel incidents sounded genuine. Similarly, a seventh grade boy thought the second story was the work of a man because of its emphasis on determination and hard work; he thought that a girl would drop the course because of the bad grade.

I asked twelve of the seventh graders about *when* they had thought about the author's gender. All indicated that they had developed some image of the author's gender *while* they listened to the story. Six seventh graders were asked about the author's race as well. Many said it made no difference, and they were hesitant to answer. "I don't think color had anything to do with it," one student responded frostily. Those who did venture a guess speculated that the author must be white, usually on the basis of internal evidence when any explanation was offered. There were not enough of these questions or replies on which to draw conclusions, though the reasons that were given are provocative, suggesting the remoteness that black students might feel even from African-American authors whose work was selected for inclusion in school curricula because it would somehow represent the life experiences of black students. Students who did specify an author's race were asked when they had drawn this conclusion. Unlike the case with gender, none of these students had thought about race during the reading. According to them, this part of their author constructions had not taken place until I asked the question. For these seventh graders, race did not appear to be as salient an interpretive tool as gender.

One African-American boy indicated that the author of "Trombones" must be white. As he explained it, "They [white people] are different; they don't think the same." Another boy was amazed at the quiet response of the mother to her son's low grade, and as a result he assumed a white author: "Because most black people's mother wouldn't be that calm." These students, in their efforts to attribute gender and race, were evidently engaged in the type of rhetorical reading envisioned by Rabinowitz,[50] trying to distinguish author, narrator, and characters.

I asked about the author's opinions of the main character and the story itself in my attempts to get at issues of tone and perspective, though I never used those words and neither did the children. None of the students talked about tone with any sophistication. Nevertheless, in a couple of cases, students did note the "seriousness" or "happiness" inherent in the text—possibly nascent forms of those concepts. For instance, one student indicated that the author probably liked the story: "It seems like when she was writing it she had a smile on her face." For the most part, the students assumed that writers liked what they had written ("because she wrote it") and liked their characters ("because he wrote about him").

These interviews, along with my earlier work on this subject, represent an attempt to explore elementary students' inventions of authors. The findings are in basic agreement with those of Lea McGee, who found that younger children knew fewer, and less communicative, reasons for why authors wrote.[51] McGee interviewed thirty-six second graders, thirty-six fifth graders, and thirty-six adults to find out why they thought authors wrote stories. Younger children proposed fewer reasons for writing stories, and the reasons that they gave rarely included communication or social interaction. Fifth graders were aware of more reasons authors write, and these reasons did show some understanding of the social purposes of text. Adult responses were even more complete in these regards. Despite the obvious limitations of work thus far in children's awareness of author, it seems safe to conclude that children do think about authors, and that the ways they do this thinking seem to change over time. As the research reviewed in the first sections of this chapter indicates, as people grow older and have more experience with texts they begin to use author both as a subjective individual presence and in more abstract ways as a construct that helps them consider theme, tone, and perspective.

The source of these changes is as yet unclear. One can only speculate on whether they are due to social maturation, author-oriented literary experiences, or the development of reading proficiency, or, more likely, a combination of all these.

Conclusions

Thus, we have seen that the author is very much alive in the bodies of work that comprise literary studies. After a brief dismissal, the author has returned to literary theory, as scholars have become interested in rhetorical aspects of reading, such as voice, invention, and purpose. The author has also become quite important in studies of disciplinary discourse, which examine the workings of academic disciplines as authoring communities. Both bodies of work—the one dealing with literary reading and the one dealing with disciplinary reading—are showing that awareness of author is a facet of sophisticated reading by people who have experience in the kind of reading they are doing, who are knowledgeable about the discourse practices in which they are engaging.

In addition, text analysts have begun to pay attention to how authors are reflected by various linguistic devices and what effects those devices have on readers. I began this chapter with the example of Walt Whitman, who used a photograph to assert his place within the text. Other authors stick with linguistic cues to connect with their readers. Which devices make the author more apparent? And is it best to have an author of whom we are more aware? At the present time, we have some answers to the first question. We know something about the linguistic devices that point to author, such as evaluations, hedges, first person pronouns. With respect to the other question, the major conclusion that can be drawn from this work is that the issue is a very complex one. One cannot say that it is always best to have "voiced" texts, that readers do better when they have a strong sense of author; nor can we say that readers do better with "unvoiced" texts. Much depends on the readers, on the context, and on what we mean by "do better." As indicated by the work in audience adaptation, discussed by Rubin in chapter 2 of this volume, authors must think about their readers (what they know, why they are reading, and so on) and be selective in the cues they provide for their readers. In other words, they must make rhetorical choices based on their own "reading" of the situation.

As for development, it seems safe to say that children start with little sense of the author behind the text but they come to see texts as intentional, communicative acts. Over time, people develop more knowledge of rhetorical aspects of communication that they can apply to their reading as well as their writing. At the present time, much pedagogical attention is being directed to various ways to help children develop the author construct and to heighten their awareness of author. Some are intended to help them become better readers and some to help them become better writers, too.

NOTES

1. Gay Wilson Allen, *Walt Whitman* (Detroit, Mich.: Wayne State University Press, 1969).

2. See, for example, Marion Crowhurst and Gene L. Piche, "Audience and Mode of Discourse Effects on Syntactic Complexity at Two Grade Levels," *Research in the Teaching of English* 13 (1979): 101-109; Moshe Cohen and Margaret Reil, "The Effect of Distant Audiences on Students' Writing," *American Educational Research Journal* 26 (1989): 143-159; Marion Crowhurst, "Two-way Learning in Correspondence Between Pen-Friend Pairs," *English Education* 23 (1991): 212-224; Laura A. Frank, "Writing to Be Read: Young Writers' Ability to Demonstrate Audience Awareness When Evaluated by Their Readers," *Research in the Teaching of English* 26 (1992): 277-298; Karen A. Schriver, "Teaching Writers to Anticipate Readers' Needs," *Written Communication* 9 (1992): 179-208. Also see Donald Rubin's chapter in this volume.

3. Melanie Sperling, "Revisiting the Writing-Speaking Connection: Challenges for Research on Writing and Writing Instruction," *Review of Educational Research* 66 (1996): 55.

4. Timothy Shanahan, "Reading as a Conversation with an Author," in *Promoting Academic Competence and Literacy in School*, eds. Michael Pressley, Karen Harris, and John Guthrie (Orlando, Fl.: Academic Press, 1992), pp. 129-148.

5. In recent years the reader-response theory of Louise Rosenblatt, as presented in *The Reader, the Text, the Poem: The Transactional Theory of the Literary Work* (Carbondale: Southern Illinois University Press, 1978), has become influential in elementary and secondary education. This theory, with its emphasis on the experience of the reader when reading, may appear to teachers and curriculum designers to be more relevant to the needs of younger readers than more text-centered approaches.

6. Cleanth Brooks and Robert Penn Warren, *Understanding Poetry*, 3rd ed. (New York: Holt, Rinehart, and Winston, 1960).

7. Monroe C. Beardsley and William K. Wimsatt, Jr., "The Affective Fallacy," *Sewanee Review* 57 (1949): 31-55.

8. David Bleich, *Subjective Criticism* (Baltimore, Md.: Johns Hopkins University Press, 1978); Norman N. Holland, *5 Readers Reading* (New Haven, Conn.: Yale University Press, 1975); Norman N. Holland, *The Critical I* (New York: Columbia University Press, 1992); Stanley Fish, "Literature in the Reader: Affective Stylistics," *New Literary History* 2 (1979): 123-162; Wolfgang Iser, *The Act of Reading: A Theory of Aesthetic Response* (Baltimore, Md.: Johns Hopkins University Press, 1978); Rosenblatt, *The Reader, the Text, the Poem*.

9. David Bleich, *Readings and Feelings: An Introduction to Subjective Criticism* (Urbana, Ill.: National Council of Teachers of English, 1975), p. 4.

10. Rosenblatt, *The Reader, the Text, the Poem*, p. 50.

11. Roland Barthes, "The Death of the Author," in Roland Barthes, *Image, Music, Text*, trans. Stephen Heath (New York: Hill and Wang, 1977), p. 146.

12. Michel Foucault, "What Is an Author?" in *Poststructuralist Criticism*, ed. Josue V. Harari (Ithaca, N. Y.: Cornell University Press, 1979), pp. 141-160.

13. Roland Barthes, *The Pleasure of the Text* (New York: Hill and Wang, 1975), p. 27.

14. Mikhail M. Bakhtin, *The Bakhtin Reader: Selected Writings of Bakhtin, Medvedev, and Voloshinov*, ed. Pam Morris (London: E. Arnold, 1994). See also James V. Wertsch, *Voices of the Mind* (Cambridge, Mass.: Harvard University Press, 1991).

15. Bakhtin, as cited by Wertsch, *Voices of the Mind*, p. 13.

16. Robert Scholes, *Protocols of Reading* (New Haven, Conn.: Yale University Press, 1989), p. 9.

17. Harold J. Bloom, "Enfolding an Author" in *The Book of J*, trans. David Rosenberg, interpreted by Harold Bloom (New York: Grove Weidenfeld), p. 19.

18. Douglas Vipond and Russell A. Hunt, "Point-driven Understanding: Pragmatic and Cognitive Dimensions of Literary Reading," *Poetics* 13 (1984): 261-277.

19. Barbara Graves and Carl H. Frederiksen, "Literary Expertise in the Description of a Fictional Narrative," *Poetics* 20 (1991): 1-26.

20. David S. Miall and Don Kuiken, "Aspects of Literary Response: A New Questionnaire," *Research in the Teaching of English* 29 (1995): 42. A related study conducted by Theresa Rogers suggested that ninth grade students rarely thought about author as they read literature. See "Students as Literary Critics: The Interpretive Beliefs and Processes of Ninth-Grade Students," *Journal of Reading Behavior* 23 (1991): 391-420.

21. Stanley Fish, *Is There a Text in This Class? The Authority of Interpretive Communities* (Cambridge, Mass.: Harvard University Press, 1980).

22. Peter J. Rabinowitz, *Before Reading* (Ithaca, N. Y.: Cornell University Press, 1987).

23. For example, Tony Becher, *Academic Tribes and Territories* (Milton Keynes, Great Britain: Open University Press, 1989); Bruno Latour and S. Woolgar, *Laboratory Life: The Social Construction of Scientific Facts* (Beverly Hills, Cal.: Sage, 1979).

24. Charles Bazerman, "Physicists Reading Physics: Schema-Laden Purposes and Purpose-Laden Schema, *Written Communication* 2 (1985): 3-23.

25. Cheryl Geisler, "Toward a Cognitive Model of Literacy: Constructing Mental Models in a Philosophical Conversation," in *Textual Dynamics and the Professions: Historical and Contemporary Studies of Writing in Professional Communities*, ed. Charles Bazerman and James Paradis (Madison: University of Wisconsin Press, 1991), pp. 171-190.

26. Samuel S. Wineburg, "On the Reading of Historical Texts: Notes on the Breach between the School and Academy," *American Educational Research Journal* 28 (1991): 495-519; idem, "The Cognitive Representation of Historical Texts," in *Teaching and Learning in History*, eds. Gaea Leinhardt, Isabel L. Beck, and Catherine Stainton (Hillsdale, N. J.: Lawrence Erlbaum, 1994), 85-135; idem, "Historical Problem Solving: A Study of the Cognitive Processes Used in the Evaluation of Documentary and Pictorial Evidence," *Journal of Educational Psychology* 83 (1991): 73-87.

27. Christina Haas, "Learning to Read Biology: One Student's Rhetorical Development in College," *Written Communication* 11 (1994): 43-84.

28. David R. Olson, *The World on Paper* (New York: Cambridge University Press, 1994).

29. Avon Crismore, "The Use of Author Roles in Improving Textbooks and Learning," Technical Report No. 365 (Urbana, Ill.: Center for the Study of Reading, 1985); Avon Crismore, Raija Markkanen, and Margaret S. Steffensen, "Metadiscourse in Persuasive Writing," *Written Communication* 10 (1993): 39-71; William J. Vande Kopple, "Some Exploratory Discourse on Metadiscourse," *College Composition and Communication* 36 (1985): 82-93; Mark Sadoski, "Imagination, Cognition, and Persona," *Rhetoric Review* 10 (1992): 266-278.

30. Avon Crismore, "The Rhetoric of Textbooks: Metadiscourse," *Journal of Curriculum Studies* 16 (1984): 279-296.

31. Susan Bobbitt Nolen, "Effects of a Visible Author in Statistical Texts," *Journal of Educational Psychology* 87 (1995): 47-65. Nolen's texts came from Stephen Jay Gould, *The Mismeasure of Man* (New York: Norton, 1981) and Gene Glass and Kenneth Hopkins, *Statistical Methods in Education and Psychology*, 2nd edition (Englewood Cliffs, N. J.: Prentice Hall, 1984).

32. Gould, *The Mismeasure of Man*, pp. 242-243.

33. Nolen, "Effects of a Visible Author in Statistical Texts," 55-56.

34. Susan Bobbitt Nolen, Nia Johnson-Crowley, and Samuel S. Wineburg, "Who Is This 'I' Person, Anyway? The Presence of a Visible Author in Statistical Text," in *Beliefs about Text and Instruction with Text*, eds. Ruth Garner and Patricia A. Alexander (Hillsdale, N. J.: Lawrence Erlbaum, 1994), p. 50.

35. Isabel L. Beck, Margaret G. McKeown, and Jo Worthy, "Giving a Text Voice Can Improve Students' Understanding," *Reading Research Quarterly* 30 (1995): 220-238.

36. Jean Fritz, *Can't You Make Them Behave, King George?* (New York: Coward-McCann, 1977); Silver Burdett, *The United States and Its Neighbors* (Morristown, N. J.: Author, 1984).

37. Avon Crismore, "Metadiscourse and Discourse Processes: Interactions and Issues," *Discourse Processes* 13 (1990): 191-205.

38. Ibid., p. 196.

39. Jill A. Hatch, Charles A. Hill, and John R. Hayes, "When the Messenger Is the Message: Readers' Impressions of Writers' Personalities," *Written Communication* 10 (1993): 569-598.

40. Don Graves and Jane Hansen, "The Author's Chair," *Language Arts* 60 (1983): 176-183.

41. Ibid, p. 182.

42. Robert J. Tierney, Jill LaZansky, Taffy Raphael, and P. Cohen, "Authors' Intentions and Readers' Interpretations," in *Understanding Readers' Understanding*, eds. Robert J. Tierney, Patricia Anders, and Judy Mitchell (Hillsdale, N. J.: Lawrence Erlbaum, 1987).

43. Gail E. Tomkins, "The Literature Connection: How One Teacher Puts Reading and Writing Together," in *Reading and Writing Together*, ed. Timothy Shanahan (Norwood, Mass.: Christopher-Gordon, 1990), pp. 201-224; Linda M. Clary, "Getting Adolescents to Read," *Journal of Reading* 34 (1991): 340-345; Sharon C. Freedman, "Reflections on a Visiting Author Program—9 Years Later," *Journal of Reading* 36 (1992-93): 312-313; M. Cyrene Wells, "At the Junction of Reading and Writing: How Dialogue Journals Contribute to Students' Reading Development," *Journal of Reading* 36 (1992-93): 294-302; Cindy Dooley, "The Challenge: Meeting the Needs of Gifted Readers," *Reading Teacher* 46 (1993): 546-551.

44. Margaret G. McKeown, Isabel L. Beck, and Jo Worthy, "Grappling with Text Ideas: Questioning the Author," *Reading Teacher* 46 (1993): 563.

45. Shanahan, "Reading as a Conversation with an Author."

46. Timothy Shanahan, "Starting a Conversation: The Development of Author Awareness During Reading" (Paper presented at the Annual Meeting of the American Educational Research Association, New Orleans, April 1993).

47. Barbara Cooney, *Miss Rumphius* (New York: Viking Press, 1982); Walter Dean Meyers, *Fast Sam, Cool Clyde, and Stuff* (New York: Puffin Books, 1988).

48. Vipond and Hunt, "Point-driven Understanding."

49. There have been a number of studies of readers' construing a gendered author, and most suggest that many readers think they can accurately attribute author's gender on the basis of text alone, but they are unable to do so reliably when put to the test. See review in Donald L. Rubin and Kathryn Greene, "Gender-Typical Style in Written Language," *Research in the Teaching of English* 26 (1992): 7-40.

50. Rabinowitz, *Before Reading*.

51. Lea M. McGee, "Perceptions of Authors' Intentions: Effects on Comprehension," in *Searches for Meaning in Reading/Language Processing and Instruction*, Yearbook of the National Reading Conference, ed. Jerome A. Niles and Larry A. Harris (Rochester, N. Y.: National Reading Conference, 1983), pp. 148-157.

CHAPTER V

Talking to an Author: Readers Taking Charge of the Reading Process

MARGARET G. MCKEOWN AND ISABEL L. BECK

What sort of author-audience relationship is established when children read their textbooks? The answer to this "rhetorical" question is that typically little connection is made. Students scarcely ever consider an author behind the words they read to master "facts," and textbook authors seem to give little attention to their audience of readers, answering instead to the demands of publishers and the educational establishment. In work with young readers and their textbooks, we found this lack of connection to be a source of problems for students, and we developed an approach to reading called "Questioning the Author," which changed the relationship between textbook author and student audience, at least from the student side.

In prior work in the intermediate grades, we had repeatedly seen students experiencing difficulty in understanding their textbooks and blaming themselves for not understanding the material. Our observations came from a series of studies, conducted in fifth to eighth grades, in which we probed students' interactions with textbook passages and interviewed students to trace their understandings of social studies topics they had studied in school, chiefly through reading textbooks.[1] When asked to read passages, students tended to disengage quickly from their reading, and then, when asked to tell about what they had read, they produced retellings that often had little apparent relationship to the ideas presented by the text. For example, one such retelling described the events of the French and Indian War as: "The Indians wanted to be free from the British . . . And they both fought and the Indians won; they got their freedom."[2] Some students even told us that they felt embarrassed that they could not remember the information they read in social studies.

Margaret G. McKeown is a Research Scientist at the Learning Research and Development Center at the University of Pittsburgh. Isabel L. Beck is a Senior Scientist at the same Center. She is also Professor of Education at the University of Pittsburgh.

What Underlies the Problem?

The difficulty students have in understanding their textbooks is rooted in a complex set of factors that begins with the quality of the materials themselves. In an analysis of textbooks in four commercial elementary social studies programs, we concluded that two major problems with the texts contributed to the difficulty.[3] One problem was that the writers of the texts made unrealistic assumptions about the knowledge of the students for whom the texts were intended. Important ideas often seemed to slide into the text as if they were already part of a familiar context rather than being introduced and foregrounded.

The other problem was that the presentation of information in the textbooks was often sparse and lacked the kind of explanatory information that would allow students to make connections among events and ideas. We found that, although facts about actions and events were often portrayed quite clearly, the information needed for students to understand those events and to see why one event would lead to another was missing. For example, the actions at the Boston Tea Party, when colonists dumped tea into Boston Harbor, were explicitly described in all texts we examined, but none of the texts explained how those actions related to colonists' disputes with the British over taxes.

Our analysis of textbook presentations as lacking explanation and coherence coincides with other analysts' studies of the "inconsiderateness" of textbooks. Bonnie Armbruster and her colleagues have used the term "inconsiderate" to describe text that presents facts in a fashion that is almost listlike without stating the interrelations among those facts that a reader would need for understanding.[4] Also missing from the presentations were devices to support coherence, such as clear referents to related information and explicit statements of causality and temporal sequence.

To illustrate the problems of assumed knowledge and inadequate explanation and coherence, let us consider some examples from our research that dealt with events leading to the American Revolution.[5] In particular, let us take the case of the First Continental Congress, which was a meeting convened in the colonies to respond to the set of harsh laws, known in the colonies as the Intolerable Acts, that Britain had enacted after the Boston Tea Party. The calling of such a meeting held great significance, as it represented the beginning of united action on the part of the colonies. There was no central governmental body in the colonies that could speak for all the colonies, so the First Continental Congress was, in essence, an ad hoc government being called into emergency session.

The textbooks, however, fail to convey the urgency and significance of this meeting—how it foreshadowed the birth of a nation. Only one of the four social studies textbook programs states why the meeting was called. The other three introduce it as if it were an entirely new topic, unrelated to the events of the Boston Tea Party and the Intolerable Acts. No program explicitly states that this Congress was not a standing body, an explanation that is likely needed given students' modern-day understanding of the term "Congress." The following is how one textbook introduces the meeting of the First Continental Congress:

In 1774, a group of Americans met in Philadelphia. Among those present were Patrick Henry, Richard Henry Lee, Peyton Randolph, Sam and John Adams, and George Washington. This was the meeting of the First Continental Congress. The Congress met to discuss the important issues of the day.[6]

Typical of the handling of the Congress in all four texts, this description makes the activities seem rather mild. Most of the description is a roll call of who was present, which may be intended to communicate that the most influential colonists had gathered. However, since that idea is not made explicit and the purpose for the gathering is not made clear, the point may be lost on young readers. The presentations of the First Continental Congress differ somewhat across the four textbooks, and one does explicitly state what the delegates demanded of Britain. However, the precipitating events of the meeting, its charged atmosphere, and its place in the chain of events leading to revolution are absent from the textbook presentations.

Readers of this chapter may think that such an elliptical way of handling information about the First Continental Congress could suffice, since something as central to United States history as events surrounding the American Revolution might already be familiar to the fifth grade students for whom the texts are intended. Our research found that this is not the case. We investigated students' background knowledge about pre-Revolutionary America before they read the textbook accounts and analyzed their understanding of the events leading up to the Revolution after reading the texts. Interviews with students about particular topics just before they studied those topics verified that there was a mismatch between students' prior knowledge related to text topics and the knowledge the text assumed students had. Responses from thirty-five fifth graders suggested that about half of them had some vague knowledge about the American Revolution, but most could not describe the reasons for the war, and three-quarters did not know that the war was between England and the colonies.[7]

We also found that, after reading a textbook presentation about events leading to the Revolution, students' understanding did not include knowledge about causes, consequences, and the significance of key events such as the Boston Tea Party and the Intolerable Acts. For example, after reading the passage about the Boston Tea Party, none of the forty students interviewed mentioned that the colonists' reason for refusing the tea was the tax levied by Britain.[8] Analyses of textbooks and studies of students' reactions to text topics and presentations indicate that the textbooks' inadequate explanation and coherence and lack of attention to background information present obstacles to student understanding.

These stylistic features can be blamed, at least in part, on the procedures used for selecting textbooks for use in schools, which in turn determine how they are produced. Coverage of sanctioned topics is extremely important, and mere mention of the topics serves to satisfy the coverage criterion. Visual appearance is also important, and thus there is the infamous "flip test" in which committee members flip the pages and, if they are caught by lively colors and appealing graphics, it is "thumbs up." Since textbook publishing is a commercial business and textbooks are produced to sell, the factors by which they are selected are the factors to which publishers pay attention. School texts are not written by individual authors, but are produced by teams of editors who coordinate authors' individual contributions. Utmost in the editorial priorities is covering all the requisite topics in the amount of space allotted and producing a graphically appealing package.[9]

To some extent, the problems students have with textbooks can be attributed to their authoritative nature, both in terms of their authoritative language and also in terms of their use as authorities in the classroom. The linguistic aspect has been addressed by David Olson, who sees the authority of textbooks as deriving largely from the kind of language that is used.[10] In Olson's view, the neutral, objective tone of textbooks provides for separation between author and audience, giving the texts a voice that is above criticism. Their language seems to issue from elsewhere, beyond a human author and beyond any immediate context of production. This detached quality of textbook prose has been noted by many who have spent time examining texts. Avon Crismore's assessment was that the role of the writer in textbooks seemed to be to report facts but not to explain them or their significance, while the reader's role seemed to be to "receive the facts passively from the truth-giving authority who wrote them and [to] memorize them."[11] Other descriptions of contemporary textbook prose label it as flat and voiceless, leaden and impersonal.[12] Such descriptions seem to coincide with what Mikhail Bakhtin has referred to as *authoritative text*, which he describes as text that has a static and dead meaning structure, making it unable to enter into contact with other voices.[13]

The role of textbooks in schooling has been discussed by Carmen Luke, Suzanne DeCastell, and Allan Luke, who view the authority of the textbook as a product of the textbook's being "authorized" in the school context.[14] Schools tend to treat textbooks as the embodiment of knowledge, particularly of the knowledge that students are expected to master while in school. Students spend 75 percent of their classroom time using textbook materials, making the textbook a cornerstone of American education.[15]

Teachers depend heavily on textbooks for the content they teach and for the lessons and activities through which the content is conveyed to students. The traditional pattern through which teachers convey text information in classroom lessons further supports textual authority. That pattern, which has been documented for decades, is known as the IRE.[16] It consists of Initiation (the teacher asks a question), Response (a student responds, usually briefly), and Evaluation (the teacher assesses the correctness of the response and then moves on to a new question). Typically, the questions require students to seek information directly from the text and students are evaluated as performing well if they simply retrieve the information. Thus the IRE reinforces the textbook as the authoritative source of knowledge, above criticism, and the teacher as the text's intermediary. Because of teachers' heavy reliance on them, textbooks are a major factor in shaping instructional programs around the nation and have the status of a kind of national curriculum.[17]

The authoritative status of textbooks seems to have ample support, whether viewed as deriving from their linguistic sources or from the school context. In either case, the upshot is that students are not within the appropriate and sanctioned social group entitled to criticize school texts. The student's role is to accept, respect, and understand the text.

Students often respond to the difficulty and authority of textbooks by limiting their engagement with them. We observed throughout our studies that students typically used a kind of hit-and-run strategy for reading textbooks. They read, taking in as much information as they could skim in one pass. Then when asked to recall what they had read or to answer questions about it, they responded without much reflection on the completeness or quality of the information they presented.

The hit-and-run reading style seems to support observations of student readers made by other investigators. David Pearson and Robert Tierney saw little pausing, rethinking, and reflecting on the part of the secondary students they observed.[18] Darren Smith described one high school student's reading strategy, typical of the students he worked with, as "she read everything once and if she didn't get it the first time, she didn't care."[19] Contrary as it may seem, students appear to limit their engagement with difficult texts because of the importance they assign to them. Students often seem to develop the attitude that if they are not able to grasp the information presented to them by this endowed authority, their textbooks, the problem lies with them. So disengaging from texts saves students from admitting to inadequacies as readers and taking the blame for comprehension problems.

How Can This Problem Be Addressed in Instruction?

Efforts have been made to foster students' engagement with texts by counteracting the voiceless and detached nature of textbook prose. One such effort was to modify a test by adding metadiscourse, language by which the author directly addresses and guides the reader.[20] Another direction was trying to give a text qualities of "voice," so that it would speak to a reader. Aspects of voice included using more active, concrete verbs to communicate immediacy of actions, using a conversational tone (as in oral language), and stressing connections between events and reactions to the events.[21] Both of these efforts met with some success, albeit limited. But the use of metadiscourse and voice represents authors speaking to readers. What about readers speaking to authors?

To deal with text information effectively, students need to understand reading as a process of figuring out what the content is all about. But interacting with text by reflecting on and grappling with ideas presented by an author is rarely a part of traditional elementary classroom experiences. In order to get students to dig in and apply active effort as they read, a first step is to get past the obstacle of textual authority.

Based on our studies of how young readers interact with what they read in school, we developed an intervention to help students engage with what they read. Our starting point was to "depose" the authority of the text by creating the perspective of reading as "questioning the author."[22] We did this by invoking a human author who had written down ideas in creating the text. The intent here was not to give students the impression that authors merely write down whatever comes into their heads and that everything in a text must be called into question. The purpose was to communicate to students that what was written in a text was not something that sprang forth in perfect form, but a verbal product created by a person. In this way we deliberately gave students the right to criticism that, as Olson and Luke et al. describe, is usually denied.[23]

The orientation to text on which the Questioning the Author approach is based begins with the notion that text is the product of human beings, who are fallible in their ability to communicate their ideas in writing. It follows then that text is specific to the particular author, that is, there is not just one way to present specific information or certain ideas. Someone else might have written it differently. It also follows that text is open-ended and inherently incomplete. A reader has to make something of a text in order to "complete" it. Relatedly, although text is directed to an audience, an author has incomplete knowledge, and sometimes inappropriate expectations, of the audience.

The view of reading that underlies Questioning the Author is that reading is a constructive process in which the reader interacts with print, assigning meaning to what is read by connecting ideas and integrating them with prior knowledge.[24] In this way, a reader builds a model of the situation that the author is trying to communicate. The consequence we presented to students was that a reader has to work to figure out the ideas that an author is trying to get across. In setting up reading as an effortful, active process, we gave students both the permission to criticize text and the responsibility for figuring it out. In essence, the message was "You sometimes have to work to get it."

In using Questioning the Author in a classroom, a teacher sets up reading as an active search for meaning through questioning of ideas as they are initially encountered. That is, the teacher stops the reading at selected places and presents an open-ended probe, or query, such as "What's the author trying to say?"; "Why do you think the author is telling us that?"; "What do you think the author means by that?"; or "Does that make sense?" As students respond, collaborative discussion is encouraged to make sense of ideas that an author has presented and to build meaning.

Support for Putting the "Author" in the Comprehension Process

There is support in the literature for the notion that a reader's awareness of an author enhances his or her interactions with text.

Timothy Shanahan has written of the importance to the reading process of a reader's consideration of an author's intentions, craft, and voice. He characterizes reading comprehension as a "conversation with an author" and describes considerations of author as "fruitful interpretive tools that help us look deeper into a text to construct a richer meaning."[25] Robert Tierney and Theresa Rogers discuss how students' sense of themselves as readers and their views of text develop as classroom discussions and activities include a focus on authorship and authors' intentions.[26] Linda Flower and Christina Haas have used the term "rhetorical reading" for the kind of reading that involves making inferences about an author's plans, goals, and context. Through rhetorical reading, readers build a link between themselves and the author, and use that relationship in constructing meaning for a text.[27]

Several studies have indicated that awareness of author can enhance comprehension. James Mosenthal found, as did Jill LaZansky and Robert Tierney, that increased recall of text resulted from training students to consider authors' intentions. Tierney, LaZansky, Raphael, and Cohen found that students who exhibited the greatest awareness of author also evidenced the greatest critical interpretation of a text. In observations of elementary classrooms, Shanahan found that students who were given instruction and experience in becoming aware of the author were consistently better in noticing errors in the logic, facts, syntax, and spelling of a text. Flower's observations of proficient adult readers led her to conclude that consideration of author's purpose seemed to play a meaningful role in resolving comprehension problems.[28]

Raymond Gibbs, Julia Kushner, and Robert Mills demonstrated the effect that awareness of author can have on readers' perception of the meaningfulness of a text. As the researchers presented similes to college students, they told the students one of two things: that the simile was written by a poet or that it was randomly generated by a computer. Students were asked to rate the degree of meaningfulness of the similes and to write interpretations of the similes. The researchers found, first, that students rated similes more meaningful if they had been told they were written by poets and, second, that students produced more interpretations for similes attributed to poets.[29]

There seems to be a consensus that more sophisticated readers are more likely to give consideration to an author as they read. Researchers who study writing have noted that students who have already developed fluency in writing are also those who approach their reading of a text with an awareness of authorship.[30] Studies, including those by Linda Flower, first alone and then in collaboration with Haas, comparing readers who have different levels of experience, revealed that more sophisticated readers were more cognizant of an author as they read and made use of that awareness in interacting with a text.[31] The readers in Flower's initial study included a graduate student, English teachers, and a psychologist. Based on observations of these proficient readers' use of a rhetorical reading strategy, Haas and Flower then conducted a controlled study to examine the reading strategies of experienced readers compared with less experienced readers (college freshmen). The distinction between the more experienced and less experienced readers resided in the use of rhetorical strategies. Student readers seemed to focus almost exclusively on content, while all the experienced readers went beyond content to construct a rhetorical situation for the text. Haas and Flower concluded that rhetorical reading was an important element used by expert readers to develop a richer representation of a text.

A study conducted by Samuel Wineburg in the discipline of history supports the notion that a sophisticated reading process includes awareness of author. In this case, historians and high school students were asked to think aloud as they reviewed documents about the Battle of Lexington. Wineburg found that a major difference in the way the two groups operated related to awareness of author. Whereas students seemed to view author attribution as the last bit of information to be considered, for historians "attribution was the 'bit' from which all else emanated."[32] For the historians, attributing the document to a person and a context was a primary concern. They used author attribution to construct entire scenarios about the author and the circumstances under which the document was produced.

Researchers' observations of author awareness indicate that it is an approach most often called on when the going through a text gets difficult. In the study mentioned earlier, Flower documented the points in the text where the six experienced readers struggled to understand the text. She found that in 60 percent of those trouble spots, the readers turned to a rhetorical reading strategy, making inferences about the author's purpose to help resolve comprehension problems.[33] In related work, Sarah Martin also noted the usefulness of author awareness in situations where students had difficulty comprehending. Her study, which focused on seven high school students, showed that these students, all of whom were good readers, made connections with the author more often as they read more abstract text.[34]

An important note on readers' use of author awareness can be found in Julia Kushner's research as well as that by Haas and Flower.[35]

Kushner learned that the college readers she studied needed training in order to bring author awareness to bear on reading tasks. In several experiments, she found that simply asking readers to attend to the source of a text or using language that brought attention to the author's voice was not sufficient to enhance reading comprehension. But prompting students to think aloud as they read did succeed in getting them to use awareness of an author in comprehending text. Similarly, Haas and Flower found that simply introducing the notion of rhetorical reading and suggesting that readers apply it were not sufficient. They concluded that getting readers to read rhetorically is "genuinely difficult" and will likely require active teaching efforts that include direct instruction and modelling.

Findings from these studies of awareness of author seem to provide some strong leads into what is still relatively unexplored territory. It seems reasonable to say, based on the work thus far, that an instructional approach that promotes the connection between reader and author would be advantageous for young readers. In the next section we explore the results that were indeed found in classrooms using the Questioning the Author approach where connection to the author was a key to constructing understanding of text.

Overview of Results of Implementing Questioning the Author

At this point in our work, we have implemented Questioning the Author over three years with five teachers and about 120 fourth and fifth grade students. The result has been dramatic changes in classroom discourse. The findings come from comparing transcripts of baseline lessons, taught by our collaborating teachers before they implemented Questioning the Author, to lessons with Questioning the Author across the year. Analyses were made of a total of twenty-nine lessons, which included lessons in reading as well as social studies. The materials students used in the reading lessons were not written in the same sort of authoritative, voiceless language as that of the texts used in the social studies lessons. Instead, for the reading classes, the materials were typically fiction—stories credited to particular authors and anthologized in a basal reader. However, even these texts can seem quite authoritative for young readers, as they form a central place in the curriculum and are usually approached as complete, closed entities rather than as representations of choices that people who happen to be authors have made. The findings, which we summarize here, indicate changes in the roles of both teachers and students in classroom discussion. They come from both the reading lessons and the social studies lessons.[36]

In the baseline transcripts, questions that asked students to retrieve information directly from text had dominated most lessons. In Questioning the Author lessons, the focus of teachers' questions changed to considering and extending meaning. Teachers were more likely to ask why something happened or why certain information was presented and how it related to other information in a text rather than asking for a replay of the information. Teachers' responses to students' comments also changed. In baseline lessons, after a student's comment the teacher had most often simply repeated what the student had said. However, in Questioning the Author, teachers responded to students in ways that extended the conversation. Teachers gave consideration to the content of students' responses and often rephrased the comment, shaping ideas by clarifying or focusing them, or giving emphasis to certain aspects. In this way, teachers were able to use student comments as a basis for continuing the discussion rather than putting closure on each comment as if it were an isolated bit.

Students were much more active participants in Questioning the Author discussions. They did more than twice as much talking as in the baseline reading lessons and three times as much talking in social studies class. Teachers did proportionally less talking. Students were also much more likely to initiate questions and comments, something they rarely did in baseline lessons. We found an average of ten instances per lesson in which students brought up their own questions.

The nature of responses that students gave also changed. Students began to focus on constructing meaning and integrating ideas rather than on retrieving information from the text. Students were more likely to phrase their contributions in their own language, going beyond verbatim responses 90 percent of the time in reading class and nearly 85 percent of the time in social studies. A quarter of students' responses in both reading and social studies showed evidence of integrating prior knowledge, hypothesizing solutions to problems, or extrapolating consequences about what they were reading. In contrast, no such integration was found in baseline social studies lessons, and it was found less than 10 percent of the time in baseline reading lessons. Another change in students' responses was that student-to-student interactions during discussions became common. Students expressed agreement or disagreement with each other's ideas, responded to each other's questions, and explicitly built on ideas that other students had presented. This kind of interaction had occurred about once per lesson in baseline reading transcripts, and not at all in social studies. In the Questioning the Author lessons, about 10 percent of students' comments were explicitly directed toward their peers.

Students' New Perspective from Questioning the Author

Accompanying the changes in discourse, students under Questioning the Author seemed to exhibit a changing perspective toward author and text, toward their role as readers, and toward their peers. This new perspective showed itself in the way students framed their comments during classroom discussions and also was revealed in interviews we conducted with them at the end of the school year. We will consider how this changing perspective may have influenced the changes in classroom discourse just presented and what the shift in perspective may suggest about the strength and permanence of the changes in discourse.

AN AUTHOR'S PRESENCE

Classroom responses during lessons provide evidence that students under Questioning the Author are aware of dealing with another person on the other side of the print. Students frequently framed their comments in terms of what the author was doing. The following are typical of comments found in transcripts of Questioning the Author lessons:

Antonio: I think that the author thinks that . . .
Heidi: The author tells us in this paragraph . . .
Betty: Um, I have a question. What did the author mean . . .

Not only did students seem to have an author in their mind's eye, but they also seemed to recognize that what is in a text is an author's expression of certain information or ideas, rather than objective reality. Students' comments during discussions suggested that, as students read, they considered how well a text was "working," and how else ideas might have been expressed. For example:

Roberta: The author didn't just like, come out and say it. You have to figure it out.
Temika: I think the author wants us to think that . . .
Reggy: Well, I think the author coulda said . . .
Alvis: Well, why didn't the author just come out and say . . .

Comments such as these are suggestive of Pearson and Tierney's notion that effective readers read like a writer, constructing and revising a text for the reader in their heads.[37] Students' comments that reflect consideration of how ideas were expressed in a text also imply that students are developing a new perspective on reading, seeing it as an active process of figuring out ideas. Embodied in this perspective is a view of themselves as capable of dealing with and making sense of what they encounter in texts.

A VIEW OF READING

When we interviewed students at the end of the year, we asked them to describe what goes on in their reading or social studies class and how they might explain it to someone new to the class. Students' new perspectives on reading and on themselves as capable readers were much in evidence in their responses. After their experiences with Questioning the Author, they described their reading process as figuring things out, thinking about what an author was saying, asking questions, and discussing ideas. Asked why they did those things while reading, the response they gave most often involved "understanding." The following is a sampling of what students told us about their classroom reading:

Zack: We question the author so we can get a clear picture of what the story is about, and also we might, because, so that we can understand the book more and we won't have to, like, 'what the heck's going on?' We know it's clear to us after we question the author awhile.

Peter: Reading is, like, finding out what the author's thinking in the book and what the people are doing. . . . We ask a lot of questions . . . because the books we read are very interesting and there's a lot of questions to be asked.

Michael: Like she [the teacher] will read a paragraph or two or maybe a whole page, and, like, she'll say, what's the author trying to say, and then kids will raise their hand and they'll, like, sort out the paragraph, like, pull it apart and so you can see, like, hear actually what the paragraph is about.

Janet: Well, we basically just ask questions and talk like the author's really sitting there, like the author's right there sitting and that you're asking a question. . . . It's more creative than just asking regular questions or just plain reading you know, like, if you don't think about what you're reading and you just read, that's not reading. You're just looking at scribbles on a piece of paper. You know.

The way in which these students described reading is particularly interesting when contrasted with what other students their age say about school reading. We obtained such a perspective because, for two of the Questioning the Author classrooms, we were able to interview comparison groups of students. The comparison students were also fourth graders from the same district as the Questioning the Author classes, and they had read the same classroom text materials.

Of the forty-seven students in the two Questioning the Author classes for which we had comparison students, thirty-three of them characterized reading as involving aspects such as figuring things out, working on what an author is saying, asking questions and discussing, and moving toward understanding. In contrast, of the forty-seven students in the comparison classrooms, only thirteen students mentioned anything about reading having to do with figuring things out, asking questions, or understanding. Only one student mentioned that an author might be involved. Students in these two classes most often spoke of reading in terms of working on vocabulary words, answering teachers' questions, and taking tests.

PEERS AS PARTNERS

Another change in students' roles as readers is that they saw their peers as valuable partners in the meaning-building process. Students' contributions during discussions illustrate the different ways in which students interacted with each other during Questioning the Author lessons. Often the students began by stating agreement or disagreement with a peer. In agreeing, they often went on to elaborate or clarify what the other student had said, as with Thomas and Shanelle in the following excerpts. These first examples come from reading lessons, but we found similar patterns in social studies classes.

Thomas's response followed comments from Darleen, who had said that Toby, a character in the story they were discussing, was trying to make his brother admit that he is real by acting like a robot.

Thomas: Um, I agree with Darleen because, I agree with her and I'm going to add something too. I think, um, Toby is acting like a robot because, um, when his brother's gonna get sick of him acting like that and saying I was just joking, you're a real person, then he's gonna say, gonna go acting like a robot for Alistair's attention.

In the same discussion, a student named Alvis had talked about what the character was doing in terms of getting on his brother's nerves. Shanelle offers support for Alvis's idea, commenting:

Shanelle: He might be doing that to Alistair because—Alvis is right—because I have a big brother that does this to me.

This next comment, from a different lesson, in fact a different class, demonstrates another function of peer interaction, clarifying what a peer has said:

Mark: I have two things to say. Um, for one I agree with Tracey they did want to improve, like, conditions of the work and their pay. And number two, I think Joshua meant by very little, the author told us very little. I think that's what he's trying to say.

Notice how this comment illustrates the multiple lines of processing in which Mark is engaged. In the first part of his comment, he contributes to issues of ongoing discussion, while the latter part demonstrates a monitoring function; he notes that a peer's earlier comment may have been misunderstood. Finally, the following comment shows a student tracking contributions of several peers:

Darleen: I agree with Tammy and April and I disagree with Alvis, 'cause I would think that women, back in those days would like their job. I think that if they really knew who Nellie Bly was, they probably woulda, um, did what Tammy said. They probably woulda wanted to not do women things.

In the end-of-year interview, Jermaine's comments summed up the role that peers played in classroom text discussion:

Jermaine: I would say I like to discuss 'cause it's fun discussing with somebody else, like, when you disagree, when you don't disagree. And I like reading and when um, say, like, when I disagree, I like to tell why I disagree and when I agree with somebody I tell why I agree with them.

Changing Roles in Classroom Reading

In Questioning the Author classrooms, the responsibilities of author, text, teacher, and student have shifted from what is typically encountered in traditional recitation lessons that still dominate elementary classrooms. Students no longer seem to approach text as a daunting authority, but as information communicated to them by another person. As students' comments indicate, the author becomes more visible through text and is held responsible for text. In a sense, the author submits text for consideration and evaluation by the class, rather than the text being delivered as something that is complete and objective. Students' responses to text in Questioning the Author suggest that the approach helps them link the text to the author and, in doing so, diminish the authority of textbooks. Students feel more at ease with questioning and transforming what an author has said, and even criticizing how it has been said.

The text is no longer viewed as the authoritative standard to which students are held, in the sense described by Luke et al.[38] Instead, the text serves as a resource for building understanding. The teacher becomes more clearly the students' ally rather than the text's ally, no longer acting as the text's agent by holding students responsible for precisely reflecting the text. Rather, the teacher's role is to facilitate consideration of text by stimulating discussion through general, meaning-focused prompts. Students are now credited for making meaning from what is presented rather than being held responsible for having received what is in the text. Instead of the text being assumed as having "all the right stuff" (all the information) and the students judged on how much of it they can reflect, the student is assumed to have the right stuff (the ability to understand the text). The text is judged on how much sense can be made of it. Students view reading as a highly interactive process of exploring and sorting out information and view themselves as equal to the challenge of that exploration.

Abundant evidence of students' changing perspective on the reading process and their relationship to an author comes from spontaneous comments during classroom discussions. The spontaneous nature of these comments suggests that students are developing habits of mind. They have not merely learned new responses to instructional prompts; rather, they are demonstrating this new perspective in use.

Questioning the Author affected students' perspectives on author and the reading process, and the procedure prompted more meaningful classroom discourse. But a remaining question is: What caused what? The Questioning the Author environment seemed to open up a space for students to explore meaning, but did the focus on meaning *cause* author awareness or was that focus the result of the fallible author perspective that was presented to students? Our hunch is that merely telling students that the author is fallible would not be effective. What is called for is to help students construct that perspective, and constructing that perspective is intertwined with examining the text—what ideas it presents, what their meaning might be, and why the author chose to present them. So constructing a new perspective on the author is inherently engagement with meaning.

The development of this chapter was supported by funds from the Office of Educational Research and Improvement (OERI) in the U.S. Department of Education and from the Spencer Foundation. The opinions expressed do not necessarily reflect the position or policy of OERI or the Spencer Foundation and no official endorsement should be inferred.

NOTES

1. Isabel L. Beck and Margaret G. McKeown, "Outcomes of History Instruction: Paste-up Accounts," in *Cognitive and Instructional Processes in History and the Social Sciences*, ed. James F. Voss and M. Carretero (Hillsdale, N.J.: Lawrence Erlbaum, 1994), pp. 237-256; Margaret G. McKeown and Isabel L. Beck, "Making Sense of Accounts of History: Why Young Students Don't and How They Might," in *Teaching and Learning in History*, ed. Gaea Leinhardt, Isabel L. Beck, and Catherine Stainton (Hillsdale, N.J.: Lawrence Erlbaum, 1994), pp. 1-26; Margaret G. McKeown and Isabel L. Beck, "What Young Students Understand from Their Textbooks about the American Revolution" (Paper presented at the Annual Meeting of the American Educational Research Association, Boston, April 1990); Gale M. Sinatra, Isabel L. Beck, and Margaret G. McKeown, "A Longitudinal Characterization of Young Students' Knowledge of Their Country's Government," *American Educational Research Journal* 29 (1992): 663-661.

2. Beck and McKeown, "Outcomes of History Instruction."

3. Isabel L. Beck, Margaret G. McKeown, and Erika Gromoll, "Learning from Social Studies Texts," *Cognition and Instruction* 6 (1989): 99-158; Isabel L. Beck and Margaret G. McKeown, "Toward Meaningful Accounts in History Texts for Young Learners," *Educational Researcher* 17 (1988): 31-39.

4. Bonnie B. Armbruster, "The Problem of Inconsiderate Text," in *Comprehension Instruction: Perspectives and Suggestions*, ed. Gerald G. Duffy, Laura R. Roehler, and Jana Mason (New York: Longman, 1984), pp. 202-217. See also Robert N. Kantor, Thomas H. Anderson, and Bonnie B. Armbruster, "How Inconsiderate Are Children's Textbooks?" *Journal of Curriculum Studies* 15 (1983): 61-72.

5. Heath and Company, *Social Studies* (Lexington, Mass.: Author, 1985); Macmillan, *Macmillan Social Studies* (New York: Author, 1985); Scott, Foresman, *Scott, Foresman Social Studies* (Glenview, Ill.: Author, 1986); Silver Burdett, *The World and Its People* (Morristown, N.J.: Author, 1984).

6. Scott, Foresman, *America Past and Present* (Glenview, Ill.: Author, 1986), pp. 148-149.

7. Margaret G. McKeown and Isabel L. Beck, "The Assessment and Characterization of Young Learners' Knowledge of a Topic in History," *American Educational Research Journal* 17 (1990): 688-726.

8. Margaret G. McKeown, Isabel L. Beck, and Gale M. Sinatra, *The Representations that Fifth Graders Develop about the American Revolutionary Period from Reading Social Studies Textbooks,*" Project Report to the Office of Educational Research and Improvement (Pittsburgh: University of Pittsburgh, 1989).

9. For a discussion of these issues, see chapters in *Textbooks and Schooling in the United States*, 89th Yearbook of the National Society for the Study of Education, Part 1, ed. David L. Elliott and Arthur Woodward (Chicago: University of Chicago Press, 1990).

10. David R. Olson, "On the Language and Authority of Textbooks," *Journal of Communication* 30 (1980): 186-196.

11. Avon Crismore, "The Rhetoric of Textbooks: Metadiscourse," *Journal of Curriculum Studies* 16 (1984): 281.

12. Gilbert Sewall, "American History Textbooks: Where Do We Go from Here?" *Phi Delta Kappan* 69 (1988): 552-558; Diane Ravitch, "The Revival of History: A Response," *Social Studies* 80, no. 3 (1989): 89-91.

13. Mikhail M. Bakhtin, *The Dialogic Imagination*, ed. Michael Holquist and trans. Caryl Emerson and Michael Holquist (Austin: University of Texas Press, 1981).

14. Carmen Luke, Suzanne DeCastell, and Allan Luke, "Beyond Criticism: The Authority of the School Text," *Curriculum Inquiry* 13 (1983): 111-127.

15. Armbruster, "The Problem of 'Inconsiderate Text.'"

16. Arno Bellack, Herbert M. Kliebard, Richard T. Hyman, and Fred L. Smith, Jr., *The Language of the Classroom* (New York: Teachers College Press, 1966); Hugh Mehan, *Learning Lessons: Social Organization in the Classroom* (Cambridge, Mass.: Harvard University Press, 1979); Courtney Cazden, "Classroom Discourse," in *Handbook of Research on Teaching*, 3rd ed., ed. Merlin C. Wittrock (New York: Macmillan, 1986), pp. 432-462.

17. Arthur Woodward and David L. Elliott, "Textbooks: Consensus and Controversy," in *Textbooks and Schooling in the United States*, ed. Elliott and Woodward, pp. 146-161.

18. P. David Pearson and Robert J. Tierney, "On Becoming a Thoughtful Reader: Learning to Read Like a Writer," in *Becoming Readers in a Complex Society*, 83rd Yearbook of the National Society for the Study of Education, Part 1, ed. Alan C. Purves and Olive S. Niles (Chicago: University of Chicago Press, 1984), pp. 144-173.

19. Darren Smith, "Common Ground: The Connection between Reader-response and Textbook Reading," *Journal of Reading* 35 (1992): 632.

20. Crismore, "The Rhetoric of Textbooks," p. 281.

21. Isabel L. Beck, Margaret G. McKeown, and Jo Worthy, "Giving a Text Voice Can Improve Students' Understanding," *Reading Research Quarterly* 30 (1995): 220-238.

22. Margaret G. McKeown, Isabel L. Beck, and Jo Worthy, "Grappling with Text Ideas: Questioning the Author," *Reading Teacher* 46 (1993): 560-566.

23. Olson, "On the Language and Authority of Textbooks"; Luke et al., "Beyond Criticism."

24. Isabel L. Beck and Patricia A. Carpenter, "Cognitive Approaches to Understanding Reading: Implications for Instructional Practice," *American Psychologist* 41 (1986): 1098-1105; Marcel Just and Patricia A. Carpenter, *The Psychology of Reading and Language Comprehension* (Rockleigh, N.J.: Allyn & Bacon, 1987); George J. Spilich, Gregory T. Vesonder, Harry L. Chiesi, and James F. Voss, "Text Processing of Domain-Related Information for Individuals with High and Low Domain Knowledge," *Journal of Verbal Learning and Verbal Behavior* 18 (1979): 275-290; Harry L. Chiesi, George J. Spilich, and James F. Voss, "Acquisition of Domain-Related Information in Relation to High and Low Domain Knowledge," *Journal of Verbal Learning and Verbal Behavior* 18 (1979): 275-290.

25. Timothy Shanahan, "Reading Comprehension as a conversation with an Author," in *Promoting Academic Competence and Literacy in Schools*, ed. Michael Pressley, Karen Harris, and John Guthrie (New York: Academic Press, 1992), pp. 129 and 131.

26. Robert J. Tierney and Theresa Rogers, "Exploring the Cognitive Consequences of Variations in the Social Fabric of Classroom Literacy Events," in *Learning to Use Literacy in Educational Settings: Literacy as a Social and Cognitive Process*, ed. David Bloome (Norwood, N.J.: Ablex, 1989), 250-265.

27. Linda Flower, "The Construction of Purpose in Writing and Reading," *College English* 50 (1988): 528-550; Christina Haas and Linda Flower, "Rhetorical Reading Strategies and the Construction of Meaning," *College Composition and Communication* 39 (1988): 167-183.

28. James Mosenthal, "Instruction in Interpretation of a Writer's Argument: A Training Study" (Ph.D. diss., University of Illinois, 1983); Jill LaZansky and Robert J. Tierney, "The Themes Generated by Fourth-, Fifth-, and Sixth-Graders in Response to Stories" (Paper presented at the Annual Meeting of the National Reading Conference, San Diego, November 1987); Robert J. Tierney, Jill LaZansky, Taffy Raphael, and P. Cohen, "Authors' Intentions and Readers' Interpretations," in *Understanding Readers' Understanding*, ed. Robert J. Tierney, Patricia Anders, and Judy Nichols Mitchell (Hillsdale, N.J.: Lawrence Erlbaum, 1987); Timothy Shanahan, "Authorship and Critical Reading" (Paper presented at the Annual Meeting of the National Reading Conference, Austin, Texas, November 1989); Flower, "The Construction of Purpose."

29. Raymond W. Gibbs, Julia M. Kushner, and W. Robert Mills, "Authorial Intentions and Metaphor Comprehension," *Journal of Psycholinguistic Research* 20 (1991): 11-30.

30. Lucy Calkins, *Lessons from a Child* (Portsmouth, N.H.: Heinemann, 1983): Don Graves and Jane Hansen, "The Author's Chair," *Language Arts* 60 (1983): 176-182; Robert J. Tierney and Timothy Shanahan, "Research on the Reading-Writing Relationship: Interactions, Transactions, and Outcomes," in *Handbook of Reading Research*, vol. 2, ed. Rebecca Barr, Michael L. Kamil, Peter B. Mosenthal, and P. David Pearson (New York: Longman, 1991), pp. 247-280.

31. Flower, "The Construction of Purpose"; Haas and Flower, "Rhetorical Reading Strategies"; Julia Kushner, "The Role of Author Information in Text Processing" (Ph.D. diss., University of Pittsburgh, 1996); Samuel S. Wineburg, "Historical Problem-Solving: A Study of the Cognitive Processes Used in the Evaluation of Documentary and Pictorial Evidence," *Journal of Educational Psychology* 83 (1991): 73-87.

32. Wineburg, "Historical Problem Solving."

33. Flower, "The Construction of Purpose."

34. Sarah Martin, "The Meaning-Making Strategies Reported by Proficient Readers and Writers" (Paper presented at the Annual Meeting of the National Reading Conference, St. Petersburg, Fl., November 1987).

35. Kushner, "The Role of Author Information in Text Processing"; Haas and Flower, "Rhetorical Reading Strategies," p. 182.

36. Isabel L. Beck, Margaret G. McKeown, Jo Worthy, Cheryl Sandora, and Linda Kucan, "Questioning the Author: A Year-Long Classroom Implementation to Engage Students with Text," *Elementary School Journal* 96 (1996): 385-414; Margaret G. McKeown, Isabel L. Beck, and Cheryl Sandora, "Questioning the Author: An Approach to Developing Meaningful Classroom Discourse," in *The First R: Every Child's Right to Read*, ed. Michael Graves, Barbara Taylor, and Paul van den Broek (New York: Teachers College Press, 1996): pp. 97-119.

37. Pearson and Tierney, "On Becoming a Thoughtful Reader." See also Frank Smith, *Joining the Literacy Club: Further Essays into Education* (Portsmouth, N.H.: Heinemann, 1988).

38. Luke et al., "Beyond Criticism."

Section Three
THE CLASSROOM CONTEXT

CHAPTER VI

Teachers as Readers of Students' Writing

MELANIE SPERLING

The red pen that signals the writing teacher at work should probably be on the endangered symbols list. Process approaches to teaching
writing, with their focus on the teacher as facilitator of students' writing and thinking processes,[1] have rendered all but obsolete the error-
centered teacher whose primary role is to "read with her pen." Yet the
red pen as a symbol of the teacher's approach to reading students'
writing is tenacious in school culture and, despite approaches to writing instruction that discount such behaviorist-influenced images, continues to reflect some strongly held assumptions about what it means
to read as a teacher ("mark papers"), what the teacher's role is in the
process ("prescriptive"), and how much students learn about writing
when teachers as readers focus on the errors of their written ways
("much").

Assuming for the sake of argument a less odious image of the
teacher-reader, assuming, say, that instead of a red pen the teacher
were seen to wield something like an orchestral baton, possibilities for
perceiving not only the aims and functions but also the processes of
reading students' writing expand enormously. Bestowed with a baton
(at once sturdy and delicate), the teacher-reader can be seen as a sensitive interpreter of text, filtering as well as animating the range of sen-
sibilities that are reflected in the reading of a single composition. As
fanciful as the orchestral image may be, the fact is that two to three
decades of writing research focusing on the teacher as reader and
responder to students' writing, as well as the evolving theories of
writer-reader relationships that have both shaped and reflected this

Melanie Sperling is an Assistant Professor in the School of Education at Stanford
University.

research, invite our serious consideration of this image as a metaphor for reading students' work and directing the social interchanges that may shape it, even though the old image may linger.

Evolving Guises of the Teacher as Reader

Theories of writing and learning to write have evolved over the past five to six decades, reflecting the epistemological movement toward postmodernism also seen in the broader educational research community.[2] This evolution is generally parsed into three theoretical emphases, each emphasis characterizing successive decades of the second half of this century and each reflected in writing research and classroom practice. The first emphasis, said to characterize in particular the 1950s and early 1960s, is on *text*, with writing research and pedagogy addressing the formal correctness of students' written products. The second emphasis, prominent in the late 1960s and 1970s, is on the *individual*, with research and pedagogy addressing the cognitive processes of composing. The third emphasis, ascendant in the 1980s and 1990s, is on *social and cultural contexts*, with research and pedagogy addressing the broader societal and discourse contexts in which writers and texts function and in which written language assumes meaning.[3] With each successive emphasis, the teacher as reader is also differently conceived.

From the textual perspective, writing is defined in terms of formal constitutive text structures—for example, sentences and paragraphs or the number of paragraphs of which a particular type of text is comprised. (In school, the number of paragraphs still, notoriously, is five, the five-paragraph essay maintaining even today a kind of iconic force.[4]) Given this formal emphasis, learning to write means, for the most part, producing structures that are grammatical and in other ways well-formed while at the same time learning to avoid grammatical errors and other formal infelicities. This focus on formal structures suggests the need for students to practice such structures, for example, imitating published prose models or doing exercises such as sentence combining, and such practice becomes central to the instructional process. For teachers, combing students' writing—both their exercises and their original texts—for formal problems, for places where written structures veer from standard or conventional form, is an appropriate way to focus their reading of this writing. Relatedly, marking errors is both a necessary and sufficient way to reflect this reading to students.

In contrast, a cognitive-process perspective defines writing as a translation of writers' thoughts, their ideas, plans, and goals.[5] Learning to write means learning to turn ideas, plans, and goals into written language. From this perspective, it is not sufficient for a teacher to read students' writing as if she were on a search-and-destroy mission, shooting down the linguistic infelicities along the path. She must, instead, focus on her students as thinkers who, in order to produce a written text at all, rely on strategies for generating and shaping ideas, planning texts for particular audiences, and revising ideas and plans to fit evolving purposes. The teacher as "cognitive" reader must read and respond to students' texts with these cognitive strategies in mind; in fact, she must "read" the strategies themselves and respond to them. From this perspective, simply reading with a red pen, pointing out grammatical and other formal errors after students have struggled to turn thought into writing, can stymie the very composing processes that the teacher wants to foster. Such reading puts the emphasis in the wrong place by telling students that conforming to features of formal written language is more important than expressing what and how they think.[6] Given a cognitive-process emphasis, it is not only appropriate but critical for teachers to read and respond to work in progress, even before words hit paper, and to keep doing so as the work, and the students' thinking, unfolds.[7]

A focus on the social and cultural contexts of composing also expands and redirects the focus on composing processes by seeing written language as a social and cultural construction as well as a translation of individual thought[8]—by seeing cognitive processes themselves as socially and culturally shaped. Language, then, shapes thought as much as the other way around.[9] From this perspective, writing is understood as language in context, that is, as discourse, reflecting writers' mediations in the social world. Put another way, texts are defined as socially and culturally situated conversations.

Reflecting this view of writing, learning to write becomes a process in which students construct hypotheses about the ways writing functions and how it is used and interpreted by particular readers in particular contexts.[10] A major goal for instruction is to allow writers to interact with their readers around their writing and thinking, in effect making explicit the conversation that is implicit in writing.[11] From this perspective, the teacher is, like all readers, a particular and situated reader (albeit a particularly knowing one) and not a simple reification of "the" universal reader. It follows that students learn by interacting not only with the teacher-reader but with other readers as well, in particular with peers in the classroom community, for the multiplicity of interactions or conversations in a shared context is the stuff of their developing ideas and strategies. The teacher-reader's role, then, is only partly to interact with the writer; it is also to orchestrate (hence the baton), through multiple writings and conversations, the multiple readings through which the writer may see and shape her work. In this process, the writer's text both reflects and contributes to a dialogic world.[12]

A DIALOGIC MODEL OF INSTRUCTION

This social-cultural perspective suggests a model of instruction in which student writers interact with teacher-readers in a process organized like the following: teacher assigns (oral and written); students think, read, talk, write; teacher (and students' peers) read, think, talk, write a response; student reads, thinks, talks, rewrites—and so on until the teacher or student calls stop.

For the past several years, I have been studying the writer-reader relationship, including the role of the teacher as reader of students' texts, and have found several examples of this dialogic process in classrooms. Looking closely at interactions among students and teachers, I have found that the voice of the red-pen teacher-reader continues to shape students' writing and ideas about writing, but that this voice can be heard as one of many cultural voices that work together in the instructional process and that students as writers negotiate in the context of school writing. For teachers working in this context, realizing the scholarly shifts that have occurred from text-centered perspectives to cognitive perspectives and on to social-cultural perspectives does not necessarily mean moving from one perspective to the next, never looking back. Instead, teachers' perspectives as readers of students' work can reflect the accumulation of this scholarly knowledge, knowledge that adds to and enriches their repertoire of roles and functions rather than simply "replacing" older perspectives with newer.

A rich and complex repertoire of roles and functions fits the assumption that teachers possess a range of purposes in reading students' writing. In particular, teachers' reading, like students' writing, changes depending on when in the writing process they are reading students' work, as the preceding instructional model suggests. It also changes depending on the kind of writing. For example, correcting students' language is one pedagogical purpose for reading students' writing, but this purpose is not necessarily compatible with, say, reading a student journal that was written to explore ideas rather than to represent a finished story or argument. Helping students to generate ideas is another pedagogical purpose, compatible with reading a draft of an essay and probably more useful at the draft stage than when the student presents a final version.

Characteristics of a class and of individual students in it also influence the teacher-reader's roles and purposes. However, even though teachers as readers can be sensitive to the needs of individual student writers, red flags should be raised when teachers respond stereotypically as hard-nosed editors to the writing of students who are struggling to learn English as a new language or those who have weak grammatical skills, and as sympathetic friend to the writing of other students who are more familiar with school language.

The point for scholars of reading and writing is that the reading process that teachers experience as they read students' work is varied, nuanced, and contextualized, and in this sense is complementary to students' writing processes. In both processes, multiple roles and purposes are at play. Yet in the classroom context, teachers still have a position of power, with implications for both students as writers and themselves as readers of students' work. This position of power is found in the most innovative classrooms, where at the very least teachers and students carry the weight of their past classroom experiences as they interact in present moments.

THE MULTIROLED READER: A LESSON FROM THE CLASSROOM

In several articles, I have described interactions among students and their teacher in a tenth grade English class[13] as the students shared drafts of their assigned research papers. Students in this classroom often read drafts or related their research experiences to one another, sharing both successes and problems in undertaking these tasks. Francoise chose to write her research paper about society's attitude toward death. As part of her research, she had visited a clinic specializing in psychological therapy for children and adolescents with terminal illnesses. There she had observed group therapy sessions in which participants spoke candidly about their illnesses and dying. When Francoise shared with the class what she had written about her visit to the clinic, the discussion soon turned to a topic that she and her teacher had discussed in conference prior to the beginning of class: her difficulty in writing down the youngsters' actual words. The youngsters had spoken in a rush of emotion and urgency—as Francoise indicated, they spoke "without punctuation"—and Francoise was not sure how to render their language in written form that was also readable. She expressed particular concern about the following two passages from her paper:

Ellie [a child at the clinic] described feelings as "a feeling is what your insides feel and from deep in your heart and it circulates your body and so if you are happy you know it most of the time you know it . . . unless you are very confused which could also be a feeling."

Jerrod [another child at the clinic] said: "It's a cell that has the part that says stop building chopped off and it just keeps on building and building until it reaches a stage where it can be seen on an MRI scan."

While these two passages are especially poignant, what is interesting about Francoise's difficulty with the question of punctuation is that most writers, wittingly or not, wrestle with the same difficulty when setting down almost any spoken language on paper. All speech occurs "without punctuation," and setting down speech on paper requires coming up with satisfactory conventions or contextual description to indicate to readers the full measure of how spoken words are delivered and heard in spoken contexts. Alas, what is heard in spoken contexts seldom matches what can be put in writing, and what is "heard" in reading the written version is not necessarily what is heard in live interaction. Francoise's experience of this phenomenon led to the following discussion with her teacher and peers:

Ms. Smith: Now, what can we do to help Francoise with her problem? She has these two quotations by people [i.e., children at the clinic]. Picky English teachers would call those run-on sentences. I'm not going to pick about it, but how can she explain that [i.e., how the children spoke] to the reader in such a way that it's clear. How can she treat that? Any ideas?

Beth: Um. You could—I mean for instance [for] the English teachers or whatever, you could punctuate it [i.e., the quotations], but then you could say like "he said (in a rush) or something like that you know, so—I don't know.[14]

Fran: Well, the thing is that I don't know where to put the punctuation pause . . . because there were no pauses or ends of sentences kind of things [when the children spoke]. So if I put in stuff [i.e., punctuation], it wouldn't be what he said.

Beth: Oh, then I have no idea.

Jody: I just think you should leave it [i.e., keep the run-on sentences]. I mean no one is—only people that are gonna like say anything about it is Ms. Smith [i.e., the

teacher], and she understands that the—why you're
um doing it [i.e., writing run-on sentences], so I mean—

Fran: But what if you [as a reader] were reading it, and you
suddenly came to this big fat quote that had absolutely
no punctuation?

Jody: Well, if you say, if you say kind of like Beth said, just
say [to the reader] like "After he says um, after he said
in an excited voice finally explaining—" you know
"explaining something that he knew," 'cause you know
how like kids get really excited about explaining something *they* know to someone else. Say something like
that. I mean, just to like explain [to the reader] *why*
they're saying something like that [i.e., speaking in a
rush].

John L.:   Why don't you, before the quote, introduce it as, you
know um uh, "it's uh written with no punctuation." . . .
No punctuation. And you'd introduce it and then say
the quote.

Ms. Smith: Does that sound workable? That's better [for the
reader] than the idea I had [in her prior conversation
with Francoise about the paper].

Fran: That's the *same* idea you had.

We see this interaction among Francoise, the other students, and
the teacher as a critical moment of teaching and learning because it
was an explicit moment of writer-reader interaction. Furthermore, it
surfaced a number of responding voices, including the teacher as one
voice, that vied—necessarily—for Francoise's attention. First were the
voices of the children at the clinic, whose language tumbled out with
no perceptible pauses or breaks, and who implicitly made claims on
Francoise to make this situation as real as possible in her paper. Then
there were the implicit cultural voices that she and the others invoked
and with which they all seemed quite familiar—specifically the canonical voices of the "trusting reader" (who might innocently stumble on
a big fat quote with absolutely no punctuation—and who could be
helped to understand the big fat quote) and of the "picky English
teacher" (with her care about run-on sentences). Additionally there
were the present voices of these students and this teacher, situated in
real time in a real classroom, with their own histories as participants in
this classroom and others, as they expressed their differing perspectives and advice on Francoise's work-in-progress.

Given these sometimes competing, sometimes overlapping, readers' voices, it is not surprising that the class's suggestions for remedying Francoise's "writing problem"—to punctuate in the text but to write a disclaimer or, conversely, not to punctuate and to explain why—were not fully satisfactory to any of them, even though the teacher in her earlier meeting with Francoise had made the latter suggestion herself. Moreover, during the class discussion, Francoise never reached a satisfactory resolution to the matter, which she seemed to recognize as far more significant than surface correctness.

In fact, the participants in this discussion implicated at least two critical tensions that sit at the heart of the literacy process itself—the tension between written text that is "proper" and written text that is effective, and the tension between language that is spontaneously spoken and language that is deliberately written. When Francoise acknowledged her role as writer vis-à-vis an interconnected web of reader respondents, she pressed on these tensions and, doing so, complicated her writing task as well as the class's notions of their reading of her work. Yet, as the discussion suggests, her task was incomplete without such complications.

The conversation between Francoise and her class offers the potential to reveal the sometimes enormous conceptual gap separating the solely prescriptive teacher-reader from the orchestrating one. It also indicates, however, how real the prescriptive teacher-reader is for both teachers and students in classroom settings, in particular, in being integral to students' and teachers' beliefs and observations about how student writing normally functions in the context of school learning. The teacher has power in the classroom, and the English teacher in particular has a history of valuing and promoting written conventions over issues of arguably more genuine communication.

More importantly, though, if we take Francoise's classroom conversation to be a serious model for teaching and learning, one that sees writing as a process of negotiation of internalized voices as much as one of following rules, it suggests how fluent and explicitly multi-roled a teacher-reader must be—and how responsive student writers must be to the frequent ambiguities among these roles.

A FRAMEWORK FOR THINKING OF THE TEACHER AS READER

My colleagues and I had the opportunity to develop a framework for thinking about the teacher-reader's multiple roles in a recent study of an eleventh grade English class.[15] The framework was a result of studying the classroom interactions between the teacher and her students that centered on the students' writing, and examining as well the comments that the teacher wrote on students' papers.

The framework is shown in Figure 1. It indicates that multiple orientations toward the students' writing converged to both shape and reflect the teacher's perspective as a reader of students' work. As the figure shows, these orientations included her different *social* roles in relationship to students, for example, fellow literary critic, sympathetic friend or colleague, school authority; her different *interpretive* lenses for reading their texts, for example, personal, cultural, popular, or academic lenses; her changing *cognitive and emotive* stances toward students' work, for example, fully articulated analyses of their work vs. summarily holistic reactions (the latter indicated in comments such as "great!"); her different *pedagogical* aims, for example, to support students' ideas, correct their formal writing problems, expand their writing goals or plans; and, not least, the different *evaluative* stances, indicating whether the student's writing has or has not worked for her as a reader.

It is important to underscore that all these orientations to the student's writing worked together—they overlapped. The following example of a writer-reader exchange in this class, seen in a passage of

FIGURE 1

Orientations Characterizing the Teacher's Perspective as Reader

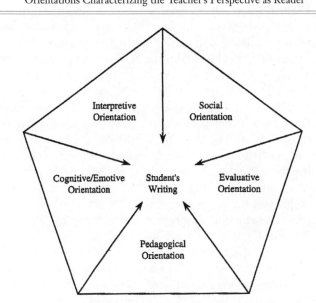

student writing and the teacher's written comment on it, should help make this overlap clear. The passage is from a paper written about Arthur Miller's *The Crucible*, a play derived from the Salem witch trials. To write the paper, the student assumed the persona of one of the characters in the play and wrote the paper in the form of a prayer created from the character's perspective. The teacher addressed her comments to the student writer, not to the persona in which he wrote, and many such comments sprinkled the paper, of which the following is a small part.

The student had written:

But now, Lord, I do not know what to do, for this is the first time that my unique knowledge of religion and witchcraft has been called upon. What if I make the wrong decision?

The teacher commented:

He thought it would be easy—in black and white, like his books.

In this comment, the teacher appears to speak directly to the student's interpretation of the character in the play and in this sense may be said to have related to the student as one literary scholar to another. Put another way, her comment reflects at least one particular social orientation (that of literary scholar), both to the student writer and to the written passage. Further, the comment suggests that she interprets the passage not only drawing on her academic knowledge of this particular character but also on some kind of personal or cultural knowledge of those who would see the world "in black and white." That is, her comment reflects at least one particular interpretive orientation (i.e., academic plus personal/cultural). The comment, relatedly, is relatively analytic as it penetrates the character the student is writing about (as opposed, say, to an emotive "Yes!") and in this sense reflects a particular cognitive/emotive orientation (i.e., an analytic one). We might also presume that through her comment she tries to expand or develop the student's understanding of the character in *The Crucible*, in this way reflecting at least one particular teaching purpose or pedagogical orientation. Finally, the comment seems to imply that the passage is on the right track—at least, she does not "correct" the student's interpretation of the character or try to rewrite his words—and in this sense reveals a likely (positive) evaluative orientation. These multiple orientations reflect the multilayered nature of all communication. Attempting to name the critical layers of teacher response to student writing trains light on how much about a teacher's reading and related response a student must unpack.

In this eleventh grade classroom, neither the teacher nor the students ever actually talked about the teacher's many orientations as a reader of their writing. Yet these orientations followed a consistent pattern across the semester and seemed to explain much about the nuanced nature of her readings. Specifically, in this class, where students wrote everything from journals to expository essays, the teacher's readings shifted systematically depending on the type of paper a student had written and depending on who the student writer was. For example, her readings of journals as compared to essays were more collegial, more aimed at expanding the student's insights, more emotive, more reflective of her personal/cultural interpretations of their writing rather than academic/school-like interpretations, and more positively evaluative. Her readings similarly shifted to accommodate the most skillful compared to the least skillful writers in the class. This classroom does not represent all classrooms, but it suggests how strategically and systematically—yet how implicitly—teachers can adjust their reading of students' writing depending on the shifting circumstances of that reading and writing in the classroom. In this sense, their readings both reflect and help define such shifting circumstances.

Classrooms that value the writing-reading relationship reveal how sensitive instruction can unpack the layers of the relationship. Unfortunately, such unpacking—or making explicit—seldom if ever happens when teachers read students' writing or when students interpret teachers' readings of their work.

Research on the Teacher as Reader and Responder

Research on the teacher as reader and responder to student writing has, in many ways, foreshadowed the need to understand the teacher-reader as multiroled. What research has said about the teacher as reader and responder to student writing is taken up in this section, where I focus on two frequently researched approaches that teachers use in responding to students' writing: commenting in writing on students' papers and holding one-on-one teacher-student conferences about the student's writing or writing process. The first approach, rooted in the history of instruction in writing, is commonplace even today, and is the first thing in most students' minds when they think of their teachers as their readers.[16] It is strongly associated with teachers' attention to surface features of text, even when they might wish to look for the deep structure and content of students' writing. The second approach has gained popularity among many teachers as they work to make their reading as responsive as possible to an individual student's writing processes and as visible as possible to the student. While commonplace in many college composition courses and frequently used in elementary school, teacher-student writing conferences are less frequent with high school teachers pressed for time and faced with 150 students or more to teach each day. Yet research indicates that, kindergarten through college, conferences can be worth the logistical shifts necessary to make them possible if teachers can jump the basic hurdle to deeper readings of students' writing.

TEACHERS COMMENTING ON STUDENTS' PAPERS

It is not surprising that, given its formalist underpinnings, the activity of marking students' papers is traditionally viewed as "correcting." In practice, this activity has meant a focus on mechanics rather than ideas. A flurry of research on teachers' written comments on students' papers occurred in the 1970s and early 1980s, when formalist approaches to writing instruction were challenged along with the attendant notion of the teacher as healer, the student as patient, and the writing as illness in need of remedy.[17] In fact, while eschewing a product-centered framework for teaching and learning, most of this research found that, despite teachers' written comments on their work, students were often not "corrected" as the teacher expected.[18] Additionally, written comments alone did not affect students' learning to write.[19]

Several reasons could be cited for these findings. Teachers often wrote formulaic comments on students' papers, even when they meant to do otherwise. Given the enormous paper load, the tendency toward quick, ready-made comments is understandable. Such comments often mimic the editing abbreviations found in composition glossaries and handbooks, which teachers more than students find easy to understand. One key study showed these written comments to be so vague as to be interchangeable from text to text, to be, essentially, "rubber-stamp" markings.[20] In this study, comments functioned more to justify a grade than to help the student improve writing skill, an observation corroborated by other studies.

Investigations also showed teachers' written comments to mean more for the teacher than for the student;[21] to be discounted by students, who believe that they reflect not their own writing weaknesses but their teachers' "confused readings" of their papers;[22] and to confirm for some students what they suspect of themselves throughout their school careers—that they are not smart enough to write the papers that can get them through their course work.[23] In short, the practice of writing comments on students' papers—especially when commenting was the reflection of the prescriptive teacher-reader focused on remedying students' problems—appeared mainly to sustain a culturally familiar yet pedagogically questionable teacher-student relationship in which the teacher is the authoritative reader and the student, too often, is the puzzled or resistant writer.

Despite the flurry of studies on written comments in the 1970s and 1980s, and the association between written comments and a now receding product-centered pedagogy, educators have more reason than ever to suspect that, in some classrooms, written comments still play a primary role in reflecting to students a teacher-reader focused on correcting surface features. Recent studies conducted by the National Assessment of Educational Progress[24] as well as studies conducted by individual researchers[25] indicate that, in contrast to students in top-performing schools, students in bottom-performing schools populated by users of minority languages and students from diverse sociocultural backgrounds tend to receive traditional instruction that not only favors the use of teacher-written comments over other response practices but, relatedly, emphasizes skills-based response divorced from concerns about students' broader rhetorical and social purposes in writing. If, as social theories of language suggest, written discourse reflects the social and cultural subtexts of the contexts in which it is used, then students, especially those who because of their cultural or language backgrounds may not be conversant with those subtexts, need to have them clarified as part of the process of learning to write.[26] Partly for the reasons indicated earlier, the teacher's written comments are seldom explicitly expected to serve this clarifying purpose.[27]

Nor do teachers' comments seem easily able to serve that purpose. Even in classrooms where the social purposes of writing and students' writing processes are at the center of instruction, students demonstrate an uncanny persistence in misreading the written responses they receive on their papers because they, too, bring subtextual expectations to their readings of these responses.

In a case study of a highly interactive process-based classroom, Sarah Freedman and I examined how one high-achieving student interpreted her teacher's comments on her papers.[28] The teacher wrote these comments to suggest alternative ideas or language and to move the student to think critically about her writing. However, rather than interpreting the comments as intended, and rather than questioning the teacher's judgment compared to her own, we discovered that the student's reading of the comments was rooted in her own prescriptivist assumptions about the role of these comments in her writing process. In particular, we found that while the student interpreted the comments by drawing on her store of factual information about writing as presented in this classroom and on her already well-developed writing skills, she also drew on her underlying beliefs regarding the teacher's unassailable authority in the classroom, in her words, "You do it because they [teachers] want you to." So this otherwise successful student, working in a highly regarded writing classroom, misinterpreted her teacher's written comments as directives to change faults or errors and always revised accordingly.

The study suggested that student-writers and teacher-readers abide by complex and context-bound assumptions about one another that comments cannot necessarily mediate. Further, as with all reading, students' reading of teachers' comments is influenced by social and cultural assumptions about the purpose and function of such reading in school contexts.

TEACHERS RESPONDING THROUGH ONE-ON-ONE CONVERSATIONS

Given the limitations of written comments to fairly convey to students the teacher's reading of their work, the activity of responding to students' writing has been extended to teacher-student writing conferences. Such conferences attempt to avoid the pitfalls of writing comments on students' papers because, through extended interactions, student and teacher expand and clarify their sense of and response to each other. With the teacher present, the student can clarify the ways the teacher has read and interpreted his writing, and, conversely, with the student present the teacher can clarify the student's intended ideas and language strategies. This conversational process helps to make visible the implicit writer-reader negotiation that is believed to occur when writers write and readers read.[29]

Because writing conferences are conversations, much of the research on writing conferences has been strongly influenced by linguists working in the area of conversational and discourse analysis. Such analyses are based on the premise that conversations are two-sided cooperative events that take shape or direction as they unfold. As participants engage in taking turns, as they relate the meaning of one turn to that of the next, and as they relate talk to a shared context,[30] they continuously negotiate meanings and shape interpretations.[31]

We see a major theoretical contrast between teachers' responses in such interactions and response through written comments on students' papers. Written comments are often expected to "stand on their own" in mediating student writing and teacher reading, with a shared social-interpretive context assumed between student-writer and teacher-reader. Because the "shared" context does not necessarily hold true, students tend to interpret written comments as simply as possible, misconstrue them, or ignore them altogether. Relatedly, written comments easily cut short the opportunity for students to learn the principle that their written texts reflect meaning that is implicitly negotiated between themselves and their readers. In contrast, the theory behind teacher-student writing conferences is that, being face-to-face conversations, they allow the teacher's reading and response to a student's written piece to evolve and take shape through extended interaction with the student writer himself. In this process, writer-reader negotiation becomes real.

Despite the theoretical ideal, research has revealed important discrepancies in the ways that conferences are conducted in different classrooms and for different students, and has asked if their conceptual promise is fulfilled in practice.

An important concern has been whether all students receive similar treatment in conferences. For example, do conferences reflect the teacher as reader to all students in the same way? If conferences take shape through the action of the particular participants, the answer to this question has to be "No." Moreover, in and of itself, such individualization is all to the good. For example, in addressing individual student needs, a conference with one student may last fifteen minutes, covering one concern in depth; for another student a conference might last six minutes, covering four topics quickly. Both conferences can reflect the teacher as reader in important ways and be equally effective for the purpose at hand. Yet if certain types of students systematically experience less effective conference conversations than others, the situation is at best troublesome.

In fact, such differential experiences have been found. Noticeable differentiation occurs among students with different levels of writing skill and also among those from different ethnic and cultural backgrounds. It is generally believed that the more conversational a dyadic conference, that is, the less it resembles teacher-led whole-class talk, the more chance students have to grapple with and develop writing ideas and strategies.[32] Given this premise, more useful and more interactive conferences have been seen with high-achieving students and with students whose ethnic or cultural backgrounds match the teacher's. Conversely, less useful and less interactive conferences have tended to occur more often with lower-achieving students and with students whose ethnic or cultural backgrounds differ from the teacher's. This discrepancy among students does not mean that teachers intentionally foil the conversational process for students who are, along one dimension or another, unlike themselves. Rather, it reveals how through their discourse teachers and students together can shape as well as reflect such discrepancies.

For example, one case study found that conferences between the teacher and higher-achieving students were longer compared to those with lower-achieving students, with more time spent between the teacher and the higher-achieving students paving the way for students to come back for more conferences.[33] In this study and in others, higher-achieving students and the teachers also made more opportunities to speak about higher-level writing concerns.[34] Studies have also found that, rather than being the dialogic events predicted by theory, conferences with some students are monologic events in which the teacher dominates and the student's input counts for little.[35] Designed to explore situations in which teacher's and student's ethnic backgrounds differ, one group of studies[36] found that teachers' preformed agendas for what counted as acceptable writing precluded true conversation, especially between the white teacher and nonwhite students.

Such findings suggest that the teacher-reader whom some students encounter in writing conferences can be just as static or impenetrable as the comments written on their papers; for other students, even with the same teacher, such may not be the case. It appears that the value of conferences in exposing a rich writer-reader conversation depends, as do most other instructional strategies, on how such conferences are used.

In my own research on writing conferences in a ninth grade English class,[37] I looked at conferences held regularly over the course of different writing assignments and found that conferences could be effective if they occurred frequently and for different purposes because they then opened up opportunities for different students to flourish in conference talk. In this classroom, conferences were held before students had written anything for the purpose of generating ideas, during drafting for the purpose of revision, and during drafting for the purpose of clarifying the teacher's written comments. These changing circumstances reflected the differing functions of conferences at various points in the writing process, and these shifting functions influenced how different students participated and benefitted, even during very short (one to two minute) conversations. In this particular classroom, however, the teacher placed a high value on students' writing processes, and conferences occurred as part of other interactive work such as peer-response groups and whole-class discussion.

This last point is not incidental. Hidden in most studies of teacher-student writing conferences is an argument for the connection between conference effects and the fuller instructional context in which conferences figure. It is rare—in fact, hardly possible—that single conversations act in isolation from the many other social-pedagogical factors that work to influence students' writing decisions. Conference conversations, only one such factor, both shape and are shaped by the others. Even casual observation reveals how commonly echoes of prior conversations appear in current ones: peer conversations, teacher-student conferences, whole-class discussions, and the written communications that occur in classrooms day-to-day influence and are reflected in one another.

From a social-cultural perspective, such a conversational network is the point of it all and exactly what curriculum and instruction need to exploit. To extend this last point through an earlier example, recall Francoise's conversation with her classmates about her written draft and remember how her earlier private conversation with her teacher was echoed in this later discussion. As that earlier teacher-student conversation became part of a broader one, the students, in effect, both reinforced and expanded the teacher-reader's presence. Writing conferences held in this kind of interactive classroom stand a good chance of positively affecting students' writing and sense of the writing process, not because in and of themselves they "teach" students how to write, but because, as reflections of one reader's point of view, they are taken up and assume relevance in a broader social fabric.[38]

The Teacher-Reader in Practice: Learning from What We Know

The different strands of teacher-reader studies have often addressed or been motivated by different theories of writing, and synthesizing these studies does not promise a fully realized portrait of the teacher-reader. Yet such a synthesis does allow some reasonable reflections on what it means to read students' writing in classroom contexts. It should be clear first and foremost that reading and responding to students' writing is a complex and nuanced communicative process. How a teacher reads students' work can depend on several factors, including the genre the student has produced, what purpose it serves in the broader curriculum, when in the student's writing process the reading takes place, and, not least, who the student writer is. Such a portrayal of a teacher's reading suggests how the process is, by its very nature, contextually constrained.

How the teacher reflects this reading through response to the student is itself a process influenced by its context, in large part because the teacher has traditionally been seen as a prescriptive and evaluative reader, and teachers' responses are often given as well as viewed with this underlying role in mind. Therefore, the teacher's response reveals only more or less effectively the multiple orientations toward students' work that characterize a teacher's reading at any given moment. A descriptive framework that captures the teacher's social, interpretive, cognitive-emotive, pedagogical, and evaluative orientations to students' writing is the foundation for thinking of the teacher as reader of students' work.

Over and above the social and cultural constraints on teachers' responses to students' writing, we know that the way teachers reflect their readings to students also depends on the mode through which they communicate to students, including the two covered in this chapter—writing comments on students' papers and talking to students face-to-face. We know that any mode through which teachers reflect their readings has built-in limitations. Of the two modes discussed in this chapter, however, the teacher-student writing conference has particular promise for immediately involving the student in the teacher's response. Moreover, through interaction with the student, the teacher's response—and reading—can also evolve and take shape. Written comments can become interactive in this way, but to be so they must be incorporated in a larger interactive process. To be more interactive, for example, written comments can become the basis of a teacher-student conference, a group discussion among peers, a whole-class conversation, or an extended written dialogue between the student and teacher.

Finally, we know that teachers as readers are situated readers. While at times they seem metaphorically to stand for "all readers" from their own or students' perspectives, at root they both contribute to and reflect the social, cultural, and political contexts of writing and reading in school.

This portrait of the teacher as reader strongly suggests the importance of instruction that incorporates the following aims:

1. to increase students' understanding of and involvement with their teacher-readers;

2. to heighten the teacher's role in the classroom community as "reader among readers";

3. to focus attention on the underlying motivations and beliefs of the network of readers that form the classroom community.

These aims reflect the epistemological direction in which writing research and instruction have headed over the past decades. They help demystify the prescriptive power of the red-pen teacher-reader by emphasizing the purposes and functions of conventional text structures in the context of a *reader's experience* of written text. They do so by placing the reader's experience in its social and cultural moment, allowing students to better understand how as writers they both contribute to and are influenced by the social and cultural world that they share with other writers and readers.

These aims also give social immediacy and real-world relevance to the cognitive processes students employ when composing. When students plan, revise, and in other ways think critically about ideas, rhetorical strategies, and language choices, they contemplate an interconnected range of readers, with an interconnected range of expectations and needs, to help guide this thinking. When writing aims not simply to "please" a prescriptive teacher but rather to address a complex and interested readership, and when individual students play a critical role as reader as well as writer in the classroom, a school-based writing task more closely resembles the vicissitudes of both writing and reading in the world outside the classroom.

To achieve such aims we need instructional tasks that allow students, as readers, to explore different points of view about writers' strategies and ideas, including different beliefs about and perspectives on the conventions of written discourse across writing situations. Such instructional tasks may lead to consensus about ideas and strategies but will just as profitably raise dilemmas or evoke questions about what is valuable in students' writing and why. Above all, such instructional tasks should allow students to explore explicitly the social and cultural contexts of writer-reader communication—an element of writing and learning to write that current research strongly indicates we cannot afford to take for granted.

To reform instruction in the classroom, however, we need a school-wide view of teaching and learning that supports the development of social and cultural awareness along with and as part of acquiring the "basics" of reading and writing. Such a view sees reading and writing not only as transportable skills that help students to learn and display knowledge in their different classrooms, but as interconnected processes that reflect the social and cultural worlds that students and teachers inhabit. Such changes in schoolwide views about reading and writing must go hand in hand with valuing forms of teaching that best serve these views. While this teaching needs to be developed and fostered within the environments of supportive schools, it must also be developed in teacher preparation programs where novice teachers first learn to orchestrate literacy learning in their classrooms.

NOTES

1. See Martin Nystrand, Stuart Greene, and Jeffrey Wiemelt, "Where Did Composition Studies Come From? An Intellectual History," *Written Communication* 10, no. 3 (1993): 267-333.

2. Ibid. See also, Melanie Sperling, "Revisiting the Writing-Speaking Connection: Challenges for Research on Writing and Writing Instruction," *Review of Educational Research* 66, no. 1 (1996): 53-86.

3. See Lester Faigley, "Nonacademic Writing: The Social Perspective," in Lee Odell and Dixie Goswami, eds., *Writing in Nonacademic Settings* (New York: Guilford, 1985), pp. 231-248; Sarah Warshauer Freedman, Anne Haas Dyson, Linda Flower, and Wallace Chafe, *Research in Writing: Past, Present, and Future*, Technical Report No. 1 (Berkeley, Calif.: University of California, Center for the Study of Writing, 1987).

4. See Janet Emig, *The Composing Processes of Twelfth Graders* (Urbana, Ill.: National Council of Teachers of English, 1971).

5. These ideas reflect especially the cognitive model of composing developed by Linda Flower and John R. Hayes. See Linda Flower and John R. Hayes, "A Cognitive Process Theory of Writing," *College Composition and Communication* 32, no. 4 (1981): 365-387. See also, Lee Gregg and Erwin Steinberg, eds., *Cognition Processes in Writing* (Hillsdale, N. J.: Erlbaum, 1980).

6. See Anne Ruggles Gere and Ralph S. Stevens, "The Language of Writing Groups," in S. W. Freedman, ed., *The Acquisition of Written Language: Response and Revision* (Norwood, N. J.: Ablex, 1985), pp. 85-105.

7. See Sarah Warshauer Freedman (with Cynthia Greenleaf and Melanie Sperling), *Response to Student Writing*, Research Report No. 23 (Urbana, Ill.: National Council of Teachers of English, 1987).

8. See Nystrand, Greene, and Wiemelt, "Where Did Composition Studies Come From?"

9. Criticizing especially the strong cognitivist version of the notion of "translation" (the process of putting thoughts into words), which appears to assume that thought precedes language, some scholars have forced a rethinking of this assumption by emphasizing the interactive and reciprocal nature of the thought-language relationship and the theoretical two-way street that it implies. See, for example, Martin Nystrand and Jeffrey Wiemelt, "On the Dialogic Nature of Discourse and Learning" (Paper presented at the Annual Meeting of the National Council of Teachers of English, Pittsburgh, 1993). For seminal scholarship on the relationship between thinking and language, with a focus on the effects of written language on thought, see Jack Goody and Ian Watt, "The Consequences of Literacy," in *Comparative Studies in Society and History* 5 (1963): 304-326, 332-345, and the response to the assumptions of their work by Sylvia Scribner and

Michael Cole, *The Psychology of Literacy* (Cambridge, Mass.: Harvard University Press, 1981), who put a social-contextual perspective on the thought-language relationship.

10. See Sperling, "Revisiting the Writing-Speaking Connection."

11. Ibid.

12. This view of writing and literacy is inspired largely by the language theories of Lev Vygotsky, *Thought and Language* (Cambridge, Mass.: MIT Press, 1962) and Mikhail Bakhtin, *The Dialogic Imagination* (Austin: University of Texas Press, 1981), for both of whom language represents a process rooted in the social world. Vygotsky linked language and thinking, asserting that what begins in the social context as actively constructed verbal and nonverbal interactions between a child and others is internalized by the child as the raw material of thought. Bakhtin linked language and text to the ongoing dialogue between individuals and social context, discourse itself reflecting such social interaction in being "entangled, shot through with shared thoughts, points of view, alien value judgments and accents" (p. 276).

13. See, for example, Melanie Sperling and Laura Woodlief, "Two Classrooms, Two Writing Communities: Urban and Suburban Tenth Graders Learning to Write," *Research in the Teaching of English* 31, no. 2 (1997): 205-349.

14. Parentheses indicate that the audiotape was unclear here, but that these words approximate what the student said.

15. Melanie Sperling, "Constructing the Perspective of Teacher-as-Reader: A Framework for Studying Response to Student Writing," *Research in the Teaching of English* 28, no. 2 (1994): 175-207.

16. See, for example, the national survey findings reported in Freedman (with Greenleaf and Sperling), *Response to Student Writing*.

17. See, for example, Glynda Hull, "The Editing Process in Writing: A Performance Study of More Skilled and Less Skilled College Writers," *Research in the Teaching of English* 21, no. 1 (1987): 8-29.

18. Melanie Sperling and Sarah Warshauer Freedman, "A Good Girl Writes Like a Good Girl: Written Response and Clues to the Teaching/Learning Process," *Written Communication* 4, no. 4 (1987): 343-363.

19. George Hillocks, *Research on Written Composition: New Directions for Teaching* (Urbana, Ill.: ERIC Clearinghouse on Reading and Communication Skills, 1986).

20. Nancy Sommers, "Responding to Student Writing," *College Composition and Communication* 33, no. 2 (1982): 148-156.

21. John Butler, "Remedial Writers: The Teacher's Job as Corrector of Papers," *College Composition and Communication* 31, no. 3 (1980): 270-277.

22. James Hahn, "Students' Reactions to Teachers' Written Comments," *National Writing Project Network Newsletter* 4, no. 1 (1981): 7-10.

23. Mina Shaughnessy, *Errors and Expectations: A Guide for the Teacher of Basic Writing* (New York: Oxford University Press, 1977).

24. Arthur N. Applebee, Judith A. Langer, Ina V. S. Mullis, Andrew S. Latham, Claudia A. Gentile, *NAEP 1992 Writing Report Card* (Washington, D.C.: Office of Educational Research and Improvement, U.S. Department of Education, 1994).

25. See Guadalupe Valdes, "Bilingual and Language Issues in Writing: Toward Profession-wide Responses to a New Challenge," *Written Communication* 9, no. 1 (1992): 48-136.

26. See Worth Anderson, Cynthia Best, Alycia Black, John Hurst, Brandt Miller, and Susan Miller, "Cross-Curricular Underlife: A Collaborative Report on Ways with Academic Words," *College Composition and Communication* 41, no. 1 (1990): 11-36.

27. But for a look at written responses to students' writing made by leading composition scholars, see Richard E. Straub and Ronald P. Lunsford, *Twelve Readers Reading: Responding to College Student Writing* (Cresskill, N. J.: Hampton Press, 1995).

28. Sperling and Freedman, "A Good Girl Writes Like a Good Girl."

29. See Linda Flower, *The Construction of Negotiated Meaning: A Social Cognitive Theory of Writing* (Carbondale: Southern Illinois University Press, 1994); Martin Nystrand, *The Structure of Written Communication: Studies in Reciprocity between Writers and Readers* (Orlando, Fl.: Academic Press, 1986).

30. Gordon Wells, "Language as Interaction," in Gordon Wells, ed., *Learning through Interaction: The Study of Language Development*, Vol. 1 (Cambridge, England: Cambridge University Press, 1981), pp. 22-72.

31. John Gumperz, *Discourse Strategies* (Cambridge, England: Cambridge University Press, 1982).

32. Sarah Warshauer Freedman and Melanie Sperling, "Written Language Acquisition: The Role of Response and the Writing Conference," in Sarah W. Freedman, ed., *The Acquisition of Written Language: Response and Revision* (Norwood, N. J.: Ablex, 1985), pp. 489-505; Suzanne E. Jacobs and Adela B. Karliner, "Helping Writers to Think: The Effect of Speech Roles in Individual Conferences on the Quality of Thought in Student Writing," *College English* 38, no. 5 (1977): 489-505; Carolyn P. Walker and David Elias, "Writing Conference Talk: Factors Associated with High- and Low-Rated Writing Conferences," *Research in the Teaching of English* 21, no. 3 (1987): 266-285.

33. Freedman and Sperling, "Written Language Acquisition."

34. Ibid. See also, Jacobs and Karliner, "Helping Writers to Think"; Walker and Elias, "Writing Conference Talk."

35. Susan Florio-Ruane, "Teaching as Response: The Problem of Writing Conferences" (Paper presented at the Annual Meeting of the American Educational Research Association, San Francisco, 1986); Sarah Michaels, "Text and Context: A New Approach to the Study of Classroom Writing," *Discourse Processes* 10, no. 4 (1987): 321-346; Polly Ulichney and Karen Watson-Gegeo, "Interactions and Authority: The Dominant Interpretive Framework in Writing Conferences," *Discourse Processes* 12, no. 3 (1989): 309-328.

36. Michaels, "Text and Context"; Ulichney and Watson-Gegeo, "Interactions and Authority."

37. For example, Melanie Sperling, "Dialogues of Deliberation: Conversation in the Teacher-Student Writing Conference," *Written Communication* 8, no. 2 (1991): 131-162; idem, "I Want to Talk to Each of You: Collaboration and the Teacher-Student Writing Conference," *Research in the Teaching of English* 24, no. 3 (1990): 279-321.

38. See Sarah Warshauer Freedman, *Exchanging Writing-Exchanging Cultures: Lessons in School Reform from the United States and Great Britain* (Cambridge, Mass.: Harvard University Press and Urbana, Ill.: National Council of Teachers of English, 1994).

CHAPTER VII

Contextualizing Teachers' Responses to Writing in the College Classroom

PAUL PRIOR

The theme writing in English A is of the most elementary description; but the compositions in this course, over 6,000 in number during each half year, are carefully criticized by the proper instructor and returned by him to the student. They are then rewritten, and often recast. Owing to the number of these exercises and the constant accumulation of fresh papers the rewritten themes are not read by the instructors, except to determine the final grade of a student whose mark is doubtful. The work of criticizing and correcting the English A themes is not inaptly described by certain of the instructors as of a "stupefying" character, to which it is difficult to give more than four hours of intelligent attention per day; and judging by a single set of 450 papers, your Committee is disposed to consider the adjective "stupefying" as a mild term to apply to such work, while four hours per day would seem an excessive time to devote to it.—Report of the Committee on Composition and Rhetoric, Harvard University, 1892.[1]

This early report on Harvard's English A, the first modern freshman composition course, paints a bleak picture of student writing and the work of writing teachers. Teachers in any setting who assign writing regularly can probably relate to the comments about the sheer volume of text, the constant accumulation of new papers needing response, and the sometimes stupefying effects of long hours of criticism and correction. Although teacher response to student writing has been a common practice in classrooms over the last century, only in the last two decades has serious, sustained attention been focused on response practices and their consequences. In the late 1970s and early 1980s, writing research, theory, and pedagogy began to pay closer attention to response and evaluation.[2] This increased attention arose from several converging trends: the rise of process approaches to teaching

Paul Prior is Assistant Professor in the Department of English at the University of Illinois, Urbana-Champaign, where he is Acting Director of the Division of Rhetoric. He is also Director of the Graduate Student Writing-Across-the-Curriculum Programs in the Center for Writing Studies.

writing that placed new emphasis on in-progress responses, a return to direct assessment of writing, and finally the emergence of composition and rhetoric as an independent subdiscipline within English departments.[3] In universities, this attention focused first around freshman composition programs. However, with the contemporaneous rise of the writing-across-the-curriculum (WAC) movement, the focus on response soon extended to undergraduate and graduate courses across the disciplines.

In terms of the central theme of this volume, the reading-writing connection, teacher response to student writing highlights classroom connections between reading and writing (and connections of both with talk). Response occurs as a link in extended chains of reading and writing. Those chains include teachers writing assignments for students, students reading those assignments and other sources as they write their papers, teachers reading students' texts and writing comments on them, and students finally reading those comments (sometimes in anticipation of writing another draft or a related task). Both inside and outside the classroom, talk among teachers, students, and others is an integral part of such chains.

In the WAC program at the University of Illinois at Urbana-Champaign, we offer a variety of workshops for faculty and teaching assistants. Each time we offer special workshops we worry about attendance. (Once the presenters actually outnumbered the audience.) However, attendance has never been a problem with any workshop whose title refers to response to students' writing. It is clear that many instructors agonize over response for varied reasons, everything from unhappiness with the quality of students' writing to unease with the grounds for and effectiveness of their own responses. As Nancy Sommers noted fifteen years ago, response is one of the most time- and energy-consuming activities that teachers engage in—if they assign student writing.[4] In many contexts, teachers' responses to students are intended to serve as one of the primary means of instruction, not only for improving writing ability, but also for developing subject-area knowledge. However, when researchers began studying response, serious doubts were raised about the value of the kinds of responses typically provided for students.

Research on Teacher Response:
Miscommunication and Discouragement

In initial studies of teachers' written responses to students' texts in college composition programs, researchers like Sommers, Lil Brannon,

and Cyril Knoblauch did not paint an encouraging portrait of response.[5] They found that instructors' written responses typically privileged linguistic form over content, the textual product over the writing
process, and the instructor's ideal text over the student's intentions.
Worse yet, many instructors' responses were themselves poor examples
of writing. Often they were too telegraphic or too cast in jargon to
communicate well. Sometimes responses conspicuously violated their
own advice. Typical examples would include marginal comments such
as "unclear," which is likely to be unclear, and "be specific," which is
itself not specific. Too often teachers' responses even displayed
errors—misreadings or miscorrections of students' texts. Research also
uncovered gaps between teachers' stated criteria and goals for response
and their observed practices. Some studies found instructors who said
they were mainly interested in responding to content but instead
responded mainly to form, or who claimed that their responses were
largely positive whereas their actual comments appeared largely negative.[6] At least since its origins in English A, response to student writing
has also been characterized by an overwhelming emphasis on, and
often frustration with, error. This negative focus of response has often
appeared counterproductive in its effects on student writing.[7] George
Hillocks summarized much of the experimental literature at all levels
of instruction on the effects of teachers' written response on students'
writing. His basic conclusion was that teacher response generally
showed little lasting effect, except that its negativity seemed to worsen
students' attitudes toward writing.[8]

Difficulties in responding effectively to students' writing have been
found in other forms besides written commentary. The process movement in composition instruction often shifted the medium of response
from text to talk and expanded the sources of response to include not
only teachers, but also peers, self, and others in the community. Thus,
studies of response have also looked at teacher-student conferences,
peer response groups, and self-evaluation.[9] Although teachers often
feel that oral response ensures clarity of communication, research has
uncovered persistent problems with oral response as well. In research
on conference talk, for example, Thomas Newkirk and Kathryn Evans
have each described examples of miscommunication and missed
opportunities for learning.[10]

Communication breakdowns in response are found not only in
composition classes, but in courses from other disciplines as well. Analyzing the written responses of college instructors in subject-area
courses across the curriculum, Carolyn Ball, Laura Dice, and David

Bartholomae found that instructors generally failed to identify and directly address students' problems with disciplinary values, knowledge, and forms of argument. Instead, the instructors commented on them as general problems with the clarity of students' writing or simply wrote in changes on the students' texts without any explanation.[11] This rewriting-as-response was also found in an undergraduate anthropology course studied by Anne Herrington. Herrington contrasted the written responses given to a struggling student (Kate) and her subsequent revisions with the responses and revisions observed for a more successful student (Sally). The teaching assistant in the course rewrote passages of Kate's, but not Sally's, papers. For her part, Kate took a fairly passive stance, usually just incorporating that response into subsequent drafts. Herrington questioned the value of such rewriting-as-response, finding that, although Kate's *texts* changed to accommodate the proposals of the instructors, *Kate* evidently did not.[12] In fact, research across the academy on the ways students understand and act on instructor response has routinely uncovered misunderstanding, partial compliance, and resistance.[13] This research has characterized much response (written or oral) as ineffective or worse.

An important development in response research has been a shift in emphasis from the teacher's response to the teacher's interpretation of the text.[14] In one study, Linda Shamoon and Robert Schwegler found that sociologists used disciplinary criteria not only to evaluate students' texts, but to construct the basic meaning of those texts.[15] When Shamoon and Schwegler rewrote student texts to maintain the basic content but replaced disciplinary with everyday terminology, the sociologists saw the texts as failed rather than inappropriate discourse. In fact, they described them as not sociology papers at all. In contrast, when the researchers randomly scrambled the order of sentences in body paragraphs, the sociology professors did not even remark on anything odd about the papers, reading them unproblematically.

In that case, disciplinary vocabulary influenced teachers' interpretations; however, more specific contextual factors also make a difference in the way instructors read students' texts. For example, in one of my studies, a professor in a graduate seminar accounted for an inconsistency in his response to, and grading of, one student's paper by noting that he had gone out to lunch (literally) in the middle of reading the paper.[16] Evans's research has documented the ways different contexts, beliefs, and assumptions lead teachers and students to sustain different understandings of texts, responses, and tasks through conferences and textual exchanges.[17] For example, she traces miscommunication in one writing conference, where the teacher fails to connect a student's stated fear of plagiarism with the lack of sources in her paper. Teachers' reading of students' texts can also be influenced by previous classroom interactions with a particular student. For instance, Glynda Hull, Mike Rose, Kay Fraser, and Maria Castellano's research traces how a teacher developed an impression of a bilingual-bicultural student as "the queen of non sequiturs" on the basis of their classroom interactions, possibly as a result of cultural differences in communicative practices.[18] The teacher's impression of the student overpowered her reading of the student's papers, leading her to discount their strengths. From studies such as these, teachers' interpretations of students' texts have emerged as a critical issue.

The research on response has identified three key communicative problems. First, teachers' interpretations of students' texts are often problematic. These interpretations are based on students' texts that may not communicate well. They are often grounded in knowledge, beliefs, and values that students do not share, and they are produced through reading practices that are often less than optimal. Second, teachers' responses to students' texts often do not communicate effectively to students what the teacher believes they have done well, what they have done poorly, how the text might be revised, or, for that matter, what they have done at all. Third, teachers' responses appear to be problematic because their negative focus and tone convey too effectively to many students that their writing is bad—a message that seems to discourage rather than encourage further engagement and growth in writing ability.

In the face of this negative evidence, a variety of ways for improving the quality and consequences of response have been proposed. Broadly, one strategy for change can be summarized in the process-writing slogan that "writers need readers." This slogan suggests that teachers take a less evaluative, less directive role, or that they structure opportunities for others (peers, external audiences, self) to play that role. This strategy assumes that readers are more positive and content-oriented—that they respond constructively with real questions and actual reactions. Another strategy for response suggests that "less may be more," especially when a focused, strategic response is reinforcing focused, coherent instruction. In WAC workshops, I routinely introduce the results of this response research and recommend these kinds of positive, content-oriented, and focused response practices to faculty and teaching assistants.

An Expanded View of Writing and Response

The predominant conception of response, apparent in the Harvard statement and in much instruction today, is undergirded by the assumptions of two key models. The first model represents writing as a linear process, while the second represents instruction as a particular pattern of interaction between teachers and students. The model of the writing process implicit in much of education today portrays writing as a linear process of transcribing texts. This process typically includes writing a draft, receiving response, and rewriting to produce a final version. In this view, writing has clear temporal boundaries and clear authorship. However, as a number of scholars, including Deborah Brandt, Stephen Witte, and Karen Burke LeFevre, have pointed out, writing is a complex process of meaning making that is not limited to the bounded and linear acts of writing words on paper or disk. Nor is it a process in which a writer acts alone. As I have argued elsewhere, writing emerges out of a continuous stream of *literate activity*, in which histories of talking and listening, reading and writing, thinking and feeling, observing and acting, all blend together in the production and reception of texts.[19]

The second model, dealing with patterns of student-teacher interaction, carries this linear, text-focused model of writing into the institutional context of school. Looking at classroom discourse, Hugh Mehan and others have noted the dominance of a particular discourse pattern, the sequence of teacher *initiation*, student *reply*, and teacher *evaluation* (IRE).[20] The following example illustrates this IRE structure:

Teacher: What is the capital of the United States?
Student: Washington.
Teacher: Right. Washington, D.C.

Although this pattern seems obvious and natural to anyone who has been in school, it is a fairly striking form of discourse. Imagine if someone stopped you on the street to ask the time, you answered, and the person then responded with "right" or "nooo, not 9:15." Nor is this structure symmetrical; the roles cannot be reversed. The student cannot initiate IRE sequences with the teacher and cannot appropriately respond to questions like the one above with answers like, "Good question. Why don't you go look it up in the dictionary?" As Shirley Brice Heath found in her research, students' familiarity (or unfamiliarity) with this kind of discourse seems to play an important role in early school adjustment and later success.[21]

This IRE pattern of oral interaction is relevant to response to writing because an almost identical model seems to frame conceptions of writing tasks: the teacher gives an assignment (initiation), students write it up and turn it in (reply), and finally the teacher writes comments, symbols, corrections, and probably grades on the papers and returns them (evaluation). Process approaches to writing instruction have altered this basic model little in many cases, suggesting that the sequence be repeated once or twice (so that evaluations serve as reinitiations) and perhaps that someone other than the instructor, such as a peer, take the role of in-progress evaluator. Texts in this model are not viewed as means of communication (as in much everyday conversation), but as objects for evaluation. Teachers read students' texts as crystallizations of students' intelligence, knowledge, attitudes, and effort, magic mirrors into which they may gaze to discover who is the most literate on the roster. Finally, the IRE model privileges the instructor's perspective; it is a view of writing from behind the teacher's desk.

In contrast to the assumptions of these two models, response is increasingly being viewed—as it must—in the wider contexts of literate activity. In this expanded view, the way students write and the way teachers read and respond to that writing must be seen in the context of broader histories of schooling and society as well as in the specific histories of the students' and teachers' experiences, goals, attitudes, and ideologies. In one of the first ethnographic studies of response, a study of two secondary teachers' writing instruction, Sarah Freedman concluded that response was a problematic category. Her analysis suggested that the teachers, especially Ms. Glass, sometimes responded to students' writing in whole class settings before the students had begun writing. These responses, in other words, were based on their knowledge of previous students' problems with a particular task. At the end of her intensive study, Freedman offered the following expansive definition of response:

Response, as defined in this study, includes other activities [besides peer groups, conferences, and written comments] as well and may not differ much from what we call the teaching of writing. Response includes all reactions to writing, formal or informal, written or oral, from teacher or peer, to a draft or a final version.[22]

In addition to reaffirming critiques of linear models of writing, Freedman's definition of response as pre-, or even a-textual, also challenges the adequacy of the IRE model for school writing tasks. Summing up the implications of this kind of expanded perspective on response, Louise Wetherbee Phelps stresses the immense complexity of interpretive activity in classrooms:

What is going on here is not simply one-way reading, but a whole circle of reciprocal and interlocking interpretations: teachers of texts and students and situations; students of assignments and commentaries and class discussions and conferences; writers of their own writing; and so on. This is truly a hermeneutic situation because it rests on the possibility, and frequently actuality, of misinterpretation.[23]

A key implication of this widening net of concern is that we cannot read students' texts as crystallizations of students' knowledge, effort, and character. As Sommers has noted, such attributions are a fallacy because every time we read a student's text, we are seeing not only the student, but also her contexts and especially the consequences of our own pedagogy. In our WAC workshops, this broader understanding of instructor response is reflected in two linked suggestions we give participants. First, we suggest that teachers read students' papers to learn about the contexts as well as the students. Second, if teachers suspect that their unhappiness with the texts they are reading might arise from contexts that they have established, we suggest that an appropriate response to a student text could involve changes in the organization and delivery of instruction as well as, or even instead of, written or oral commentary on the text. In other words, faced with a problem in a student's text, teachers should ask whether the appropriate response is a written comment, a conference discussion, a discussion of the problem with the whole class, additional readings, a change in the resources available to students or in ways their literate activity is structured, and so on. In short, as Freedman's definition implies, responses should be drawn out of the whole kit of teaching tools.

The Tuning of Writing Tasks: Response throughout the Process

With this expanded perspective on writing and response, it becomes clear that teachers are responding to (and structuring responsive environments for) students throughout the full history of a course. It is this full history that shapes the way students engage in an assigned writing task. Borrowing Andrew Pickering's metaphor, I would suggest *tuning* as a way to think broadly about response. I use this term to refer to the mutual, interactive, emergent, open-ended processes in which students and teachers co-construct tasks, texts, and contexts.[24]

From analyses of writing and response in graduate seminars, I have concluded that writing tasks must be understood historically and from the multiple perspectives of participants. To understand how writing tasks are tuned in a classroom, we must ask a series of questions:

How is the writing task cued and communicated by the instructor and the course?

How do students understand the task?

How do students and the instructor negotiate the task?

How do students choose to undertake it?

What texts do students produce?

How does the instructor read and respond to those texts?

How do students understand and act on, or are they influenced by, that response?

When we ask these questions, we get multiple, evolving, and potentially contradictory images of a task instead of a single image.

Between the time when a teacher first assigns a writing task and the time when he or she responds to the students' "final" texts, a number of opportunities arise in the classroom (or in halls and offices) to shape students' understandings of the task, their activities, and the development of their texts. These opportunities may or may not arise in relation to a specific task or texts. They may be intentionally structured by teachers, implicit in instruction, or initiated by students. For example, situated research has made it clear that students in a class develop multiple interpretations of writing tasks.[25] Told to summarize an article, one student might produce a close paraphrase while another produces a critical interpretation. Typically, these differences between the desired tasks and the tasks students perform are read by instructors as differences in the quality of the desired task. If the instructor assigning the summary wanted a critical interpretation of the text, the student who did a close paraphrase (a different task) is likely to be seen as having simply written a poor "summary" (a difference in the quality of the desired task). Whatever shapes students' interpretations of the task is, therefore, especially crucial to the process of tuning. A variety of particular interactions can lead students' interpretations of writing tasks to converge with, or diverge from, the teacher's intended task. For that matter, through such interactions, the teacher's own interpretations of and goals for a task may shift.

Illustrations of Response in Two Graduate Seminars

While all of the kinds of events and all of the participants' perspectives discussed above are crucial in understanding writing tasks in classrooms, I will focus here on specific ways that teachers shape student writing. To illustrate these classroom processes, I will present vignettes from my own research in graduate seminars. However, these basic processes appear to be common in writing tasks across educational contexts and levels. In particular, I will take examples from two sites, a Language Education seminar taught by Professor Mead and an American Studies seminar taught by Professor Kohl, a professor of geography associated with the American Studies program.[26] In the Language Education seminar, the three writing tasks Mead gave M.A. and Ph.D. students were a critique of an article, a critique of a dissertation or thesis, and a research proposal. For the research proposal (the major assignment), Mead had students share drafts of sections (e.g., title, problem statement, questions) for whole-class discussion throughout the quarter. The American Studies seminar focused on field research. Kohl asked students to turn in a final document, which would consist of an outline for a projected report on their field research with one section of the outline written up and an annotated bibliography of primary and secondary sources. However, given students' diverse interests, he allowed considerable flexibility in what students researched and what they wrote. Here I will first focus on three kinds of classroom interactions I consider particularly salient in this expanded conception of response—emphasizing topics and issues, elaborating on assignment guidelines and goals, and co-planning processes and texts. I will then consider the process of teachers' reading to respond.

EMPHASIZING SPECIFIC TOPICS AND ISSUES

In Aristotle's rhetoric, sets of topics were fixed "places" speakers or writers could go to generate lines of arguments and to find material for those arguments.[27] By using the topic "cause," for example, a person could not only generate material, but also a means of organizing it in a cause-effect pattern. The notion of topics is currently being reworked by expanding what counts as a topic, situating topics in particular communities, and seeing topics as fluid rather than fixed. Topics in this sense are not simply issues or organizational schemes, but include propositions, concepts, stories, metaphors, images, mathematical formulas, and so on.[28] These topics may be explicitly or implicitly signalled by a text. For example, when we read the first paragraph of a newspaper story, the who-what-where-how scheme is not explicitly displayed, but can be seen to have shaped the text. On the other hand, in a research report, a scheme that elaborates methodology as subjects, instrumentation, procedures, and analysis may be explicitly signalled with subheadings. With this broadened understanding of topics, instruction can be seen as a way to introduce, rehearse, and reinforce the particular topical maps of professional and disciplinary communities.

In Mead's seminar, the sources of topics included the assigned readings, classroom talk, and texts (papers and written responses). Disciplinary discourses provided one source of special topics. For example, a major issue in second (and first) language pedagogy and research since the 1960s has been the nature of communicative competence and communicative teaching. In seminar interactions and students' writing, this issue repeatedly arose as Mead and the students considered the naturalness of language tests and language classroom interactions. However, more dominant than those specific disciplinary topics was a cross-disciplinary set of topics dealing with social scientific research (statistics, experimental design, rational argumentation, and the philosophy of science). Whether in the context of discussing class readings or students' papers, Mead stressed both specific topics and general values in research such as attention to detail, full public disclosure of methods, skeptical testing of assumptions, and careful reasoning. For example, when students presented oral critiques of research articles they had read, Mead repeatedly emphasized such topics as the importance of randomization in experimental studies, of providing reliability measures for tests used, and of providing sufficient information for replication. The consistent focus on these topics provided a powerful signal to, and resource for, students as they undertook the writing tasks.

In the American Studies seminar, Kohl emphasized another set of topics: ethnographic methods of field research with a special emphasis on cultural geography. Kohl began the first class by asking students what their research interests were. As each student mentioned a topic (many of which had to do with ethnic or other social identities), Kohl worked to tie it in to field research—to local neighborhoods and people. In seminar sessions, Kohl lectured about fieldwork, urban geography, and the history of the city. He referred regularly to maps, spending over an hour in one session showing varied maps (topographical, demographic, economic, infrastructure) of the city and its neighborhoods from their early history to the present. He emphasized the importance of place, the value of observation and interviewing, and the idea that questions are crucial and enduring while the answers are almost always transitory. In a particularly clear indication of his notion of field research, Kohl arranged for one session of the seminar to meet in a chartered bus. Microphone in hand, Kohl played the role of tour guide, pointing out the geography of the city and how it related to histories of commercial and industrial districts and residential neighborhoods. He also offered to "go out into the field" with students if it would be useful. Several students did go to his office and at least one drove around the city with Kohl in an attempt to reconstruct the setting of a 1930s trucking strike. In all of these ways, Kohl, like Mead, invoked topics that would frame the contexts in which students wrote and he would respond.

Recurring topics are part of the writing context, indicating to students what is important with respect to a course, the institution, and the discipline as well as what is important in their specific writing tasks. The topics that Mead and Kohl stressed through various interactions were clearly visible in the work students did during the semester and in the final texts students produced.[29] With topical emphases dispersed throughout interactions in a course, a teacher can powerfully shape how students engage in the task and what they finally write.

ELABORATING ON ASSIGNMENT GUIDELINES AND GOALS

The writing tasks students were to perform changed in various ways as the two courses progressed, and they were interpreted and reinterpreted variously. The first day of the seminar, Mead handed out a syllabus that included a fairly detailed representation of the research proposal. However, that static image of the writing task was not the final word. It was supplemented by oral restatements of the task in and out of class. Mead intentionally initiated some elaborations. For example, in the fifth session of the seminar, Mead was going over the research proposal, developing an outline (like that in the syllabus) on the blackboard. Where the syllabus had presented one section as "method (to include procedures for data collection and data analysis)," on the blackboard Mead represented that same section with subheadings for population, instruments, procedures, and data analysis. As Mead reviewed the organization of the research proposal, he also elaborated on the content and goals of each section. An example of this kind of elaboration came in discussions of the section described simply as "background to the study" in the syllabus. Mead spent considerable time in this seminar session discussing the content and goals for the background review of the literature. He stressed the need to define crucial terms clearly and to select only literature relevant to the specific research questions. He also characterized common problems with literature reviews, such as simply dumping the content of notecards. These elaborations assumed connections between the seminar research proposal and other institutional or disciplinary texts. For example, he talked not of previous student papers in the seminar, but of dissertation proposals and dissertations themselves. To emphasize that the review of the literature must be selective, he told a story of his negotiations with a former student who wanted to discuss every study ever published on a certain form of language testing in his dissertation. With these classroom elaborations, Mead worked to define and contextualize the goals and content of his research proposal assignment.

Mead also had opportunities to elaborate on his expectations for the research proposals when students presented drafts of sections in class. For example, the first day that students passed around drafts of "problem statements," several were fairly long; one ran two pages. Mead reminded students of the length of the entire proposal (4-6 pages) and suggested that the problem statement should be concise, probably no longer than a paragraph. In the next class, five students presented problem statements and all were one paragraph.

Elaborations of the writing tasks could contribute to divergent as well as convergent interpretations. Mead frequently referred to the research proposal as "a draft" and emphasized that a good proposal required the "shaping and molding" of ideas. This representation appeared to lower some students' concern and care in ways Mead had not intended, a fact reflected in decidedly lower grades and more critical responses on students' research proposals than on their critiques. In a session near the end of the quarter, Lin, a doctoral student from the People's Republic of China (PRC), passed out her research questions, expressing uncertainty about them. After a number of serious questions had arisen about her methodology, Mead moved to put the research proposal into perspective. Emphasizing that writing is a process, he went farther to suggest that some people might not even be able to give him an initial draft, but that what was important was that they had gone through the process. It seems likely that Mead's comments on Lin's proposal were designed to take the pressure off and encourage her, since he felt she was quite competent but that she tended to "put herself down." However, other students, overhearing this public dialogue, could easily construe Mead's comments as addressed to them and as implying that their drafts could be very rough indeed.

Han, another student from the PRC, also illustrated how talk of shaping and molding and actual dissertations affected interpretations of and decisions about the task. Asked in an interview about how Mead would grade and respond to the research proposals, she replied:

At first I was worried because I don't think I could finish this within one quarter, and in every class he said, "That's just shaping and molding" and "I don't expect a really complete proposal" . . . I have kind of a dilemma. I thought maybe I just write a kind of tentative title for this course, not really my dissertation title, or I try to find the real topic for my dissertation starting from this point. Finally I decided I would write to find a title for my dissertation—even [if] it's not very logical and the design is not very good, that's ok, Dr. Mead will understand about that. If I can't get a good grade, that's ok.

Mead, as we will see below, found Han's proposal, like those of a number of students, rougher and less carefully thought out than he had hoped. This roughness, however, must be read in light of Han's perception that Mead had invited "rough drafts" and "incomplete proposals" and of her decision to pursue the topic she was actually interested in for her dissertation rather than to seek to optimize her performance in this seminar by selecting an easier problem. In this case, we can see how the students used Mead's elaborations to construct representations of the task, although in ways Mead had not really intended.

Opportunities for clarification (or confusion) of tasks also arose from student-initiated interactions in class, in the office, and during breaks. For example, in the seventh week of the American Studies seminar, Kohl announced that he wanted the students to give him a draft of their outlines the following week. He reviewed what should be included in the outline and the bibliography. As he talked, students asked a variety of questions. Some were clearly negotiations over ways of doing parts of the task, as illustrated in the following exchange:

James: Would you mind a bibliographic essay instead of an annotated bibliography?
Kohl: Yeah, handle the bibliography in any way you want.

Asked by another student if he wanted Roman numerals, phrases, sentences, or paragraphs in the outline, Kohl indicated that it did not have to be "a formal outline," that it could include paragraphs where students said something like, "Chapter 1, I want to introduce this subject, these are the conceptual frameworks I'm thinking about." The effect of these elaborations was that students came to construe both the outline and the annotated bibliography so broadly that essays would count. For example, one student turned in a full draft of a long paper the following week. She presented no outline, but used subheadings and wrote in ink on the top of the first page: "My outline is embedded in this draft." In this case, Kohl accepted this way of doing the task.

As these examples suggest, the nature of a particular task cannot be understood simply by looking at a written assignment. Tasks are typically elaborated in various ways as teachers and students interact over time in and around a class. As the examples from Mead's and Kohl's seminars suggest, the consequences of these elaborations also vary. Taken up in diverse ways, elaborations may lead students to greater convergence with, or divergence from, the teacher's task representations.

CO–PLANNING PROCESSES AND TEXTS

In addition to emphasizing special topics and elaborating on task guidelines and goals, teachers often become involved in co-planning processes and texts. In co-planning, teachers suggest specific resources to use or activities to engage in, or they contribute specific ideas or organizational schemes to a text. Of course, structuring the process itself—as Mead and Kohl both did with their requests for drafts—is one of the primary ways that instructors co-plan students' writing. In more extreme cases (e.g., the kinds of rewriting-as-response that Herrington and Ball, Dice, and Bartholomae found), instructors actually move to co-author parts of the text.[30] Like elaborations, co-planning includes quite diverse types of interactions and can have complex consequences for different students' writing processes and texts.

In Mead's seminar, Teresa was a student who actively sought opportunities to get feedback, in part because she was finalizing actual plans to do her thesis research in Spain at the end of the quarter. She actively bid to have a draft of her methodology discussed early in the process. During the discussion of her methods, Mead focused attention on a questionnaire she had developed to elicit data on which of two languages (Catalan or Castilian) students used in different contexts (home, school, among friends) and in different activities (speaking, reading, writing, taking notes). In class, Mead suggested that Teresa might use a Likert scale for her questionnaire and that descriptive statistics might be more appropriate than the t-tests she had proposed in the draft of her analysis section. Several other students who were planning to use questionnaires participated in this discussion, moving it to a more general level. When Mead called a mid-session break, Teresa immediately went up to him to continue talking over her proposal. In this discussion, Mead asked why she needed 200 students and how many different groups she planned to sample (guessing perhaps five). When she replied "thirteen," he suggested that she cut down on the number of groups and the number of subjects. Teresa took up several of these suggestions as she revised her research proposal. She reduced the number of students she sought to 150 and the number of groups to three. She did not change her questionnaire scales, but did switch to largely descriptive statistics. In Teresa's case, co-planning the content of the research proposal for the class happened to coincide completely with co-planning her actual research. It seemed to produce good results for both Teresa and Mead. Teresa's research plan was simplified in a way that she adopted successfully; her master's committee was ultimately satisfied with her research and her thesis. For his part, Mead was impressed with Teresa's final research proposal and her overall performance in the class. However, for most of Mead's students, as the next example shows, the relevance of the study being co-planned in the class and the consequences of that co-planning were less clear.

In another example of co-planning from Mead's seminar, Han was interested in studying cultural breakdowns in communication. When she presented a draft of her research questions to the class, discussion shifted from those questions, which Mead suggested might be unanswerable, to issues of methodology. Given the kind of qualitative study she had outlined in her draft, Mead argued that it would be difficult to systematically capture breakdowns in communication or to establish that cultural differences contributed to them. He proposed an experimental design, using simulated situations. Going to the board, he sketched out a sequence of boxes and arrows to illustrate how Han could structure scenarios for those simulations. When Han expressed a concern that the design Mead proposed would not be "natural," Mead suggested several other faculty members she might talk to about her research. In her final proposal for the course, Han's design attempted, in a way that Mead found problematic, to blend her desire to do a qualitative study with his suggestion that she do a more controlled study. Although Han did not take up Mead's specific plans in this proposal, Mead was clearly engaged in co-planning a possible research design (at least for this text).

In American Studies, Kohl also demonstrated instances of co-planning. The first came on the first day, when he suggested particular local sites in relation to many students' research interests. Opportunities for co-planning are, of course, almost a given in responses to draft texts. For example, in the seminar, Kohl had strongly suggested that students take a comparative perspective, comparing their local research with studies from other cities. In a draft outline for her research on local Cinco de Mayo celebrations, Lilah had included a section titled "Comparative Perspective," a kind of place holder where she wrote that she might contrast her research with information from an article on Cinco de Mayo in San Francisco. In his written response to her draft outline, Kohl suggested that she might compare Cinco de Mayo with other local ethnic celebrations. In her final paper, Lilah followed Kohl's suggestion for that section, comparing Cinco de Mayo with the history of a local Norse-American celebration.

Co-planning is also a typical part of the tuning process that characterizes writing tasks in classrooms. One of the basic rationales for asking students to write multiple drafts and for a teacher's in-progress response to students' texts is to create opportunities for co-planning. As these examples also suggest, co-planning involves the other kinds of interactions discussed above: emphasizing topics and issues and elaborating on assignments and goals. Because co-planning involves an explicit interaction between the teacher and a student (as opposed to general classroom emphases on topics or elaborations of tasks), it also highlights the kinds of negotiations that occur between student and teacher. As the above examples indicate, co-planning may or may not result in a convergence between a student's text and the teacher's expectations.

READING TO RESPOND

Now I return to the narrower issue of how teachers interpret students' texts, or more accurately, what kinds of interpretations shape teachers' written responses. Here we are firmly back in the conventional territory of response, but exploring that territory from a contextual perspective. Especially in earlier studies of response and assessment, researchers sought to identify textual correlates or causes for teachers' readings.[31] With a better understanding of the interpretive character of teachers' reading and response, we now know that we need to look beyond the text for the contextual sources and motives of those interpretations and responses.

Mead's written responses to research proposals clearly reflected his sense that the proposals were real tasks. He imaginatively recontextualized these assigned texts, seeing them as possible or certain plans for students' M.A. or Ph.D. research and taking up the role of research advisor as much as that of seminar instructor. The following examples give the flavor of much of Mead's response to students' research proposals: "How often? Each time they meet? How many? Who will do the interviews? Of what will they consist?;" "I wouldn't trust your memory—I would record each conference and transcribe soon afterwards so as not to lose anything;" and "We need to talk about this study if you intend to go about actually doing it!" These responses were oriented to revision of the proposal (not required or even possible for the seminar) or to actually conducting the research (also not a requirement of the seminar).

Interviews with Mead about his reading practices also pointed to the multiple contexts that shaped his interpretations. First, and most obvious, he read and responded to the papers in a single block of time, a period of about four days, about one month after the seminar had ended. He waited that long because he had received the papers at the end of finals week and four days later began teaching an intensive summer course. Second, he did not read the papers in random order. He read each student's three papers (two critiques in addition to the research proposal) together. He started with a student whose research he knew well and whose papers he expected to be good, a kind of easy entry into his task. He saved one student's papers for last because he expected them to be very frustrating. Interestingly, it happened that he was frustrated by the first student's work and pleasantly surprised by the last student's. Both of these facts were reflected in his grading. Third, he reported that he usually read papers twice, once mainly for meaning and once more for response. However, he added that he read the international students' papers three times, as he wanted to ensure that he understood them clearly before he began to respond to them.

When I asked Mead to comment on students' texts, it became clear again that the texts were read, were in fact understood, in multiple and shifting contexts. His reactions were clearly affective as well as intellectual. As mentioned above, some students' texts surprised him; some frustrated him. For the critiques, the articles being critiqued were an important context. He perceived some articles as difficult to critique and took that difficulty into account when he responded. Although "missing information" was generally a very acceptable critique of any research report, he rejected that criticism of one article. In his response to a student who critiqued that article, Mead repeatedly defended missing information by putting it in the context of length limits imposed by journal editorial policies. In our interview, Mead noted the article was an extremely important one in the field and, thus, deserved a more substantive critique. Mead's responses were also oriented to students' identities. For example, he clearly responded to the international students' papers somewhat differently from those of U.S. students. In responding to their papers, he was much more attentive to lexical, syntactic, and mechanical problems than in his responses to U.S. students. This attention was reflected in more editing of language and in marginal comments that often stated rules for writing.

Some of the strongest contexts for Mead's readings were his perceptions and knowledge of the individual students that arose from the seminar, from previous coursework, and from out-of-class experiences. For example, pointing to a stylistic problem in one student's critique, he said that the error had led him to conclude that the student had not spent much time on the paper because he knew she was a freshman composition instructor. In another case, he mentioned that a student had taken courses in the reverse of the normal order, completing a full-year research sequence before taking his seminar. Given this fact, he expected the student to have greater control than other students over the form for research proposals. However, he was frustrated when he found that the student had not provided the subheadings in the methodology section (from the blackboard). Although few students did provide these subheadings, this paper was the only one on which Mead wrote them as part of his written response and the only case in which he mentioned this problem in our interviews. As he discussed the papers, he also noted that some responses were directed at the person more than the text.

To illustrate the particularity of his interpretive work, it might be useful to consider some of Mead's comments on the proposal written by Han, whose work has been discussed in previous sections. Mead's response to Han's proposal revolved around notions of what a workable draft was; of what the text said about her effort, insight, and commitment; and finally of how his response could or should contribute to advancing her work on the research:

I know, if I recall this correctly, that I did not think it was very well thought through and therefore didn't feel that it had the wherewithal to be considered really solid as an initial proposal to be worked on, although, there is certainly the germ of an idea here, and I think that I did say something about a difficult idea to deal with. I just don't think that she had enough opportunity or took enough time or worked or even talked about it with other people, other than me, to think about how she could carry this out. There seem to be some ideas here that could be workable, but she just doesn't have it—it doesn't hold together—and then there are a wide variety of proofreading problems that she just didn't deal with.

Later in the interview, as he discussed one of his written comments on her proposal, Mead explained that he wanted "to keep some pressure on this individual to continue to look broader." Mead's interview comments suggest he was not simply comparing Han's proposal to an ideal proposal, but was reading and responding to it as Han's work. He was using his understanding of Han from the seminar and other contexts as well as what he inferred about her from this proposal in seeking to have an impact on her future work. His responses also revealed his sense of disappointment with Han's work, his uncertainty about its quality, and his desire to push her to develop her ideas more carefully. Overall, Mead's written responses on students' papers and his comments during our interviews suggest that his reception of students' texts was as complexly contextualized an activity as the students' interpretations of his tasks.

In the American Studies seminar, I conducted similar interviews with Kohl on students' texts. When we got to Lilah's paper on Cinco de Mayo (which he gave an 'A'), Kohl's first comment was: "Yeah, I was particularly interested in this." He then recalled at some length his own experiences with the local Hispanic community and recounted histories of Hispanic migration to the state and of Anglo-Hispanic racial tensions. He talked about his role in the 1960s with University programs designed to attract Hispanic students and faculty. He then returned to Lilah's paper, saying "I can't read this without reading myself onto every page and getting involved."

Much as Kohl read himself onto every page of Lilah's research on Cinco de Mayo, teachers I interviewed routinely read their personal experiences, institutional contexts, and disciplinary knowledge into students' texts. These kinds of open-ended, context-sensitive interpretive processes are exactly what we should expect to find when teachers act as readers of students' texts and seek to use response to teach students. These examples also suggest that teachers, as they respond to students' writing, operate within complex contexts that extend beyond the time and place of the reading and beyond the classroom. Thus situated, the teacher is reading not only the words of a student's text but the student and multiple other contexts as well.

Implications of a Contextualized Perspective for
Theory, Research, and Pedagogy

The research described here illustrates that there are no clear grounds for separating writing from reading, talking, observing, and acting. Nor are there grounds for privileging (as the IRE model of writing and response does) the perspectives of teachers and schools in defining the contexts for academic writing tasks. Through the specific history of a classroom, teachers shape students' interpretations of tasks and their writing of texts. This shaping involves such processes as emphasizing special topics, elaborating on task guidelines and goals, and co-planning processes and texts. In all of these processes, students appear as active agents as well. Students are engaged in making interpretations and decisions, initiating interactions, and negotiating task processes and texts. The specific nature of these processes, their intensity, and their consequences (positive or negative) on students' writing and learning will vary markedly across and even within specific classrooms, but the history of the classroom will always shape students' writing. What is especially important to recognize here is that these routine, everyday processes are distributed throughout the literate activity of students. Tuning is accomplished in full contexts, contexts that include much more than the draft text and specific written or oral comments.

When teachers read and respond to students' writing, their response is shaped by a multidimensional context. That context includes the history of classroom events (the tuning of tasks throughout the course), but also encompasses institutional, disciplinary, and social contexts. Contexts are imagined and projected as well. Teachers routinely recontextualize student writing for a class, imagining that students have written in another context or that the text is being read in another context. Teachers also routinely respond not only to the text, but to the student who wrote it. In all of these interpretive processes, teachers bring their own histories to their reading and response. Briefly, these points are:

- The history of the class shapes teachers' reading and response.
- Teachers' own histories shape their reading and response.
- Institutional, disciplinary, and social contexts shape teachers' reading and response.
- Teachers recontextualize texts, imagining other contexts in which the text might have been produced or might be read.
- Teachers respond to students as well as texts.

This expanded notion of writing and response has important implications for researchers as well as teachers. When writing is set in the full contexts of literate activity, we see that researchers must carefully render the contexts of production and reception for student texts. Decontextualized study of teachers' responses to student writing will fail to capture the rich dialogic activity of classrooms, those interlocking chains of interpretation that Phelps sketched.[32]

Two key implications for teachers become apparent. One is that teachers must increase their awareness of the complexity and diversity of interpretive activity in the classroom, attending carefully to students' interpretations of their goals and expectations as well as to their own interpretations of students, their contexts, and their texts. The examples in this chapter have focused on writing and response in college classrooms, but the points made here are relevant to writing at other levels of education as well. In elementary and secondary classes, students and teachers engage in processes of tuning through the means discussed here: emphasizing topics, elaborating on assignments and goals, and co-planning processes and texts. The second key implication is that teachers can and should respond in multiple ways to students' texts, that written and oral commentary are not the only, or necessarily the best, tools available to shape students' writing and their learning. This point also applies across educational contexts. In some cases, changes in instructional delivery or institutional contexts might represent the best response to problems seen in students' texts.

John Dewey pointed to the fundamental connection between the words *communication*, *community*, and *common*, suggesting that education is achieved in communication (rather than simply through it) and in joint activity.[33] A contextualized understanding of response to writing points in a similar direction. As Dewey's work would imply, building literacy is the work of bringing people together as co-participants in common literate practices. To understand the roles writing and response to writing play in learning, we must attend to the fine-grained details of such participation in classroom activities, considering the complex ways that teachers and students construct commonalities and negotiate differences.

NOTES

1. Charles Adams, Edwin Godkin, and Josiah Quincy, "Report of the Committee on Composition and Rhetoric (1892)," in *The Origins of Composition Studies in the American College 1875-1925: A Documentary History*, ed. John Brereton (Pittsburgh: University of Pittsburgh Press, 1995), p. 76.

2. See, for example, Lil Brannon and C. H. Knoblauch, "On Students' Rights to Their Own Texts: A Model of Teacher Response," *College Composition and Communication* 33 (1982): 157-166; Sarah Freedman, "How Characteristics of Students' Essays Influence Teachers' Evaluations," *Journal of Educational Psychology* 71 (1979): 328-338; Anne Ruggles Gere, "Written Composition: Toward a Theory of Evaluation," *College English* 42 (1980): 44-58; Elaine Lees, "Evaluating Student Writing," *College Composition and Communication* 30 (1979): 370-374; Nancy Sommers, "Responding to Student Writing," *College Composition and Communication* 33 (1982): 148-156.

3. In addition to the sources cited in the previous note, see, for example, Charles Cooper and Lee Odell, eds., *Evaluating Writing: Describing, Measuring, Judging* (Urbana, Ill.: National Council of Teachers of English, 1977); Susan Miller, *Textual Carnivals: The Politics of Composition* (Carbondale: Southern Illinois University Press, 1991); Stephen North, *The Making of Knowledge in Composition: Portrait of an Emerging Field*

(Portsmouth, N.J.: Boynton/Cook, 1987); Louise Wetherbee Phelps, *Composition as a Human Science: Contributions to the Self-Understanding of a Discipline* (New York: Oxford University Press, 1988).

4. Sommers, "Responding to Student Writing."

5. Ibid.; Brannon and Knoblauch, "On Students' Rights to Their Own Texts"; C. H. Knoblauch and Lil Brannon, *Rhetorical Traditions and the Teaching of Writing* (Upper Montclair, N.J.: Boynton/Cook, 1984).

6. Chris Anson, "Response Styles and Ways of Knowing," in *Writing and Response: Theory, Practice, and Research*, ed. Chris Anson (Urbana, Ill.: National Council of Teachers of English, 1989), pp. 332-366; Bennett Rafoth and Donald Rubin, "The Impact of Content and Mechanics on Judgments of Writing Quality," *Written Communication* 1 (1984): 446-459.

7. Donald Daiker, "Learning to Praise," in *Writing and Response: Theory, Practice, and Research*, ed. Anson, pp. 103-113; Sommers, "Responding to Student Writing"; Vivian Zamel, "Responding to Student Writing," *TESOL Quarterly* 19 (1985): 79-102.

8. George Hillocks, *Research on Written Communication: New Directions for Teaching* (Urbana, Ill.: National Conference on Research in English and ERIC Clearinghouse on Reading and Communication Skills, 1986). The few exceptions Hillocks notes involve highly focused responses assessed by equally focused measures.

9. Richard Beach and Sara Eaton, "Factors Influencing Self-Assessing and Revising by College Freshman," in *New Directions in Composition Research*, ed. Richard Beach and Lillian Bridwell (New York: Guilford, 1984), pp. 149-170; Carol Berkenkotter, "Student Writers and Their Sense of Authority over Texts," *College Composition and Communication* 35 (1984): 312-319; Marilyn Cooper and Cynthia Selfe, "Computer Conferences and Learning: Authority, Resistance, and Internally Persuasive Discourse," *College English* 52 (1990): 847-869; Kathryn Evans, "Writing, Response, and Contexts of Production, or Why It Just Wouldn't Work to Write about Those Bratty Kids," *Journal of Language and Learning across the Disciplines* 2 (1997): 5-21; Anne Ruggles Gere and R. Stevens, "The Language of Writing Groups: How Oral Response Shapes Revision," in *The Acquisition of Written Language: Revision and Response*, ed. Freeman, pp. 85-105; Thomas Newkirk, "The Writing Conference as Performance," *Research in the Teaching of English* 29 (1995): 193-215; Geoffrey Sirc, "Response in Electronic Media," in *Writing and Response: Theory, Practice, and Research*, ed. Anson, pp. 187-205.

10. Evans, "Writing, Response, and Contexts of Production"; Newkirk, "The Writing Conference as Performance."

11. Carolyn Ball, Laura Dice, and David Bartholomae, "Telling Secrets: Student Readers and Disciplinary Authorities," in *Developing Discourse Practices in Adolescence and Adulthood*, ed. Richard Beach and Susan Hynds (Norwood, N.J.: Ablex, 1990), pp. 337-357; For studies describing response to writing in the disciplines, see, for example, Carol Berkenkotter, Thomas Huckin, and John Ackerman, "Conventions, Conversations, and the Writer: Case Study of a Student in a Rhetoric Ph.D. Program," *Research in the Teaching of English* 22 (1988): 9-44; Anne Herrington, "Composing One's Self in a Discipline: Students' and Teachers' Negotiations," in *Constructing Rhetorical Education*, ed. Marie Secor and Davida Charney (Carbondale: Southern Illinois University Press, 1992), pp. 91-115; Paul Prior, "Tracing Authoritative and Internally Persuasive Discourses: A Case Study of Response, Revision, and Disciplinary Enculturation," *Research in the Teaching of English* 29 (1995): 288-325; Paul Prior, "Contextualizing Writing and Response in a Graduate Seminar," *Written Communication* 8 (1991): 267-310.

12. Herrington, "Composing One's Self in a Discipline." For example, after the instructor deleted Kate's challenge in one draft to the fairness of regulating Eskimo hunting, Kate complied, deleting the challenge, but then reintroduced the same issue elsewhere in the text. For comparable findings in an elementary setting, see Sarah

Michaels, "Text and Context: A New Approach to the Study of Classroom Writing," *Discourse Processes* 10 (1987): 321-346.

13. See also Larry Beason, "Feedback and Revision in Writing Across the Curriculum Classes," *Research in the Teaching of English* 27 (1993): 395-422; M. F. Hayes and Donald Daiker, "Using Protocol Analysis in Evaluating Responses to Student Writing, *Freshman English News* 13 (1984): 1-10; Nina Ziv, "The Effect of Teacher Comments on the Writing of Four College Freshmen," in *New Directions in Composition Research*, eds. Beach and Bridwell, pp. 362-380.

14. See, for example, many of the essays in Bruce Lawson, Susan Ryan and W. Ross Winterowd, eds., *Encouraging Student Texts: Interpretive Issues in Reading Student Writing* (Urbana, Ill.: National Council of Teachers of English, 1989).

15. Linda Shamoon and Robert Schwegler, "Sociologists Reading Student Texts: Expectations and Perceptions," *The Writing Instructor* (1988): 71-81.

16. Prior, "Contextualizing Writing and Response in a Graduate Seminar."

17. Evans, "Writing, Response, and Contexts of Production."

18. Glynda Hull, Mike Rose, Kay Fraser, and Maria Castellano, "Remediation as Social Construct: Perspectives from Analysis of Classroom Discourse," *College Composition and Communication* 42 (1991): 299-329.

19. Deborah Brandt, *Literacy as Involvement: The Acts of Readers, Writers, and Texts* (Carbondale: Southern Illinois University Press, 1990); Stephen Witte, "Revision, Composing Theory, and Research Design," in *The Acquisition of Written Language: Revision and Response*, ed. Freedman, pp. 250-284; Stephen Witte, "Context, Text, Intertext: Toward a Constructivist Semiotic of Writing, *Written Communication* 9 (1992): 237-308; Karen Burke LeFevre, *Invention as a Social Act* (Carbondale: Southern Illinois University Press, 1987); Paul Prior, *Writing/Disciplinarity: A Sociohistoric Perspective on Literate Activity in the Academy* (Mahwah, N.J.: Lawrence Erlbaum, in press).

20. Hugh Mehan, *Learning Lessons: Social Organization in the Classroom* (Cambridge, Mass.: Harvard University Press, 1979); Courtney Cazden, *Classroom Discourse: The Language of Teaching and Learning* (Portsmouth, N.H.: Heinemann, 1988).

21. Shirley Brice Heath, *Ways with Words: Language, Life, and Work in Communities and Classrooms* (New York: Cambridge University Press, 1983).

22. Sarah Freedman, *Response to Student Writing* (Urbana, Ill.: National Council of Teachers of English, 1987), p. 5.

23. Louise Phelps, "Images of Student Writing: The Deep Structure of Teacher Response," in *Writing and Response: Theory, Practice, and Research*, ed. Anson, p. 64.

24. Andrew Pickering, *The Mangle of Practice: Time, Agency, and Science* (Chicago: University of Chicago Press, 1995). I should also clarify here that I am not suggesting that tuning is a positive, egalitarian, or even non-coercive process; instead, I am suggesting that even the most authoritarian classroom involves emergent, interactive processes of interpretation and action.

25. Linda Flower, Victoria Stein, John Ackerman, Margaret Kantz, Kathleen McCormick, and Wayne Peck, *Reading-to-Write: Exploring a Cognitive and Social Process* (New York: Oxford University Press, 1990); Anne Herrington, "Writing in Academic Settings: A Study of the Contexts for Writing in Two College Chemical Engineering Courses," *Research in the Teaching of English* 19 (1985): 331-359; Jennie Nelson, "This Was an Easy Assignment: Examining How Students Interpret Academic Writing Tasks," *Research in the Teaching of English* 24 (1990): 362-396; Prior, "Contextualizing Writing and Response in Graduate Seminars"; Prior, *Writing/Disciplinarity*.

26. The names of seminar instructors, students, and institutional sites are pseudonyms. The research in these seminars involved observation and recording of classroom

interactions; analysis of students' papers, including drafts; analysis of instructors' written comments; and interviews with instructors and students.

27. See, for example, Aristotle, *The Rhetoric of Aristotle*, trans. Lane Cooper (Englewood Cliffs, N.J.: Prentice-Hall, 1932).

28. See Prior, *Writing/Disciplinarity*, for a fuller discussion of topics. Also see Carolyn Miller and Jack Selzer, "Special Topics of Argument in Engineering Reports," in *Writing in Nonacademic Settings*, ed. Lee Odell and Dixie Goswami (New York: Guilford, 1985), pp. 309-341. In their analysis of one specific community (transportation engineers), Miller and Selzer identified as special topics not only organizational schemes for genres (e.g., transit plans) and thematic issues (e.g., cost), but also certain graphics (e.g., land use maps), tabular presentations (e.g., tables with survey responses), corporate slogans (e.g., service to clients), and disciplinary concepts (e.g., memory scheduling, productivity analysis, zone fare structure).

29. See Prior, *Writing/Disciplinarity*, for analysis of how topics shaped writing in these two seminars.

30. Ball, Dice, and Bartholomae. "Telling Secrets: Student Readers and Disciplinary Authorities"; Herrington, "Composing One's Self in a Discipline." In this chapter, I do not present examples of co-authoring; however, see Prior, "Tracing Authoritative and Internally Persuasive Discourses" for a detailed analysis. For a detailed analysis of co-authoring through response in a sixth grade classroom, see Michaels, "Text and Context: A New Approach to the Study of Classroom Writing."

31. See Freedman, "How Characteristics of Students' Essays Influence Teachers' Evaluations"; Rafoth and Rubin, "The Impact of Content and Mechanics on Judgments of Writing Quality."

32. Phelps, "Images of Student Writing."

33. John Dewey, *Democracy and Education* (New York: Free Press, 1916).

CHAPTER VIII

"How Much Are We the Wiser?": Continuity and Change in Writing and Learning in the Content Areas

GEORGE E. NEWELL

Over the past fifteen years, as secondary school reform has included calls for "writing across the curriculum," it has become a truism to say that writing develops critical reasoning skills. "Higher order thinking," problem solving, and analytic thinking have, at times, all been linked directly to writing instruction. In *High School: A Report on Secondary Education in America*, for example, Ernest Boyer argues for making clear and effective writing a "central objective of the school."[1] In Theodore Sizer's *Horace's School*, Franklin High's curricular redesign calls for writing across the curriculum as a key to integration and for writing to become a facultywide responsibility.[2] However, regardless of how urgently writing instructors and school reformers insist on the centrality of writing in the secondary school curriculum, the case needs to be made that writing activities offer something unique to specific academic subjects and not just help for English language arts teachers. Currently, a strong professional base of writing teachers and a tradition of academic research argue for such a role for writing; yet the larger social, political, and cultural developments in American society complicate educational reform.

In this chapter, I will argue that the nature of the writing task and the kinds of learning from text that writing may foster are keys to understanding the importance of writing in academic learning, making writing an important tool as well as a "central skill" in the secondary school curriculum. Perhaps more important, I will argue that, when any school reform agenda asks teachers to select writing activities to promote learning, attention must go to the diverse nature of the cultural and institutional contexts that complicate a writing-to-learn agenda. Accordingly, my efforts will include not only a description of how, why,

---

George E. Newell is Associate Professor of English Education in the School of Teaching and Learning at Ohio State University.

and when writing-to-learn approaches work and do not work, but also an exploration of the countervailing forces that subvert them.

Specifically, I will examine (1) theoretical and empirical projects to understand the relationships between writing and learning, (2) efforts to implement process-oriented writing activities to foster learning in all content areas, and (3) more recent understanding of the complexities and importance of previously made promises to reform schools and writing. Put another way, I use this chapter to consider a question James Britton and his colleagues posed in the final chapter of their seminal study of writing across the curriculum: "Standing back from it all, how much are we the wiser?"[3]

Constructivist Notions of Teaching and Learning

In spite of rather convincing arguments for the value of writing in academic learning, two interrelated issues have plagued writing-to-learn reforms. First, earlier conceptions of writing to learn based on process-oriented writing instruction neglected the fundamental issue of "what constitutes learning," focusing instead on the development of new activities and routines. Accordingly, "transmission" views of teaching and learning that emphasize memorization and recitation, coopted the learner-centered underpinnings of writing for which theorists such as Janet Emig, James Britton, Donald Graves, and Nancy Martin had argued. Second, although writing-to-learn approaches have provided insights into the role of writing as a tool for learning, they have largely ignored, particularly in elementary and secondary education, some of the unique ways of knowing and doing in various academic disciplines and content fields. This has led to two assumptions: (1) that writing should be the primary concern of the English teacher who has the responsibility to teach generic strategies and forms for writing and (2) that writing has no practical relevance to instruction in other content areas. Accordingly, any reform will have to consider not only how students make sense of ways of knowing and doing in various disciplines, but also the realities of schooling (e.g., testing) that often complicate shifts toward such fundamental change. The challenge is to develop a coherent view of teaching and learning that offers a conceptually powerful way of supporting process-oriented, learner-centered approaches to writing as well as one that gives teachers an overarching framework for thinking about issues of teaching and learning in the content areas.

To offer new ways of conceptualizing models of teaching and learning, many educators and scholars are turning to constructivist theories of language and learning. With roots in fields as diverse as psychology, linguistics, sociology, history of science, and philosophy, constructivist approaches share a view of knowledge as active constructions, although some approaches focus on the constructions of individuals whereas others focus on the constructions of groups and even large communities. A key principle of such a framework is that, rather than viewing the content of the academic disciplines and students' learning as separate concerns, a constructivist sees learning in context—how knowledge develops within particular instructional contexts when students are actively engaged, as, for example, when they take positions on topics and issues discussed by others.[4] This view of teaching and learning is compatible with some of the motives underlying process-oriented approaches to writing instruction, and it offers, in a principled way, a description of effective teaching and learning.

What then are some of the tenets of constructivism relevant to a reconsideration of the role of writing to learn in the secondary school? Although constructivism has been discussed and examined from a range of perspectives, the view employed in this chapter is informed by James Britton's discussions of the role of language in learning and by Douglas Barnes's notion of the "interpretation" view of learning, each of which integrates the act of communication with the process of knowing.[5]

In *Language and Learning*, James Britton, following such major constructivist theorists as Jean Piaget, Jerome Bruner, Lev Vygotsky, and George Kelly, spoke of learning as organizing and reorganizing one's experience and also reflecting on that experience.[6] Britton pointed to the role of language in the shaping of experience: Language provides a means of symbolizing and of interpreting; it is not the only means but it is one means. He argued that writing "allows a writer . . . to wrestle with his [or her] thoughts, to work and re-work his [or her] formulation or projection or transformation of experience."[7] Language influences learning on a social level as well as an individual level, since through language individuals affect each other's understandings and build common meanings. In Britton's conception, there are three major uses of language: transactional, expressive, and poetic. The transactional function includes expository and persuasive writing with subcategories that constitute an abstractive scale from reporting to summarizing, analyzing, and theorizing. The expressive function gives indications of the writer himself or herself in terms of voice, thoughts, and feelings. This is best understood as corresponding to informal talk among friends, where the rules of use are relaxed. The poetic function is essentially the literary uses of language as in poetry, fictional narratives, and drama used to represent the writer's experiences, and, in turn, to represent a virtual experience for the reader.

Douglas Barnes, who, like Britton, built on the ideas of Piaget, Bruner, Vygotsky, and Kelly, and who built on Britton's ideas as well, described knowledge as "systems for interpreting the world"—systems that are transformed even as they are being used for understanding. Language plays a major role in this constructive process, as it provides "a set of strategies for interpreting the world" and also a "means for reflecting upon this interpretation."[8] In considering the transformations that occur in a person's interpretive systems, Barnes emphasized social influences, pointing out that, through communication with others, one person's interpretive systems interact with those of others. In considering how interpretive teaching might foster students' active construction of meaning, Barnes described the value of "exploratory talk." His analysis of successful small-group discussions indicates that the language students use in such contexts tends to be "marked by frequent hesitations, rephrasings, false starts and change of direction. . . . That is, such exploratory talk is one means by which the assimilation and accommodation of new knowledge to old is carried out."[9]

Expressive uses of language and exploratory talk, which are part of this constructivist tradition of language and learning, are also associated with a "process orientation" toward literacy instruction. The "process" view of teaching and learning, which emphasizes growth and development, is based on the assumption that learning is not linear and sequential but instead involves false starts and tentative explorations. Understanding will grow and change as learning progresses. Premature evaluation emphasizing correctness will short-circuit the process and stall risk taking.

In the context of American schools and colleges a learner-centered position, such as that taken by Britton and Barnes, has countered a transmission conception of education. Applebee has described the transmission view of teaching and learning with its "emphasis on memorization and rote learning" as "knowledge-out-of-context." On the other hand, a constructivist orientation toward teaching and learning can be described as "knowledge-in-action," that is, as ways of knowing that are a confluence of past and current ideas, concerns, and discussions. "Knowledge-in-action shapes our expectations about the future as well as our interpretation of the past."[10]

This is a view of curriculum and instruction that will be developed more fully later in this chapter. My point for the moment is that, when writing and reading are construed as ways of knowing and doing, the role of "literate thinking" is expanded and deepened to include the learning of content as well as the process of critical analysis. However, given that transmission views of teaching and learning are still the common sense of schooling and of the larger culture of which schools are a part, to implement writing-to-learn reforms requires a new per-spective—which John Mayher would call an "uncommon sense"—to guide teaching and learning.[11] As a field, composition has much work to do; to this point, the notion of writing to learn has been based more on favorite activities such as free writing or dialogue journals rather than on broad principles of effective teaching across the content areas. But how did we arrive at a point in time when commonsense views can, in any case, be challenged and perhaps transformed? Perhaps we can envision the future with more confidence by taking stock of past reform efforts: Just how much are we the wiser for those efforts? And what reforms emerge out of that collective wisdom?

Origins of Writing to Learn

Until recently, within the field of composition as represented in scholarly and practitioners' journals, there has been little debate over the special role of writing as an intellectual process or as a tool for learning in content areas. Eminent scholars such as David Olson and Jerome Bruner have written extensively and convincingly about the cultural consequences of literacy and the centrality of schooling in developing sophisticated and complex ways of thinking and reason-ing.[12] However, more recent scholarship that has examined the role of literacy in cultural and individual life, has questioned the notion of written language as a unitary phenomenon with specific effects on cognition that oral language cannot produce.[13] Although some of this work is discussed later in this section, the point for the moment is that just as claims for the effects of literacy have been overly simplistic, arguments for the value of learning from writing in school settings suffer from the same limitation; they have assumed that the process of writing will lead inevitably to a better understanding of the topic under consideration while ignoring various situational variables that might affect such learning. Put another way, to understand the many effects and potential benefits of writing we need to look at the func-tional roles that writing serves in specific contexts.

Because the details of the history of writing and literacy have been presented in various works,[14] I will begin with developments in the 1970s, including process-oriented writing instruction. My discussion of process-oriented writing will be followed by a consideration of the British model developed at the University of London and the American writing-across-the-curriculum (WAC) movement, both of which represent important contributions to ongoing efforts to reform teaching and learning.

PROCESS APPROACHES TO WRITING

Although the notion of "process" as a way to conceptualize how writers compose and how teachers might teach writing had been known and implemented before 1971, the publication of Janet Emig's seminal study, *The Composing Processes of Twelfth Graders*, in that year marks an important point in the development of process approaches to writing instruction and in the role of writing in academic learning.[15] As Emig studied the writing experiences of professional writers, literary artists, and students alike, she discovered that much of the conventional wisdom offered by writing and grammar textbooks (for example, the necessity of outlining before writing and the requirement that all essays be formulated with five paragraphs) confined rather than fostered writing development.

Emig's alternative to such a tradition based on rules of correct public forms for formal discourse was a new model of writing instruction anchored in the writer's own experiences. She argued that school writing imposed topics on students for which they had little commitment, leading to more concern with pleasing the teacher than exploring new ideas. This argument widened the possible role of writing not just as a way to demonstrate knowledge but also as a way to explore a topic for understanding and self-discovery. Six years after the publication of her important study, Emig again drew on various sources to consider "Writing as a Mode of Learning." She developed an argument showing why writing works so well as a tool for reasoning and illustrating the parallels between writing processes and learning strategies.[16]

Emig's study of the composing process ignored an issue that remains at the center of some controversy, that is, the potential conflict between the individual student's "learning experiences" and the collective experiences that teachers and academic disciplines represent: How can the experience of the learner be balanced with the demands of the discipline or content area? Put another way, what is the role of the teacher and what is the authority of the discipline in the student's intellectual development?

Emig's contributions were only the beginning of studies of writing processes. Her 1971 study was followed by a flood of other process studies that emphasized the exploratory, heuristic, and problem-solving nature of writing, whether from the student's experiences or from textual sources. Across these studies, several general findings have been evident: (1) writing processes include recursive operations such as planning, organizing, drafting, and editing, (2) experts compose differently than novices, and (3) processes vary according to the task and the instructional context as well as according to students' cultural background and topic-related knowledge. By the mid-1980s, as the process approach dominated the professional journals and as the National Writing Project became widely known, process supplanted more product-driven approaches as the new "writing establishment." In *What Works*, a 1986 publication of the U.S. Department of Education, Chester Finn advocated "process" as the most effective way to teach writing.[17] Although the definition of process differs from teacher to teacher, such approaches are marked by instructional activities designed to help students think through and organize a draft and to support them as they rethink and revise their initial drafts. Activities now associated with process-oriented approaches include brainstorming, journal writing, small-group discussions, teacher-student conferences, peer-response groups, multiple drafting, and delaying or even eliminating evaluation. For convenience in planning instruction, process activities are often subdivided into stages such as prewriting, drafting, revising, and editing, with consideration given to recursiveness rather than linearity and to complexity rather than simplicity.

When the history of writing instruction is told from this perspective, process studies and process-oriented approaches can appear disconnected from the writing-to-learn movement. However, by 1987 Judith Langer and Arthur Applebee opened their report *How Writing Shapes Thinking* by pointing out parallels:

Both emphasize the active role of the writer, who must organize and reformulate ideas and experiences in the process of writing about them. Both treat learning as ongoing and cumulative, with errors to be expected (and even encouraged as a natural concomitant of tackling new and more difficult problems). And both imply renewed attention to the processes rather than simply the outcomes of instruction.[18]

This statement harks back to earlier claims about the process of discovery that writing often fosters, and it also pushes forward to a new agenda for process approaches to writing—to enhance the learning of content area information. Yet by the end of their report Langer and Applebee were less sanguine and more tentative in their conclusions. Rather than assuming that without exception writing leads to learning, they pointed to the importance of the teacher's intent and of students' interpretations of the teacher's intent. Writing can be used most effectively, they argued, when the teacher's purpose is not accuracy of recall but quality of thought. Specifically, they argued that most of the content area teaching they observed easily recognized and rewarded references to "correct" information in student writing, but struggled to articulate the ways of arguing and providing evidence that govern their particular disciplines.

Accordingly, Langer and Applebee suggested a broader agenda for writing beyond the English classroom: "This is to view the classroom as a community of scholars (or of scholars and apprentices) with its own rules of evidence and procedures for carrying the discussion forward."[19] It is at this point that writing can be seen to have a "central" role in the secondary curriculum, a role that begins to connect writing to learn with writing across the disciplines. This is precisely the role that the British educator and scholar, James Britton, and his colleagues at the University of London saw as early as the 1960s when they began to formulate a research agenda to promote the development of knowledgeable and thoughtful students.

THE BRITISH MODEL

As I have pointed out, process approaches to writing would seem to have a natural connection to a broader agenda for the role of writing and language in academic learning. The Institute of Education at the University of London made this the central tenet of its research on school writing. Its principal research effort entitled *The Development of Writing Abilities (11-18)* made a major theoretical statement about the significance of writing and learning and a major criticism of the narrowness of school writing.[20] James Britton, Tony Burgess, Nancy Martin, Alex McLeod, and Harold Rosen's contributions to writing to learn were twofold: first, their classification of school writing tasks by function or purpose and, second, their documentation of the narrow range of functions employed in British schools, a pattern in American school writing that was later documented by Applebee.[21] The major categories of function in the so-called "British Model" were those discussed by Britton in his earlier work, as mentioned above: transactional, expressive, and poetic. The concern of Britton and his colleagues was that, as students moved through secondary school, their writing became more directed toward the teacher as examiner and increasingly informational with significant declines in literary and expressive or personal uses of writing. This led the team to argue for "expressive" writing as "best adapted to exploration and discovery. It is the language that externalizes our first stages of tackling a problem or coming to grips with an experience."[22]

Britton and his colleagues saw an imbalance among the various functions as used in schooling. However, there is another, more positive way to interpret the shift toward informational writing in the high school years. Clearly, the curriculum is intended to move students toward the abstractions of the academic disciplines and to such forms as critical analyses in literature and laboratory reports in science. Informational writing includes expository and persuasive functions as well as subcategories that constitute an abstractive scale moving from reporting to summarizing, analyzing, and finally theorizing. Because these language functions represent school writing that is closest to the types of writing in the academic disciplines, they have provided a useful means for discussing written discourse across subject areas and a more comprehensive alternative to less accurate and less detailed modes of discourse. Perhaps the greatest contribution of Britton's classification system in general and his transactional category in particular is that they provide a means for studying writing according to the nature of the task and possible demands on the writer. Of course, a theory that focuses so closely on school writing ought to have mechanisms for contrasting writing in different subjects. Thus, an important project for anyone employing the systems will be to examine variations within, for example, the analytic function in subject areas such as literature, biology, and history.

In 1976 Nancy Martin led an effort to follow up on Britton's earlier study by developing practical approaches to writing and learning in various content areas, especially science, and to deepen the understanding of the effects of examination pressures on such a reform agenda. This work, presented in *Writing and Learning across the Curriculum, 11-16*, made the theoretical aspects of the role of language in learning more accessible to a wider audience and pooled teachers' expertise in trying to understand language and learning in all subject areas.[23] In 1992, in a review of the watershed decades of the 1960s and 1970s, Martin pointed out that the emphasis on language, either oral or written, in the British Model is not just a new technique for teaching but is central to the nature of learning.[24] She also admitted that ideas about the centrality of language in organizing and reflecting experience have not been well "assimilated" in British schools. This lack of assimilation would also seem to hold true in the United States where the writing-to-learn and WAC movements have had little impact on secondary schools.

Efforts to bring a new vision of teaching, learning, and writing to American schools and universities are well documented, as are some of the difficulties of doing so.[25] Accordingly, my purpose here is to describe some of the differences and similarities between the British and American movements to make clear the professional and institutional conditions under which writing-to-learn efforts become supported and successful. More important, the WAC movement, which has had more play in universities than in high schools, offers a way for secondary teachers to push their instructional concerns beyond content and general writing strategies toward fundamental differences in discipline-specific ways of writing and learning.

The WAC movement in America had its origins as early as 1870 in persistent calls from university professors to solve "the writing problem." As the student population attending college increased in numbers and changed in socioeconomic status, there were few institutional structures to support the new students who entered specialized academic discourse communities. The correlated curriculum of the 1930s, the communications programs established after World War II, and the calls for social equity in the 1960s were all attempts to negotiate conflicting interests such as those, for example, between inclusiveness and disciplinary standards or between social unity and specialization.[26]

By the 1970s and 1980s WAC in higher education benefited from the confluence of several developments: for better or worse, concerns over basic literacy had the attention of the nation; a new group of writing specialists provided leadership for teaching and research efforts; the British tradition of teaching, research, and curricular reform in language education provided a theoretical basis for reform; and colleges and universities began to use WAC to reform college-level pedagogy by basing it on progressive education. These efforts coalesced around a new-found belief in the intellectual and professional importance of writing and the need to embed writing instruction in the unique curricular and pedagogical issues of the disciplines.

The British model and the American WAC movement share many features, among them the beliefs that language and writing are tools not only for student-centered learning but for faculty development and that learning, teaching, and writing are inextricably linked. Moreover, a progressive education philosophy underlies each. However, there are important differences also. For instance, WAC gives more attention to disciplinary differences in writing than does the British Model, which tends to view writing as more general, overarching all academic disciplines and content areas. A key to the success of WAC in American colleges and universities has been to appeal to faculty members from a range of departments whose primary concerns and loyalties lie in their disciplines. Yet the fact remains that both movements have sought to foster students' reasoning and thoughtfulness as they pursue their studies in the content fields.

One WAC movement at the secondary school level, the National Writing Project (NWP), borrows extensively from the British Model and has achieved national recognition and even federal funding. Beginning in 1971 at the University of California (Berkeley) as the Bay Area Writing Project, instructors and administrators began a program to improve instruction in writing in secondary schools. Rejecting the ideas of supplying secondary teachers with "teacherproof" materials or prescribing new methods using expert outsiders, NWP, which now includes elementary and college teachers as well, provides a forum for experienced and successful teachers to exchange ideas about writing instruction in a collegial atmosphere. An effort is made to create the best blend of teachers' practical knowledge of schools and students with current composition theory and practice that seem relevant to writing in schools.

Roots in the Sawdust, edited by Anne Ruggles Gere, represents one successful effort to do so.[27] For this book, classroom teachers from the Puget Sound Writing Project each contributed a chapter to document the potential of writing-to-learn activities to transform classroom life. For the most part, these activities are informal in nature—response statements, free writing, and journals—and short and ungraded. But also suggested are more formal assignments that require attention to formal constraints such as writing for critical and distant audiences. The essays in *Roots in the Sawdust* are each in their own right thoughtful excursions into teachers' minds and classrooms, and each represents "reflective practice." Yet one element that is overlooked in Gere's introduction and in the contributors' essays is that writing-to-learn assignments are likely to represent but a single element in a larger configuration of social elements at work in the teachers' practices. For instance, each essay assumes the value of an intellectual community in classrooms where students feel they can contribute to an ongoing exploration of ideas and experiences. Such a context seems just as necessary to successful teaching and learning as do imaginative writing and reading assignments.

So where do the histories of the British writing-to-learn movement and the American WAC movement leave us? Perhaps a key issue for secondary schooling is the need for researchers and practitioners to collaborate in unpacking some of the essential similarities and differences in the ways of knowing in various disciplines. If discipline-specific ways of knowing remain implicit and thus hidden from students, it seems likely that concerns over students' inability to engage in critical thinking will continue. Students are unlikely to be learning how to gather evidence and develop effective arguments when their teachers (and the field in general) have not articulated these concerns clearly to themselves. As it stands, we do not have a clear vision of how to reform secondary schooling using what we have learned from the WAC movement. However, many useful paths are beginning to form in a forest of complex social, institutional, and cultural issues. For example, Langer's analysis of conceptions of subject matter within particular disciplines as they are presented in their theoretical and pedagogical literatures suggests how useful pathfinding can be.[28]

Langer discovered that teachers in subjects as different as biology, history, and literature are likely to ask students to "provide evidence," "analyze," and "elaborate" as part of discussing and writing about academic content. However, she also discovered that the very real differences from one subject to another in the meaning of those ways of knowing were rarely, if ever, explained. The question, "How much are we the wiser?" seems all the more pertinent after some thirty years of effort to move toward more thoughtful and democratic approaches to writing and learning in the content areas. Interestingly, the social and intellectual contexts necessary for effective uses of writing-to-learn tasks are still an issue that a theory of writing across the curriculum has only recently begun to develop.

PROMISES TO KEEP: A THEORY OF WRITING TO LEARN

After analyzing the developments in theory, research, and practice in writing to learn over a twenty-five-year period, John Ackerman concluded that, although it has been promised, we have yet to make an argument for writing to learn.[29] But what are the promises that scholars and teachers have made to themselves and to their students? More important, what makes such promises so difficult not only to keep but to articulate to others not so inclined toward such ideas as student ownership or teacher empowerment? Finally, what is at stake if we do not make writing to learn a central component of school reform?

From my discussion of the origins of writing to learn it should be obvious that the British model contributes to both WAC and process-oriented approaches. Accordingly, in order to understand the theoretical roots of writing to learn, it is necessary to begin with James Britton's contributions. Britton's notion of language and learning was developed to accommodate the needs of the practitioner at least as much, if not more than, the needs of the educational researcher or social scientist. Within Britton's scholarship two questions seem ever present: How do young people develop language and literacy? How might understandings about the development of language and literacy shape instruction? These lead naturally to two more questions of particular relevance to this chapter: What promises of school reform does the theory offer? and, perhaps most importantly, To what extent, if at all, is the theory viable within the current context of schooling?

Although not the only voice in the development of the theory of writing to learn, Britton's voice, especially in *Language and Learning*,[30] was an important one. In his synthesis of the theoretical works, he stressed the importance of students using language—both oral and written—to explore, organize, and refine their understandings of experiences and content area information. Teachers could, Britton argued, use writing not only to evaluate current understandings, but also to foster students' unique interpretations of literature, history, and science. In this way, Britton's constructivist theory of language and learning is also a critique of teaching as transmission and learning as absorption.

Within his framework the promises of writing and learning become compelling for two reasons. First, the theory of writing to learn is compatible with process-oriented instruction that is based on learner-centered notions of instruction and on the importance of making meaning during the act of composing. Second, its learner-centered view of learning provides an approach to broad underlying principles that govern effective contexts for teaching and learning within the realities of schooling. For example, Langer and Applebee have used the metaphor of "instructional scaffolding" as an alternative to traditional models of writing instruction.[31] As the student attempts new tasks, the teacher provides scaffolding or support that assumes that the writing assignment must allow the student to have some ownership over the task with the teacher collaborating with the student (perhaps delaying or eliminating evaluation) in order to lead the student through effective strategies to complete the task successfully. In this way writing-to-learn theories have significant implications not only for writing instruction, but for broader rethinking of what it means to teach and to learn in all content areas.

There are, however, two caveats regarding some of the assumptions underlying Britton's theory of writing to learn. First, literacy scholars such as Deborah Brandt, Brian Street, and Shirley Brice Heath have raised important concerns over a "strong text" theory of literacy, arguing that writing and other literacy events cannot in and of themselves lead inevitably to abstract thinking.[32] Rather than being mutually exclusive, orality and literacy are "protean," that is, they constantly act in concert with one another. These scholars have also pointed out the cultural biases implicit in such strong claims for writing and learning and have reminded us that all writing practices carry cultural values and that instruction employing personal writing, informal explorations of new ideas, and challenges to authority may find resistance among students of some cultures.

Second, regardless of how neatly theory seems to explain how writing may foster learning, teaching and learning occur within certain institutional, cultural, and social contexts that may complicate how and when learning may occur. Britton's own formulation of language and learning seems, at times, to hesitate in recognizing this point. He examines learning and personal discovery in a vacuum as many of his examples come from his observations of individual children. In his subsequent thinking, however, he has recognized and argued for learning as a communal activity requiring children to learn the tacit rules of talk.[33] As Ackerman has so wisely pointed out, we need to understand writers interacting not only with content but also with the cultural codes that are part of life in school.[34] Thus, the notion of what constitutes learning differs from situation to situation. Writing does enrich reasoning and learning but only to the extent that learning is situationally supported and valued. Context factors, such as the content area, group composition, grade level, and available sources should be considered by teachers as they integrate writing into their classrooms. Choice of writing task, however, is a significant decision that teachers must make. Accordingly, it is important that teachers be selective about the kinds of writing assignments they provide for their students, as the nature of the task may foster one type of learning but short-circuit other kinds. For this reason we will examine the demands of various tasks and how they are experienced by students, that is, how writing enriches students' reasoning and learning.

"Writing Is Not Writing Is Not Writing"

As this section heading—an aphorism taken from Langer and Applebee's study of school writing tasks—warns, discussions of writing as learning go astray when they neglect to specify the kinds of learning various writing tasks might be expected to foster. Accordingly, in this section I continue the discussion of a theory of writing to learn with a brief overview of Britton's and Applebee's theories of school writing tasks. I then review several key studies that have employed writing tasks developed from Britton's writing function system in order to understand the types of learning fostered by a range of writing tasks. The point to be made in this part of the discussion is that not all writing tasks are equal and that teachers' instructional decisions regarding when, how, and why to use writing-to-learn activities should depend on the kinds of learning they envision for their students.

A THEORY OF TASK

In developing a discourse scheme for understanding the cognitive and linguistic demands of writing, Britton and his colleagues based their theory on language function, that is, the universe of possible uses of language in general and written language in particular. Writing teachers are perhaps more familiar with the traditional modes of discourse—narration, description, exposition, argumentation, and sometimes poetry. Because these categories of writing assignments are based largely on fully formed, preordained structures rather than the nature of the task itself or the demands it makes on the writer, Britton looked to other theories of language function and intention to explore the intellectual value and complexities of school writing. For Britton, writing within a particular function (e.g., to tell a story, to report on an event) enables writers to organize meaning around intention and language use.

As noted earlier, Britton's system proposed three main categories for functions of language: transactional, expressive, and poetic.[35] In his adaptation of Britton's system, Applebee renamed the three overall categories as "informational," "personal" and "imaginative."[36] He also refined and extended the system to include subcategories for both personal and imaginative writing, and streamlined and reconceptualized the subcategories for informational writing to characterize writing in American schools more accurately. Because his classroom observations and survey research revealed that a great deal of school writing required no composing, Applebee also added a category for "restricted" uses of writing such as multiple-choice and short-answer exercises.

HOW WRITING SHAPES THINKING AND LEARNING

Thus far my argument for the role of writing in academic learning has presumed a general or global effect of writing, that is, the process of writing will somehow lead inevitably to a better understanding of information gleaned from texts or from a teacher's presentation. As experienced writing teachers know, however, different writing assignments ask students to engage with ideas, information, and experiences in differing ways. For example, in writing from reading, it should usually be less demanding to outline the content of a chapter than to perform a critical analysis of ideas from that chapter. Consequently, writing research has examined under what conditions students learn from writing about texts, including the reasoning processes that accompany the generation and reformulation of ideas that enable students to understand and remember the information they read. The studies I discuss here are inquiries in social studies in the secondary school and involve writing based on the reading of single texts.[37] In these studies the kind of understanding examined was conceptual, that is, knowledge of the concepts and the relationships among concepts gleaned from reading passages in a range of content areas.

In this section I examine the effects of three types of writing as described by Britton's discourse theory (with Applebee's modifications): (1) restricted writing (requiring little or no composing) such as answering study questions, (2) summary writing, and (3) analytic writing. Not only are these three types of writing frequently assigned in secondary schools; they also represent three distinct ways to engage students in thinking and reasoning about what they are assigned to read in various content areas. The underlying assumption that frames this discussion is that the extent to which information is manipulated enhances topic understanding. For example, writing tasks would require more time to complete and more active engagement with the content of a reading passage than would nonwriting tasks such as mental review of a reading passage. In general, engagement would be associated with the constraints of the writing task. Essay writing would make more demands on the writer than answering study questions or fill-in-the-blank exercises. Accordingly, the greater the range of composing processes a writing task engenders, the more likely the writer will focus on the relationships among the ideas that give them coherence and structure and thus develop more coherent understanding of the topic. A second assumption is that different tasks focus the writer's attention in specific ways and the effects of writing on learning from text deal, for the most part, with ideas that are expressed during composing. For example, summarizing a passage would likely focus the writer's attention on a wide range of ideas but only superficially, whereas analytic writing would focus the writer's attention on a narrower range of ideas (those chosen for analysis) but in substantial ways.

One caveat. The few studies of writing and learning from texts that have measured students' prior understanding of key concepts in reading passages have found that students' knowledge affects writing quality and influences how well they can organize their written responses.[38] For example, if students' knowledge of key concepts in a reading passage is well organized, they should be able to complete such complex tasks as comparing and contrasting ideas, but if their knowledge is less well organized but extensive, then merely providing supporting evidence for a thesis is more manageable. Again, studies of the effects of prior knowledge on writing suggest that, in making instructional decisions, the teacher should consider what students bring to the task. An effort to help students generate new information before writing may be significant or may be wasted depending on how well informed they are about the topic at hand.

In answering study questions (assigned by the teacher or included in a textbook) students are usually asked to write a brief statement that suggests specific information in the text. In the following excerpt from a transcript of a student thinking aloud while responding to a study question we can see how the task shapes the student's responses to a reading passage.

What are the major manufacturing industries at the turn of the century? Uhm, looking down the page, factors of growth. No it's under . . . I'm reading over. I don't see any. . . . They're looking for specific factors. Uhh. Okay, I found it at the bottom of the page. In 1900, for example, the main manufacturing industries were meat packing. . . .[39]

The student begins by reading the question, then searches for relevant information, reconsiders the question, and locates the answer in the text. Considering that this process is largely a transcription rather than an elaborated interpretation of the information, when might such a task be pedagogically useful? My own studies of teaching with writing suggest that study questions can provide useful means for students to prepare for a more complex task or to review several elements of a text prior to class discussion.[40]

Summary writing can also provide the classroom teacher with a tool to help students review previous learning or prepare for new tasks. However, when summarizing, students must consider text-based information somewhat differently than they would when answering study questions. Two types of plans are necessary for summarizing: plans for compressing and integrating information from the text and plans for representing the organization of the text in a succinct way. Studies of summarizing have revealed that, although students order information paragraph-by-paragraph as they search for relationships among ideas, this task can result in a superficial understanding of content.[41] Analysis of the written products of summarizing suggests why this happens. Rather than evaluation or analysis of ideas, summaries provide highly distilled descriptions of events and ideas. Although summarizing enables students to get a "bird's eye view" of the information, such tasks tend to represent only the major ideas in a temporal order (i.e., the order in which they occur in the reading passage).

What, then, are the alternatives to tasks that require virtually no composing or require restatements or paraphrasing of reading passages? How might teachers, for example, foster students' reformulations and extensions of what they have read? How does this kind of learning differ from short-term recall of information? In secondary schools an entire range of both formal and informal writing assignments can be described as "analytic." In literature classes this might be an analysis of figurative language or characterization in a literary work; in history classes it might be an explanation of the significance of a historical event; in science classes it might be a comparison of two theories. In each case, students are required to move beyond reproducing or compressing information to a more specific or focused explanation.

With analytic writing students have access to a different tool for understanding new ideas and information: a focused examination of relations among ideas and events. Across a set of studies anchored in Britton's discourse theory, a consistent pattern has emerged of the kinds of thinking and reasoning fostered by analytic writing: a complex manipulation of ideas as a result of marshalling an argument to support a point of view and selecting language for representing it. All have dealt with writing based on the reading of a single text. Although analytic writing focuses on a narrow range of content in the reading passage when compared to answering study questions or summarizing, a more lasting representation of that content seems to develop through an integration and reformulation of ideas.[42]

This raises an important issue that Peter Winograd and I addressed when we studied the uses of writing made by a teacher who taught a general track class and an academic track class in U.S. history.[43] The teacher used analytic writing tasks with the academic track students, but she favored summary and review assignments for the general track. She was concerned about using analytic writing tasks with her general track students because with analytic writing they would have reviewed less information. This is the way she put it: "Knowing information and writing about it go hand-in-hand, but I still feel pressure—maybe it's just me—to make sure they know certain things and when they don't I try to get them caught up."[44] The teacher's dilemma lies not only in deciding which writing task to assign but also in deciding how to balance content coverage with students' efforts to make sense of the content. This becomes a very real and important practical problem when teaching is conceived as content coverage, a view that is a legacy of transmission notions of curriculum and instruction. This is not intended as a criticism of a particular teacher but to describe how a curricular tradition can shape a teacher's instructional decisions, in this case a teacher who was by all accounts concerned about her students' independence as thinkers. Winograd and I concluded that a large set of curricular problems needs to be resolved if analytic writing tasks, asking students to reformulate and extend their understanding, are to have purchase in secondary schools. Instead of simply calling for more writing or for reading-writing connections, we suggested a broader analysis of what is essential to knowing and doing in each subject area and of how such knowledge might be introduced in a coherent manner across the school year and across grade levels. To do so implies a new set of promises and a new vision of what it means to teach and to learn in school settings.

New Promises: Transforming Teaching and Learning

What, then, are the promises of writing to learn, especially in light of recent efforts to reform secondary schooling? First, rather than a more efficient way of covering content and of testing for memory of that content, writing assignments can become ways of exploring and making sense of new ideas and experiences. Second, writing-to-learn approaches to instruction can alter the roles of both the teacher (from evaluator to collaborator) and students (from memorizers to meaningmakers) and transform the perception of content-area information (from facts to be absorbed to ways of understanding oneself and one's cultural communities and their traditions). Third, with efforts to teach writing in all content areas, students may become more aware of a full range of conventions and genres used in various contexts, especially in the discourse communities of various academic disciplines and content fields.

This is a large agenda, much larger than that envisioned by writing professionals in the 1970s and early 1980s when WAC became a movement. How can we approach the new promises and problems fostered by emphasis on writing to learn?

Over the past twenty years, as writing has become a more central component of schooling, constructivist views of knowledge and understanding have emerged as a key part of the reform agenda. This is no coincidence. Although process-oriented and constructivist-oriented approaches to learning are not synonymous, they are compatible by virtue of the fact that both ask students to construct meanings and to work with ideas rather than passively absorb information. But process-oriented approaches to writing instruction and related arguments about the value of writing to learn have taken us just so far. They enable the conceptualization of what might be useful in a lesson or what activities might be effective for a group of students, but they do not address the issues of what knowledge is central or integral to learning in the content areas. Unless we develop a more coherent way to conceptualize curriculum as something more than lists of content, skills, and titles to be taught, teachers will continue to face the dilemma of the U.S. history teacher quoted earlier. Should students be asked to write about their growing understandings, or should teachers present facts "to get them caught up" before they write?

Accordingly, writing to learn would seem to have a more legitimate role in classrooms in which the teacher's curricular decisions are guided by, are compatible with, and are supportive of a vision of teaching and learning that enables students not only to know but to do. We need an approach to curriculum that complements constructivist approaches to writing instruction, one in which writing to learn from texts would play a central role. Students would discuss and write about their literary responses and not just memorize literary terms, authors, and titles; they would discuss and write historical analyses and not just be told the results of others' analyses. Writing would serve learning, but this would be only one of a number of factors in restructuring teaching and learning. Students' ideas and experiences would be central, especially in terms of how they contribute to the building of knowledge. These might concern, for instance, good and evil in a literature classroom or the metaphor of the "melting pot" in a U.S. history classroom. Writing and discussion would be used to explore ideas and to create a new sense of authority in students.[45] In this vision of teaching and learning, writing would have a central role as efforts are made to reform secondary schools.

Writing as Entry into Curricular Conversations

Although I cannot present a full picture of how discipline-based writing in the secondary schools might be developed, I will make some tentative suggestions based on Applebee's recent formulation of "curriculum as conversation," which suggests how students may participate in living traditions and conversation through knowledge in action.

Such knowledge arises out of participation in ongoing conversations about things that matter, conversations that are themselves embedded within larger traditions of discourse that we have come to value (science, the arts, history, literature, mathematics among many others). When we take this metaphor seriously, the development of curriculum becomes the development of significant domains of conversation, and instruction becomes a matter of helping students learn to participate in conversations within those domains.[46]

But what role might writing play in enabling students to enter into and participate in such conversations? If entering the curricular domain is contingent upon knowing the conventions of conversation of an academic domain—what is talked about, how, and why—learning to write within that domain must play a central role. Of course, participation will also be oral in the presentations and interactions that constitute the dialogue of instruction. But writing becomes a necessary medium for practicing the ways of organizing and presenting ideas that are most appropriate to a particular conversational domain within the content area. To enter the domain of literary studies, for example, students must be taught what kinds of interpretations are appropriate and how to marshal support for their arguments. However, such instructional concerns become evident only as the teacher begins to consider larger curricular issues concerning how writing and reading assignments might be integrated into an ongoing conversation about literary interpretation. For example, an issue such as whether responses should be based on literary texts or on personal experience may be revisited and reinterpreted in light of the literary themes under investigation. The use of primary sources in a U.S. history classroom becomes appropriate when such materials extend the conversation about the development of the thirteen colonies into a nation. And in a biology class writing about conclusions based on observations becomes more authentic when such activities are embedded in larger conversations about how biologists develop new theories.

Recent developments in "situated cognition" would seem to support Applebee's argument for knowledge-in-action as a way to engage students in significant cultural conversations. In their argument for the "situated" nature of cognition, John Seely Brown, Allan Collins, and Paul Duguid proposed "cognitive apprenticeship" as a means for students to acquire, develop, and use cognitive tools (such as writing and reading) in authentic domain activity.[47] Like Applebee, they see a teacher as a mentor who guides students in their learning of a tradition and their entering into a conversation. The teacher helps students become aware of strategies, offers instructional support, and removes support, when appropriate, in order to empower the students to work independently. Situated cognition and knowledge-in-action share another important feature. Both assume that conceptual knowledge can be fully understood only through use. Specific content has meaning, not in itself, but as it is used and situated in the larger context of academic traditions in which it is embedded.

As we look back on the origins of writing to learn and its continuing promises and consider just how much the wiser we are for these efforts, we can no longer expect to reconceptualize teaching and learning with theoretical arguments for, and studies of, writing and learning alone. For the exigencies of schooling are far too complex for such a narrow vision of reform. This does not negate the value of what effective teachers know about writing and learning, but it does suggest the need to rethink our original "strong text" version of reform that assumes that writing in brief, fragmented episodes is adequate. The problem is that we have focused on an approach to teaching and learning without asking the more difficult question of what is worth knowing and why. Accordingly, I have attempted to complicate and extend the promises of writing to learn by contextualizing this approach to teaching within a larger framework of curriculum. Such frameworks as the one proposed by Applebee would introduce students to the ongoing conversations about things that matter to them as individuals and to the cultural and intellectual communities in which they live. We should see a new generation of research and practice in writing to learn in the secondary school that attends to the values and conventions of different disciplines and content fields.

Notes

1. Ernest Boyer, *High School: A Report on Secondary Education in America* (New York: Harper and Row, 1983).

2. Theodore Sizer, *Horace's School* (Boston: Houghton Mifflin, 1992).

3. James Britton, Tony Burgess, Nancy Martin, Alex McLeod, and Harold Rosen, *The Development of Writing Abilities (11-18)* (London: Macmillan, 1975).

4. Arthur N. Applebee, "Environments for Language Teaching and Learning: Contemporary Issues and Future Directions," in *Handbook of Research on Teaching the English Language Arts,* eds. James Flood, Julie M. Jensen, Diane Lapp, and James R. Squire (New York: Macmillan, 1991), pp. 549-556; Nancy Nelson Spivey, "Transforming Texts: Constructive Processes in Reading and Writing," *Written Communication* 7 (1990): 256-287.

5. James Britton, *Language and Learning* (Middlesex, England: Penguin Books, 1970); Douglas Barnes, *From Communication to Curriculum* (New York: Penguin Books, 1976).

6. Jean Piaget, *Language and Thought of the Child,* trans. Marjorie Gabain (London: Routledge and Kegan Paul, 1959); Jerome S. Bruner, Ross R. Olver, Patricia M. Greenfield, and others, *Studies in Cognitive Growth* (New York: Wiley, 1966); Lev S. Vygotsky, *Thought and Language,* trans. Eugenia Hanfmann and Gertrude Vakar (Cambridge, Mass.: M.I.T. Press, 1962); George A. Kelly, *A Theory of Personality* (New York: Norton, 1963).

7. Britton, *Language and Learning,* p. 248.

8. Barnes, *From Communication to Curriculum,* p. 115.

9. Ibid., p. 28.

10. Arthur N. Applebee, *Curriculum as Conversation: Transforming Traditions of Teaching and Learning* (Chicago: University of Chicago Press, 1996), pp. 16-17.

11. John S. Mayher, *Uncommon Sense: Theoretical Practice in Language Education* (Portsmouth, N. H.: Boynton/Cook, 1990).

12. David Olson, "From Utterance to Text: The Bias of Language in Speech and Writing," *Harvard Educational Review* 47 (1977): 257-281; Jerome Bruner, *Toward a Theory of Instruction* (Cambridge, Mass.: Belknap-Harvard University Press, 1966).

13. Brian Street, *Literacy in Theory and Practice* (Cambridge: Cambridge University Press, 1984); Sylvia Scribner and Michael Cole, *The Psychology of Literacy* (Cambridge, Mass.: Harvard University Press, 1981).

14. Arthur N. Applebee, "Writing and Reasoning," *Review of Educational Research* 56 (1984): 577-596; David R. Russell, *Writing in the Academic Disciplines, 1870-1990: A Curricular History* (Carbondale: Southern Illinois University Press, 1991); James Berlin, *Rhetoric and Reality: Writing Instruction in American Colleges, 1900-1985* (Carbondale: Southern Illinois University Press, 1987).

15. Janet Emig, *The Composing Processes of Twelfth Graders* (Urbana, Ill.: National Council of Teachers of English, 1971).

16. Janet Emig, "Writing as Mode of Learning," *College Composition and Communication* 18 (1977): 122-128.

17. Chester Finn, *What Works: Research about Teaching and Learning* (Washington, D.C.: United States Department of Education, 1986).

18. Judith A. Langer and Arthur N. Applebee, *How Writing Shapes Thinking* (Urbana, Ill.: National Council of Teachers of English, 1987), pp. 6-7.

19. Ibid., p. 150.

20. Britton et al., *The Development of Writing Abilities.*

21. Arthur N. Applebee, *Writing in the Secondary School: English and the Content Areas* (Urbana, Ill.: National Council of Teachers of English, 1981).

22. Britton et al., *The Development of Writing Abilities.*

23. Nancy Martin, Pat D'Arcy, Brian Newton, and Robert Parker, *Writing and Learning across the Curriculum 11-16; Schools Council Project* (Montclair, N. J.: Boynton/Cook, 1976).

24. Nancy Martin, "Language across the Curriculum: Where It Began and What It Promises," in *Writing, Teaching, and Learning in the Disciplines,* eds. Anne Herrington and Charles Moran (New York: Modern Language Association of America, 1992), pp. 6-21.

25. See Russell's *Writing in the Academic Disciplines* for a history of writing across the curriculum at the college level. Colleges and universities have taken more seriously the agenda for writing across the curriculum than have American secondary schools.

26. Langer and Applebee, *How Writing Shapes Thinking*; Sarah Freedman, *Exchanging Writing, Exchanging Cultures* (Cambridge, Mass.: Harvard University Press, 1992); Russell, *Writing in the Academic Disciplines*; James Kinneavy, "Writing across the Curriculum," *Association of Departments of English Bulletin* 76 (1983): 7-14; Toby Fulwiler, "How Well Does Writing across the Curriculum Work?" *College English* 46 (1984): 113-125; Deborah Swanson-Owens, "Identifying Natural Sources of Resistance: A Case Study of Implementing Writing across the Curriculum," *Research in the Teaching of English* 20 (1986): 69-97.

27. Anne Ruggles Gere, ed. *Roots in the Sawdust: Writing to Learn across the Disciplines* (Urbana, Ill.: National Council of Teachers of English, 1985).

28. Judith A. Langer, "Speaking of Knowing: Conceptions of Understanding in Academic Disciplines," in *Writing, Teaching, and Learning in the Disciplines*, eds. Anne Herrington and Charles Moran (New York: Modern Language Association of America, 1992).

29. John M. Ackerman, "The Promise of Writing to Learn," *Written Communication* 10 (1993): 334-370.

30. James Britton, *Language and Learning*.

31. Langer and Applebee, *How Writing Shapes Thinking*.

32. Deborah Brandt, *Literacy as Involvement: The Acts of Writers, Readers, and Texts* (Carbondale, Ill.: Southern Illinois University Press, 1990); Brian Street, *Literacy in Theory and Practice* (Cambridge: Cambridge University Press, 1984): Shirley Brice Heath, *Ways with Words* (Avon: Cambridge University Press, 1983).

33. James Britton, "Response in Re-Presenting James Britton: A Symposium," *College Composition and Communication* 41 (1990): 166-188.

34. Ackerman, "The Promise of Writing to Learn."

35. Britton, *Language and Learning*; Britton et al., *The Development of Writing Abilities*.

36. Applebee, *Writing in the Secondary School*.

37. See reviews of other work in Ackerman, "The Promise of Writing to Learn"; Russel K. Durst and George E. Newell, "The Uses of Function: James Britton's Category System and Research in Writing," *Review of Educational Research* 59 (1989): 375-394; William McGinley and Robert J. Tierney, "Traversing the Tropical Landscape," *Written Communication* 6 (1989): 243-269; Spivey, "Transforming Texts."

38. See Langer and Applebee, *How Writing Shapes Thinking*; George E. Newell and Peter Winograd, "Writing about and Learning from History Texts: The Effects of Task and Academic Ability," *Research in the Teaching of English* 29 (1995); 133-163; Judith A. Langer, "The Effects of Available Information on Responses to School Writing Tasks," *Research in the Teaching of English* 18 (1984): 27-44.

39. Langer and Applebee, *How Writing Shapes Thinking*, p. 34.

40. George E. Newell, "Learning from Writing in Two Content Areas: A Case Study/Protocol Analysis," *Research in the Teaching of English* 18 (1984): 365-387; Newell and Winograd, "Writing about and Learning from History Texts."

41. Suzanne Hidi and Vicki Anderson, "Producing Written Summaries: Task Demands, Cognitive Operation, and Implications for Instruction," *Review of Educational Research* 56 (1986): 473-492; Russel K. Durst, "Cognitive and Linguistic Demands of Analytic Writing," *Research in the Teaching of English* 21: 347-376; Langer and Applebee, *How Writing Shapes Thinking*.

42. Newell, "Learning from Writing"; Newell and Winograd, "Writing about and Learning from History Texts"; Durst, "Cognitive and Linguistic Demands"; Langer and Applebee, *How Writing Shapes Thinking*; Stuart Greene, "The Role of Task in the Development of Academic Thinking through Reading and Writing in a College History Course," *Research in the Teaching of English* 27 (1993): 46-75; James D. Marshall, "The Effects of Writing on Students' Understanding of Literary Texts," *Research in the Teaching of English* 21 (1987): 30-63.

43. Newell and Winograd, "Writing about and Learning from History Texts," p. 160.

44. Ibid.

45. Judith A. Langer, "Literacy Instruction in American Schools: Problems and Perspectives," *American Journal of Education* 93 (1984): 107-132.

46. Applebee, *Curriculum as Conversation*, p. 3.

47. John Seely Brown, Allan Collins, and Paul Duguid, "Situated Cognition and the Culture of Learning," *Educational Researcher* 18 (1989): 32-42.

CHAPTER IX

Leading Middle Grade Students from Reading to Writing: Conceptual and Practical Aspects

ROBERT C. CALFEE

Oral language and literacy are both acquired over time, reflecting development, learning, and (ofttimes) teaching. Oral language develops naturally; literacy takes some work. This chapter reviews the reading-writing-language connection during a critical period in the educational experience of many students—the years between the primary and secondary grades, from about third through eighth grade in the United States. Before they enter this stretch, students are viewed as children, they spend the school day with a single teacher, they depend on substantial instructional support, grades are not that serious, and school is mostly "fun." On the other side of this chasm, students have become young adults, the school day is a rush from one fifty-minute class to the next, instructional support consists of assignments, grades determine lifelong outcomes, and school (other than the social milieu) is mostly hard work.

The primary student is clearly a novice. More instructional time is allocated to reading, less to writing.[1] Texts are mostly stories, the emphasis is on acquiring skills in word identification and fluent oral reading, and comprehension focuses on literal recall and retelling. The teacher directs reading instruction, often following a basal reader script. Writing is more student-centered; children are encouraged to compose using "invented spellings," and the teacher feels free to serve as "stenographer."[2] By the end of first grade, writing appears as journal entries, a sentence or two recounting a personal experience, usually prepared for the teacher's response, often evoking a smiley face and brief comment. Writing instruction remains relatively low-key; the teacher encourages student efforts and offers positive responses, relying on personal intuition more than prescribed manual. Oral language development—rich and sustained classroom discourse—is an essential

---

Robert C. Calfee is Professor in the School of Education, Stanford University, and coeditor of this volume.

curriculum goal. These trends stand against a background of diverse practices, to be sure, but by the mid-elementary years, important shifts emerge, with greater emphasis on writing, more reliance on individual student effort, and increased accountability. Student work is graded, and school effectiveness is judged by statewide assessments.

The high school student is expected to perform as an expert, in the sense of having mastered certain fundamentals. Basic reading is taken for granted, and basic writing is assigned rather than taught.[3] English classes emphasize critical interpretation and appreciation of literary works, along with grammatical and compositional skills. Other subject matters rely on expository texts to transmit content knowledge, which students are expected to absorb. The teacher's role is to provide further information and analysis, typically through lectures, and to promulgate assignments. Students are expected to work independently on complex tasks.

What happens in the middle? I address this question in this chapter, not because an enormous amount of research is available (it is not), but because the question is important for theory and practice, and because tools developed for other purposes bear on the issues. Following this introduction, I present background thoughts and a conceptual framework, and then examine *book reports* and *research papers* as practical instantiations of the reading-writing connection during the middle grades. Primary grade teachers seldom assign these tasks to their students; high school teachers give high priority to ensuring that their students perform well on assignments built upon these foundational competencies.

The contrast between narrative and expository text structures provides one focus for the chapter. Book reports typically transform narratives into expositions, while research papers begin with a writing assignment that requires analysis and synthesis of information from multiple texts. The emphasis in book reports is the movement from reading to writing, while the research paper starts with the written product, with other texts serving as resources.

A second theme is the student's development of *formal language* during the middle grades, partly through the acquisition of reading and writing, but also through a shift in language style marked by increasing sensitivity to the importance of explicitness and strategic forethought for effective communication.[4]

The final theme, more question than answer, centers around the nature of *reading-writing connections* during these years, and the "value added" from various techniques for integrating language and literacy.

The middle grades are complex and troublesome, a mixture of changing organizational arrangements, adolescent turmoil, subject matter specialization, and movement beyond the basics.[5] Questions arise, especially for students experiencing academic problems. Who should teach reading? Writing? About the connection between the two?

Background Thoughts

Like other authors in this yearbook, I have my own "spin" on the reading-writing connection. My first turn inquires about the well-springs of *disconnectedness*. My work has centered around the elementary reading side of the equation, and I have only lately arrived at writing and the middle grades. These interests emerged from the realization that (a) composing opens doors to comprehension at all developmental levels, (b) primary reading programs seldom provide students the rhetorical tools needed to communicate in various media, and (c) examination of middle and secondary literacy programs casts primary grade issues in a more informative light.

These changes in my perspective entail some embarrassment. More than a decade ago, as Priscilla Drum and I prepared the reading chapter for the *Handbook of Research on Teaching*,[6] we surveyed corollary chapters in previous handbooks; if we considered the parallel literature in writing, I cannot remember it. We are not alone. To be sure, Elfrieda Hiebert and Taffy Raphael in the *Handbook of Educational Psychology* treat reading and writing as an integrated package, but I have yet to find another handbook chapter designed in this fashion.[7] The separation of reading and writing (and the relatively slim offerings for the latter) in previous NSSE Yearbooks also speaks to the issue. On the positive side, chapters in this volume show researchers attending to the connections.

My second spin is, "What about—'If it ain't broke, break it'?" One might argue that reading and writing are so interwoven as to require no separation for either research or practice. Teach one and you foster the other; investigate one and you understand the other. Correlations between reading and writing performance appear to support the proposition that reading and writing are fundamentally connected.[8]

The case is yet to be made. For instance, high correlations, when they appear, may well reflect assessment methods of questionable validity. Reading indicators typically rely on multiple-choice tests and oral reading performance, whereas students must demonstrate their writing achievement by actually composing a paper, the quality of which a teacher judges. These are large task differences, but both are typically performed under severe time pressure in decontextualized situations. High correlations may simply mean that some students manage such situations better than others. Fundamental questions about the distinctiveness and interconnectedness of reading and writing cannot be answered by product-moment correlations.

My third puzzlement centers around the *separation of reading and writing practice* in both primary and upper elementary/middle school classrooms: different times, methods, books, language, models, purposes. My experiences in classrooms, first to observe reading, more recently to look at writing, and to try my hand at teaching, have perplexed me.

Consider, for example, the technical language of reading and writing instruction. Today's young writers talk about how they *plan, draft, revise, edit, present,* at least in the more interesting situations. These aspects of the writing process are typically quite explicit. Young readers, in contrast, *read, answer questions,* and *answer more questions.* Not very illuminating. To be sure, certain essential elements of the reading process are difficult to observe and may seem mysterious. As a consequence, *read* can come to mean translating print into speech and answering literal questions about the text.

The language of classroom practice hints that *different activities and processes underlie reading and writing;* my fourth set of background issues springs from this matter. It is complicated by overlaps and contrasts between literacy tasks. As noted above, writing "clearly" differs from reading. But both build on language, on symbol systems, on linguistic features (words, sentences, paragraphs). The psycholinguistic similarities are compelling both theoretically and practically.

For instance, both reading and writing investigators contrast *serial* with *parallel* models, offering supportive data for each position. In a popular serial model of the reading process, for example, reading moves in turn through letter perception, translation of print to speech, identification of word meaning, unpacking sentence grammar, and eventually comprehension of paragraphs and the entire passage. The corresponding model for writing reverses these steps, starting with ideas and ending with letter strings. Parallel models sometimes argue for similar components but allow complex iterations.[9] The reader may re-examine word meaning in the middle of a sentence when comprehension fails; the writer may change a word because of developments later in the sentence. Other parallel models resist the idea of distinctive components altogether, claiming that both reading and writing are inherently wholistic and cannot be decomposed into more fundamental elements.

Empirical findings do not presently permit a choice among these models—and probably never will. The iterative model offers a useful compromise; separable components exist, but these operate in a flexible fashion. This choice provides a small plot of theoretical ground on which to stand, while allowing room to maneuver. But let me question the "one model fits all" assumption. Reading and writing processes are probably a source of both between- and within-individual variation, reflecting what a student has been taught and has learned, as well as the task and situation. My early reading instruction emphasized letter-sound regularities, which now serves me well for pronouncing and spelling a word like *shinplaster* (although not with the meaning), but helps me not at all when pronouncing or spelling the name of an esteemed colleague, Mihaly Csikszentmihalyi (the meaning springs from other sources). Others might find the first-mentioned word a greater challenge on both counts, and the second word quite easy. Our thought processes reflect our experiences, and theorists will likely search in vain for the one best model of either reading or writing, which need not leave us in shambles. A question raised throughout this volume is how combining reading and writing may influence the underlying processes—for instance, by helping the student see relations among these activities.[10]

A fifth set of background connections flavoring this chapter springs from my practical encounters with the tradition of *integrated language arts*,[11] a blend of philosophy and practice, progressive education, and social constructivist techniques. This approach is grounded in linguistics, in the careful study of spoken language, and in a view of literacy as the acquisition of the formal style of language usage mentioned earlier. The assumption is that all forms of language—reading, writing, speaking, and listening—operate from a common core, and that literacy development cuts across these forms. The way then opens for discussion of the effects of literacy on oral as well as print-based activities, on the linguistic domains of phonology, semantics, syntax, and on the discourse forms of narration and exposition.

A Conceptual Framework

The preceding section raises numerous questions. In this section I present a conceptual framework, *CORE*, laying out a social-cognitive analysis of literacy instruction and acquisition as a foundation for addressing these questions.[12] The acronym, which stands for *connect, organize, reflect,* and *extend,* incorporates themes found elsewhere in this volume. The matrix in Figure 1 displays key elements and relations encompassed by the CORE framework. This structure is a placekeeper more than a model, a design for organizing the current cacophony of ideas and practices. The framework addresses deep-structure issues in comprehension and composition. It does not specify a particular process model, but identifies essential components that need to be addressed by any model, while offering a platform for examining similarities and distinctions between reading and writing.[13] The column entries along the top are pragmatic—two major domains of the middle-grades curriculum. "Reading" refers to tasks where the starting point is a text, a book or article to be understood for some purpose. "Writing" includes assignments where the starting point is a composition, a text to be created by the student.

The CORE entries along the side spring from social-cognitive research and theory.[14] *Connect*—acquisition of new knowledge proceeds most effectively when it builds on prior knowledge. *Organize*—the human mind searches for patterns, and complex information is most efficiently remembered when it can be structured or "chunked." *Reflect*—psychological research on transfer and metacognition (thinking about thinking) shows that new learning is most far-reaching when the student stands aside from the details and considers applications to other situations. *Extend*—the test of transfer occurs when the student applies short-term learning to more complex tasks. The sub-elements for each entry identify significant concepts and processes that operationalize the entry. The four components operate in dynamic rather than linear fashion; the idea is *not* that the student connects, then organizes, and so on. CORE is not a sequence of events, but a set of lenses through which to view complex reading-writing activities.

Within each cell, snippets from classroom activities aim to communicate key ideas. For example, the Author's Chair described in chapter 4 provides opportunities for young writers to reflect on their work while an audience of fellow classmates reacts to their compositions.[15] The Book Club[16] is a parallel activity in which elementary students share their personal reactions to literary works, drawing forth reflections about what it means to appreciate and interpret, to analyze an author's intent and style. As these two examples suggest, activities "slop over" from one cell to another. The idea behind the entries is to suggest how one might identify the significant contributions and multiple facets found in classroom practice.

	READING	WRITING
CONNECT		
Content Knowledge	Develop webs and semantic maps of prior knowledge, including ideas and key vocabulary	Lay out background knowledge, other sources of information, check the library
Style	Identify text as narrative or expository, casual or technical	Decide on approach: narrative, informational, explanatory, persuasive
Purpose	Find out reason for reading: appreciation, information, argumentation, etc.	Be clear about the reason for writing: an assignment, getting something, personal expression, fun, etc.
Community	Discover "what's on the test," who can provide resources during task	Who is the audience, what can they learn from the composition
ORGANIZE		
Content Structure	Look for natural clusters among the ideas, often part of webbing/mapping	Build clusters from the ideas and words that have been collected
Rhetorical Structure	Locate episodic chunks and main characters in narrative, elements and relations in exposition (headings help)	Outline the main parts of the composition (for expositions) or (probably more effective) explore various graphic organizers
Selection/ Expansion	Find main events and main ideas, think about what you can ignore and what else you need to know	Sort through the collection and decide what is most important, what can be tossed, what needs to be added
REFLECT		
Preparation	"Get ready for the story," often the start of the reading lesson, *connection* but also a chance to reflect	Hold a planning discussion of the writing assignment
Discussion/ "Digestion"	Talk with someone else during reading (often called "paired reading")	Use collaborative writing peer groups to design the composition, either as a team project or to support individual work
Review	Think about the text, including summaries and journal notes; the *Book Club* activity	Arrange a critique of the final product, as in the *Author's Chair* activity
EXTEND		
Initial Steps	Prepare a summary of main ideas from the initial reading of the text	Prepare a rough draft, turning organizational sketches into sentences and paragraphs
Refinement	Reread the article, looking for additional information and ideas	Finetune the draft, revising and polishing at various levels, including grammar/spelling
Presentation	Decide on the main points for focus, and how to communicate what you have understood and enjoyed	"Publish" the final work, by sharing with classmates and parents, posting on the bulletin board, or presenting to a real "audience"

Fig. 1. CORE: A social-cognitive analysis of middle grade literacy instruction and acquisition

I will rely on the CORE framework throughout the following sections on *book reports* and *research papers*. A few words about the choice of these two activities. As we approach a new millennium, one might think that these apparent anachronisms would have gone the way of McGuffey's Readers. In fact, just as McGuffey's mutated into the basal readers that now range from phonics-based to literature-centered programs, so the essentials of book reports and research papers remain an essential part of classroom practice, often under different names. *Response journals* and *personal reading logs* are more "personal" and reader-writer-friendly than *book reports*, though they may serve the same purposes. For *research papers*, the emphasis is more likely to fall on the first word—hence, *RESEARCH paper*—and who can complain about doing "research"? My aim in choosing these two activities is to span a broad range of reading-writing tasks that encompass both narrative and expository genres. In the middle grades, *book reports* range from a brief journal note about "Why I liked _____" to a three-page review of thematic issues in Hemingway's *The Old Man and the Sea*. Research papers might be a short paragraph on "My favorite mammal" or a two-page essay explaining the effect of geographic features on the local environment.[17]

Data on the frequency with which such tasks are assigned is hard to come by, perhaps because of the assumed demise of the genres. National Assessment of Educational Progress (NAEP) surveys offer a glimpse through students' eyes. In 1994, when asked about writing assignments, 38 percent of fourth graders said they wrote a book report every week, dropping to 28 percent by eleventh grade. Essays and "other reports" were a weekly occurrence for 60 percent of fourth graders, while 70 percent of eleventh graders wrote one or more reports per week. NAEP did not record teacher perceptions, but Applebee's[18] survey of high school English teachers supports the previous findings. Teachers assigned three to four pages of writing per week, more book reports for freshmen, more research papers for seniors, the latter more text-based than student-centered. The teachers reported attending writing-process workshops, but their bottom line, especially for college-bound students, was the quality of the final product.

The point is that these two genres are far from dead, and can serve as springboards for conceptual analysis and research review. The discussions that follow may exaggerate some distinctions. We can imagine a student picking a book based on personal interest and preparing a report, but he or she may instead decide on a writing topic and then select a narrative to fit. Research papers usually begin with an assigned problem for which the student must track down resources (primary texts, encyclopedias, Encarta or the Web), but an expository piece may be selected by the student or assigned by the teacher as the starting point. The contrast between narratives and expositions is a fundamental distinction, however, as is the difference between preparing to read versus preparing to write.

Book Reports: From Reading to Writing

"We are going to the library. Pick a book to read. When you have finished it, write a report. Tell what it was about, and what you really liked." This experience is so ubiquitous for my readers that you have probably not thought of it as an object for review and research. Educators have tried to stamp it out in recent years,[19] but like the five-paragraph essay, it has survived the assaults and remains a mainstay in the middle grades. As the practical centerpiece for this section, it embodies a significant classroom activity that joins reading with writing.[20]

How should a student read a story to prepare for the task? How should a student write a book report? Why should a student perform this task? Answers to the "Why" question actually appear in the research literature. Teachers employ book reports for a variety of reasons: as a demonstration to parents that students are "reading," as a homework assignment, and as a context for applying skills in grammar and punctuation.[21] These purposes are practical enough, but lack intrinsic motivation and do little to promote either literary appreciation or skills of literary criticism, which may be why students (and others) often view book reports as boring and pointless.

Answers to the "how" questions are harder to come by; neither research literature nor contemporary books on methods of teaching reading offer much help, nor are teachers especially articulate. Experience offers some help for students. Generations have passed along the dust jacket strategy: be sure the book has a jacket, and paraphrase the summary and comments found there. It solves the "how to read" problem, and usually works unless you simply copy. Scarcely what most teachers have in mind, but students who do not learn an effective and efficient strategy are in trouble.

Ten years ago I spent several months as a teacher's assistant in a middle school remedial class. Students spent most of the class period completing worksheets, but each month they read a book of their choosing, for which they then prepared a report summarizing the story and selecting ten words to "define." One student conveyed to me the frustration felt by many in the class: "I read the book, and that's ok. But then I have to go back and read it again for the report, and that's boring. . . ." My recommendation—and it worked for many students—was to make notes along the way, keeping track of characters, plot episodes, and "vocabulary words," being sure to record page numbers for later reference. Part of the answer to the question "How to read a book for a book report?" is to write as you read, and so I designed a *Story Notes* sheet for this purpose. One might argue that note-taking interferes with aesthetic experience, and it certainly may. For these students, however, literary appreciation was beside the point, and *Story Notes* offered a practical solution to a practical problem.

In the remainder of this section I look more closely at the assignment and purpose of book report tasks, and then the process of completing the assignment, including the interplay of instruction and learning outcomes, bringing available research on the reading-writing connection to bear as I proceed.

ASSIGNMENT AND PURPOSE

The book report assignment appears simple enough on the surface: select a book, read it, and write a report. Behind this apparent simplicity reside numerous decisions for both teacher and student. One is the choice of a story or narrative, what teachers and students call a "chapter book," as the starting point. The student who selects an informational book on volcanoes or Native Americans may confront complexities that neither he nor (most likely) the teacher can easily negotiate. The assignment seldom clarifies the genre distinction; in the primary grades, directions may be to "Pick a book that you like," while in the later grades length may be the chief criterion (a short story will not suffice).

Another decision centers around *content*. Before third grade, the report may be an entry in a "response journal," a sentence or two about "What I liked best" as a reading record and an opportunity for teacher response.[22] By eighth grade, the report *must* include a summary and *may* include commentary. As it turns out, summarizing a narrative poses a challenge. One approach is a brief retelling, but what to include and what to leave out? Another approach is to analyze a key literary element—a significant character or episode. Or the student may attempt a thematic strategy, organizing various elements around a central concept. I have encountered interesting anecdotes describing how teachers guide students in structuring a report,[23] but have found little systematic research from the middle grades on this question.

A final decision centers around the *appearance* of the final product. In high school and college, quality and depth of the analysis may matter, but elementary and middle school teachers have limited background and time for mulling a student's review of Katherine Paterson's *Bridge to Terebithia*, and are more likely to assess spelling, punctuation, and grammar. Preservice textbooks often characterize student response to literature as an intensely personal matter, not to be disrupted by the threat of critical response, and with little advice about how to design an assignment to support particular learning outcomes.[24] Suggestions range from art (sketches, dioramas) to acting out (class discussion, a play, a radio broadcast) and written products (a letter to the author, an alternative ending). Creative alternatives, but the teacher is left to connect the assignment to definable outcomes.

To summarize, book report assignments tend to be rather diffuse at all grades, focused on practical purposes like record keeping and opportunities to practice basic writing skills. I did locate one example of a more structured and comprehensive approach. Stewig[25] describes strategies for connecting children's literature to a variety of writing exercises that (a) motivate transfer from reading to writing, (b) lead students through discussions that help explicate story structure, and (c) promote strategic text-based writing similar to that described in the next section. The monograph was written over two decades ago, and offers no empirical evidence of program outcomes, but is notable for the contrast with current practice.

COMPLETING THE ASSIGNMENT: INSTRUCTION AND LEARNING

How do students and teachers move from assignment to product to response? This section is organized around three issues: the role of the text, the process of writing, and developmental trends. The CORE model serves throughout as a lens.

What might a student learn by reading a story for purposes of literary analysis? After all, relatively few workplace opportunities depend on an individual's skill in recounting and analyzing a work like Conrad's *Heart of Darkness*. One answer is that literary works offer a relatively engaging situation for learning about *content*, *structure*, and *style*, although transfer to more demanding expository texts is not guaranteed. Second, good literature can lead to exploration of moral issues that are important in their own right, and familiarity with cultural artifacts is a mark of the educated person.[26] Finally, digging more deeply into a variety of stories offers students an understanding of why some stories are judged more highly than others, and of their own personal likes and dislikes.

At a practical level, the assignment prepares students for close textual reading (see chapter 11), a task that they will encounter throughout high school and college, and a foundation for analyzing increasingly difficult material. A close reading begins with content, with the "stuff" of the story.[27] Comprehending this "stuff" entails a *connection* with the student's background knowledge and interests (for both narrative and expository texts). Story content exists at a variety of levels, and an important issue in composing a book report is the choice of level. The student who reads E. B. White's *Charlotte's Web* may come away with thoughts about spiders and pigs, but a deeper message comes from connecting to an experience in which an antagonistic relationship develops into intense friendship. Missing in current research are systematic studies of how connectedness, both surface-level and more profound, affects the comprehension-composition linkage, and vice versa. Stories convey content; how can new information combine with previous knowledge to help a student construct a work that is rather unique.

Much is known about narrative *organization* from the work of both literary analysts and story grammarians. The basic elements of character, plot, setting, and theme are familiar to most of us, as is experience with the broad range of edifices that can be constructed upon these foundations.[28] Knowledge of these structural features offers two outcomes for students. First is the analysis of simple models as a basis for composing book reports, and second is the blueprint for authoring complex narratives.[29] As to the second point, researchers have demonstrated that students can learn to use model stories to good advantage as templates for their own works, especially when the underlying structure is made clear. An 11-year-old's statement is typical: "I think about what I've read and kinda put it the way I read it." A second grader talks about "borrowing" structure (and style) from other authors in writing to her aunt (who guided these efforts). More important for present purposes is the use of structural features as the basis for summarization and analysis. Most work on this matter has focused on either text analysis or summarization as a strategy for reading comprehension, or on graphic organizers and prewriting notes for writing, with only a few asides on the linkage between these two domains.[30]

I have found little research or practical advice on "model book reports," and nothing that employs narrative structure as the starting point.[31] A large gap exists between the New York Times *Book Review* (most high school and college teachers would probably accept these contributions as appropriate models) and the typical middle-grades reading log entry ("*The Count of Monte Cristo*, by Alexander Dumas, this thrilling adventure story is about a dashing young hero, named Edmond Dantes, who is betrayed by his enemies, and thrown into a secret dungeon. Eventually, he escapes, and gets revenge"[32]). How should a student design a book report and connect various story structures to this design? The literary criticism described by Mathison in chapter 11 is the end point; the path to this goal is less clear.

Reflection, the third component of the CORE model, appears infrequently in either research or practice on book reports. One instance springs from research on oral discussions of literary works (e.g., the Book Club), but these are seldom coupled to written analysis. An interesting (but defunct) example appears in the California Learning Assessment System. Students first read a passage (either narrative or expository), adding marginal notes and answering factual and analytic questions about the text. They then gathered in groups to discuss reactions to the story and to prepare a composition around a thematic prompt based on the initial passage. Each student then wrote an essay on the theme. Missing from the assessment (and from most instructional practice), however, was reference to the structural features of narrative writing (character, plot, setting).[33]

Style is seldom mentioned in the book report literature. I have uncovered a few allusions to the value of literary works for illustrating word choice and figurative language. Practically speaking, however, these examples are mostly decontextualized exercises in which students search for metaphors and similes in fairly rote fashion, without consideration of the value of these devices for supporting an author's goals in a particular instance.

Beyond analyzing and preparing for the task, how does actual writing take place for book reports—the *extension* element of the CORE model? As noted in chapter 1, writing-process methods have been widely adopted in schools in the United States, balancing "how to compose" and the final product. The writing-process movement spans the spectrum from preschool through college, but has found especially comfortable niches in the narrative genre, in free writing, and in the early grades. The second grader writing about a personal experience is encouraged by advice to plan, to draft, to "risk," assured that the product will be celebrated rather than critiqued. The tenth grader preparing an analytic essay on Orwell's *1984* for an advanced placement English class might welcome the same support, but he or she is also aware of the importance of the final product. The middle grades book report must somehow bridge these two situations.

Both reading and writing change dramatically during this developmental transition, but the biggest impact shows up in the actual writing. The third grader possesses some degree of comfort with the writing process—planning, drafting, and final revision. The book report format offers a setting for this process that places reasonable demands on the student. The narrative genre is familiar, attractive stories are available in wide variety, and "product quality" is tolerable. By the end of eighth grade, students need to have mastered the essentials of this format, so that they can run on "automatic" in planning literary essays around more complex and less accessible narratives, while directing mental energy to the more strategic and analytic tasks of literary critique expected in high school and college. Automaticity and the capacity to see beneath the surface features distinguish the expert from the novice.[34] Unfortunately, in the area of literary analysis as elsewhere, we know more about end points than movement from beginner toward mastery.

Research Papers: From Writing to Reading

Monday morning in a sixth grade classroom. "This week's assignment is a paper on a historical hero. The main thing is that the person has to be dead. You may already have someone in mind. No matter, the librarian will help you find where to look for famous people in the card catalogue and the biography section. You have to use at least three different sources for the report. The paper has to be at least two pages long. You need a title and a reference section—the librarian can also help you with the references. We go to the library at 10 o'clock. You'll have an hour this morning and another hour on Wednesday for your research. Remember to take some paper for note taking. The paper is due on Friday. Hand in the outline on Tuesday, and show me your draft on Thursday morning. Remember big margins and neat handwriting." Once more, these words should strike a chord. Two pages or twenty, a week or a month, the starting point is a writing assignment that requires the student to locate one or more texts as background resources, where crafting the composition is chiefly the student's responsibility.[35]

The research paper can be serious business. Most teacher textbooks on literacy instruction cover this topic, and they do not berate the activity. They may complain about the "unreality" of such assignments, but they do not reject them out of hand. Research papers reveal what a student has learned about a topic: "reading to learn" links naturally to "writing to learn." Students do find shortcuts, most notably the "encyclopedia approach."[36] We have all read student papers that are little more than regurgitation, lacking the depth of processing that is the instructional goal.

Research papers demand advanced skills and strategies, and typically appear around fifth or sixth grade. One difficulty springs from the use of exposition both as the source material and the form of the report. Expository texts are tougher to comprehend, and students prefer to write personal narratives. Research papers often require students to hunt for multiple sources—another challenge. Finally, who has the responsibility for teaching students how to handle these assignments? From the middle school onward, English teachers see their job as literature (including literary critique) and composition (grammar); research papers are the province of social studies and science teachers. To be sure, teacher textbooks abound in "reading across the content areas," but "writing across the content areas" is less common at this level.[37]

ASSIGNMENT AND PURPOSE

Research papers typically begin with a topic and a writing task. States or countries, inventions or imaginations, animals, vegetables, or minerals—"pick an item from the category, look it up in the library or an encyclopedia, and write a two-page paper." A model may be offered, and the five-paragraph essay is still a popular starting point. Technical details like citations and graphics may be required. The assignment often prescribes length and form. Reproduction of information is the implicit goal in these compositions. Assignments infrequently call for analysis, explanation, or argument, and external assessments demonstrate that few students can handle such tasks. For instance, the 1994

National Assessment of Educational Progress (NAEP) writing surveys showed that the majority of eighth graders performed at the "Adequate" level when asked to report information from a text, but fewer than one in eight could write "Adequate" analytic papers or persuasive refutations of a position paper.[38]

Purpose and audience for research papers in the middle grades are straightforward: typically to demonstrate content knowledge and writing skills for the classroom teacher, and as a basis for grading. The following section describes attempts to develop and evaluate programs in some of which students encounter more authentic reading-writing tasks, where the purpose is convincing and the audience is genuine.

COMPLETING THE ASSIGNMENT: INSTRUCTION AND LEARNING

How can teachers most effectively support student learning and assess performance outcomes? The literature provides more answers for research papers than for book reports. The advice is partly process-oriented—pick a theme, locate sources, take notes and summarize, write and revise.[39] Many suggestions cover technical details: library procedures, citational style, titles and headings, proper punctuation, and so on. A few programs have probed deeper issues. In *Making Thinking Visible*, a project of Linda Flower and colleagues, adolescents at risk for academic failure are immersed in "real writing," mostly around argumentative texts prepared by collaborative groups on hot topics like drugs, teen pregnancies, and school reform.[40] The project relies on personal knowledge more than text resources, to be sure, but the latter (including newspapers and magazines) could certainly serve a useful role. Flower's findings are quite encouraging about the potential for adolescent students to perform these tasks remarkably well when the proper stage is set.

The CORE model offers perspectives on the research paper assignment that help integrate existing studies and point out missing pieces in the puzzle. *Connect* encompasses the broad range of activities and information used by the student to make sense of the task. Since the ultimate outcome is a written work, students should review basic matters like audience, purpose, and voice—matters that are too often missing from the assignment. The implicit answers may not satisfy, to be sure—"You are writing this paper because I have decided to assign it, I will read it and grade it, and spelling and length matter." Raphael and Boyd interviewed fourth and fifth graders about how they approached an integrative writing task, and found them largely unclear about the purpose; students seldom considered audience or voice, but instead mimicked the source texts.[41] These facets are more significant for research papers than for book reports, partly because of the expository nature of the task, and partly because the content may be less personally engaging. Informational texts and tasks sometimes have intrinsic motivational force,[42] but most readers would probably rather curl up with Michael Crichton than Stephen Hawking, and would rather discuss themes in *Jurassic Park* than the physics of black holes.

A second domain of connections centers around content; how to find out about armadillos, for instance. Research papers typically require students to go beyond personal knowledge to locate new information from complex textual sources. A large research literature is available on expository comprehension, showing the importance of text structure.[43] When the reading task is not thorough digestion of the details but previewing, skimming, selecting, and note taking, a sparser literature is available.[44] *Connecting* to prepare a research report in the middle grades requires the student to develop efficient "search strategies," the capacity to identify informational categories and conduct rapid scans of data bases, homing in or specific sources when appropriate. Reading must shift quickly from broad ranging overviews to selective and intense examination.

Once a student has assembled an information base for a paper, next comes the task of arranging the material into a coherent form—*organize* in the CORE model. This job depends partly on the topic. To recount a historical event like Pearl Harbor Day, the most natural plan is sequential; describing the differences between the dog and cat families may better begin with similarities as a foundation for laying out the contrasts. Purpose also determines form. Describing the events of Pearl Harbor Day may call for a time line, but an argumentative piece comparing the role of various nations in precipitating the attack requires a compare-contrast matrix.

Structural features also play a vital role in organizing the research. paper. "Writing from models" is a commonplace activity for teaching text structures. While not the favorite of many English teachers, examples of well-organized texts (five-paragraph essays, compare-contrast compositions, thesis-development arguments) can help students achieve greater coherence than when left to their own devices.[45] The concern, of course, is that writers may hew too closely to the model. College-level "basic writers" (i.e., remedial students) tend to stick so tightly to the source that they fail to achieve teachers' goals of analysis and commentary.[46] Note that *text models* serve a different function than *text resources*. The texts that a student discovers while hunting for information may not provide good models for the research paper, although one can imagine counterexamples (e.g., newspapers). Teachers using writing-process procedures often recommend graphic organizers as a foundation for expository writing, a promising idea, and a few investigations have studied the impact of direct instruction on text structures (including graphic organizers) as a design strategy for middle grades writing.[47]

Reflection for research papers shares much in common with book reports, but with a change in developmental context. Group projects are acceptable and even encouraged in the elementary grades, but individual work is more typical in junior high school. Research suggests that collaboration and the opportunity to discuss writing projects promotes reflective learning at all grades, whether in group projects or peer review of individual tasks.[48]

A passing thought: school newspapers, which begin to emerge in the middle school years and are relatively commonplace in high school, would seem fertile soil for examining the reading-writing connection in the creation of research papers, including informational and explanatory reports as well as persuasive essays, all within a context of genuine purpose and audience. The newspaper is pertinent to *reflection* because of its fundamentally collective character; a group comes together to discuss and debate, to construct and critique, confronted by deadlines and the demand to produce a product. Unfortunately, I have found little significant research on this topic in the middle grades.[49]

Finally, the bottom line comes when background sources and the plan for the paper come together in the actual composition—*extension*. One research question focuses on the linkages between source texts and final papers, exploring the degree to which the two come to resemble one another, even when the assignment requires the student to go beyond the information given, to employ a different structure, or to pursue a different purpose. This question goes to the heart of how to help students move beyond encyclopedic writing toward genuine analysis.

I have found no substantive research on this question in the middle grades, but the issues are informed by Flower's think-aloud studies of college students who talked while reading and writing.[50] These informants are presumably almost experts. What do they have to say about how they pull the pieces together? Flower organized her findings around four issues: the *organizing plan, task representation, costs and benefits*, and *strategic moves*. These issues cut across the CORE model, but address the bottom line for *extension*—the written product. Flower found that most informants possessed organizing techniques for handling information, although many fall into the "3x5 cards" category. Task representation described students' perspectives on the final goal: they aimed to finish the paper with minimum effort and maximum grade, sensitive to the practicalities of costs and benefits. As to strategic moves, students worked individually, and evidence of reflectivity was rare. In completing the paper, students focused on Warriner's "four problems: the word, the sentence, the paragraph, and the longer composition."[51] The results resemble those of Raphael and Boyd, who found fourth and fifth graders insensitive to audience, overreliant on personal knowledge and unanalyzed factual details from source texts (i.e., they copied the material), and reliant on narrative more than expository genre in writing the paper. These data are consistent with holistic ratings of writing quality from the NAEP surveys mentioned earlier.[52]

The lack of comprehensive developmental studies is even more serious for the research paper paradigm than for book reports, because the task is more complex and more significant. We know that young students have difficulty with expository reading and writing, and high schoolers are not much better. The NAEP writing survey found that barely 12 percent of eighth graders could perform "adequately" when asked to analyze a short exposition on "Frontier Food." By eleventh grade, only 22 percent could handle the task. It seems that we have a problem.

Final Thoughts

Learning to read and write, and to connect the two, poses a challenge in the middle grades. Despite widespread interest in literacy and the reading-writing connection, middle-grades instruction is rather scattershot, tending to emphasize surface features of writing and literal content of reading. Genuine communication between readers and writers—the interactive exchange of information that is the ultimate goal of the literacy enterprise—requires technical skill, but even more important are social and cognitive strategies, the habits of mind that lead the student to move back and forth across the reading-writing boundary regardless of the assignment.

The primary theme of this chapter has been the potential of mundane activities like book reports and research papers to serve as windows on the development of this integrative capacity during the middle grades of schooling. As with many educational domains, research offers more snapshots than moving pictures. The snapshots do provide some important leads about promising areas for the future:

- Further exploration of the potential of text *structures* to link reading and writing is an obvious candidate. A related issue is the role of text *models* to aid students in developing explicit schemata, not through rote exercises, but through the dialogic interactions found in exemplary instructional practice.
- Another domain is the educational value of *small-group activities*—collaborative learning and peer review—to support reflective learning and to teach strategic thinking. The special "bounce" that comes when students work together on substantial reading-writing projects has yet to be demonstrated by existing research, but the idea certainly merits further study.
- A third area is the *teacher's role* in supporting the reading-writing connection, not only through special activities like the Book Club and the Author's Chair, but as an intrinsic, ongoing, and self-initiated feature of virtually all literacy assignments.
- The teacher as "*adaptive expert*" provides a promising model for instruction on complex tasks during the middle grades.[53] Adolescence is a critical period in a student's education, a time of movement from egocentric and concrete activities toward reflective and abstract thought. This movement can be nurtured by the teacher who sees situations through adolescent eyes.

Introspecting on an activity while performing it can lead to considerable interference—try to think about how you process or produce a text while actually reading and writing, and you immediately understand the meaning of "short-term memory limitations"—it is hard to tap your mental belly and metacognitive head both at the same time. While constructing this chapter, I have found myself attempting along the way to trace the process, to "think-aloud," as it were. Have my mental processes mirrored my conceptual claims, especially the CORE framework? I can offer no evidence; introspection failed long ago as a source of trustworthy data. The framework seems to me to have merit, but the processes of theory construction and effective instruction are both iterative and interactive. And I must admit that many of my reflections are based on memories of middle grade teachers and their assignments—which I remember vividly as book reports and research papers.

NOTES

1. Judith A. Langer, *Children Reading and Writing* (Norwood, N.J.: Ablex, 1986).

2. Composing and writing are quite different matters. Before children have mastered the technology of print, they can invent stories; moreover, they can also invent spellings that allow them to put their ideas in print. See Linda K. Clarke, "Invented versus Traditional Spelling in First Graders' Writing: Effects on Learning to Spell and Read," *Research in the Teaching of English* 22 (1988): 281-309.

3. This characterization typifies the college-bound high school student. A different picture emerges for youngsters in the lower tracks, for whom the curriculum changes little across the grades, and whose teachers, prepared for subject matter specializations, work under conditions that vitiate their ability to handle student needs that often emerge from a decade of missed opportunities.

4. The literature on literacy as a formal language style or *register* is quite extensive. For entry points see Suzanne de Castell, Allan Luke, and Kieran Egan, eds., *Literacy, Society, and Schooling: A Reader* (Cambridge, England: Cambridge University Press, 1986). In "A Sisyphean Task: Historical Perspectives on the Relationship between Writing and Reading Instruction," in *Collaboration through Reading and Writing*, ed. Anne H. Dyson (Urbana, Ill.: National Council of Teachers of English, 1989), pp. 25-84, Geraldine Jonçich Clifford recounts the position of the 1984 Committee of Ten: "The chief function of language is communication. . . . The pupils must speak or write to or for somebody, with a consciously conceived purpose to inform, convince, inspire, or entertain." (pp. 47-48). Chapter 1 in this volume recounts the history of swings in definitions of literacy in the United States.

5. The formal education of adolescents remains a substantial challenge and a moving target. See S. Shirley Feldman and Glen R. Elliot, eds., *At the Threshold: The Developing Adolescent* (Cambridge, Mass.: Harvard University Press, 1990).

6. Robert C. Calfee and Priscilla A. Drum, "Research on Teaching Reading," in *Third Handbook of Research on Teaching*, ed. Merlin Wittrock (New York: Macmillan, 1986), pp. 804-849.

7. Elfrieda H. Hiebert and Taffy E. Raphael, "Psychological Perspectives on Literacy and Extensions to Educational Practice," in *Handbook of Educational Psychology*, ed. David C. Berliner and Robert C. Calfee (New York: Macmillan, 1996), pp. 550-602. Several other handbooks deal with reading and writing, but usually in separate chapters. Where the topics are treated in the same chapter, they are separated. Overlap between reading-writing citations is virtually nil. See Judith A. Langer and Richard Allington, "Curriculum Research in Writing and Reading," in *Handbook of Research on Curriculum*, ed. Philip W. Jackson (New York: Macmillan, 1992), pp. 687-721, and Arthur N. Applebee and Alan Purves, "Literature and the English Language Arts," ibid., 726-752; Jane Hansen and Donald Graves, "The Language Arts Interact," in *Handbook of Research on Teaching the English Language Arts*, ed. James Flood, Julie Jensen, Diane Lapp, and James Squire (New York: Macmillan, 1991), pp. 805-819; Mary Healy and Mary Barr, "Language Across the Curriculum," ibid., pp. 820-826; Marlene Scardamalia and Carl C. Bereiter, "Research on Written Composition," in *Handbook of Research on Teaching*, 3rd ed., ed. Merlin Wittrock (New York: Macmillan, 1986), pp. 778-803; Robert J. Tierney and Timothy Shanahan, "Research on the Reading-Writing Relationship: Interactions, Transactions, and Outcome," in *Handbook of Reading Research*, vol. 2, ed. Rebecca Barr, Michael Kamil, Peter B. Mosenthal, and P. David Pearson (New York: Longman, 1984), pp. 246-280; Calfee and Drum, "Research on Teaching Reading."

In sharp contrast to the divisions found in handbook articles are the works of Spivey and her colleagues, several of which are cited in chapter 1. In particular, see Nancy Nelson Spivey, "Transforming Texts: Constructive Processes in Reading and Writing," *Written Communication* 7 (1990): 256-287.

8. Judith W. Irwin and Mary Anne Doyle, eds., *Reading/Writing Connections: Learning from Research* (Newark, Del.: International Reading Association, 1992); see especially the appendix on correlations. See also Melanie Sperling and Sarah Warshauer Freedman, "Research on Writing," in *Handbook of Research on Teaching*, 4th ed., ed. Virginia Richardson (New York: Macmillan, forthcoming). The bottom line is that correlations between reading and writing are sporadic, to say the least, and may be meaningless as well.

9. Describing the ongoing battles among reading and writing models would require far more space than is available in this chapter. The handbook references in previous notes provide important background. Variations in reading models can be found in Robert Ruddell, Martha Rapp Ruddell, and Harry Singer, eds., *Theoretical Models and Processes of Reading*, 4th ed. (Newark, Del.: International Reading Association, 1994). A variety of writing models are presented in Carl C. Bereiter and Marlene Scardamalia, *The Psychology of Written Composition* (Hillsdale, N.J.: Lawrence Erlbaum Associates, 1987). A companion volume for writing is presently in progress under the editorship of James Squire and Roselmina Indrisano. For an attempt to link reading and writing processes, see William Page, "The Author and Reader in Writing and Reading," *Research in the Teaching of English* 8 (1974): 179-183.

10. Judith A. Langer and Arthur N. Applebee, *How Writing Shapes Thinking* (Urbana, Ill.: National Council of Teachers of English, 1987).

11. Robert C. Calfee, "Language-oriented Curriculum," in *Encyclopedia of English Studies and Language Arts*, ed. Alan Purves (New York: Scholastic Press, 1994); James Moffett and Betty Jane Wagner, *Student-centered Language Arts: K-12*, 3rd ed. (Portsmouth, N. H.: Boynton/Cook, 1992); Sandra Strotsky, "Research on Reading/Writing Relations: A Synthesis and Suggested Directions," in *Composing and Comprehending*, ed. Julie M. Jensen (Urbana, Ill.: National Council of Teachers of English, 1984).

12. Robert C. Calfee and Cynthia P. Patrick, *Teach Our Children Well* (Stanford, Cal.: Alumni Association/Portable Stanford Series, 1995), chap. 3. Constructivist concepts are also described in chapters 1 and 12 of this volume. See also, Nancy Nelson Spivey, *The Constructivist Metaphor: Reading, Writing, and the Making of Meaning* (San Diego, Cal.: Academic Press, 1997).

13. The relation between print literacy and spoken language could have been developed as a significant counterpoint in this chapter; the critical issues in the middle grades are about neither the medium nor the message, but about students' acquisition of the tools of formal language style. Virtually every argument in the chapter applies as well to listening and speaking in academic situations.

14. The social-cognitive perspective on school learning and literacy is described in Hiebert and Raphael, "Psychological Perspectives on Literacy and Extensions to Educational Practice," and throughout in Berliner and Calfee, *Handbook of Educational Psychology*.

15. The Author's Chair was first described by Janes Hansen and Donald Graves, "The Author's Chair," *Language Arts* 60 (1983): 176-183.

16. Susan I. McMahan and Taffy Raphael, eds., *The Book Club Connection* (New York: Teachers College Press, 1997).

17. The middle grade examples are from *Performance Standards, vol. 2, Middle School* (Pittsburgh, Pa.: University of Pittsburgh and the National Center on Education and the Economy, 1997).

18. Arthur N. Applebee, *Literature in the Secondary School: Studies of Curriculum and Instruction in the United States* (Urbana, Ill.: National Council of Teachers of English, 1993).

19. For a sampling of comments on alternatives to the dreaded book report, see Evelyn Krieger, "Stamping Out Book Reports: The Book Report Battle," *Journal of Reading* 35 (1992): 340-341. In *Reading Instruction: Diagnostic Teaching in the Classroom*, 3rd ed. (New York: Holt, Rinehart and Winston, 1980), Larry A. Harris and Carl B. Smith write "Sharing of books can encourage exploration," but the results of book reports are "seldom happy" (pp. 88-90). See also Patricia M. Cunningham, Sharon A. Moore, James W. Cunningham, and David W. Moore, *Reading in Elementary Classrooms* (New York, Longman, 1983), pp. 380-396; Kathy H. Au, Jana M. Mason, and Judith A. Sheu, *Literacy Instruction for Today* (New York: Harper Collins, 1995), pp. 97-100.

20. In chapter 11 of this volume Mathison addresses similar issues, but from the college perspective. The chief parallel is between narrative and expository (literary and disciplinary) texts. Mathison emphasizes situations in which the text is the starting point, and the task is a close reading, and then looks at the prototypic college assignment of an expository piece—the "research article." For present purposes, the most important contrast is between the critical analysis expected at the college level (and in the upper track in high school courses) and the more mechanical tasks typical of the middle grades.

21. Rose Marie Codling, Linda B. Gambrell, Aileen Kennedy, Barbara M. Palmer, and Mary Graham, *The Teacher, the Text, and the Context: Factors that Influence Elementary Students' Motivation to Write*, Reading Research Report 59 (College Park, Md.: National Reading Research Center, 1996); Langer, *Children Reading and Writing*.

22. Julie E. Wollman-Bonilla and Barbara Wechadlo, "Literature Response Journals in a First Grade Classroom," *Language Arts* 72 (1995): 562-570; Pamela L. Grossman, "Research on the Teaching of Literature," in *Handbook of Research on Teaching*, ed. Virginia Richardson (New York: Macmillan, forthcoming).

23. Wollman-Bonilla and Wechadlo, "Literature Response Journals in a First Grade Classroom"; Martha Waggoner, Clark Chinn, Hwajin Yi, and Richard C. Anderson, "Collaborative Reasoning about Stories," *Language Arts* 72 (1995): 582-589.

24. In "Research on the Teaching of Literature," Grossman discusses the canon and goals of the literature curriculum and expresses concern that elementary teachers have little preparation in literary analysis. For textbook advice on book reports, response journals, and so on, see Harris and Smith, *Reading Instruction*, Cunningham et al., *Reading in Elementary Classrooms*, Au et al., *Literacy Instruction for Today*. See also, Robert Tierney, John E. Readance, and Ernest K. Dishner, *Reading Strategies and Practices: A Compendium* (Needham Heights, Mass.: Allyn and Bacon, 1995).

25. James W. Stewig, *Read to Write: Using Children's Literature as a Springboard to Writing* (New York: Hawthorn Books, 1975).

26. On the use of stories for moral development, see Paul C. Vitz, "The Use of Stories in Moral Development," *American Psychologist* 45 (1990): 702-720, and Victoria Evans and Robert C. Calfee, "Teaching Moral Values through Literature," *California Reader* 31, no. 1 (1997): 14-18. As to the importance of "cultural literacy," see E. D. Hirsch, Jr., *The Schools We Need* (New York: Doubleday, 1996).

27. Today's educators sometimes emphasize instructional techniques that downplay the text. Teachers are encouraged to draw out students' prior experience before and during the reading of a story, and ask students to write personal responses that are virtually textfree. See Leslie M. Morrow, "The Impact of a Literature-based Program on Literacy Achievement, Use of Literature, and Attitudes of Children from Minority Backgrounds," *Reading Research Quarterly* 27 (1992): 251-275, and Shelby A. Wolf, Angela A. Carey, and Erikka L. Mieras, "'What is this Literachurch Stuff Anyway?': Preservice Teachers' Growth in Understanding Children's Literary Response," *Reading Research Quarterly* 31 (1996): 130-157.

28. Hiebert and Raphael, "Psychological Perspectives on Literacy and Extensions to Educational Practice." See also, Susan S. Lehr, *The Child's Developing Sense of Theme* (New York: Teachers College Press, 1991); Rebecca J. Lukens, *A Critical Handbook of Children's Literature*, 4th ed. (New York: Harper Collins, 1990).

29. On the use of models, see Langer, *Children Reading and Writing*. In "How Reading Model Essays Affects Writers," in Irwin and Doyle, eds., *Reading/Writing Connections: Learning from Research*, Peter Smagorinsky cautions that a novice may be tempted to "copy" without thinking. "A model is most beneficial when learners have appropriate content knowledge and need to learn how to transform it into text; the model can illustrate how to relate the bits of knowledge into a coherent structure." (p. 174). See also George Hillocks, Jr., "The Writer's Knowledge: Theory, Research, and Implications for Practice," in *The Teaching of Writing*, Eighty-fifth Yearbook of the National Society for the Study of Education, ed. Anthony R. Petrosky and David Bartholomae (Chicago: University of Chicago Press, 1986), pp. 71-94. Positive effects of models in college writing are described in Davida H. Charney and Richard A. Carlson, "Learning to Write in a Genre: What Student Writers Take from Model Texts," *Research in the Teaching of English* 29 (1995): 88-125.

30. Scardamalia and Bereiter, "Research on Written Composition"; Thomas G. Devine, "Studying: Skills, Strategies, and Systems," in *Handbook of Research on Teaching the English Language Arts*, ed. Flood et al., pp. 743-753.

31. Beach discusses related issues in chapter 10 of this volume. His example is a poem, but the main point is how dialogue can inform the connection between text and personal reaction, resulting in a genuine critique.

32. This example is from Performance Standards, vol. 2, Middle School, p. 49.

33. In "Issues in Portfolio Assessment: Assessing Writing Processes from Products," *Educational Assessment*, in press, Maryl Gearhart and Shelby A. Wolf illustrate the incorporation of structural features into an assessment exercise.

34. A thread running throughout this section is the tension between the ideal and the practical. English/Language Arts teachers must balance aesthetics and skills. At a practical level, the eighth grade teacher is well advised to emphasize skills, even in his or her upper track course. The instructor in a college track introductory course in English can aim toward aesthetic appreciation and critique. The remedial instructor, perhaps the same individual, must shift attention back to skills. This chapter offers no resolution for this tension, but rather points toward the middle grades as the nexus for resolving issues like the "undoing" of the "book report" mentality mentioned by Mathison in chapter 11 of this volume. As to the contrast between novices and experts, see Michelene T. Chi, Robert Glaser, and Marshall J. Farr, eds., *The Nature of Expertise* (Hillsdale, N.J.: Erlbaum, 1988).

35. As the reader probably realizes, the focus on book reports and research papers is a rhetorical device in this chapter to describe endpoints on a continuum. Reading-writing tasks can take a variety of different shapes.

36. For a personal experience with encyclopedic writing by a young student, see Mary Ellen Giacobbe, "Learning to Write and Writing to Learn in the Elementary School," in *The Teaching of Writing*, ed. Petrosky and Bartholomae, pp. 131-147. She also offers curious advice about alternative strategies: "Read until you are filled up. Then start writing notes without looking at the book."

37. But see Allen Glatthorn, "Thinking, Writing, and Reading: Making Connections," in *Content Area Reading and Learning*, ed. Diane Lapp, James Flood, and Nancy Farnan (Englewood Cliffs, N.J.: Prentice-Hall, 1989), pp. 283-296.

38. Jay R. Campbell, Clyde M. Reese, Christine O'Sullivan, and John A. Dossey, *Trends in Writing Achievement from 1984-1994, Part IV* (Washington, D.C.: U.S. Dept of Education, Office of Educational Research and Improvement, 1996); Jay R. Campbell,

Kristin E. Voekl, and Patricia L. Donahue, *NAEP 1996 Trends in Academic Progress, Part IV* (Washington, D.C.: U.S. Dept. of Education, Office of Educational Research and Improvement, 1997).

39. For samples of textbook advice on research papers, see James Flood and Peter H. Salus, *Language and the Language Arts* (Englewood Cliffs, N.J.: Prentice-Hall, 1986), pp. 147-149; Richard Robinson and Thomas L. Good, *Becoming an Effective Reading Teacher* (New York: Harper and Row, 1987), pp. 287-288; Au et al., *Literacy Instruction for Today*; Tierney et al., *Reading Strategies and Practices*.

40. Linda Flower, "Collaborative Planning and Community Literacy: A Window in the Logic of Learners," in *Innovations in Learning: New Environments for Education*, ed. Leona Schauble and Robert Glaser (Mahwah, N.J.: Erlbaum, 1996); Linda Flower, David L. Wallace, Linda Norris, and Rebecca E. Burnett, eds., *Making Thinking Visible* (Urbana, Ill.: National Council of Teachers of English, 1994).

41. Taffy E. Raphael and Fenice B. Boyd, *Synthesizing Information from Multiple Sources*, Center Series No. 45 (East Lansing, Mich.: Center for the Learning and Teaching of Elementary Subjects, Michigan State University, 1991).

42. Codling et al., *The Teacher, The Text, and The Context*; Patricia A. Alexander, "Knowledge-seeking and Self-schema: A Case for the Motivational Dimensions of Exposition," *Educational Psychologist* 32 (1997): 83-94.

43. Bruce K. Britton and John B. Black, eds., *Understanding Expository Text* (Hillsdale, N.J.: Lawrence Erlbaum Associates, 1985); Charles A. Weaver, III and Walter Kintsch, "Expository Text," in *Handbook of Reading Research*, vol. 2, ed. Barr et al., pp. 230-245.

44. Victoria C. Hare, "Summarizing Text," in *Reading/Writing Connections*, ed. Irwin and Doyle: "Examining the process involved in summarizing provides an opportunity for studying a unique relation between reading and writing" (p. 96). In "Writing to Learn," ibid., pp. 145-159, Richard T. Vacca and Wayne M. Linek make the point that simply copying text has little effect on growth in comprehension or composition.

45. Smagorinsky, "How Reading Model Essays Affects Writers"; Miles Myers, "The Teaching of Writing in Secondary Schools," in *The Teaching of Writing*, ed. Petrosky and Bartholomae, pp. 148-169; Elizabeth Curtin, "The Research Paper in High School Writing Programs: Examining Connections between Goals of Instruction and Requirements of College Writing" (Doct. diss., Carnegie Mellon University, 1988). The structural models for research reports encompass many of the same genre as for book reports, which are typically expository analyses of narrative works. For example, the compare-contrast structure applies in one way to man and marlin in *The Old Man and the Sea*, and in a different way to marlin and dolphin for a science paper. Beyond the middle elementary grades, assignments that call for writing original stories are not very common.

46. For a review of research on Basic Writing, see Sperling and Freedman, "Research on Writing."

47. Marilyn Chambliss and Robert C. Calfee, *Today's Textbooks, Tomorrow's Minds* (London: Blackwell, forthcoming) describe a variety of expository structures designed for instructional purposes.

48. George E. Newell and Peter Winograd, "The Effects of Writing on Learning from Expository Text," *Written Communication* 6 (1989): 196-217; Vacca and Linek, "Writing to Learn." "Talking about ideas [presumably from text?] before writing about them generates motivation that is absent when students are simply directed to produce written answers to study questions." (p. 150).

49. But see Sharon J. Derry, "Cognitive Schema Theory in the Constructivist Debate," *Educational Psychologist* 31 (1996): 163-174, especially pp. 169ff.

50. Linda Flower, "The Role of Task Representation in Reading-to-Write," in *Reading-to-Write: Exploring a Cognitive and Social Process*, ed. Linda Flower, Victoria Stein, John Ackerman, Margaret J. Kantz, Kathleen McCormick, and Wayne C. Peck (New York: Oxford Press, 1990), pp. 35-75.

51. John E. Warriner and Francis Griffith, *English Grammar and Composition*, rev. ed. (New York: Harcourt Brace, 1965).

52. Campbell, Reese, et al., *Trends in Writing Achievement from 1984-1994.*

53. Giyoo Hatano, "Cognitive Consequences of Practice in Culture-Specific Procedural Skills," *Quarterly Newsletter of the Laboratory of Comparative Human Cognition* 4 (1982): 15-18.

Section Four
THE DISCIPLINARY CONTEXT

CHAPTER X

Writing about Literature:
A Dialogic Approach

RICHARD BEACH

Discussions of writing about literature inevitably raise questions about the ultimate purpose or value of such writing. In this chapter, I argue for the value of a dialogic approach to writing about literature. This dialogic approach goes beyond much of traditional formalistic analysis of character, setting, plot, and theme. It encourages students to use their writing in the following ways:

- to describe and analyze their experiences with conflicts and tensions portrayed in a text;
- to reflect on the reasons for these conflicts and tensions as related to a text's multiple voices, perspectives, beliefs, and attitudes;
- to connect their experiences with texts to real-world experiences;
- to relate their written responses to the social context of the classroom.

First I will describe a dialogic theory of language meaning, applying that theory to responses to a poem. I will next discuss how readers respond to dialogic language use in literature and will draw some implications for formulating writing assignments. Then I will conclude with some suggestions for evaluating students' written responses.

The Dialogic Nature of Language and Literature

A dialogic approach builds on Mikhail Bakhtin's theory of language meaning.[1] Bakhtin argued that the meanings of utterances are

Richard Beach is Professor of English Education in the Department of Curriculum and Instruction, University of Minnesota—Twin Cities.

based on how those utterances are used within a social context and how they relate to other utterances. He used the term "answerability" for the referral of an utterance to previous utterances or its anticipation of future utterances.[2] As an illustration of answerability, let us imagine that Bob says, "There's a new restaurant opening up down the street," and Ann responds, "That's nice." The meaning of Bob's utterance depends on how Bob anticipates Ann will react. His utterance could be an invitation to Ann to go with him to the restaurant, in which case he seeks an acceptance from her, but, instead of an acceptance, he receives a rejection of his invitation. Or Bob could simply be describing the fact that there is a new restaurant, and Ann affirms Bob's observation.

If these utterances occur in a literary text, readers then sort out these competing meanings by constructing a larger context constituting Bob's and Ann's roles, traits, beliefs about and knowledge of each other, agendas, and social setting. Bakhtin argued that literary texts are comprised of multiple, competing meanings constituted by characters' complex social intentions and agendas. The meanings of these intentions and agendas vary according to how the characters construe these contexts—and also how readers construe these contexts. Readers who construe the exchange between Ann and Bob as a romantic interlude may infer that Bob is attempting to woo Ann but Ann is resisting Bob's advances. They may also infer other voices: that Bob is speaking in the voice of the "lover," while Ann is speaking in the voice of a "tease."

In addition to the characters' voices, there is yet another voice to consider in a literary text: that of a narrator. A narrator who embellishes Ann's "That's nice" with "she stated in a flat, uninterested tone, as she kept her eyes on the newspaper," adds an additional voice to the mix as distinct from the voices of Bob and Ann. Readers construct these voices by drawing on their knowledge of social genres or discourses that constitute certain systematic ways of knowing or acting.

Readers also use their knowledge of genres and discourses to construct discourse worlds shaping characters' actions. For instance, in responding to *The Great Gatsby*, readers infer the worlds of the outsider midwesterner (Nick), the "rags-to-riches" Puritan Ethic (Gatsby), the gangster-hero (Gatsby), the upper-class snob (Daisy), and the down-and-out (Muriel).[3] Tensions among these discourse worlds increase the complexity of each character's utterances, creating conflicts, tensions, gaps, and contradictions that enhance the narrative power of the novel. For example, the discourse of Gatsby's gangster world conflicts with the discourse of Nick's midwestern or Daisy's upper-class values.

These multiple, complex, dialogic meanings contrast with what Bakhtin described as "monologic" language, such as that of official bureaucratic pronouncements, that precludes expression of alternative voices.[4]

In a dialogic approach to responding to literature, students write about their experiences with the conflicts and tensions among these multiple voices and perspectives. They make explicit the processes they employ in constructing social contexts in order to infer differences in characters' traits, beliefs, knowledge, agenda, and power. They also relate the conflicts and tensions evoked by the text to their own real-world experiences. Through this sort of writing, they acquire different ways of understanding and valuing their own social experiences. By experiencing the multiple voices and perspectives of the text world, they develop their sense of the multiple meanings of utterances in real-world contexts.[5] As students experience the multiple meanings of literary texts, they gain a sensitivity to the multiple meanings of everyday speech, which continually evokes previous and anticipated utterances, voices, and discourses. To quote Marshall Gregory, such literary experiences serve to "call students out of themselves, to create for student readers compelling invitations to imagine different conditions of the world and different kinds of human feelings and motives far beyond their own experiences."[6]

Bakhtin's theories of meaning have also served as the basis of a dialogic pedagogy that celebrates the questioning of conflicted meanings. As Bakhtin noted, "Without one's own questions, one cannot creatively understand anything other or foreign."[7] Through this questioning, readers explore what Bakhtin described as an array of different potential meanings that transcend even an author's intended meaning.

In a dialogic approach, instead of simply summarizing texts or responding to an assigned topic, students use their writing to raise questions about texts, questions that open up conflicts, tensions, gaps, and contradictions. For example, in writing about texts set in past historical periods, students raise questions about the gap between their own perspectives and the speaker's perspective, seeing how both are influenced by cultural eras. Such questions broaden the scope of writing about literature to include larger historical and cultural aspects.

An Illustration of Dialogic Reading and Writing

To illustrate a dialogic approach to writing about literature, I will use a poem written by Langston Hughes, "Theme for English B."

Hughes wrote this poem during the period of the Harlem Renaissance. Having recently arrived in New York from the South, he was overwhelmed by the artistic expression and economic development occurring in Harlem. Based on his experiences as a student at Columbia University, he depicts a speaker having to write an essay for his white instructor. The speaker compares his experiences growing up as a black in North Carolina with what he assumes is the quite different experience of his white instructor:

Theme for English B

The instructor said
   Go home and write
   a page tonight
   And let that page come out of you—
   Then it will be true.
I wonder if it's that simple.
I am twenty-two, colored, born in Winston-Salem.
I went to school there, then Durham, then here
to this college on the hill above Harlem.
I am the only colored student in my class.
The steps from the hill lead down to Harlem,
through a park, then I cross St. Nicholas,
Eighth Avenue, Seventh, and I come to the Y,
the Harlem Branch Y, where I take the elevator
up to my room, sit down, and write this page:

It's not easy to know what is true for you or me
at twenty-two, my age. But I guess I'm what
I feel and see and hear. Harlem, I hear you:
hear you, hear me—we two—you, me talk on this page.
(I hear New York, too). Me—who?
Well, I like to eat, sleep, drink, and be in love.
I like to work, read, learn, and understand life.
I like a pipe for a Christmas present,
or records—Bessie, bop, or Bach.

I guess being colored doesn't make me not like
the same things other folks like who are other races.
So will my page be colored that I write?
But it will be
a part of you, instructor.

You are white—
yet a part of me, as I am a part of you.
That's American.
Sometimes perhaps you don't want to be a part of me.
Nor do I often want to be a part of you.
But we are, that's true!
As I learn from you,
I guess you learn from me—
although you're older—and white—
and somewhat more free.

This is my page for English B.

Readers experience conflicts, tensions, ambiguities, complexities, human vulnerabilities, and differences as they read the poem and vicariously participate in the speaker's social practices. They also experience different meanings depending on their teacher's or their peers' social agendas and purposes operating in a classroom. A teacher may use "Theme" as part of a unit on the Harlem Renaissance to illustrate the work of an African-American poet writing about the world of Harlem, and students in the class may experience it that way. However, the students may instead see "Theme" as an illustration of the difficulties students encounter when having to write for an unfamiliar teacher audience without a clear sense of purpose. Readers adopt perspectives and stances relative to the context in which they are responding. For example, readers of this chapter would make assumptions about my use of the poem within the context of this essay and within the larger context of theoretical positions on reading and writing.

Not only do readers *work within* contexts but they also *bring* contexts to their reading. For "Theme," the evoked real-world contexts would likely include the world of school and the world of home, as readers make connections to their own experience of tensions between the two worlds. Readers may also apply their experience of cultural differences, inferring the gap between the speaker's boyhood in the rural South versus the world of an elite Ivy League university. These tensions between contexts are further complicated by the racial differences between the speaker and his white instructor. Readers might also bring their experiences of writing essays—how they learned to "psyche out" or rhetorically read their teachers' agendas and expectations and decided whether they wanted to conform to or to resist those agendas and expectations.

In applying knowledge of such contexts, readers recall their own stances typically adopted in these contexts. Having grown up in what was the segregated city of Durham, North Carolina (referred to in the poem) during the 1950s and having experienced the civil rights movement of the late 1960s and 1970s, I bring some sense of shifting institutional and historical forces of past decades. At the same time, from a dialogic perspective, I recall the conflicts and tensions associated with any historical change—the backlash resistance fueled by economic warnings from segregationist politicians. By reflecting on the conflicts and tensions associated with my own beliefs and attitudes about race relations, I bring these beliefs and attitudes back to my reading of the poem. I thus experience the complexity of the poem by interrogating my own conflicts and tensions.

Unfortunately, writing about literature in school often entails a monologic, singular perspective, failing to invite exploration of these dialogic complexities. Literature is thus perceived as a means of imparting a coherent, singular set of values or thematic message. Given this didactic approach, students are often given a theme or asked to formulate a thematic message and then to apply that theme to their own lives. For example, students reading the poem might be asked to write about how the speaker's diligence in completing the essay should lead to "success in life." What is problematic with this approach is that it creates a rhetorical context that limits the focus to one topic. It also presupposes a direct causal link between the kind of experience portrayed in the poem and real-world experiences.

Another common kind of writing assignment reflects a formalistic approach to teaching literature. Much of this formalistic approach builds on the New Critical assumption, discussed in previous chapters, that the meaning of the text lies within the text's linguistic structure, as opposed to what the reader brings to the text. In a formalistic approach, the primary purpose of literature instruction becomes to teach conceptual knowledge of such terms as "main character," "point of view," "theme," "setting," "attitude," "metaphor," "alliteration," and "plot development" so that students can analyze literature according to these aspects. Students are given writing assignments in which they write literary analyses based on their close readings. For example, in responding to "Theme for English B," students might be asked to analyze the sound patterns in the poem or to describe the nature of the setting and how that setting shaped the speaker's attitude. These kinds of assignments are typical in American schooling. As one national survey found, three-fourths of the assigned writing in secondary literature courses consisted of "text-based essays," while only a small portion of the other writing consisted of "reader-based essays."[8]

This formalistic approach does not encourage students to apply their own experiences to the text or to engage in any critical self-reflection on social or political issues. It treats literary language as having singular, as opposed to multiple, contradictory meanings. Assignments based on a formalistic approach often employ a thesis-support text structure with a focus on citing illustrative evidence from the text. Once students define their primary thesis and cite some supporting evidence, they often impose a premature closure, assuming that once they have said what they wanted to say, they are done.[9] This writing, with its definitive, authoritative stance, represents what Marcia Farr described as an "essayist literacy" that encourages the formulation of one's own original position, but rewards a depersonalized, abstract treatment. Likewise, Ruth Spack also noted the contradictory nature of an "essayist literacy" when she pointed out that, despite privileging individuality and originality, it requires an impersonal stance.[10]

While it is certainly important that students learn to cite textual evidence, they also need to learn how to relate their own experiences to texts. In reaction to limitations of formalistic approaches, many literature instructors have embraced a reader-response approach that emphasizes writing about one's "living-through" experience with a text. Drawing on Louise Rosenblatt's notion of an "aesthetic stance," students are asked to write about their emotional experience with texts.[11] For example, they might write about the empathy they felt with the speaker in "Theme." Such writing moves away from the confines of a text-based approach to encourage students to describe and reflect on their own unique experience with a text. It also encourages students to explore reasons for their responses in terms of their beliefs and attitudes.

However, some versions of a reader-based, experiential mode can be just as monologic as a formalistic approach in that students may simply formulate their reactions—"I felt sorry for the speaker having to write an essay for someone he doesn't know"—without any further exploration or reflection on the complexity of their own or the characters' experiences. Moreover, reader-response theorists often encourage expression of students' own so-called "authentic" experience with a text. As George Kamberelis and K. D. Scott observed, this notion of authenticity assumes that, by peeling away the "false" voices, students will ultimately discover their one single, authentic voice, a notion that runs contrary to the idea of multiple voices inherent in language use.[12] An alternative approach to writing invites students to describe the different voices operating within a text as well as the voices inherent in their own responses. In this manner, they are using writing to explore and entertain different social perspectives. And, by reflecting on tensions between these voices, they begin to reflect on how these voices represent different beliefs and attitudes, recognition central to interpretive analysis.

Dialogue and Writing about Literature

I have argued that writing assignments based on a text-based, formalistic model often invite a monologic perspective and so can some reader-response assignments. By simply describing one's experience, students may not necessarily adopt a self-reflective, self-interrogating orientation. Gordon Pradl characterized a monologic approach as reflecting a "discourse of certainty," while a more dialogic approach entails a "discourse of possibilities" in which students "are constantly weighing and choosing among alternative linguistic representations of reality."[13] In adopting a dialogic approach, students write about the conflicts, tensions, contradictions, complexities, gaps, competing voices, or multiple perspectives evoked by their literary experiences. However, these conflicts and tensions are not simply "in" the text. It is readers who construct these conflicts and tensions by drawing on their own experiences with conflicts and tensions from their own lives or with other texts. In responding to Hughes's "Theme," readers perceive conflicts and tensions between the speaker's past and present perspectives, black-versus-white experience, academic versus nonacademic worlds, and being "more free" versus less free, or raise questions as to what it means to be "true."

In a dialogic approach, students adopt a range of different, competing stances. Adopting different stances entails assuming different imagined identities and having different kinds of experiences related to those identities. In responding to the conflicts and tensions in "Theme," they might adopt the stance of the dutiful student attempting to succeed in school, the "outsider" in an alien environment, the member of a different or "other" race, or the artist who resists formal structures. In adopting these evoked stances, students then reflect on the contradictions between them.

This dialogic approach is more self-reflective and less definitive than that associated with a text-based approach or an "authentic voice" reader-based approach. For example, in a traditional text-based assign-ment for "Theme," students would be asked to analyze the speaker's use of sounds and rhyme in the poem. While this formalistic analysis helps students appreciate poetic devices, it may not engage them with ideas and issues evoked by the poem. A more dialogic assignment leads to stu-dents generating these ideas and issues by posing questions, entertaining doubts, exploring conflicts and tensions, and reflecting on the meaning of those conflicts and tensions. By posing questions about their experi-ence with the poem, students are continually open to exploring new possibilities of meaning. They may, for example, write their perceptions of a text on one side of the page and their questions and reflections about these perceptions on the other side. They may also treat their hypotheses or explanations as tentative passing theories that are open to refutation and further exploration. For example, a student formulates the idea that the speaker is trying to persuade his instructor that his life experiences are of value. Having generated that hypothesis, the student then shares that idea with her peers. In analyzing the speaker's use of persuasive techniques, she also draws on her everyday experience with people attempting to persuade others of their self-worth.

It is up to the teacher to create writing contexts in the classroom that encourage exchange of conflicting perspectives and can lead to self-reflectiveness as well as to alternative stances and perspectives. For instance, by sharing their responses in peer-dialogue journal exchanges, students can build on the tentative, exploratory stances they have taken in conversational exchanges.[14] Exchanges can also take place electroni-cally. One analysis of computer exchanges in response to multicultural literature found that students generated twice as much talk on the com-puter as in oral discussions and were more likely to engage in disagree-ments on the computer than in oral discussions.[15]

In writing to and for their peers, students can construct a shared stance that transcends each of their own individual perspectives. In doing so, they experience disagreements, misunderstandings, conflicts, resistances, and divergent understandings that create dialogic tensions between their own and others' stances. They also begin to experience Bakhtin's answerability—that all utterances anticipate some potential reaction from another person. In anticipating potential reactions, they extend their responses. Knowing their partner might disagree with their position, they formulate a counter argument. Or they pose questions of their partner: "What do you think about the character's behavior?" These "outer" or "public" questions then form the basis of an "inner" set of questions for further thinking about a text.

And in this written exchange they are learning how to respond socially to others' messages. They are learning to ascertain whether or not to reply, what they will say, how they want to present themselves, and how they perceive their audience. For example, to discern the relevance of a message to a conversation, they have to infer the underlying social point of that conversation and to see that certain norms and conventions are operant in their social context. They are learning how to include and exclude others in events, manage conflict, construct social identity or roles, and establish their position of authority or status.[16] And by participating in these written exchanges, students are learning to read and write rhetorically. They are learning to contextualize both literary texts and others' responses according to their own and others' social agendas.

INTERTEXTUALITY IN READING AND WRITING

A major limitation of thematic, formalistic, and some forms of reader-response approaches is the assumption that readers can understand a text apart from other texts. In contrast, a dialogic perspective emphasizes the "double-voiced"[17] nature of writing, the echoing of other voices and languages from different text-world and real-world contexts. The "double-voiced" language within a text world does not occur simply in characters' dialogue, but also in authors' and speakers' languages and in the tensions among them. Speakers and characters may directly quote other languages operating in the text world, but they are more likely to evoke, mimic, or parody these different languages as representative of different genres or discourses. The meaning of language, therefore, derives from intertextual references to different genres and discourses. For example, the speaker's references to hearing or listening to Harlem and New York in the lines "Harlem, I hear you:/hear you, hear me—we two—you, me talk on this page./(I hear New York, too). Me—who?" as well as the rhythmic repetition of words and allusions to "Bessie, bop, or Bach" evoke intertextual references to music and jazz, something central to Hughes's life and poetry. Readers then apply their own knowledge of jazz to analyze the poem as a jazz lyric—an expression of African-American identity during that historical period in New York.

In a text world characters are caught in competing languages, what Bakhtin referred to as "heteroglossia."[18] As Gary Morson and Caryl Emerson noted in discussing the heteroglossia or dialogue between languages in novels: "Each language of heteroglossia is allowed to view other languages, each is viewed by others, and each glimpses its own image in the eyes of others."[19] Bakhtin gave the example of the narrator of Dickens's *Little Dorrit* who employs two different languages to describe the actions of a character called Mr. Merle:

The conference was held at four or five o'clock in the afternoon, when all the region of Harley Street, Cavendish Square, was resonant of carriage-wheels and double-knocks. It had reached this point when Mr. Merle came home *from his daily occupation of causing the British name to be more and more respected in all parts of the civilized globe capable of appreciation of world-wide commercial enterprise and gigantic combinations of skill and capital.*[20]

The language in italics mimics the language of political rhetoric, which is set against the narrative language used for the busy, domestic upper-class life of the setting. Thus, there is tension between the two discourse worlds: the world of political power and the world of domestic life.

Readers play a key role in defining the meaning of these uses of "double-voiced" language. They draw on their knowledge of language uses to construct intertextual links with other discourses and make inferences about the conflicts and tensions within the text world. For example, a reader may associate Mr. Merle's use of political rhetoric with his or her beliefs about the arrogance of British imperialism, which have come, in large part, from intertextual references to texts such as Conrad's *Heart of Darkness*.

In writing about their experience with "double-voiced" languages, students could describe the tensions between different languages operating within a text world, and the ways in which these languages represent different beliefs and attitudes. For example, the previously cited lines beginning "Harlem, I hear you" suggest the notion of Harlem itself speaking a particular language distinct from the language of the speaker or of New York. The language of Harlem reflects a world of art, music, and ethnicity that is set against the language of the speaker's own more pedestrian past world of growing up in North Carolina as well as the language of the larger world of New York.

In making these intertextual links, readers also make links between the contexts of the text world with other real-world or text-world contexts—a process that might be labeled "intercontextualizing."[21] Applying their historical and cultural knowledge, readers make these intercontextual links to understand and judge characters' actions as normal, appropriate, relevant, or typical relative to the beliefs and attitudes operating in a particular social and cultural context. For example, they may be judging the speaker's sharing his personal experience with his instructor as somewhat unusual and even risky within the world of Columbia University at that time. This creates a tension between their sense of what is normal in the current real-world context versus their sense of what was considered to be normal in the poem's historical context. For literature set in a past historical period or in other cultural contexts, readers could write about the tension between their experience in current contexts of college classrooms of the 1990s versus their experience of the speaker's classroom of the 1940s. Reflecting on this tension then leads them to consider how perceptions are shaped by beliefs and attitudes. For example, in response to the lines, "You are white—/yet a part of me, as I am a part of you./That's American," a reader may reflect on the ways in which categories of race, as in "You are white," and nationality, as in "That's American," shape the speaker's beliefs about his instructor.

In a dialogic approach to literature, students can write other sorts of responses that parody, mimic, extend, or recreate the text. They can rewrite story endings, construct a diary for a character, retell a story through the eyes of a different character, place characters in a different time period or cultural context, or parody a writer's style or techniques—activities in which they assume the ventriloquist's ability to mimic or adopt others' voices. For example, in response to "Theme," students could write the instructor's reaction to the speaker's essay or write an alternative version of the speaker's essay as if the speaker were an African-American student in a contemporary composition classroom. Students could then reflect on the tensions between their own voices and the text's voices, in terms of who is speaking, what attitudes and beliefs are being espoused, what the motives are for assuming a certain voice, and how these voices define relationships with others.

Hypertext response software can be used to make some intertextual links explicit.[22] By clicking on certain words or phrases in a text, readers gain access to background information, other chunks of text, alternative scenarios, or, in web-based texts, other web pages. By making these links, readers create their own versions of texts. Teachers can also employ computer authoring software to construct assignments that facilitate intertextual links. For example, an assignment for writing about "Theme" could include links to descriptions of the Harlem Renaissance, Hughes's own autobiography[23] and other poems, other literary texts about school, and other students' previous writing about the poem. Students can also use the authoring software to write their own hypertext responses with multiple links for their teachers or peers.

DEVISING GUIDED RESPONSE ASSIGNMENTS

All of this suggests that a dialogic approach to constructing text meaning is an unfolding, cyclical process in which readers formulate initial responses, link their knowledge and experience to their responses, define conflicts and tensions between responses, and reflect on how their beliefs and attitudes shape their responses. To foster this dialogic process, writing assignments need to provide some guidance for students, particularly younger or less able students, that will help them to extend and explore their responses in a systematic manner. In many classes, students are given assignments similar to the following essay assignment, which comes from the 1991 Advanced Placement literature examination based on a list of particular novels and plays:

Many plays and novels use contrasting places (for example, two countries, two cities or towns, houses, or the land and the sea) to represent opposed forces or ideas that are central to the meaning of the work. Choose a novel or a play that contrasts two such places. Write an essay explaining how the places differ, what the place represents, and how their contrast contributes to the meaning of the work.[24]

While this may be a relatively appealing topic, the problem with such an assignment is that many students do not know what to do with it, do not know "what to say" about their topic. They lack the heuristics or systematic thinking skills necessary to develop their ideas. In the case of the assignment in the Advanced Placement examination, a writer needs to define the symbolic meanings of a setting, infer thematic meanings, and relate the two—strategies he or she may not have learned. It is not enough simply to formulate a thesis, for example, that the culture of Harlem in the 1920s as reflected in art, music, and literature, differed from that of Columbia University. The writer must develop the thesis. Based on an analysis of two students who were having difficulty developing their topics, Patricia Sullivan found that "it was not in the act of reading or interpretation or analysis of works themselves that [the students in her study] found themselves at a loss as to what to say, but in what each as a writer had to bring to those texts, to the topics they had discovered through their transactions with texts."[25]

Furthermore, students often seek only evidence that confirms their position and avoid contradictory evidence.[26] They need assistance in generating hypotheses and then reflecting on alternative perspectives and conflicting evidence. In completing traditional "worksheet" or textbook questions, students often answer each question and move on to the next without using their writing to reflect on or relate their responses to other contexts. As a result, they do not learn how reflecting on their previous thoughts may help them generate more.

A dialogic approach can do much to foster development of ideas. Guided response assignments consist of a sequence of activities (e.g., free writing, listing, note taking, drawing, mapping, question asking, discussing, and role playing), based on a range of different response strategies involved in formulating and extending one's thinking.[27] Each activity serves to prepare students for subsequent activities. A listing activity prepares students for a mapping activity (drawing out the various connections and tensions that are seen), or a freewriting activity prepares students for a role play activity. As students develop and elaborate their initial responses, the more ideas they carry forward to responses in subsequent activities. In my own research on eighth grade students' use of mapping in responding to and comparing two short stories, I found that the more elaborate the students' maps of characters and their traits or beliefs, the more likely the students were to formulate complex explanations and interpretations of characters' actions.[28] In responding to "Theme," students might initially list the different worlds portrayed by the poem. Based on this list, they could use overlapping circles to create a map showing the relationships between the worlds of North Carolina, Harlem, Columbia University, and America. They could then place the speaker, the instructor, and his classmates within these circles to represent their allegiances to these different worlds. Through completing such sequenced activities, students begin to acquire the heuristics involved in dialogic thinking.

It is also important that, as part of inquiry instruction, students learn to formulate their own questions about their experience with a text. For example, students might use Kenneth Burke's pentad to list questions about the speaker in the poem. This heuristic provides a means of analyzing different aspects of an event: "act" (What is the speaker doing or thinking?), "agent" (Who is the speaker? What is his status and power?), "scene" (What is the context or social world shaping the act?), "agency" (What does the speaker use to accomplish his goals?), and "purpose" (What is the speaker trying to accomplish?).[29] They then reflect on which of these questions is most worth pursuing or investigating.

Question asking as well as question answering can lead to important insights. In one study, second graders learned to generate written questions that served as the basis for their discussions.[30] Over time, as these second graders recognized that certain kinds of questions elicited certain kinds of responses, they learned to improve the quality of their questions. Teachers participating in the study used time-out sessions during a discussion for students to write their reflections on the discussion. At the end of the discussion, students then wrote about what they learned by synthesizing their perceptions of that discussion as well as listing unanswered questions which served as the basis for future discussions.

In formulating guided assignments, teachers may include statements of the purpose of and the criteria for assessing the use of each activity. Because many students have difficulty engaging in self-reflection, teachers may also want to include some models of the self-reflection process. (Computer versions of these guided assignments could include options for students to access information about purpose, criteria, or models.)

Teachers can also foster self-reflection across a series of assignments. Each assignment would be designed to build on the previous assignment so that students interrogate their responses and stances adopted in previous assignments. For example, in an initial assignment I have used, students write about their beliefs about equal opportunity for persons relative to their class, gender, or race, as well as how they define "opportunity" and the factors that serve to enhance or deny equal opportunity. They are also asked for the criteria they use for assessing fulfillment of opportunity, such as financial success, self-fulfillment, social recognition or status. In doing this assignment, students often espouse a relatively idealistic view of equality of opportunity and see opportunity as entirely dependent on an individual's own initiative. Then, in the next assignment, they respond to the novel *Invisible Man* by Ralph Ellison,[31] and discuss the ways in which, given their previous definition, the main character is or is not denied equal opportunity. Some students begin to recognize a tension between their previously stated assumptions about opportunity and their descriptions of the character being consistently denied opportunity. They also reexamine some of their criteria for what constitutes opportunity. For example, students note that, while the narrator may not achieve the financial success valued by middle-class America, he does achieve a sense of his own identity through resisting these values. Then, in a third assignment, they read selections from Jonathan Kozol's *Savage Inequalities*,[32] which depicts the disparities between schools located in poor and those in wealthy communities. They then write about the extent to which students from these disparate school systems can achieve equal opportunity. Those students who initially argued for an individualistic conception of opportunity as achievable for those who just want to work hard begin to realize that institutional forces such as poor schools can play a role in limiting opportunity. Through self-interrogation fostered by these assignments, students are continually rethinking their beliefs and attitudes.

A series of assignments can also be built around analysis of cultural representation of the same phenomenon portrayed by different texts, for example, portrayals of gender roles, class differences, the family, or religion. Kathleen McCormick and her colleagues developed a course around a series of assignments to help students analyze the social forces at work on individuals' positions.[33] For the first assignment, students write about a conflict in their lives and how their perspective on that conflict has changed over time. They discuss their own position relative to the positions of other students in the class, highlighting the notion of competing stances within the classroom. They then study shifts in the representations of specific phenomena in texts, for example, the portrayal of love, gender roles, evil, and spirituality. Students then write about changes in cultural attitudes toward what is considered to be "normal" or "commonsensical" in certain contexts. In the final section of the course, students choose an issue and examine the different stances or positions on that issue, including their own contradictory stances. In this process, they begin to understand how past and present stances are ideologically constructed, an understanding they can then apply to their own responses.

By building each assignment on previous assignments, students begin to perceive patterns in their responses. They may note, for example, that they are consistently dealing with the same ideas or adopting a similar stance across different papers. In reflecting on reasons for these patterns, they may identify certain stances that reflect their beliefs and attitudes.

Using Dialogic Evaluation to Foster Self-Reflection

I have argued that students' writing about literature should be dialogic; it should entertain and interrogate the multiple voices and stances portrayed in texts. I have also argued that students are more likely to adopt a dialogic stance within a social context that is itself dialogic—one in which both students and teachers collaboratively share oral and written responses, not as definitive interpretations, but as open to further inquiry and exploration. How a teacher evaluates students' writing can either foster or discourage this collaborative inquiry.

Unfortunately, teachers often evaluate students' writing about literature simply in terms of the degree to which the students provide supporting evidence from the text. They are less likely to respond in a dialogic manner to the students' ideas. Based on an analysis of college instructors' comments on three thousand papers, Robert Connors and Andrea Lunsford attributed this "text-based" evaluation to the impersonal, evaluative stance adopted by the instructors: "Many of the comments seemed to speak to the student from empyrean heights, delivering judgments in an apparently disinterested way. Very few teachers, for instance, allowed themselves the subjective stance implicit in telling students simply whether they liked or disliked a piece of writing."[34] This distanced tone predominated in 83 percent of the comments.

In a more dialogic approach to evaluation, teachers engage in mutual inquiry with students. They react to students' responses in a descriptive, conversational mode that encourages students to reflect further on their responses. They also provide an external, alternative perspective that challenges students to rethink their responses. In providing dialogic feedback, teachers model the kinds of responses they hope students will employ in responding to literature.

For example, teachers may describe students' use of different voices and stances in their responses, as well as what they perceive as the tensions between these voices and stances. In reflecting on these tensions, students may then recognize the conflicted nature of their own response as symptomatic of their own ambivalent attitudes. For example, a teacher might note that, in responding to "Theme," a student adopts both the voice of a "teacher," who hopes that the speaker will conform to the instructor's demands if he is to succeed in school, and a "student," who applauds the speaker's sense of the need to share his own experience as a means of potentially challenging the instructor's world view. By using feedback to foster students' awareness of these different voices and stances, teachers help students begin to assess the value of these voices relative to their own voices. As Thomas Recchio argued, students can thereby begin to understand the complexity of the relationships between competing voices: "In order for the student to begin to realize her own voice, she has to liberate it from the other voices in the paper, not in a process of rejecting those voices, but in managing them, using them as a background against which she can sound her own."[35]

Students can also, as part of a portfolio evaluation, select essays or journal entries from the beginning, middle, and end of a course that represent changes in their responses during a course. Students can reflect on how these selected responses reflect shifts in their response strategies, voices, and stances. They may note that in the beginning of a course they simply summarized plots, while at the end of the course, they analyzed texts. They can also reflect on reasons for differences or changes in their voices or stances, for example, reasons related to increased social exchange of their responses with their peers.

In his eighteenth-century literature course, Russell Hunt had students share their responses with each other on a computer network.[36] Students then used material from the computer chat exchange to develop drafts, which they then shared with peers for further feedback. As the students became more accustomed to this informal chat mode, they recognized that they were responding in a different voice or discourse. One student, Barb, began the course by writing in a formal mode, for example, "Ultimately, the relationship between comedy and its audience cannot be measured because society is not homogenous in nature." Toward the end of the course, after much experience with computer exchanges, she wrote, "From what I've read about the often diseased food at the time, I don't think I would have wanted to have eaten back then." In reflecting on the differences between her more formal and her informal responses, Barb noted:

I found my initial report to be more formal. I think we were trying to impress you, the professor, rather than our classmates because that is what we are used to doing . . . we try to sound as academic as possible. When we write for the benefit of our classmates, we know that they are at the same academic level, so we don't have to sound so professional. The writing in class is more friendly; more personal and less formal.[37]

Barb related the differences between her formal essay writing and her more informal computer-chat writing to differences in purpose and audience, impressing the professor versus sharing responses to inform her classmates. She recognized that noting differences in social contexts is itself an important aspect of learning literature.

In summary, through dialogic writing about literature, students learn to appreciate the complexity of literary language as constituted by multiple, competing voices and stances. They open themselves to the playfulness of language and become more resistant to monologic uses of language. And through adopting different stances evoked by certain kinds of text-world experiences, they experiment with multiple forms of real-world identities, beliefs, and attitudes.

Notes

1. Mikhail Bakhtin, *The Dialogic Imagination*, ed. Michael Holquist; trans. Caryl Emerson and Michael Holquist (Austin: University of Texas Press, 1981); idem, *Speech Genres and Other Late Essays*, trans. Vern W. McGee (Austin: University of Texas Press, 1986); idem, *Art and Answerability: Early Philosophical Essays by M. M. Bakhtin*, ed. Michael Holquist and Vadim Liapunov (Austin: University of Texas Press, 1990); idem, *Problems of Dostoevsky's Poetics*, ed. and trans. Caryl Emerson (New York: Manchester University Press, 1984). For summaries of Mikhail Bakhtin's work, see David Danow, *The Thought of Mikhail Bakhtin* (London: Macmillan, 1991); Simon Dentith, *Bakhtinian Thought: An Introductory Reader* (London: Routledge, 1995); Michael Holquist, *Dialogism: Bakhtin and His World* (London: Routledge, 1990): Gary Saul Morson and Caryl Emerson, *Mikhail Bakhtin, Creation of a Prosaics* (Stanford, Cal.: Stanford University Press, 1990). For applications to literature, see Don Bialostosky, *Wordsworth, Dialogics and the Practice of Criticism* (New York: Cambridge University Press, 1992); David Lodge, *After Bakhtin: Essays on Fiction and Criticism* (New York: Routledge, 1990); Lynne Pearce, *Reading Dialogics* (New York: Edward Arnold, 1994).

2. Bakhtin, *Art and Answerability*.

3. F. Scott Fitzgerald, *The Great Gatsby* (New York: Scribner, 1981).

4. Bakhtin, *The Dialogic Imagination*. See discussion by James Wertsch in *Voices of the Mind: A Sociocultural Approach to Mediated Action* (Cambridge, Mass.: Harvard University Press, 1991), p. 144. Margaret McKeown and Isabel Beck suggest in chapter 5 in this volume that this authoritative voice, described by Bakhtin, characterizes the language of textbooks.

5. For a discussion of this point, see George Kamberelis and K. D. Scott "Other People's Voices: The Coarticulation of Texts and Subjectivities," *Linguistics and Education* 4 (1992): 359-403. Kamberelis and Scott suggest that other people's voices provide a Vygotskian "zone of proximal development" for young people, who appropriate and transform those voices.

6. Marshall Gregory, "The Hydra of Theory vs. the Unifying Mission of Teaching," *College English* 59 (1997): 49.

7. Bakhtin, *Speech Genres*, p. 7.

8. Arthur N. Applebee, *Literature in the Secondary School* (Urbana, Ill.: National Council of Teachers of English, 1993).

9. Elise Earthman, "Creating the Virtual Work: Readers' Processes in Understanding Literary Texts," *Research in the Teaching of English* 26 (1993): 351-384.

10. Marcia Farr, "Essayist Literacy and Other Verbal Performances," *Written Communication* 10 (1993): 4-38; Ruth Spack, "The Acquisition of Academic Literacy in a Second Language," *Written Communication* 10 (1993): 3-62.

11. Louise Rosenblatt, *Literature as Exploration* (New York: Modern Language Association, 1996).

12. Kamberelis and Scott, "Other People's Voices."

13. Gordon Pradl, *Literature for Democracy: Reading as a Social Act* (Portsmouth, N. H.: Boynton/Cook, 1996).

14. Michael A. K. Halliday, *Spoken and Written Language* (New York: Oxford University Press, 1989).

15. Lynne Anderson-Inman, Carol Knox-Quinn, and Peter Tromba, "Synchronous Writing Environments: Real-time Interaction in Cyberspace," *Journal of Adolescent and Adult Literacy* 40 (1996): 134-138. See also, Scott Christian, *Exchanging Lives: Middle School Writers Online* (Urbana, Ill.: National Council of Teachers of English, forthcoming).

16. Stephen P. Witte and Jennifer Flach, "Notes Toward an Assessment of Advanced Ability to Communicate," *Assessing Writing* 1 (1994): 207-246.

17. Bakhtin, *The Dialogic Imagination.*

18. Ibid.

19. Morson and Emerson, *Mikhail Bakhtin,* p. 312.

20. Bakhtin, *The Dialogic Imagination,* p. 303.

21. Anne Floriani, "Negotiating What Counts: Roles and Relationships, Texts and Contexts, Content and Meaning," *Linguistics and Education* 5 (1993): 214-274; Richard Beach and Margaret Phinney, "Students' Uses of Intercontextual Links in Responding to and Writing Stories," *Linguistics and Education* (in press).

22. Jay Bolter, *The Writing Space: The Computer, Hypertext, and the History of Writing* (Hillsdale, N. J.: Lawrence Erlbaum, 1991).

23. Langston Hughes, *The Big Sea: An Autobiography* (New York: Hill and Wang, 1993).

24. *Advanced Placement Course Description* (Princeton, N. J.: College Entrance Examination Board and Educational Testing Service, 1991), p. 18.

25. Patricia Sullivan, "Writing in the Graduate Curriculum: Literary Criticism as Composition," in *Composition Theory for the Postmodern Classroom,* ed. Gary Olson and Sidney Dobrin (Albany, N. Y.: SUNY Press, 1994), p. 41.

26. Elise Ann Earthman, "Creating the Virtual Work: Readers' Processes in Understanding Literary Texts," *Research in the Teaching of English* 27 (1992): 351-384.

27. Richard Beach and James Marshall, *Teaching Literature in the Secondary School* (San Diego, Cal.: Harcourt Brace, 1991).

28. Richard Beach, Deborah Appleman, and Sharon Dorsey, "Adolescents' Uses of Intertextual Links to Understand Literature," in *Developing Discourse Practices in Adolescence and Adulthood,* ed. Richard Beach and Susan Hynds (Norwood, N. J.: Ablex, 1990), pp. 224-245.

29. Kenneth Burke, *A Rhetoric of Motives* (Berkeley: University of California Press, 1969).

30. Michelle Commeyras, "Questions Children Most Discuss: What Teachers and Students Learn in a Second Grade Classroom" (Paper presented at the annual meeting of the National Reading Conference, Charleston, South Carolina, 1996).

31. Ralph Ellison, *The Invisible Man* (New York: Modern Library, 1992).

32. Jonathan Kozol, *Savage Inequalities* (New York: Crown, 1991).

33. Kathleen McCormick, *The Culture of Reading and the Teaching of English* (New York: Manchester University Press, 1994).

34. Robert Connors and Andrea Lunsford, "Teachers' Rhetorical Comments on Student Papers," *College Composition and Communication* 44 (1993): 214.

35. Thomas Recchio, "A Bakhtinian Reading of Student Writing," *College Composition and Communication* 42 (1991): 450.

36. Russell Hunt, "Speech Genres, Writing Genres, School Genres, and Computer Games," in *Learning and Teaching Genre,* ed. Aviva Freedman and Peter Medway (Portsmouth, N. H.: Boynton/Cook, 1994), pp. 243-262.

37. Ibid., p. 254.

CHAPTER XI

Students as Critics of Disciplinary Texts

MAUREEN A. MATHISON

Much academic writing is based on reading. Writers refer to other writers' texts, summarize them, dismantle them, and synthesize them. Often they also judge the texts, providing commentary for other readers about their value. The term for this evaluative kind of writing from reading is *critique*, which refers sometimes to the type of text that is produced and other times to the practice of producing it. In this chapter I consider the genre and practice of critique not only in English studies but in other areas of study, where responding to other writers' texts is also a part of the educational process. I begin with a brief historical background on written forms of critique and a discussion of the role of critique in the academic disciplines. That introduction provides a context for my major focus, which is student critiquing. Incorporated in my discussion of student critiquing is an extended illustration from a study I recently conducted in an undergraduate sociology course. The study examined two aspects of critiquing: how the students critiqued a disciplinary text and how the students' critiques were, in turn, evaluated by professors in that discipline. I conclude with some comments about the importance of critique as an educational practice at various levels of education and suggestions for a "pedagogy of critique."

The Role of Critique in Disciplinary Thinking

The beginnings of contemporary critique go back to classical antiquity, when scholars examined texts to identify and clarify the principles that were at work in particular types of discourse. By seeing the principles applied, students could learn and appropriate them for their own use. Contemporary forms of critique are related to the Roman tradition of "studium,"[1] which involved the very close reading of texts for an explanation of the work, but did not require an explicit evaluation of its claims.

Maureen A. Mathison is Assistant Professor in the Communication Department and a faculty member of the University Writing Program at the University of Utah, where she coordinates the Writing Emphasis/Intensive Program.

It was not uncommon for the critic to write commentary on the text itself so that those remarks could be read alongside the author's words, sometimes line by line. Thus the content of the critique was limited to the topics presented, and its order was dictated by the organization of the original text. The discourse originated by the critic, therefore, served as a type of supplementary reading that added a new dimension to the original work. And because individual critics could supply their own interpretations, the types of comments made about a text were idiosyncratic. According to James Murphy, each commentary was "an expression of the glossator's personal views as well as his understanding of what the original author intend[ed]."[2] Commentary was supplied to various types of texts including literary, religious, and rhetorical treatises for the purpose of elucidation.

Through time, the role of commentary expanded. By the Middle Ages it found its place across educational levels in the pedagogical practices of "lecture" and "commentary," both of which were applied to the disciplines of theology, philosophy, law, and medicine, some of the foundations of the curriculum.[3] During the Renaissance, however, the role of commentary became more limited. Commentary associated with critical inquiry became the province of logic, and rhetoric became the province of eloquence, or the art of writing and speaking well. Liberal education as it was practiced by the humanists was based more on oral disputation than on written commentary as it had been in earlier historical periods. Textual commentary related to eloquence tended to emphasize style and delivery over issues of content. In their schooling, students were more apt to be asked to respond orally to questions of timely interest, among them, those dealing with education, religion, and politics, and to demonstrate the plausibility of their position. Written texts, influenced by this oral emphasis, often were conversational in tone. Through time, though, this emphasis shifted in response to social needs, and essays and written examinations became incorporated into education. The emphasis on eloquence, however, continued until the eighteenth century, when rhetoricians began examining the relationship between understanding and emotion, and rhetorical inquiry turned to the psychological mechanisms associated with texts.[4]

In their introductory chapter, Nancy Nelson and Robert Calfee describe the centrality of criticism in rhetoric, particularly the eighteenth-century rhetoric that was influential through much of the nineteenth century. As the authors of that chapter have already shown, rhetoric lost literary criticism when its focus became composition, and those two—rhetoric/composition and literary criticism—have been separate components of the discipline of English since its inception in the last decades of the nineteenth century.[5]

Critique has been important in the discipline of English, which even has a component labeled *literary criticism*. It has also been important in other disciplines that do not have such a branch. During the Scientific Revolution, for example, scientists began to use the texts of others to originate their own texts and, in so doing, questioned established order. This was an important moment because it opened up the possibility for alternative conjectures regarding phenomena. As scientific inquiry grew, so did the use of critique, expanding into the social scientific disciplines as they developed during the nineteenth century and adopted the scientific method as their own. Scholars continued analyzing and evaluating information with the goal of improving upon it. It became routine for readers to respond critically to the texts of others and to present their positions to an audience of other readers, who in turn would read their texts and respond critically to them. Through the critique of others' claims, an author could demonstrate the validity and novelty of his or her own.

Although critique has been an important feature of inquiry, its nature has changed over time. This was due in part to the expansion of the academic community and its move toward specialization. Charles Bazerman examined the history of the research article as seen in the longest-running English language journal, *Philosophical Transactions of the Royal Society of London*, founded in 1665.[6] He found that the valued intellectual disposition related to critique was not evident in the earlier volumes, but became increasingly prominent and more standardized by the nineteenth century, when a contemporary version of a research article could be identified. Traces of critique in this particular genre can be found today in the review of related research, where gaps and discrepancies are cited, and in the methods section, where scientists and social scientists are able to fill such gaps and resolve discrepancies by employing rigorous methods.

Critique has become an important feature of the knowledge-making endeavor, as undertaken by scientific disciplines and other disciplines emulating the method of science. It is used to position theoretical issues and results of studies and thus transforms or reproduces extant claims about the world. By evaluating the written texts of others doing similar work, scientists determine the relevance of theoretical perspectives and the appropriateness of the methods employed to answer or resolve problems. They then apply this new knowledge to think through and improve upon issues related to their own work, and in so doing, further the work done in their respective areas of inquiry.

In addition to its role in positioning claims, critique flourishes as a means of gatekeeping in the disciplines for ensuring quality (a practice started long ago with the establishment of editorial boards). Through peer review, the worth and soundness of claims are adjudicated by members of a scholarly community. Robert K. Merton has argued that one of the basic norms of science is *organized skepticism*, the taking of a critical stance toward one another's work.[7] Through skepticism and criticism, science is able to maintain its ethical standards, or ethos, ensuring rigor and honesty.

This notion of critique as gatekeeping has been generalized to all academic areas, although the criteria, forums, and customs differ across disciplines. Whereas a scholar is encouraged to be creative, the community judges the worth of the end product to some extent on its fit with convention. If the result does not seem to be within the realm of normal academic inquiry, it is disregarded, or the researcher is asked to go back and modify his or her thinking to craft it more closely to disciplinary concerns.[8] Thus, when scholars evaluate a text, or some aspect of it, they do so based upon established principles.

On the Importance of Becoming a Critic

Within both traditions of academe—the liberal arts tradition and the scientific tradition—it is important for young scholars pursuing disciplinary studies to be able to assess the texts of others. Critiquing has been quite visible in the liberal arts tradition, as it has been a major facet of rhetoric itself and is the central practice of a community within English known as literary critics. Students following this tradition are expected to analyze and often evaluate literary texts according to literary principles. In the scientific and social-scientific disciplines, students, particularly at upper levels, are expected to evaluate claims as they read disciplinary texts. To become disciplinary scholars themselves, they must not only learn the content, the undergirding theories, and the methods of a discipline, but must also be able to evaluate particular contributions.[9] This entails the careful analysis, and perhaps reconsideration, of extant claims for the purposes of constructing a position.

By critiquing in a manner appropriate for a discipline, students demonstrate that they have learned one facet of the discourse of that discipline. Critiquing is a part of a discipline's ways of "being-doing-thinking-valuing-speaking-listening (-writing-reading)," to use James

Paul Gee's phrasing.[10] One history professor recently described for me
what critical thinking means in his discipline, not only on the part of
historians but also on the part of students:

Number one, it means not to believe anything you read the first time. Number
two, it means to read enough different people's versions of a subject so that you
have a pretty reasonable spectrum. And then number three [is] to be able to
collect and filter those materials in your own way of making a reasonable
explanation, whether it's the French Revolution or the Counter-Reformation.[11]

In their disciplinary studies, students have opportunities to read,
analyze, and evaluate the texts of others, to use them as resources in
order to address pertinent issues and problems, which might be win-
nowing instances from historical documents or searching out patents
in government offices. In assigning tasks that engage students in valued ways of thinking, professors provide opportunities for students to
appropriate source material into their own work, with the expectation
that students' perspectives are recognized instances of that discipline's
"ways." And students—some of them, anyway—do acquire those
"ways." For instance, in a study of enculturation that is well known in
English studies, Nate, a first-year graduate student in a rhetoric program, produced writing over the course of the year that became progressively more characteristic of writing valued by members of the disciplinary community for which he was being prepared. One important
indicator of the change was a decrease in the use of the first-person
pronoun, which had been a prominent feature of the personal-expres-
sivist discourse he used at the beginning of the year.[12]

Undergraduates, too, undergo important changes throughout their
higher education experience that are reflected in the writing they do
from their reading. They tend to begin as more naive readers and
writers focusing only on *what* information is presented, but over time
many become more aware of the rhetorical dimension of texts, paying
attention to *how* information is presented and in what contexts. Also
the texts they produce become more easily recognized as instances of
conventional writing for a disciplinary community.[13] One study in particular demonstrates this transition. Six psychology students were followed throughout their undergraduate careers to examine their development as authors. Over time, all six showed a growing awareness of
the discourse of psychology, using more disciplinary concepts and
phrasings in their written texts, which increasingly approximated conventional forms or genres for the discipline. Some even began creating

their own identifiable bodies of work by writing texts that were inter-related thematically and repeatedly referred to the same issues and sources. As "emergent authors," these students were learning the forms—and the thinking that accompanies those forms.[14]

The expectations for writing differ across the scholarly divisions of the humanities, natural sciences, and social sciences, and the individual disciplines within them. Students pursuing an interest in one of these divisions may be asked to perform tasks that are unique to the intellectual problems associated with it. In the humanities, the individuality and uniqueness of a position is important, although scholars approach their work from broad philosophical orientations, such as Marxism and feminism. In the sciences, there is more of an assumption of shared understandings and procedures. When a scientific problem is identified, the community of scientists is portrayed as approaching it incrementally, building on previous findings. The tasks students are assigned in science tend often to presume this sort of consensus about what knowledge is and how knowledge is to be developed. In the social sciences, where problems are not as clearly defined as in the natural sciences, reading-writing tasks are more likely than in the sciences to encourage students to identify an issue and then to construct their own position, placing it within the concerns of the discipline and those whose work is related.[15]

Sociologists, for example, are not as likely to assume shared frameworks in their thinking about social and group behavior as are scientists in their thinking about the natural world. Consequently, professional sociologists must identify pertinent issues for an audience and argue their relevance for the disciplinary community. One of the ways in which they accomplish their identification and argument is by citing work of other authors, not simply to build upon it but to lay the foundation for the novelty of their own perspective. They must, in effect, persuade readers that the phenomenon and claims made about it are warranted. Once they have established the issue, they persuade the reader that what is novel is not the phenomenon itself but the manner in which it is viewed. In doing so, they employ the particularized language and other means of communication, such as visuals and numbers, used by other sociologists.[16]

Students of sociology must learn to identify issues and argue their relevance, while at the same time they learn the conventions for writing in the discipline. The results of one study showed that, when evaluating research reports written in an introductory sociology class, instructors focused on the students' ability to employ the sociological language associated with particular issues and to develop those issues with appropriate sociological lines of reasoning.[17]

More specific to this chapter, critique itself would vary somewhat across divisions and disciplines.[18] Students in the natural sciences, for example, may be expected to critique the work of others in order to identify gaps in knowledge as a basis for proposing solutions. Students writing in the social sciences may be expected to demonstrate the importance of a problem so that they can offer a particular position on it. And in the humanities the goal of the reading-writing tasks may not be the solution of a problem but the construction of a unique way of looking at the problem that opens up new areas of possibility. One problem begets another.

Instructors assigning reading-writing tasks expect disciplinary ways of understanding, analyzing, and commenting on texts. Depending on the discipline and the course, these objects of critique can be research reports, theoretical explanations, or literary texts.

An Example of Student Critiquing in Sociology

When scholars in the various academic disciplines critique a text, they provide commentary about it, which may be negative or may be positive, and they provide support for the various evaluative comments they make. In doing so, they indicate either disagreement, which means transforming claims by providing a different perspective, or agreement, which means providing reasons to maintain the claims as they are. Student critiquing can involve much the same thing, according to some analyses I have recently conducted on critiques written for a sociology class. For their critiques, student critics selected topical material, made comments about it, and provided support for their comments. There were, however, certain ways of setting up the critique, certain kinds of comments, and certain sorts of support that were favored over others by sociology professors who rated them for me.

The critiques were written by thirty two undergraduate students in a Sociology of Religion class, a junior-level elective, at a public university in the Northeast.[19] All except six of the students were juniors or seniors, and twelve were sociology majors. The professor, who referred to herself as a critical sociologist, regularly incorporated features of critique into class discussions and assignments. She believed it was important for students to "think like sociologists" and explained that this meant examining issues from a perspective that was systematic and attentive to the discipline's assumptions (its objects of inquiry and the questions posed about them).

To engage students in some of the debate regarding contemporary issues, the professor asked students to read and respond to "On the Margins of the Sacred," a fourteen-page scholarly article that challenged traditional definitions of religion.[20] In effect, she was asking her students to critique the usefulness of this new position for other sociologists who study religion. This was not an unreasonable task, according to the professor, because students had been in the course for nine weeks and had covered the material they would need to inform their evaluation. Students were given one week, outside of class, to complete the assignment.

I analyzed these critiques for patterns of topics and comments. For example, a student might select the topic "definition of quasi-religion," discussed by the authors of the article, and respond to that topic with positive commentary ("The authors are correct when they say that people will react differently, depending upon whether they think of themselves as 'doing religion.'"). Or the student might present the topic but make negative commentary ("By doing this [categorizing] they are doing essentially the same thing they are being critical of other sociologists for doing."). Or the student might simply present that particular topic without evaluative commentary ("Some of the quasi-religions mentioned by the authors do not want to be typed as religious since some people might be scared off by the idea of a different religion.").

My discourse analyses also focused on the kind of support that was given for the evaluative comments. The support tended to be of two types: disciplinary and personal. For example, the following sentence that one student wrote to back up a positive comment was considered disciplinary support: "While people still have the same needs that caused them to turn to religion—need to have answers to the unanswerable, a sense of order in the world, a sense of community, help in dealing with human dilemmas—many of these needs have grown due to changes in society." The following sentence that another student wrote to back up a positive comment was considered personal support: "I feel that I learned a great deal about what these organizations stood for, believed in, and why they would choose to be the way that they were."

By examining the topics students selected and the comments they made about them, I could determine larger discourse patterns.[21] Some students set up their critiques in two parts with the first part presenting topical material for the entire text they read and the second presenting their evaluative commentary upon it. I called this pattern the

Topic-Comment Separate Configuration. Other students interwove their topics and comments throughout their critiques. They would introduce a topic, such as the therapeutic services provided by these "quasi-religious" organizations, would comment on that topic, then move on to another topic, such as the socialization of children into the Judeo-Christian tradition, and comment on it, and so on. I called this pattern the Topic-Comment Integrated Configuration.

From these analyses, I found that the students wrote two major kinds of critiques, which could be differentiated from each other not only by organizational pattern but also by amount and kinds of commentary and types of support. Approximately half of the critiques were set up with the Topic-Comment Separate Configuration, and the other half were set up with the Topic-Comment Integrated Configuration. Students using the Topic-Comment Separate pattern wrote critiques that tended to be summaries with very little commentary; they presented lengthy overviews of the source article first, in which they moved from one topic to another, suspending judgment, and provided very brief evaluative commentary at the end. For example, one student began her critique with the authors' definition of "quasi-religion" and then described several of the organizations mentioned in the article that fit into that category. It was not until the end of her critique that she provided any kind of evaluative comment. Although enrolled in a course in which the professor regularly emphasized examining issues from a sociological framework, students writing these critiques primarily summarized claims from the source text and offered little commentary about any sociological issue that was raised.

For many of these critiques written with the Topic-Comment Separate Configuration, any evaluative commentary that was included tended to receive support from the students' personal experiences. Instead of making their evaluation of the source text relevant for a community of scholars for whom the concept might have important implications, students writing these critiques seemed to be more self-focused, in most cases considering how the concept related to their own religious views. Some statements were similar to the expressivist discourse students might be encouraged to write in a journal in a reader-response oriented literature class. The following conclusion from one student's critique illustrates this type of stance:

The essay caused me to think about my ways of defining religion. . . . It made me think about where I draw the line on what is religious or religion. I found it difficult to separate myself from my strong Catholic upbringing.

In contrast, the students whose critiques suggested the Topic-Comment Integrated Configuration tended not only to provide more evaluative commentary but also to provide commentary of a different type. Their commentary, which could be positive but was more likely to be negative, tended to receive disciplinary support, as students contextualized their responses for a scholarly community. Consider the following conclusion from one of these students' papers, which assesses the contribution the article makes to sociological knowledge:

I feel that although the authors have attempted to introduce a logical argument toward their theory of quasi-religions, they have ignored or simplified too many facets of religion as it relates to the critical function of society.

This conclusion is a summing up of more specific critical commentary that had been integrated throughout the critique as particular subtopics were addressed. This contrasts with the previously cited conclusion from the Topic-Comment Separate critique; that other conclusion was not a summary of previous commentary but *was* the commentary.

The students' critiques were rated holistically for quality by four sociology professors who taught at the same university the students attended; one was the students' own professor. In performing the rating, these sociologists were asked to apply their own criteria for disciplinary standards. After I examined the ratings in relation to the discourse features, I discovered that the critiques that received the highest quality ratings were those that used proportionately more negative commentary and had those comments substantiated with disciplinary support. These two measures—amount of negative commentary and of disciplinary support—were the strongest predictors of the quality ratings. The critiques with largest proportions of negative commentary and disciplinary support tended to be those written with the Topic-Comment Integrated Configuration. The negative commentary, supported with disciplinary evidence, was interwoven with material from the source text.

In subsequent interviews conducted individually, these four sociology professors were asked to discuss what constitutes a quality critique. Although they had different ways of talking about such matters, all of them mentioned four features that were strongly related to the ratings. First, students had to show an understanding of the article they were critiquing. To do this, professors expected some summarizing, which would demonstrate an understanding of the material. Second, students had to go beyond summarizing and evaluate the source text. Professors tended to value negative commentary because those kinds of comments showed that students were intellectually engaged with the issues presented by the authors. Positive commentary indicated students were reproducing rather than transforming the source article. Third, students had to substantiate their claims with evidence. Three of the professors stated that the evidence should be discipline-based. But one said that, although he expected discipline-based support for general points, it was fine also for students to apply experience from their own lives on smaller points, because the goal of sociology is to get students to think about their own lives in relation to sociological issues. And, fourth, students had to place the article in a broader context. This meant they had to demonstrate some knowledge of the article's value to the sociological community.

In summary, then, students' written texts suggested different approaches to the critique, from presenting a detailed account of the source article with little evaluative commentary to presenting an evaluative analysis substantiated with disciplinary support. The critiques more highly valued by the professors, though, were those that positioned students more as agents of change, that is, as authors who could disagree with authors of the source text.

While this study of students as critics of disciplinary texts has provided some insights into student critiquing, there are many questions that remain concerning the use and value of critique in other contexts. The study I reported on was conducted in a university setting in a third-year sociology course as students commented on one text. To help us understand critique more fully, subsequent research might address how critique is performed and evaluated at other levels, in other courses, in other disciplines, and at other professional sites. In addition, research concerning multiple texts would provide information on how students interpret the task of evaluating various (and perhaps conflicting) positions.

Critique as an Academic Practice

Disciplinary writing is one way for students to learn about a field of study, its assumptions, its objects of inquiry, and the questions posed about them. The tasks that are assigned to students in their courses are a means for them to begin to acquire the habits of thinking associated with a particular discipline, for instance, sociology as it has been discussed in this chapter. At the same time, the expectations for student writing differ from those for professional writing and students often find themselves demonstrating a mastery of content in their written assignments as much as they do an understanding of the tenets and methods associated with the discipline. Students who wrote the summary and response critiques in the sociology class, for example, may have been demonstrating their mastery of content by emphasizing summary of the main points over commentary in their texts, cutting short the space allocated for response. They may have thought they were being "good" students, a lesson learned from earlier educational experiences that emphasized only the mastery of content.

In disciplinary reading and writing, students are required to participate in a community's practices as they are learning about them. By practices, I mean the tasks and the types of disciplinary thinking associated with them. This could be anything from setting up an experiment to writing a critique. As students learn disciplinary genres, they are learning social practices. Genres, such as critique, are associated with particular kinds of social actions in academic disciplines,[22] and each genre has a particular kind of rhetorical force insisting that a text be read or heard in a particular way. The kind of action intended is signaled, in part, through recognized discourse conventions. In the social sciences, a research report, with its introduction, method, results, and discussion sections, solves a problem or answers a question. A summary, through compressing information, presents some work or thought—in gist form—without explicit assessment. A critique is presentation and assessment; it presents a person's work and assesses its value. A reader of critique, seeing topics selected for commentary and commentary provided, knows a critical disposition is to be taken toward what is discussed.

In this sense, genres help a writer and audience "co-create meaning."[23] By employing the written conventions of a community, a writer is more likely to connect with readers, who can anticipate the social action suggested by the text. Information may be more easily recognized and considered by the reader because of an assumed shared understanding that directs attention in particular ways. Thus, when writers perform a given task, they are guided by certain parameters of the task that have been socially designated and accepted by community members as sanctioned types of communication.

Learning the practices also means learning the more particular emphases given by one's own institution and the people there. Although much attention today is given to the shared assumptions and conventions of a discipline, there are differences as well. Particular institutions of higher education, for example, are recognized for their own emphases and their own specialized approaches to a discipline, and students' education can reflect these differences.[24]

Also, within a program at a particular university, individual professors vary in their practice of their discipline: what they consider important and how they approach their work. In the critique study discussed earlier, all four sociology professors agreed to some extent about what constitutes a quality text. However, the analyses also revealed individual preferences.[25] While all four are sociologists, they bring their own individual perspectives about sociology and its practices to the classroom and, in doing so, they influence student expectations and, consequently, student learning. Students juggle multiple constraints in education, from institutional values to individual professors' preferences for evaluating papers to their own personal histories, motivations, and goals.

Toward a Pedagogy of Critique

While critique may be an integral part of disciplinary practices, it is often not explicitly taught in educational settings, even though it is implicit in assignments. Actual instruction in critiquing might help students, like the sociology students just discussed, to meet the expectations of their professors. They could be shown that more is required than summarizing. Many students have been schooled to believe that there are "right" and "wrong" answers, and that if the information is in a textbook, it must be correct.[26] Many classroom practices at all educational levels contribute to this kind of thinking and preclude students' learning that disciplinary claims are often in transformation—being improved upon, updated, and even discarded.

Students must, therefore, be given opportunities to dismantle texts, to examine others' claims, and determine their own stance relative to those claims. In some settings, personal criteria are appropriate. In other settings, it is not enough for students to apply personal criteria to disciplinary problems and issues, as many of the students in the sociology class did. As Judith Roof and Robyn Wiegman explain:

When personal experience is the basis for critical knowledge, such knowledge may be premised on a fairly unexamined opinion, whose rhetorical force comes from the appeal of the "authentic." When opinion claims to be unassailable because it is based on experience, authority becomes tautological. . . . This tautology fixes ultimately on the person of the speaker who becomes both the subject and object of critical attention while criticism becomes an extension of personal essence. Although the "in se" authority of self appears to grant a certain kind of experiential authority, it also limits authority.[27]

Effective critique in much disciplinary writing signals the value of information for a community of readers, not for a single individual. When writers make judgments about the texts they read, their critiques are supposed to be in accord with academic standards in terms of form and substance, but at the same time bear the mark of individual thought.

The very nature of the genre requires students to read the text of another with a critical disposition toward the ideas and issues presented in order to construct their own written positions about them. Explicit instruction in critiquing the text of another should help students overcome their difficulties in taking a stance and arguing a position. Moreover, reading the text of another for the purpose of evaluating that person's claims has the potential to facilitate thoughtful and independent thinking in students, a skill that is valued not only throughout one's academic career, but in one's professional and personal life as well.

Students at various levels of education should engage in some literate activities that authorize them to challenge received knowledge—to get them to go beyond what has been called a "recitation literacy."[28] There are some pedagogies that do just that. For example, Yager explains that in the Science/Technology/Society Movement, a student in elementary or secondary school "locates, collects, analyzes, and evaluates sources of scientific and technological information and uses these sources in solving problems, making decisions, and taking action."[29] Students' assignments may involve reading the local newspaper as well as textbooks, and their writing may involve writing not only reports to the class but also letters to manufacturers.[30] These uses of reading-writing make science accessible and practical to students while teaching them ways of evaluating evidence and marshaling it in order to persuade others.

Also, in social studies, programs such as the Questioning the Author approach described in an earlier chapter, teach students that authors, even textbook authors, are real people and therefore can be challenged. Students can also learn to challenge each other. Excerpts from some of the participants quoted in a study by Beck et al. demonstrate that allowing students to dismantle texts encourages independent thinking and taking a stance: "We always disagree with each other. Then we read on and start disagreeing with ourselves. Then we find out about our disagreement and why we were wrong. We disagree with ourselves if we're wrong."[31] Also in the humanities, some new pedagogies encourage students to examine situations from multiple perspectives, to begin to understand that constructing accounts is contingent upon the point of view of the person evaluating the evidence. Students in secondary history courses may read about the same event as told by different individuals, some authors representing one side of the American Revolution and others representing the other side.[32] Students learn that knowledge is often not straightforward and that historians must evaluate and weigh many factors when creating an account. Pedagogical initiatives such as these assist students in taking steps toward critique by helping them understand that claims are transformed through some of the skills related to these activities.

A "pedagogy of critique" would teach the major aspects of social action: to determine major points made by an author, to analyze underlying assumptions, to judge the strength and weaknesses of the support the author provides, and to engage in argument as a critic, persuading others of the validity of a critique by providing lines of reasoning. These features overlap with some of those considered important to critical thinking in general.[33] It is important to note that, while critique and critical thinking are related, critique emphasizes the ability of students to construct a new text that is grounded in the tenets and methods of the community for whom the argument is relevant. To achieve authority as writers of critiques, students must learn to recognize that particular information is valued and is valued in particular ways.

In teaching students to perform the social action of critique, the emphasis is neither on the students as writers (process) nor on the texts they produce (product) but on the appropriateness of the writer's efforts for particular rhetorical situations. In this manner students can begin to understand that reading and responding critically to the texts of others is not just a school-based exercise, but a literate practice that can potentially further thinking about important issues—their own thinking as well as the thinking of readers of their texts.

NOTES

1. Edwin Black, *Rhetorical Criticism: A Study in Method* (Madison: University of Wisconsin Press, 1978), p. 3; Donald Lemen Clark, *Rhetoric in Greco-Roman Education* (Morningside Heights, N. Y.: Columbia University Press, 1957); Karlheinz Stierle, "Studium: Perspectives on Institutionalized Modes of Reading," *New Literary History* 22 (1991): 116.

2. James J. Murphy, *Rhetoric in the Middle Ages: A History of Rhetorical Theory from St. Augustine to the Renaissance* (Berkeley: University of California Press, 1974), p. 144.

3. Stierle, "Studium," p. 18.

4. John O. Ward, "Renaissance Commentators on Ciceronian Rhetoric," in *Renaissance Eloquence*, ed. James J. Murphy (Berkeley: University of California Press,

1983), pp. 126-173; T. O. Sloane, "Rhetorical Education and Two-Sided Argument," in *Renaissance-Rhetorik/Renaissance Rhetoric*, ed. Heinrich F. Plett (Berlin: De Gruyter, 1993), pp. 163-178; James L. Golden and Edward P. J. Corbett, eds., *The Rhetoric of Blair, Campbell, and Whateley* (New York: Holt, Rinehart and Winston, 1968).

5. See also Nan Johnson, *Nineteenth-Century Rhetoric in North America* (Carbondale: Southern Illinois University Press, 1991).

6. Charles Bazerman, *Shaping Written Knowledge: The Genre and Activity of the Experimental Article in Science* (Madison: University of Wisconsin Press, 1988).

7. Robert K. Merton, *Social Theory and Social Structure*, 3rd ed. (New York: Free Press, 1968).

8. Norman Storer, *The Social System of Science* (New York: Holt, Reinhart and Winston, 1966); Greg Myers, *Writing Biology: Texts in the Social Construction of Knowledge* (Madison: University of Wisconsin Press, 1990); Carole Blair, Julie R. Brown, and Leslie A. Baxter, "Disciplining the Feminine," *Quarterly Journal of Speech* 80 (1994): 383-409.

9. Brent Bridgeman and Sybil B. Carlson, "Survey of Academic Tasks," *Written Communication* 1 (1984): 247-280; Mark L. Waldo, "Inquiry as a Non-Invasive Approach to Cross-Curricular Writing Consultancy," *Language and Learning across the Disciplines* 1, no. 3 (1996): 6-19.

10. James P. Gee, *Social Linguistics and Literacies: Ideology in Discourses* (London: Falmer Press, 1990), p. 174.

11. Maureen A. Mathison and Linn Bekins. "Writing in Disciplines: Enculturating Students into Academic Ways of Knowing" (working paper, 1998).

12. Carol Berkenkotter, Thomas N. Huckin, and John M. Ackerman, "Conventions, Conversations, and the Writer: A Case Study of a Student in a Rhetoric Ph.D. Program." *Research in the Teaching of English* 22 (1988): 9-44.

13. Christina Haas, "Learning to Read Biology: One Student's Rhetorical Development in College." *Written Communication* 11 (1994): 67; Robert K. Schwegler and Linda K. Shamoon, "Meaning Attribution in Ambiguous Texts in Sociology," in *Textual Dynamics of the Professions: Historical and Contemporary Studies of Writing in Professional Communities*, eds. Charles Bazerman and James Paradis (Madison: University of Wisconsin Press, 1991); Sharon Stockton, "Writing in History: Narrating the Subject of Time," *Written Communication* 12 (1995): 47-73; Dorothy A. Winsor, *Writing Like an Engineer: A Rhetorical Education* (Hillsdale, N. J.: Lawrence Erlbaum, 1996).

14. Nancy Nelson Spivey and Maureen A. Mathison, "Development of Authoring Identity," in Nancy Nelson Spivey, *The Constructivist Metaphor: Reading, Writing, and the Making of Meaning* (San Diego, Cal.: Academic Press, 1997), pp. 223-234.

15. Susan Peck MacDonald, "Problem Definition in Academic Writing," *College English* 49 (1987): 315-331.

16. Richard Harvey Brown, *A Poetic of Sociology: Toward a Logic of Discovery for the Human Sciences* (Chicago: University of Chicago Press, 1977); Ricca Edmondson, *Rhetoric in Sociology* (London: Macmillan Press, 1984); Christine R. Casanave, "The Role of Writing in Socializing Graduate Students into an Academic Discipline in the Social Sciences," (Ph.D. diss., Stanford University, 1990); Paul Prior, "Girl Talk Tales, Causal Models, and the Dissertation: Exploring the Topical Contours of Context in Sociology Talk and Text," *Languages and Learning across the Disciplines* 1, no. 1 (1994): 5-34.

17. Schwegler and Shamoon, "Ambiguous Texts." See discussion of this study in Paul Prior's chapter in this volume.

18. MacDonald, "Problem Definition."

19. Maureen A. Mathison, "Writing the Critique, a Text about a Text," *Written Communication* 13 (1996): 314-354.

20. Arthur L. Greil and David R. Rudy, "On the Margins of the Sacred," in *In Gods We Trust*, 2nd ed., ed. Thomas Robbins and Dick Anthony (New Brunswick, N. J.: Transactions Publishers, 1990): 219.

21. Joseph E. Grimes, *The Thread of Discourse* (New York: Mouton Publishers, 1975); Bonnie J. F. Meyer, *The Organization of Prose and Its Effects on Memory* (Amsterdam: North Holland Press, 1975); Lawrence W. Rosenfield, "The Anatomy of Critical Discourse," *Speech Monographs* 35, no. 1 (1968): 50-69.

22. Carolyn Miller, "Genre as Social Action," in *Genre and the New Rhetoric*, ed. Aviva Freedman and Peter Medway (Bristol, Penn.: Taylor and Francis, 1994), pp. 23-42; John Swales, *Genre Analysis* (Cambridge: Cambridge University Press, 1990); Kathleen M. Jamieson, "Generic Constraints and the Rhetorical Situation," *Philosophy and Rhetoric* 6, no. 3 (1973): 162-170; Carol Berkenkotter and Thomas N. Huckin, *Genre Knowledge in Disciplinary Communication: Cognition/Culture/Power* (Hillsdale, N. J.: Lawrence Erlbaum, 1995).

23. Richard Lee Enos and Janice M. Lauer, "The Meaning of *Heuristic* in Aristotle's *Rhetoric* and Its Implications for Contemporary Rhetorical Theory," in *A Rhetoric of Doing: Essays on Written Discourse in Honor of James L. Kinneavy*, ed. Stephen P. Witte, Neil Nakadate, and Roger Cherry (Carbondale: Southern Illinois University Press, 1992): p. 80.

24. See, for example, Arjo Klamer and David Colander, *The Making of an Economist* (Boulder, Colo.: Westview Press, 1990).

25. Mathison, "Writing the Critique."

26. Kathleen McCormick, *The Culture of Reading and the Teaching of English* (New York: St. Martin's Press, 1994).

27. Judith Roof and Robyn Wiegman, "Speaking Parts," in *Who Can Speak?: Authority and Critical Identity*, ed. Judith Roof and Robyn Wiegman (Urbana: University of Illinois Press, 1995), p. 93.

28. Daniel Resnick and Lauren Resnick, "The Nature of Literacy: A Historical Exploration," in *Perspectives on Literacy*, ed. Eugene R. Kintgen, Barry M. Kroll, and Mike Rose (Carbondale: Southern Illinois University Press, 1988), pp. 190-220.

29. Robert E. Yager, "History of Science/Technology/Society as Reform in the United States," in *Science/Technology/Society as Reform in Science Education*, ed. Robert E. Yager (Albany: State University of New York Press, 1996), p. 8.

30. Robert E. Yager, ed., *What Research Says to the Science Teacher: The Science, Technology, Society Movement* (Washington, D.C.: National Science Teachers Association, 1993).

31. Isabel L. Beck, Margaret G. McKeown, Cheryl Sandora, Linda Kucan, and Jo Worthy, "Questioning the Author: A Year-long Classroom Implementation to Engage Students with Texts." *Elementary School Journal* 96 (1996): 409.

32. Robert J. Swartz, "Teaching for Thinking: A Developmental Model for the Infusion of Thinking Skills into Mainstream Instruction," in *Teaching Thinking Skills: Theory and Practice*, ed. Joan Boykoff Baron and Robert J. Sternberg (New York: W. H. Freeman and Company, 1987), pp. 106-126.

33. Robert H. Ennis, "A Taxonomy of Critical Thinking Dispositions and Abilities," in *Teaching Thinking Skills: Theory and Practice*, ed. Baron and Sternberg, pp. 9-26.

CHAPTER XII

Reading and Writing Contextualized

NANCY NELSON

> From time to time . . . it is imperative that we stand aside from the
> movement of affairs to review trends, to assay products, to map out
> new paths.
>
> Harold Rugg, *26th NSSE Yearbook*

Some occasions invite, even force, us to reflect on the past, to imagine historical figures with whom we have some kinship, and to consider past events that affected the course of our lives. This is one of those times for me, as I write a concluding chapter for this volume, the ninety-seventh yearbook of the National Society for the Study of Education. My thoughts go to the early 1900s, as I imagine what it must have been like when those first yearbooks were published, when education was a new frontier. From all accounts, there was much optimism about what lay ahead, about what would be accomplished from the study of education, as *new* theories of learning were being developed, *new* instructional methodologies were being implemented, and *new* approaches were being taken to the study of education. In the first NSSE yearbook the historian Lucy Maynard Salmon pointed to "newness," not only the newness of history as a subject in the school curriculum but also to the newness of the study of education, as evidenced by the recent formation of the Society.[1]

Now near the end of the century, we educators are looking in two directions: assessing what we have accomplished even as we anticipate what the future might hold. Like the Roman god Janus, we look backward as we also look forward, aware of endings as well as beginnings. With respect to literacy education, the first chapter of this volume highlighted some of the century's developments: the early decades in which two movements, scientific measurement and progressive education, had profound effects on education that persist today; the

Nancy Nelson, coeditor of this volume, is Professor in the College of Education at Louisiana State University. She is also Director of the LSU Writing Project.

mid-century years, when some people sought educational quality through a return to traditional education and others sought it either through development of further innovations or through research into existing methods; and the last three decades, during which our theories and pedagogies, some directed more toward cognitive processes and others more toward social processes, emphasize reading comprehension and the compositional aspects of writing.

This chapter centers on one fairly recent development: the adoption of a constructivist orientation toward communication, which portrays reading and writing as the building of meaning from and for texts. As pointed out in the first chapter, this perspective made apparent the parallels in reading and writing processes, which had been viewed as the inverses of each other. Constructivism began to impact education in the 1970s at a time when linguists had developed tools for analyzing texts, when cognitive psychologists had begun investigating mental processes, and researchers in artificial intelligence were modeling some of those mental processes on computers. Literacy educators began studying the processes of comprehension and composition and through the years learned a great deal about different kinds of strategies, different sorts of texts, and different groups of readers and writers.[2] Now in the late 1990s, after two decades, there is general acknowledgment of the variability in the constructive processes that we study and teach. Much of that variability in the processes, we are realizing, is due to the contexts in which reading and writing occur. Meaning making is socially situated: when the context changes, the processes change, and what we think of as *the text* changes.

Sources of New Thought about Communicative Contexts

As the turn of the century approaches, we are rethinking our categories and reconceptualizing the reading and writing processes that we study and teach. This reflectiveness and this re-vision have been motivated by three sources of new thought about communicative contexts: (a) the various "post" theories of our times, particularly postmodernism and poststructuralism; (b) the work being done with electronic means of communication; and (c) a large-scale shift in perspective that has educators looking at social groups as well as individuals as makers of knowledge and meaning. First I consider these three components of our current intellectual milieu, and then I turn to specific aspects of reading and writing processes that are being reconceptualized as we move into the twenty-first century.

THE "POST" CRITIQUE

Various "posts" characterize our times, particularly the big post—postmodernism—and the related position known as poststructuralism. Postmodernism, which blurs lines between what is real and what is not real, questions a stable reality, and it also questions any kind of stable identity for a person or for a society.[3] Instead of stability, there is indeterminacy. Instead of permanence, there is ephemerality. Instead of wholes, there are fragments. Postmodernism points to losses, particularly a loss of coherence, as old logical patterns (e.g., hierarchical structures, narrative forms, causal relations) no longer seem to hold together fragmented parts of knowledge and experience. In these times of "inauthentic authenticity," old forms seem to yield to new hybrids, such as "infotainment," which are not one thing or another but something in between.[4] This "post" critique can become so extreme and reactive, when longstanding categories and forms of thought are called into question, that it borders on nihilism (approached, ironically, through clever, almost playful, parody). However, a "post" stance is not necessarily pessimistic, since a shift to something new is not necessarily a shift to something worse.

In discussions of postmodernity, context issues become preeminent. What a particular text means now is not what it will mean moments from now; what it means here is not what it means somewhere else. These changes can occur almost instantaneously, now that our electronic media have compressed time and space. Texts are transplanted rapidly into other contexts. David Harvey made this point: "The temporary contract in everything . . . becomes the hallmark of postmodern living." So did Katherine Hayles: "The disappearance of a stable context for our texts is the context of postmodern culture."[5]

Poststructuralism, a set of interrelated theoretical positions regarding texts and contexts, is a more specific critique whose point of departure is structuralism.[6] The major object of this critique is, of course, structure: the notion that a text has a set structure. Structure, according to the poststructuralists, is collapsible; there is no determinate structure for a text, since texts can be read in multiple ways. Another target is the notion of discreteness. For instance, poststructuralists have attempted to show how concepts conventionally set in opposition to each other are not so separate after all, such as the dichotomies of philosophy/literature, understanding/misunderstanding, and central/marginal. Poststructuralists have questioned the discreteness of texts and have developed a conception of *intertextuality*, which is arguably their most important theoretical contribution.[7] Intertextuality, which refers to interconnections among texts, can be envisioned in two different ways: either by seeing a text as a kind of pastiche of bits and pieces from other texts or seeing it as part of a vast interrelated network composed of prior texts, present texts, and even future texts. For example, this chapter can be viewed as a patchwork, pieced together from material from different texts, some scarcely recognizable, or can be seen as part of a network, in which links to other texts come through the borrowed or repeated material.

"Post" claims, which often seem flamboyant and overwhelmingly negative, may appear at odds with the serious educational endeavor of understanding and teaching literacy processes. I would argue, though, that instead of being disruptive they have been quite generative, that literacy educators have experienced beneficial effects from this "post" sort of theorizing.

The major benefit, I think, is that we have begun to question our assumptions and our categories, have become more reflective. We engage in the "both/and" thinking that Robert Venturi argued was the hallmark of postmodernism (as opposed to the "either/or" thinking of modernism).[8] In the 1970s and 1980s, before the "post" critique became so pervasive, the text was seen as separate or separable from its context. Now we are beginning to see how texts can also be contexts for other texts as they combine into ever-shifting intertexts. Before the "post" critique became so pervasive, reading was viewed as a different process from composing. Now we are beginning to see how both work together in hybrid acts of literacy. Both of these insights will be discussed further in this chapter. We are also beginning to question other dichotomies that have been so much a part of our discourse, such as process/product, author/audience, social/cognitive, narrative/expository, and orality/literacy.

THE COMMUNICATION REVOLUTION

The re-vision of communication processes has also been forced upon us by new developments in electronic technology, which have transformed the contexts of reading and writing in major ways.[9] One contextual change is time, since communication is now so rapid across great distances; and another is place, which becomes virtual in networked communication. A person can navigate, surf, and jump through cyberspace, following trails or creating paths, and can even get lost.

Of particular theoretical interest to literacy educators is hypertext, a system of interlinked textual units—texts or portions of texts— through which a reader can move.[10] Hypertext connects textual chunks of variable sizes, and it becomes hypermedia when the interlinked components include video, images, and sounds instead of or in addition to sequences of written words. The hypertext can appear as a single text, as, for instance, an interactive tale that can be read in various ways. It can also be a whole set of interlinked texts, such as those that students might read for a course, and can also be as large as all major works of a culture. Hypertexts can themselves be contextualized within larger networks—conceivably a kind of "docuverse" to include, eventually, all texts.[11] Major features of hypertext are multiplicity, flexibility, and indeterminacy, because there are numerous ways to move through the set and readers have choices. A reader jumps from one chunk to another, choosing among various preset trails or creating one's own, and can often perform transformations, such as making additions or writing commentary.

With the development of hypertext, the vision Vannevar Bush described back in 1945 has been realized.[12] This early cyber theorist had envisioned a device, which he called the "memex" (short for "memory extender"), for threading through a maze of texts in the "world's record." It was a means by which someone could move rapidly from the relevant portion of one text to the relevant portion of another. For example, an attorney might easily locate relevant parts of relevant cases, a physician might locate relevant findings in a number of research reports, a chemist might find relevant portions of articles in the chemical literature and other publications, and a historian might find relevant accounts of a particular event. The "essential feature" of the memex, Bush pointed out, was tying together two items: "any item may be caused at will to select immediately and automatically another."[13] This was the kind of associative linking that an expert would do in working on a subject.

The hypertext concept was further developed by Douglas Englebart, who, like Bush, talked about a means of augmenting memory; but it was Theodor Nelson who coined the term *hypertext*.[14] Nelson created a hypertext, which he described in a report with the provocative, whimsical, and almost overwhelming title *Literary Machines: The Report on, and of, Project Xanadu Concerning Word Processing, Electronic Publishing, Hypertext, Thinkertoys, Tomorrow's Intellectual Revolution, and Certain Other Topics Including Knowledge, Education, and Freedom*. Nelson claimed: "There is no Final Word. There can be no final version, no last thought."[15]

Here too, in the cyber theorizing as in "post" theorizing, there is questioning of accepted boundaries and conventional dichotomies. There are obvious similarities between the hypertext concept and the poststructuralists' concept of intertextuality. As George Landow put it, hypertext is the "literal embodiment" of intertextuality.[16]

Technology is changing communication in numerous other ways. Consider, for example, the options that are now available to writers who compose and publish with their computers—all the fonts, formats, and layouts, which can be varied according to one's purpose, audience, and persona, and the visuals, which can be easily incorporated. Consider the reading process, when words are on screens instead of pages and readers scroll backward and forward. Also consider the various forms of networked communication, such as electronic mail and bulletin boards and even electronic conferences and journals. For example, with electronic mail we have a form of discourse that seems to be somewhere between written correspondence and oral conversation. E-mail messages are written forms, but writers tend not to take the care in preparing them that they take with paper texts and readers tend not to read them as carefully either,[17] since speed—rapid turnaround—is a major factor in both writing and reading. These texts seem to have some of the ephemeral characteristics and the casualness of many oral communications, even though they are archived in written form. An interesting body of multidisciplinary scholarship is now accumulating that deals with the principles users employ and the conventions they follow in e-mail use—a kind of rhetoric of e-mail. For instance, in group e-mail use there has been demonstration of the "equalization phenomenon," less reticence about sending messages to those with higher status than when communicating face to face.[18]

In the last decades of this century, communication has been changed dramatically by computer-assisted, networked communication and by other technological developments, such as beepers, cellular phones, voice mail, and fax machines. Our machines make it easy to communicate rapidly across great distances, and they also make it difficult to avoid communication—to avoid what Langdon Winner referred to as the "bombarding" of formerly sheltered corners of our lives by "the insistent call of incoming and outgoing messages."[19] These forms of communication, as well as printed materials, are part of the culture in which our students live. They affect literacy in profound ways, and they force changes in our conceptions of literacy education.

THE SOCIAL CONSTRUCTIVIST TURN

Other recent developments in literacy education are associated with the perspective known as social constructivism that has become increasingly important in educational theory, research, and practice.

Along with the "post" critique and the communication revolution, this social shift is a major influence on the re-vision of literacy educators at the end of the century.[20] The new attention to social groups contrasts with the dominant focus on the individual during much of the 1900s. In the first half of the century, the scientific measurement movement had its attention on the individual, whose capabilities were assessed through the newly developed tests so that instruction could be customized. The attention of the progressive education movement was also on the individual, whose uniqueness (in terms of experience, interests, and talents) was of prime importance, even though social processes were considered critical for individual development. When constructivism first became so influential in literacy studies in the late 1970s and early 1980s, the individual was portrayed as the constructive agent, building meaning and building knowledge cognitively through reading and writing and other experiences. Although much research still goes to individuals as constructive agents, there has been growing interest in groups as constructive agents. When attention goes to groups, the object of interest is not only *shared* knowledge but also *shared* understandings and *shared* conventions.

In one line of social constructivist scholarship, attention is on the collaborative processes of relatively small groups with identifiable members, such as classes of students and their teachers, discussion groups, and peer response groups.[21] Activities of these groups tend to be situated in contexts that are relatively constrained as to time and place, and most occur when members are together spatially and temporally. However, not all communications occur so directly; they can take place through various kinds of correspondence, including electronic media.

Those studies situated in classroom settings have revealed much about implicit "rules" that participants follow in group activities and the power relations that they honor as they work together. For instance, in recitations about the texts students have read, it is the teacher who initiates a sequence by asking a question, who nominates a student for response, and who evaluates the correctness of the response. Students participating in recitations have speaking rights only when nominated for a response, but teachers have the right to speak at almost any point. In contrast, in discussions of their reading students have more equality with the teacher in terms of speaking rights and nomination is not required.[22] Social factors, including "rules" about what topics are relevant, who can talk about them, what can be said, and how it can be said, influence what counts as knowledge when shared understandings are being constructed.

Another line of social constructivist scholarship—more *macro* in perspective—has examined the knowledge-making activities of relatively large groups, such as people associated with a particular academic discipline, whose members do not all know one another or come into direct contact with one another.[23] A disciplinary group, such as historians or computer scientists or literary critics, can be seen as a single agent, building its meanings for texts and building its knowledge in a social fashion. Such groups have been likened to communities or tribes going about their communal work in accordance with their own "ways"—their own values, norms, language, forums, customs, and so on. Their work is directed toward knowledge making—conducting the studies, writing the articles, getting the work published, disseminating it, and enculturating new community members to continue it—all of which occur in social fashion. Social determinations, accomplished through various kinds of reviews and responses, influence which work gets funded, which gets published, and who gets accepted into which subgroups. The territories of various disciplinary communities are bounded, but instead of geographic boundaries, the boundaries are conceptual (i.e., the group's specialized topics and issues). Within these large groups are smaller communities with their own more specialized customs and interests. These academic disciplines, associated mainly with colleges and universities, help shape the school subjects, which are affected by other cultural influences as well.[24]

Meaning making can thus be seen at two social levels—an immediate kind of social level where group members interact rather directly and a more abstract social level—as well as an individual level. Individuals' contributions can effect changes in community knowledge and customs; and social constructs, such as ways of knowing or ways of writing or speaking, become cognitive matters when the focus is on individuals. A social perspective provides a broad lens for a re-vision of some key concepts in light of the critique of the post theorists and the virtual realizations of the cyber theorists.

Rethinking Our Concepts

At this point, I will discuss five literacy concepts that are being rethought at this time, now that the "post" critique has been heard, the new electronic forms of communication have been introduced and experienced, and the social nature of the construction of meaning has been pointed out. My discussion begins with literacy itself, and then moves to authorship, text, reading and writing, and identity.

LITERACIES AS WELL AS LITERACY

Literacy, one of the concepts undergoing transformation, is being re-seen in three major ways. The first reconceptualization, discussed briefly in the first chapter, is the notion of *emergent literacy*, the idea that literacy does not have a clear beginning point in children's development.[25] Very young children experience written language, when, for example, they listen to their parents read storybooks, see others using computers, notice the special, recurring marks on such items as cereal boxes and street signs, or watch family members writing notes or lists and try doing so themselves. Through such experiences, children begin to build knowledge that can be called literacy. It continues to develop through other experiences, including the more formal experiences associated with schooling.

The second reconceptualization is the realization that forms of discourse considered "literate" forms are not always restricted to written language. They can be "both/and"—*both* written forms *and* oral forms as well—to use the shorthand of the "post" theorizing. This both/and way of thinking differs from the either/or distinctions that characterized previous discussions of orality and literacy. A prominent example of a literate form is the essay, which plays such an important role in academic discourse. In several studies, some historical and others observational, the kind of knowledge display required by the essay has been linked to students' earlier productions, mostly oral, such as responses to their teachers' questions.[26]

The third reconceptualization, which builds on the previous two, is that, instead of a single literacy, people acquire multiple *literacies* over their lifetimes. When used in plural fashion, the term refers to the specialized languages belonging to particular social groups. These literacies include semantic and syntactic knowledge of the specialized terminology, genres, and phrasings used by the group as well as pragmatic knowledge of the conventions for participation in its practices.[27] In their schooling, students encounter a variety of languages associated with the school subjects and academic disciplines, such as history or physics or English literature. Students' development of literac(y/ies) is interwoven with their learning of "content" in school subjects.

AUTHORSHIP AS COLLABORATION

Another concept undergoing transformation is authorship. The "traditional" way of thinking about authorship, which dates back to the Romantic period, ties a text to a particular individual, who originated it and "owns" it as intellectual property. In this conception an author is considered a special individual, endowed with special gifts (even perhaps a kind of genius), who produced a unique work in solitary fashion, untainted and unconstrained by others.[28] This individualistic view of author, which is still held by many people, has come under critique. One attack has come from the poststructuralists, who sought to undermine the authority of the author in literary interpretation. Through their conception of intertextuality, they showed how a text, rather than originating with the single named author, was composed of traces of other texts.

A more social conception of authorship has come from researchers conducting contextualized studies of composing.[29] They have shown how collaborative the writing process is, not only when there are co-authors but also when there is only one named author. One major kind of collaboration in which writers engage is that which goes by the label *response*. A respondent, who might be a colleague, friend, fellow student, family member, referee, editor, or teacher, is not simply in the role of reader. He or she typically moves into a role that is very much like the writer's: considering purposes, thinking about what the audience's reception might be, construing other aspects of the context, and assessing the success of the piece in those terms. Often a respondent envisions a somewhat different piece, and makes suggestions for how that other text might be created. The exchange of drafts and suggestions, which often involves much reading as well as writing, can occur in various ways, including e-mail, which can speed up the response process and can also make it possible for writers to involve more respondents quite easily. Stevan Harnad uses the term "skywriting" for what happens when writers send their ideas out, through group e-mail and networked discussion groups, for immediate and wide review.[30] Response has become an important component of writing instruction from elementary to secondary to college, not only with teachers as respondents but peers as respondents too, as the authors of two chapters in the section of this volume entitled "The Classroom Context" have shown.

Other collaborators are authors of related texts, who contribute across time and space to the text that a writer (student writer, literary writer, technical writer, disciplinary writer, or other kind of writer) produces. These collaborators include those whose work a writer has read at some other point and draws on when writing as well as those whose work he or she reads as part of the composing process. Sometimes writers are aware of the influences of these other contributors whom they read in the past; many times they are not. Sometimes they acknowledge assistance; many times they do not. In disciplinary writing, known debts to other authors are often made quite explicit through citations and acknowledgments. In literary writing, where the appearance of originality can be more important, indebtedness may be explicitly noted only in acknowledgments.

Appropriation and transformation of others' work—common but often hidden parts of composing—are becoming easier, and more problematic, with the new technologies. With computers, a writer can "re-use" material, can copy what someone else has written and insert it immediately in the new text or, if producing a multimedia composition, can copy an image, a video excerpt, even sounds and can make various transformations until the borrowed item is no longer identifiable with the "original." Computers known as samplers can digitally duplicate recorded songs and play them back in other sequences or keys or pitches. The ownership issue is raised: How much transformation is necessary before something stops being one author's and becomes another author's? Issues surrounding authorship have been with us since the printing press, but the re-use becomes more visible and immediate in electronic production. Writers today must deal with complex issues of authorship, and it is no longer adequate for writing teachers simply to present a definition of plagiarism and warn against it.

In considering collaborative authorship, I have given most of my attention to two kinds of collaborators: respondents and other authors. There are other collaborators whose relationships to writers challenge some conventional distinctions. I mentioned, briefly, the role of the computer as an assistant in reproducing material. It can, of course, do much more to assist in the generation, selection, and organization of material in writing—can contribute to such an extent that it is often difficult, if not impossible, to distinguish the machine's intelligence from the human's.[31] I should also mention that, if a broad social perspective is taken on authorship, the line between author and audience is removed, since whole communities become *both* author *and* audience. A particular discourse community, such as a disciplinary group, can be seen as the collective author of its texts and also the collective audience for those texts.

TEXTS WITHOUT BORDERS

Although much discussion in literacy education still focuses on texts, there is now an acknowledgment that texts are not discrete units. Instead, they are interconnected intertextually and sometimes hypertextually too. Texts—essays, stories, jokes, newspaper articles, conversations, research reports—are produced within a context of other texts. When composing, writers draw from experiences they have had with other texts, and the writings they produce reflect those experiences. For instance, when children create stories, their creations relate to previous stories they have read, heard, and have composed themselves.[32] Some connections are to content, such as particular kinds of characters or settings or events. Others are to form, such as story elements (setting, protagonist, goal, conflict, resolution) and story conventions ("once upon a time," "they all lived happily ever after").

Intertextual connections are also made by readers, who vary in the experiences they bring to their reading and thus vary in the connections they make. For example, this chapter would mean different things to those readers who are familiar with many of the texts that are cited or implied than it would mean to other readers. It will mean something different to readers in the future, since they will make connections between this chapter and texts that have not yet been written. The understanding of a text changes, in part, because of the ever-shifting intertext.

To illustrate intertextuality in reading, I will use an excerpt from "The Coyote Clan," the first piece in a book titled *Coyote's Canyon*.[33] At the very beginning of the book, the author, Terry Tempest Williams, provided an epigraph, an intertextual borrowing from another text, an essay by Judith Fryer.[34] Fryer had written the words as a sentence— just one sentence in a rather lengthy paragraph—but Williams laid them out in the form of a poem:

These things are real:
    desert,
    rocks,
    shelter,
    legend.

A reader would likely build meaning for this "poem," and, in intertextual fashion, that meaning would influence the reader's understanding of the book *Coyote's Canyon* and also the piece "The Coyote Clan." In addition, readers might relate the "poem" to other texts they had read previously. For example, if they have read Byrd Baylor, they might remember such books as *Everybody Needs a Rock* and *The Desert Is Theirs*.[35]

The text of "The Coyote Clan" begins with these paragraphs:

When traveling to southern Utah for the first time, it is fair to ask if the redrocks were cut would they bleed. And when traveling to Utah's desert for the second or third time, it is fair to assume that they do, that the blood of the rocks gives life to the country. And then after having made enough pilgrimages to the slickrock to warrant sufficient separation from society's oughts and shoulds, look again for the novice you once were, who asks if sandstone bleeds.

Pull out your pocketknife, open the blade, and run it across your burnished arm. If you draw blood, you are human. If you draw wet sand that dries quickly, then you will know you have become part of the desert. Not until then can you claim ownership.

This is Coyote's country—a landscape of the imagination, where nothing is as it appears. The buttes, mesas, and redrock spires beckon you to see them as something other: a cathedral, a tabletop, bears' ears, or nuns. Windows and arches ask you to recall what is no longer there, to taste the wind for the sandstone it carries. These astonishing formations invite a new mythology for desert goers, one that acknowledges the power of story and ritual, yet lies within the integrity of our own cultures. The stories rooted in experience become beads to trade. It is the story, always the story, that precedes and follows the journey.

Just when you begin to believe in your own sense of place, plan on getting lost. It's not your fault—blame it on Coyote. The terror of the country you thought you knew bears gifts of humility. The landscape that makes you vulnerable also makes you strong. This is the bedrock of southern Utah's beauty: its chameleon nature according to light and weather and season encourages us to make peace with our own contradictory nature. The trickster quality of the canyon is Coyote's cachet.[36]

Readers would bring their experiences with other texts to bear in the reading of this one. Early on, they might make intertextual connections to texts they can remember only vaguely, for example, when they experience the repeated patterns of the first sentences or the cyclical chronology, which seems to be going somewhere but then gets back to the starting point. At some points their connections might be to specific texts, perhaps prior treatments of myth or story in response to "power of story" and "It is the story, always the story." When reading the references to coyote, some people would likely remember trickster stories they have read previously. Some readers might even think of a coyote analogy that has been used in discussions of postmodernism—the claim that in postmodernity nothing is as it appears.[37] These are, of course, just a few places where intertextual connections might be made. If there were a hypertext version of "The Coyote Clan," such intertextual linkages would be more apparent in jumps that readers could make. The hypertext might include, for instance, the full essay by Fryer, the Byrd Baylor stories, various trickster tales, a piece about cyclical chronology and an illustration, an article about postmodernism that used the coyote analogy, and any number of other texts or other media forms.

Our example here has been literary, but the making of intertextual connections is important in the reading of other sorts of texts too. Disciplinary learning within academic fields is intensely intertextual. It involves reading contributions that have been made to disciplinary knowledge and being able to interrelate them—becoming familiar with the "conversations" of the discipline. It involves making those linkages that Vannevar Bush described when he conceived the memex.

PERMEABLE BOUNDARIES BETWEEN READING AND WRITING

Within the last two decades, as pointed out throughout this volume, parallels have been noted between reading and writing. Both involve use of similar kinds of knowledge, and both are constructive processes that involve building meaning. In reading, meaning is built *from* texts; and in composing, meaning is built *for* texts.

Now there is an awareness that many acts of literacy are hybrid in nature, in that they involve *both* composing *and* comprehending. In these hybrid acts the two processes cannot be neatly separated at some point where one stops and the other starts.[38] Imagine, for instance, a person reading a news article in order to summarize it for his or her own audience. The purpose—to produce a summary for other people—would be an important part of the context for reading and would affect the very nature of the reading process. The writer would approach the text with some ideas about the to-be-written text that would affect the reading. Meaning would be constructed for the to-be-written text even as meaning is being constructed for the article being read. Or consider a person reading a children's book in order to produce a critique of it. In that situation too, meaning for the critique would be built even as the person was reading the book.

In such acts, reading and writing processes tend to blend and a person is in two roles concurrently—a reader building meaning from a text and a writer building meaning for a text. If we look only at behaviors in such acts, there might *seem* to be two phases, first a reading phase, in which a writer finds a relevant text and moves his or her eyes over the pages, and then a writing phase, in which the writer puts pen to paper or begins typing at the computer and eventually produces a text. However, if we consider the constructive nature of the process—reading as building meaning from a text and writing as building meaning for a text—rather than behaviors, we cannot say that there are two phases: a building-meaning-from-a-text phase and a building-meaning-for-a-text phase. We cannot say where construction from reading stops and construction for writing starts, since, before putting pen to paper, a person can already be composing meaning mentally for the new text.

Quite often, these hybrid acts of literacy involve reading multiple texts, instead of only one, to produce one's own. For example, a person writing a report would likely find several texts on the topic and select material that seems relevant to the purpose and audience. For the new text, the material (that which is generated by the writer as well as that selected from reading) would be arranged in some kind of order and connections would be provided. This process of organizing, selecting, and connecting, which I call *discourse synthesis*,[39] is a common form of composing, not only in writing reports but in producing various other sorts of texts as well, such as essays, arguments, and proposals. Even though the texts being read suggest possible methods of organizing, prioritizing, and linking content, the writer must supply new connections and most likely a different sort of arrangement to integrate the content. In disciplinary reading and writing, the synthesis process often involves tying particular authors to particular positions, aligning authors with those who agree and distinguishing them from those who disagree. It can be important to acknowledge the prior work, making one's own contribution by building on what others have done.

Hybrid acts of literacy are not new. What is new is awareness of them, since, to a great extent, they have been rather invisible in schooling. Attention in writing instruction has been on students' writing "original" texts, which tend to be stories or essays, and attention in reading instruction has been on students' reading texts to decode or comprehend them, not to use them in producing one's own. Students might be assigned "the" research paper and taught rather mechanical matters (e.g., taking notes on cards, producing footnotes and bibliographies), but such instruction has not typically included strategies for transforming others' writing to create one's own.[40]

IDENTITY AS COMMUNITY

The final concept to receive attention here—identity—has been implicit in much of the previous discussion. Throughout the discussion of the other concepts, there was an emphasis on the social, the multiple, and the indeterminate. These same descriptors might be used for the notion of identity to be discussed now. It too emphasizes the social, the multiple, and the indeterminate.

In a social fashion, individuals create identities for themselves, and others create identities for them. Identities come through social ties, perceived membership in particular groups or communities, which might, for instance, be geographic groups, gender groups, ethnic groups, interest groups, professional or vocational groups.[41] Language plays a major role here, since, as noted in the discussion of literacies, different groups have their own ways of speaking or writing, their own particular forms, as well as their own favored topics. A great deal of attention has gone to cultural identities of people belonging to particular ethnic groups and to their forms of discourse, how the "ways" of some groups contrast with the conventions of schooling.

Literacy acquisition can be seen as a process of social identification—joining a "literacy club," to borrow Frank Smith's metaphor[42]—in which people construct social identities as readers and writers, even as particular kinds of readers and writers. For instance, one important feature of the writing workshop approach to language arts is students' perceptions of themselves as authors—seeing themselves as belonging to a community of authors with whom they share interest, knowledge, and approaches, and even some specialized jargon. Kathryn Davinroy has recently reported on a study of students gaining membership in the specialized community of a journalism class.[43] Newcomers went through an apprenticeship period in which they spent time observing and working under more experienced students and stayed with "safe" stories. Over time, they acquired the group ways of writing and interacting and earned the right to take on more controversial assignments.

During their college years, possibly earlier, many students begin to develop disciplinary identities. They "place" themselves in particular disciplinary groups and also in smaller more specialized groups within that discipline (i.e., people interested in particular topics, people doing particular kinds of work).[44] Some aspects of identity construction are associated with the writing they do for their courses. For instance, a student may begin identifying with a particular group by adopting its style of writing, by pursuing topics or issues that "belong" to that group, and by repeatedly citing others in the field who are doing or have done related work.

Social identity is multifaceted. Throughout their lives, people add discourses, acquire other literacies, and gain membership in other communities. Identities shift as contexts shift, since some social ties are salient in some contexts and other ties are in other contexts.

Conclusion

At the beginning of this chapter, I referred to the two faces of Janus, one looking backward and one looking forward. The first chapter of this yearbook began with a look back—as far back as colonial times—and it traced the historical developments in American education that have pulled reading and writing together toward some common center and those that have pushed them apart. Much attention went to the developments of this century, including what happened during the early decades when the study of education was just beginning. The chapter ended with a discussion of the current status of connections and disconnections. As that review showed, particular kinds of context, including rhetorical contexts, classroom contexts, and community contexts, have tended to draw reading and writing together. Or, to use a more etymologically correct metaphor (since *context* is derived from *com-*, together, and *texere*, to weave), they have *woven* reading and writing together. The ten chapters coming between that introduction and this conclusion have dealt with specific aspects of those three contexts. Their authors have provided fuller discussions of specific topics, reviewing major accomplishments but focusing particularly on what is *new*. They provided background, but most emphasized what is current and also did some looking ahead, suggesting what might be done by educators.

This chapter too has centered on the *new*. From my perspective, what is new is the rethinking of some central concepts in literacy studies at a time when the conceptual boundaries that worked in the past no longer hold. The concepts considered here included literacy itself as well as text, authorship, reading and writing, and identity. All these revisions have instructional implications, which present challenges for the future: (a) supporting students' growth in the literacies associated with various subject areas and specializations, (b) fostering connections between texts (with and without hypertext applications), (c) acknowledging the social aspects of authorship and helping students take advantage of collaborations, (d) giving more instructional attention to the hybrid acts of literacy that have thus far received so little attention in education, and (e) helping students develop social identities as members of literate communities. All are critical and complex elements in students' literacy development, and all need further study by educators.

NOTES

1. Lucy Maynard Salmon, *Some Principles in the Teaching of History*, 1st Yearbook of the National Society for the Scientific Study of Education (Chicago: University of Chicago Press, 1902). The society dropped "scientific" from its name in 1910.

2. For historical treatments, see Nancy Nelson Spivey, "Construing Constructivism: Reading Research in the United States," *Poetics* 16 (1987): 169-192; idem, *The Constructivist Metaphor: Reading, Writing, and the Making of Meaning* (San Diego, Cal.: Academic Press, 1997).

3. Ihab Hassan, *The Postmodern Turn: Essays in Postmodern Theory* (Columbus: Ohio State University Press, 1989); Jean-Francois Lyotard, *The Postmodern Condition: A Report on Knowledge*, trans. Geoff Bennington and Brian Massumi (Minneapolis: University of Minnesota Press, 1984); Hans Bertens, *The Idea of the Postmodern: A History* (London: Routledge, 1995). For a discussion of postmodernism and education, see William E. Doll, Jr., *A Post-Modern Perspective on Curriculum* (New York: Teachers College Press, 1993).

4. Lawrence Grossberg, *It's a Sin: Politics, Postmodernity, and the Popular* (Sydney: Power, 1988).

5. David Harvey, *The Condition of Postmodernity: An Enquiry into the Origins of Cultural Change* (Oxford: Blackwell, 1989), p. 291; N. Katherine Hayles, "Text out of Context: Situating Postmodernism within an Information Society," *Discourse* 9 (1987): 28.

6. Roland Barthes, "From Work to Text," in *Textual Strategies: Perspectives in Post-Structural Criticism*, ed. Josue V. Harari (Ithaca, N.Y.: Cornell University Press, 1979, essay published in French in 1971), pp. 73-81; Jacques Derrida, "Structure, Sign, and Play in the Discourse of the Human Sciences," in *The Structuralist Controversy: The Language of Criticism and the Discourse of the Human Sciences*, ed. Richard Macksey and Eugenio Donato (Baltimore, Md.: Johns Hopkins University Press, 1970); Michel Foucault, "What Is an Author?" in *Textual Strategies: Perspectives in Post-Structuralist Criticism*, ed. Harari (essay published in French in 1969).

7. Julia Kristeva, "Word, Dialogue and Novel," in *The Kristeva Reader*, ed. Toril Moi (New York: : Columbia University Press, 1980, original work published in 1967), pp. 34-61; Barthes, "From Work to Text." For a discussion of the conception, see James E. Porter, "Intertextuality and the Discourse Community," *Rhetoric Review* 5 (1986): 34-47.

8. Robert Venturi, *Complexity and Contradiction in Architecture* (New York: Museum of Modern Art and Graham Foundation, in association with Doubleday, 1966).

9. See, for example, Gretchen Bender and Timothy Druckery, eds., *Culture on the Brink: Ideologies of Technology* (Seattle, Wash.: Bay Press, 1994); David B. Whittle, *Cyberspace: The Human Dimension* (New York: W. H. Freeman, 1997).

10. Edward Barrett, ed., *The Society of Text: Hypertext, Hypermedia, and the Social Construction of Information* (Cambridge: MIT Press, 1989); J. David Bolter, *Writing Space: The Computer, Hypertext, and the History of Writing* (Hillsdale, N. J.: Lawrence Erlbaum, 1991); George P. Landow, *Hypertext: The Convergence of Contemporary Critical Theory and Technology* (Baltimore, Md.: Johns Hopkins University Press, 1992).

11. Theodor H. Nelson, *Literary Machines* (Swarthmore, Penn.: Author, 1981).

12. Vannevar Bush, "As We May Think," *Atlantic Monthly* 176, no. 1 (1945): 101-108.

13. Ibid., p. 34.

14. Douglas C. Englebart, "A Conceptual Framework for the Augmentation of Man's Intellect," in *Vistas in Information Handling*, vol. 1, ed. Paul W. Howerton and David C. Weeks (Washington, D. C.: Spartan Books, 1963), pp. 1-29; Theodor H. Nelson, "Getting It Out of Our System," in *Information Retrieval: A Critical Review*, ed. George Schecter (Washington, D. C.: Thompson, 1967), 191-210.

15. Nelson, *Literary Machines*, p. 48.

16. Landow, *Hypertext*, p. 53. For another perspective on this connection between the two bodies of work, see Ned J. Davison, "Literacy and Electronic Hypertext: Borges, Criticism, Literary Research, and the Computer," *Hispania* 74 (1991): 1159-1161.

17. Gail E. Hawisher and Charles Moran, "Electronic Mail and the Writing Instructor," *College English* 55 (1993): 627-643.

18. Vitaly J. Dubrovsky, Sara Kiesler, and Beheruz N. Sethna, "The Equalization Phenomenon: Status Effects in Computer-Mediated and Face-to-Face Decision-Making Groups," *Human-Computer Interaction* 6 (1991): 119-146. For a review of research on various aspects of electronic communication, see Julie Foertsch, "The Impact of Electronic Networks on Scholarly Communication: Avenues for Research," *Discourse Processes* 19 (1995): 301-328.

19. Langdon Winner, "Three Paradoxes of the Information Age," in *Culture on the Brink: Ideologies of Technology*, ed. Gretchen Bender and Timothy Druckery (Seattle, Wash.: Bay Press, 1994), p. 194.

20. This is not to say that the work focusing on individuals was unconcerned with social factors. In fact, much attention was given to socially acquired knowledge and to intersubjective aspects of communication. See Donald Rubin's chapter, this volume, and Nancy Nelson Spivey, "Written Discourse: A Constructivist Perspective," in *Constructivism in Education*, ed. Leslie P. Steffe and Jerry Gale (Hillsdale, N. J.: Lawrence Erlbaum, 1995), pp. 313-329.

21. Judith L. Green and Catherine Wallat, eds., *Ethnography and Language in Educational Settings* (Norwood, N. J.: Ablex, 1981); David Bloome and Ann Egan-Robertson, "The Social Construction of Intertextuality in Classroom Reading and Writing Lessons," *Reading Research Quarterly* 28 (1993): 304-333.

22. Courtney Cazden, *Classroom Discourse: The Language of Teaching and Learning* (Portsmouth, N. H.: Heinemann, 1988); Hugh Mehan, *Learning Lessons: Social Organization in the Classroom* (Cambridge, Mass.: Harvard University Press, 1979); see also Donna Alvermann and David A. Hayes, "Classroom Discussion of Content Area Reading Assignments," *Reading Research Quarterly* 24 (1989): 305-335.

23. Porter, "Intertextuality and the Discourse Community"; Barrett, ed., *The Society of Text*; Tony Becher, *Academic Tribes and Territories* (Milton Keynes, Great Britain: Open University Press, 1989).

24. See discussion by Barbara Stengel, " 'Academic Discipline' and 'School Subject': Contestable Curricular Concepts," *Journal of Curriculum Studies* 29 (1997): 585-602.

25. William Teale and Elizabeth Sulzby, eds., *Emergent Literacy: Reading and Writing* (Norwood, N. J.: Ablex, 1986).

26. Shirley Brice Heath, *Ways with Words: Life and Work in Communities and Classrooms* (New York: Cambridge University Press, 1982); idem, "The Sense of Being Literate: Historical and Cross-Cultural Features," in *Handbook of Reading Research*, vol. 2, ed. Rebecca Barr, Michael L. Kamil, Peter Mosenthal, and P. David Pearson (New York: Longman, 1991), pp. 3-25; Heath and Leslie Mangiola, *Children of Promise: Literate Activity in Linguistically and Culturally Diverse Classrooms* (Washington, D. C.: National Education Association, 1991).

27. James Paul Gee, "Literacy, Discourse, and Linguistics," *Journal of Education* 171 (1989): 5-17.

28. For accounts of this conception, see Meyer H. Abrams, *The Mirror and the Lamp: Romantic Theory and the Critical Tradition* (Oxford: Oxford University Press, 1953); James Stillinger, *Multiple Authorship and the Myth of Solitary Genius* (New York: Oxford University Press, 1991).

29. For example, James A. Reither and Douglas Vipond, "Writing as Collaboration," *College English* 51 (1989): 855-867. See also the studies conducted by Stillinger, *Multiple Authorship*.

30. Stevan Harnad, "Scholarly Skywriting and the Prepublication Continuum of Scientific Inquiry," *Psychological Science* 1 (1990): 342-344.

31. Donna Haraway, *Simians, Cyborgs, and Women: The Reinvention of Nature* (New York: Routledge, 1991).

32. Trevor Cairney, "Intertextuality: Infectious Echoes from the Past," *The Reading Teacher* 43 (1990): 478-484.

33. Terry Tempest Williams, "The Coyote Clan," in John Telford and Terry Tempest Williams, *Coyote's Canyon* (Layton, Utah: Gibbs Smith, 1989), pp. 16-20.

34. Judith Fryer, "Desert, Rock, Shelter, Legend: Willa Cather's Novels of the Southwest," in *The Desert Is No Lady*, ed. Vera Norwood and Janice Monk (New Haven, Conn.: Yale University Press, 1987), p. 44.

35. Byrd Baylor, *Everybody Needs a Rock* (New York: Macmillan, 1974); idem, *The Desert Is Theirs* (New York: Macmillan, 1975).

36. Williams, "The Coyote Clan," pp. 16-18. Reprinted with permission.

37. Donna Haraway, "The Actors Are Cyborgs, Nature Is Coyote, and the Geography Is Elsewhere: Postscript to 'Cyborgs at Large,'" in *Technoculture*, ed. Constance Penley and Andrew Ross (Minneapolis: University of Minnesota Press, 1991), pp. 21-26.

38. See the discussion of hybrid acts in Robert J. Bracewell, Carl H. Frederiksen, and Janet D. Frederiksen, "Cognitive Processes in Composing and Comprehending Discourse," *Educational Psychologist* 17 (1982): 146-164. For a description of the transformations writers make, see Nancy Nelson Spivey, "Transforming Texts: Constructive Processes in Reading and Writing," *Written Communication* 7 (1990): 256-287.

39. Nancy Nelson Spivey, *Discourse Synthesis: Constructing Texts in Reading and Writing* (Newark, Del.: International Reading Association, 1984); Nancy Nelson Spivey and James R. King, "Readers as Writers Composing from Sources," *Reading Research Quarterly* 24 (1989): 7-26; Spivey, "The Shaping of Meaning: Options in Writing the Comparison," *Research in the Teaching of English* 25 (1991): 390-418.

40. Elizabeth Curtin, "The Research Paper in High School Writing Programs: Examining Connections between Goals of Instruction and Requirements of College Writing" (Doctoral diss., Carnegie Mellon University, 1988).

41. Henri Tajfel, *Human Groups and Social Categories* (New York: Cambridge University Press, 1981); Dominic Abrams and Michael A. Hogg, eds., *Social Identity Theory: Constructive and Critical Advances* (New York: Springer-Verlag); Bernardo M. Ferdman, "Literacy and Cultural Identity," *Harvard Educational Review* 60 (1990): 181-204.

42. Frank Smith, *Joining the Literacy Club: Further Essays into Education* (Portsmouth, N. H.: Heinemann, 1988).

43. Kathryn H. Davinroy, "Developing a Writer-ly Identity through Participation on a School Newspaper" (Paper presented at the annual meeting of the National Reading Conference, Charleston, S. C., November, 1996).

44. Nancy Nelson Spivey and Maureen A. Mathison, "The Development of Authoring Identity," in Spivey, *The Constructivist Metaphor*, pp. 223-234.

Name Index

Abrams, Dominic, 285
Abrams, Meyer H., 284
Ackerman, John M., 49, 175, 176, 189, 201, 227, 264
Adams, Charles, 174
Afflerbach, Peter, 52
Aiken, Wilford M., 48
Alexander, Patricia A., 111, 227
Allen, Gay Wilson, 109
Allington, Richard, 223
Altmann, Irwin, 44
Alvermann, Donna, 284
Anders, Patricia, 111, 130
Anderson, Richard C., 27, 48, 49, 225
Anderson, Thomas H., 128
Anderson, Vicki, 201
Anderson, Worth, 151
Anderson-Inman, Lynne, 247
Anson, Chris, 175
Anthony, Dick, 265
Applebee, Arthur, 30, 45, 46, 50, 70, 151, 181, 184, 185, 190, 192, 198, 199, 200, 201, 202, 210, 223, 224, 247
Appleman, Deborah, 248
Aristotle, 4, 6, 44, 57, 74, 77, 78, 79, 87, 177
Armbruster, Bonnie, 113, 128, 129
Atwell, Nancie, 30, 50
Au, Kathy H., 225

Bakhtin, Mikhail M., 33, 51, 91, 92, 109, 116, 129, 151, 230, 231, 239, 247, 248
Ball, Carolyn, 155, 167, 175, 177
Barnes, Douglas, 180, 181, 200
Baron, Joan Boykoff, 265
Barr, Mary, 223
Barr, Rebecca, 44, 223, 227, 284
Barrett, Edward, 283
Barthes, Roland, 90, 91, 109, 283
Bartholomae, David, 71, 156, 167, 175, 177, 226, 227
Bauman, Richard, 51
Baxter, Leslie A., 264
Baylor, Byrd, 277, 278, 285
Bazerman, Charles, 94, 110, 251, 263, 264
Beach, Richard, 29, 43, 92, 175, 176, 226, 229, 248
Beardsley, Monroe C., 48, 109
Beason, Larry, 176

Becher, Tony, 110
Beck, Isabel L., 28, 40, 41, 98, 99, 101, 110, 111, 112, 128, 129, 130, 247, 265
Bekins, Linn, 264
Bellack, Arno, 129
Bender, Gretchen, 283, 284
Bennington, Geoff, 283
Bereiter, Carl C., 223, 224, 226
Berger, Peter I., 51
Berkenkotter, Carol, 72, 175, 264, 265
Berlin, James A., 45, 200
Berliner, David C., 223
Bertens, Hans, 283
Best, Cynthia, 151
Bestor, Arthur, 48
Bialostosky, Don, 247
Bizzell, Patricia, 71
Black, Alycia, 151
Black, Edward, 71
Black, Edwin, 263
Black, James B., 227
Blair, Carole, 264
Blair, Hugh, 6, 7, 45
Bleich, David, 28, 29, 49, 90, 109
Bloom, Harold J., 92, 110
Bloome, David, 284
Bolter, Jay, 248, 283
Bonk, Curtis J., 71, 72
Booth, Wayne, 71
Boyd, Fenice B., 218, 227
Boyer, Ernest, 178, 199
Bracewell, Robert J., 285
Braddock, Richard, 23, 29, 48
Brandt, Deborah, 158, 176, 191, 201
Brannon, Lil, 154, 174, 175
Bransford, John D., 26, 48
Brereton, John, 174
Brewer, William F., 48
Bridgeman, Brent, 264
Bridwell, Lillian, 175, 176
Britton, Bruce K., 227
Britton, James, 25, 29, 30, 42, 50, 54, 61, 70, 87, 179, 180, 181, 185, 186, 190, 192, 193, 199, 200, 201
Brodinsky, Ben, 51
Broek, Paul van den, 130
Brooks, Cleanth, 48, 109
Brossell, Gordon, 71
Brown, John Seely, 51, 199, 202

Subject Index

Accountability movement, impact of, on reading-writing connections, 37

Audience: categories of, in school writing, 54-55; determinate-indeterminate character of, 59-61; discourse community as a type of, 60-61; limited attention to, in writing instruction, 54-55; multiple nature of, 62-63; preeminence of, in composing, 53; the self as, 61-62

Author (as interpretive construct): emphasis on, in historical-biographical approach to the study of literature, 89; lack of attention to, by reader-response theorists, 90; place of, in literary theory, 89-94; poststructuralist conception of, as an abstract form, 90-91; rejection of, by the New Criticism in literary theory, 89-90; renewed interest in, in current conceptions of reading, 91-94; role of, in disciplinary discourse, 94-96

Authorship, changes in concept of, 274-276

Awareness of audience: cultivation of, through reading and response, 67-70; importance of, in all phases of writing, 63-66; role of social cognition in development of, 68-69

Awareness of author: effects of, on reader's comprehension of text, 117-121; instructional activities to increase, among young readers, 101-102; interview studies of, in children, 102-108; studies of changes in text features to increase, 96-101

Back to basics movement (1950s-1960s): emphasis in, on separation of reading and writing, 23; major attention to reading in, 23

Bay Area Writing Project, 30, 188

Book reports, as example of an activity that joins reading and writing, 211; decisions to be made in assigning, 212-213; purposes of, 211; potential learning outcomes of, for students, 213-216

Center for the Study of Reading, 26-27
Center for the Study of Writing, 27

Commission on Reorganization of Secondary Education (1918), 19-20

Committee of 15 (1895), report of, on English in elementary schools, 13

Committee of Ten (1894), recommendations of: on English as a high school subject, 10; on teaching of reading and composition in elementary schools, 12

Committee of Thirty (1917), report of, on reorganization of English in secondary schools, 19

Communication, changes in, due to technology, 269-271

Communicative contexts, sources of new thought regarding, 267-273

Comprehension-as-construction movement, impact of, on studies of reading and writing, 26-27

Conference on College Composition and Communication, 22

Constructivist theories of language and learning, 180-181

CORE (Connect, Organize, Reflect, Extend) framework for analysis of middle grade literacy instruction and acquisition, 207-208, figure, 209

Critique: changing nature of, 251; desirability of explicit instruction in, 261-263; differences among disciplines in expectations for, 254-55; important role of, in contemporary knowledge making, 251-252; origins of, 249-250

Dartmouth Conference (1966), 25, 30

Dialogic approaches to writing about literature: contrasted with a formalistic approach, 234-236; developing guided response assignments in, 241-244; illustration of, 231-234; nature of, 229-231; students' learning in, 246; teachers' evaluation of students' writing in, 244-246

Discourse communities: impact of, on reading-writing connections, 33-35; nature of, 32-34

Eight Year Study, lack of attention to findings of, in postwar years, 23

INFORMATION ABOUT MEMBERSHIP IN THE SOCIETY

Membership in the National Society for the Study of Education is open to all individuals who desire to receive its publications. Membership dues for 1998 are $30. All members receive both volumes of the current Yearbook.

For calendar year 1998 reduced dues are available for retired NSSE members and for full-time graduate students *in their first year of membership*. These reduced dues are $25.

Membership in the Society is for the calendar year. Dues are payable on or before January 1 of each year.

New members are required to pay an entrance fee of $1 in addition to the annual dues for the year in which they join.

Members of the Society include professors, researchers, graduate students, and administrators in colleges and universities; teachers, supervisors, curriculum specialists, and administrators in elementary and secondary schools; and a considerable number of persons not formally connected with educational institutions.

All members participate in the election of the Society's six-member Board of Directors, which is responsible for managing the affairs of the Society, including the authorization of volumes to appear in the series of Yearbooks. All members whose dues are paid for the current year are eligible for election to the Board of Directors.

Each year the Society arranges for meetings to be held in conjunction with the annual conferences of one or more of the major national educational organizations. All members are urged to attend these sessions at which the volumes of the current Yearbook are presented and critiqued. Members are also encouraged to submit proposals for future Yearbooks.

Members receive a 33 percent discount when purchasing past Yearbooks that are still in print from the Society's distributor, the University of Chicago Press.

Further information about the Society may be secured by writing to the Secretary-Treasurer, NSSE, 5835 Kimbark Avenue, Chicago, Illinois 60637.

PAST PUBLICATIONS OF THE SOCIETY STILL AVAILABLE

1. The Yearbooks

Ninety-seventh Yearbook (1998)

Part 1. *The Adolescent Years: Social Influences and Educational Challenges.* Kathryn Borman and Barbara Schneider, editors. Cloth.

Part 2. *The Reading-Writing Connection.* Nancy Nelson and Robert C. Calfee, editors. Cloth.

Ninety-sixth Yearbook (1997)

Part 1. *Service Learning.* Joan Schine, editor. Cloth.

Part 2. *The Construction of Children's Character.* Alex Molnar, editor. Cloth.

Ninety-fifth Yearbook (1996)

Part 1. *Performance-Based Student Assessment: Challenges and Possibilities.* Joan B. Baron and Dennie P. Wolf, editors. Cloth.

Part 2. *Technology and the Future of Schooling.* Stephen T. Kerr, editor. Cloth.

Ninety-fourth Yearbook (1995)

Part 1. *Creating New Educational Communities.* Jeannie Oakes and Karen Hunter Quartz, editors. Cloth.

Part 2. *Changing Populations/Changing Schools.* Erwin Flaxman and A. Harry Passow, editors. Cloth.

Ninety-third Yearbook (1994)

Part 1. *Teacher Research and Educational Reform.* Sandra Hollingsworth and Hugh Sockett, editors. Cloth.

Part 2. *Bloom's Taxonomy: A Forty-year Retrospective.* Lorin W. Anderson and Lauren A. Sosniak, editors. Cloth.

Ninety-second Yearbook (1993)

Part 1. *Gender and Education.* Sari Knopp Biklen and Diane Pollard, editors. Cloth.

Part 2. *Bilingual Education: Politics, Practice, and Research.* M. Beatriz Arias and Ursula Casanova, editors. Cloth.

Ninety-first Yearbook (1992)

Part 1. *The Changing Contexts of Teaching.* Ann Lieberman, editor. Cloth.

Part 2. *The Arts, Education, and Aesthetic Knowing.* Bennett Reimer and Ralph A. Smith, editors. Cloth.

Ninetieth Yearbook (1991)

Part 1. *The Care and Education of America's Young Children: Obstacles and Opportunities.* Sharon L. Kagan, editor. Cloth.

Eighty-ninth Yearbook (1990)

Part 1. *Textbooks and Schooling in the United States.* David L. Elliott and Arthur Woodward, editors. Cloth.

Part 2. *Educational Leadership and Changing Contexts of Families, Communities, and Schools.* Brad Mitchell and Luvern L. Cunningham, editors. Paper.

301

Eighty-eighth Yearbook (1989)

Part 1. *From Socrates to Software: The Teacher as Text and the Text as Teacher.* Philip W. Jackson and Sophie Haroutunian-Gordon, editors. Cloth.

Part 2. *Schooling and Disability.* Douglas Biklen, Dianne Ferguson, and Alison Ford, editors. Cloth.

Eighty-seventh Yearbook (1988)

Part 1. *Critical Issues in Curriculum.* Laurel N. Tanner, editor. Cloth.

Part 2. *Cultural Literacy and the Idea of General Education.* Ian Westbury and Alan C. Purves, editors. Cloth.

Eighty-sixth Yearbook (1987)

Part 2. *Society as Educator in an Age of Transition.* Kenneth D. Benne and Steven Tozer, editors. Cloth.

Eighty-fifth Yearbook (1986)

Part 1. *Microcomputers and Education.* Jack A. Culbertson and Luvern L. Cunningham, editors. Cloth.

Eighty-fourth Yearbook (1985)

Part 1. *Education in School and Nonschool Settings.* Mario D. Fantini and Robert Sinclair, editors. Cloth.

Eighty-third Yearbook (1984)

Part 1. *Becoming Readers in a Complex Society.* Alan C. Purves and Olive S. Niles, editors. Cloth.

Part 2. *The Humanities in Precollegiate Education.* Benjamin Ladner, editor. Paper.

Eighty-second Yearbook (1983)

Part 1. *Individual Differences and the Common Curriculum.* Gary D Fenstermacher and John I. Goodlad, editors. Paper.

Eighty-first Yearbook (1982)

Part 1. *Policy Making in Education.* Ann Lieberman and Milbrey W. McLaughlin, editors. Cloth.

Part 2. *Education and Work.* Harry F. Silberman, editor. Cloth.

Eightieth Yearbook (1981)

Part 2. *The Social Studies.* Howard D. Mehlinger and O. L. Davis, Jr., editors. Cloth.

Seventy-ninth Yearbook (1980)

Part 1. *Toward Adolescence: The Middle School Years.* Mauritz Johnson, editor. Paper.

Seventy-eighth Yearbook (1979)

Part 1. *The Gifted and the Talented: Their Education and Development.* A. Harry Passow, editor. Paper.

Part 2. *Classroom Management.* Daniel L. Duke, editor. Paper.

The above titles in the Society's Yearbook series may be ordered from the University of Chicago Press, Book Order Department, 11030 Langley Ave., Chicago, IL 60628. For a list of earlier titles in the yearbook series still available, write to the Secretary, NSSE, 5835 Kimbark Ave., Chicago, IL 60637.

2. The Series on Contemporary Educational Issues

This series has been discontinued.

The following volumes in the series may be ordered from the McCutchan Publishing Corporation, P.O. Box 774, Berkeley, CA 94702-0774. Phone: 510-841-8616; Fax: 510-841-7787.

Academic Work and Educational Excellence: Raising Student Productivity (1986). Edited by Tommy M. Tomlinson and Herbert J. Walberg.

Adapting Instruction to Student Differences (1985). Edited by Margaret C. Wang and Herbert J. Walberg.

Choice in Education (1990). Edited by William Lowe Boyd and Herbert J. Walberg.

Colleges of Education: Perspectives on Their Future (1985). Edited by Charles W. Case and William A. Matthes.

Contributing to Educational Change: Perspectives on Research and Practice (1988). Edited by Philip W. Jackson.

Educational Leadership and School Culture (1993). Edited by Marshall Sashkin and Herbert J. Walberg.

Effective Teaching: Current Research (1991). Edited by Hersholt C. Waxman and Herbert J. Walberg.

Improving Educational Standards and Productivity: The Research Basis for Policy (1982). Edited by Herbert J. Walberg.

Moral Development and Character Education (1989). Edited by Larry P. Nucci.

Motivating Students to Learn: Overcoming Barriers to High Achievement (1993). Edited by Tommy M. Tomlinson.

Radical Proposals for Educational Change (1994). Edited by Chester E. Finn, Jr. and Herbert J. Walberg.

Reaching Marginal Students: A Prime Concern for School Renewal (1987). Edited by Robert L. Sinclair and Ward Ghory.

Restructuring the Schools: Problems and Prospects (1992). Edited by John J. Lane and Edgar G. Epps.

Rethinking Policy for At-risk Students (1994). Edited by Kenneth K. Wong and Margaret C. Wang.

School Boards: Changing Local Control (1992). Edited by Patricia F. First and Herbert J. Walberg.

The two final volumes in this series were:

Improving Science Education (1995). Edited by Barry J. Fraser and Herbert J. Walberg.

Ferment in Education: A Look Abroad (1995). Edited by John J. Lane.

These two volumes may be ordered from the Book Order Department, University of Chicago Press, 11030 S. Langley Ave., Chicago, IL 60628. Phone: 312-669-2215; Fax: 312-660-2235.